BRITISH HISTORICAL FACTS, 1688–1760

BRITISH
HISTORICAL FACTS,
1688–1760

CHRIS COOK

Head of the Department of History, Philosophy and European Studies,
Polytechnic of North London

and

JOHN STEVENSON

Reader in History, University of Sheffield

St. Martin's Press   New York

First published in the United States of America in 1988

Printed in Hong Kong

ISBN 0–312–02106–2

Library of Congress Cataloging-in-Publication Data
Cook, Chris, 1945–
British historical facts, 1688–1760/Chris Cook and John
Stevenson.
p.   cm.
ISBN 0–312–02106–2 : $35.00
1. Great Britain—History—George I, II, 1714–1760—Handbooks,
manuals, etc.   2. Great Britain—History—1689—1714—Handbooks,
manuals, etc.   3. Great Britain—History—Revolution of 1688–
—Handbooks, manuals, etc.   I. Stevenson, John, 1946–   .
II. Title.
DA498.C66 1988
941.07—dc19   88–7047
                                                          CIP

CONTENTS

v

vi

CONTENTS

PREFACE

This volume has attempted to present, within a single medium-sized book, a reference work on English history from 1688 to 1760 that will be of value to teachers, to students and to research workers in this important period of modern history. Within this book we have attempted to bring together as many of the important historical facts as can be reasonably assembled. Inevitably, however, no book of this type can be entirely comprehensive. In some areas the data is unreliable or indeed non-existent. Reasons of space also dictate the amount of information that can be presented.

In any book of this sort, the compilers owe a deep debt both to existing published works and to individual scholars who have offered help and advice, in particular to Stephen Brooks who compiled the chapter on the armed forces.

Finally, we would like to appeal to scholars and others working in this field to point out any omissions or errors in this book, so that the volume may be expanded or enlarged in future editions.

14 November 1987

CHRIS COOK
JOHN STEVENSON

ACKNOWLEDGEMENTS

The authors and publishers wish to thank the following who have kindly given permission to reproduce copyright material:

Cambridge University Press for tables from *Abstract of British Historical Statistics*, 2nd edn, by B. R. Mitchell and P. Deane (Cambridge University Press, 1971).

Longman for permission to use a table from *Religion and Society in Industrial England* by A. D. Gilbert (Longman, 1976).

Oxford University Press for a table from *The Population of Ireland, 1750–1845* by K. H. Connell (Oxford University Press, 1950).

1 THE MONARCHY

BIOGRAPHICAL DETAILS OF MONARCHS AND THEIR ISSUE

WILLIAM III

Born 4 Nov 1650, the son of William II, Prince of Orange and Mary Stuart, daughter of Charles I. On 13 Feb 1689 William and Mary were made King and Queen for their joint and separate lives. William had married Mary, the daughter of James II on 4 Nov 1677.

ANNE

Born 6 Feb 1665, the daughter of James II and Anne Hyde. She acceded to the throne 8 Mar 1702 and died 1 Aug 1714. On 28 July 1683 she married Prince George, the son of Frederick III of Denmark. The marriage produced:

William Born 24 July 1689. Created Duke of Gloucester, 27 July, he died on 30 July 1700.

Her other children were still-born or died in infancy.

GEORGE I

Born 28 May 1660, the son of Ernest Augustus, Elector of Hanover and Sophia, daughter of Frederick, the Elector Palatine. He acceded to the throne 1 Aug 1714 and died on 11 Jun 1727. On 21 Nov 1682 he married Sophia Dorothea, daughter of George William, Duke of Luneberg-Celle. The marriage produced the following children:

1. **George**   later George II (q.v.). Born 30 Oct 1683.
2. **Sophia Dorothea** Born 16 Mar 1687. Died 28 June 1757. On 17 Nov 1706 she married Frederick William, later King of Prussia.

George I's illegitimate children (by the Duchess of Kendal) were Petronille Melusine (born 1693) and Margaret Gertrude (born 1703).

GEORGE II

Born 30 Oct 1683, the son of George I and Sophia Dorothea. He acceded to the throne on 11 Jun 1727, and died 25 Oct 1760. On 22 Aug 1705 he

1

married Caroline, the daughter of John Frederick, Margrave of Brandenburg-Anspach. The marriage produced the following children:

1.	**Frederick**	Born 20 Jan 1707. Died 20 March 1751. Created Prince of Wales 7 Jan 1729.
2.	**Anne**	Born 22 Oct 1709. Died 12 Jan 1759. On 14 March 1734 she married Prince William IV of Orange.
3.	**Amelia (Emily)**	Born 30 May 1711. Died 31 Oct 1786.
4.	**Caroline Elizabeth**	Born 30 May 1713. Died 28 Dec 1757.
5.	**George William**	Born 2 Nov 1717. Died in infancy.
6.	**William Augustus**	Born 15 Apr 1721. Died 31 Oct 1765. Created Duke of Cumberland 27 July 1726.
7.	**Mary**	Born 22 Feb 1723. Died 16 Jan 1772. On 8 May 1740 she married Frederick, later Landgrave of Hesse-Cassel.
8.	**Louisa**	Born 7 Dec 1724. Died 8 Dec 1751. On 27 Oct 1743 she married Frederick, later King of Denmark.

GEORGE III

Born 24 May 1738, the son of Frederick, Prince of Wales, and Augusta, daughter of Frederick II, Duke of Saxe-Gotha. He acceded to the throne on 25 Oct 1760 and died on 29 Jan 1820. On 8 Sep 1761 he married Charlotte, daughter of Charles Louis, Duke of Mecklenburg-Strelitz. Because of his insanity, the Prince of Wales became regent on 5 Feb 1811.

His marriage produced the following children:

1.	**George**	Later George IV. Born 12 Aug 1762. Died 26 Jun 1830.
2.	**Frederick**	Born 16 Aug 1763. Created Duke of York 29 Nov 1784. Died 5 Jan 1827.
3.	**William**	Later William IV. Born 21 Aug 1765. Died 20 June 1837.
4.	**Charlotte**	Born 29 Sep 1766. Died 5 Oct 1828. Married, 18 May 1797, Frederick Charles, later King of Wurttemberg.
5.	**Edward**	Born 2 Nov 1767. Created Duke of Kent 24 Apr 1799. Died 23 Jan 1820.
6.	**Augusta**	Born 8 Nov 1768. Died 22 Sep 1840.
7.	**Elizabeth**	Born 22 May 1770. Died 10 Jan 1840. Married, 7 Apr 1818, Frederick Joseph, Prince of Hesse-Homburg.
8.	**Ernest Augustus**	Born 5 June 1771. Died 18 Nov 1851. Created Duke of Cumberland, 24 Apr 1799. Succeeded as King of Hanover 20 June 1837.
9.	**Augustus**	Born 27 Jan 1773. Died 21 Apr 1843. Created Duke of Sussex 27 Nov 1801.

10.	**Adolphus**	Born 24 Feb 1774. Died 8 July 1850. Created Duke of Cambridge 27 Nov 1801.
11.	**Mary**	Born 25 Apr 1776. Died 30 Apr 1857. Married, 22 July 1816, William, Duke of Gloucester.
12.	**Sophia**	Born 3 Nov 1777. Died 27 May 1848.
13.	**Octavia**	Born 23 Feb 1779. Died 3 May 1783.
14.	**Alfred**	Born 22 Sep 1780. Died 26 Aug 1782.
15.	**Amelia**	Born 7 Aug 1783. Died 2 Nov 1810.

Allowances to Members of the Royal Family in 1760

Grantees, with their Relationship to the Sovereign

		£
Dowager Princess of Wales	Mother	60 000
Duke of York	Brother	12 000
Duke of Gloucester (Wm. Henry)	Brother	8 000
Duke of Cumberland (Hy. Fredk.)	Brother	8 000
Princess Amelia	Aunt	12 000
Duke of Cumberland (son of Geo. II)	Uncle	15 000

ROYAL ABSENCES

WILLIAM III

11 Jun–6 Sep 1690	Ireland
16 Jan–13 Apr 1691	United Provinces
2 May–19 Oct 1691	United Provinces – Netherlands
5 Mar–18 Oct 1692	United Provinces – Netherlands
31 Mar–29 Oct 1693	United Provinces – Netherlands
6 May–9 Nov 1694	United Provinces – Netherlands
12 May–10 Oct 1695	United Provinces – Netherlands
6 May–6 Oct 1696	United Provinces – Netherlands, Cleves
26 Apr–14 Nov 1697	United Provinces – Netherlands
20 Jul–3 Dec 1698	United Provinces
2 Jun–18 Oct 1699	United Provinces
5 Jul–18 Oct 1700	United Provinces
4 Jul–4 Nov 1701	United Provinces

GEORGE I

1 Aug–18 Sep 1714	Hanover

7 Jul 1716–18 Jan 1717	Hanover
11 May–14 Nov 1719	Hanover
15 Jun–10 Nov 1720	Hanover
5 Jun–28 Dec 1723	Hanover and Brandenburg
4 Jun 1725–23 Jan 1726	Hanover
3 Jun–11 Jun 1727	Hanover

GEORGE II

22 May–11 Sep 1729	Hanover
7 Jun–26 Sep 1732	Hanover
17 May–26 Oct 1735	Hanover
24 May 1736–14 Jan 1737	Hanover
23 May–13 Oct 1740	Hanover
7 May–20 Oct 1741	Hanover
11 May–15 Nov 1743	Hanover and the German campaign
10 May–31 Aug 1745	Hanover
19 May–23 Nov 1748	Hanover
17 Apr–4 Nov 1750	Hanover
6 Apr–18 Nov 1752	Hanover
28 Apr–15 Sep 1755	Hanover

TABLE OF REGNAL YEARS
1688–1760

WILLIAM AND MARY

1	13 Feb 1689 12 Feb 1690	**WILLIAM III**		
2	13 Feb 1690 12 Feb 1691	7	28 Dec 1694 27 Dec 1695	
3	13 Feb 1691 12 Feb 1692	8	28 Dec 1695 27 Dec 1696	
4	13 Feb 1692 12 Feb 1693	9	28 Dec 1696 27 Dec 1697	
5	13 Feb 1693 12 Feb 1694	10	28 Dec 1697 27 Dec 1698	
6	13 Feb 1694 27 Dec 1694	11	28 Dec 1698 27 Dec 1699	

12	28 Dec 1699 27 Dec 1700	14	28 Dec 1701 8 Mar 1702
13	28 Dec 1700 27 Dec 1701		

ANNE

1	8 Mar 1702 7 Mar 1703	8	8 Mar 1709 7 Mar 1710
2	8 Mar 1703 7 Mar 1704	9	8 Mar 1710 7 Mar 1711
3	8 Mar 1704 7 Mar 1705	10	8 Mar 1711 7 Mar 1712
4	8 Mar 1705 7 Mar 1706	11	8 Mar 1712 7 Mar 1713
5	8 Mar 1706 7 Mar 1707	12	8 Mar 1713 7 Mar 1714
6	8 Mar 1707 7 Mar 1708	13	8 Mar 1714 1 Aug 1714
7	8 Mar 1708 7 Mar 1709		

GEORGE I

1	1 Aug 1714 31 July 1715	8	1 Aug 1721 31 July 1722
2	1 Aug 1715 31 July 1716	9	1 Aug 1722 31 July 1723
3	1 Aug 1716 31 July 1717	10	1 Aug 1723 31 July 1724
4	1 Aug 1717 31 July 1718	11	1 Aug 1724 31 July 1725
5	1 Aug 1718 31 July 1719	12	1 Aug 1725 31 July 1726
6	1 Aug 1719 31 July 1720	13	1 Aug 1726 11 June 1727
7	1 Aug 1720 31 July 1721		

GEORGE II

1	11 June 1727 10 June 1728	18	11 June 1744 10 June 1745
2	11 June 1728 10 June 1729	19	11 June 1745 10 June 1746
3	11 June 1729 10 June 1730	20	11 June 1746 10 June 1747
4	11 June 1730 10 June 1731	21	11 June 1747 10 June 1748
5	11 June 1731 10 June 1732	22	11 June 1748 10 June 1749
6	11 June 1732 10 June 1733	23	11 June 1749 10 June 1750
7	11 June 1733 10 June 1734	24	11 June 1750 10 June 1751
8	11 June 1734 10 June 1735	25	11 June 1751 10 June 1752
9	11 June 1735 10 June 1736	26	11 June 1752 10 June 1753
10	11 June 1736 10 June 1737	27	11 June 1753 10 June 1754
11	11 June 1737 10 June 1738	28	11 June 1754 10 June 1755
12	11 June 1738 10 June 1739	29	11 June 1755 10 June 1756
13	11 June 1739 10 June 1740	30	11 June 1756 10 June 1757
14	11 June 1740 10 June 1741	31	11 June 1757 10 June 1758
15	11 June 1741 10 June 1742	32	11 June 1758 10 June 1759
16	11 June 1742 10 June 1743	33	11 June 1759 10 June 1760
17	11 June 1743 10 June 1744	34	11 June 1760 25 Oct 1760

CONTEMPORARY EUROPEAN SOVEREIGNS
1688–1760

BAVARIA (Electors)

1679	Maximilian II
1726	Karl Albrecht I
1745	Maximilian III
1777	Karl Theodor I

BRANDENBURG (Electors of)

1640	Frederick William (The Great Elector)
1688– 1713	Frederick III (became King Frederick I of Prussia in 1701)

DENMARK

1670	Christian V
1699	Frederick IV
1730	Christian VI
1746	Frederick V
1766	Christian VII

FRANCE

1643	Louis XIV
1715	Louis XV
1774	Louis XVI

HOLY ROMAN EMPIRE

1658	Leopold I
1705	Joseph I
1711	Charles VI
1740	Charles VII of Bavaria
1745	Francis I
1765	Joseph II

OTTOMAN EMPIRE

1687	Suleiman II
1691	Ahmed II
1695	Mustafa II

1703	Ahmed III
1730	Mahmud I
1754	Osman III
1757	Mustafa III
1773	Abdul Hamid I

THE PAPACY

1676	Innocent XI
1689	Alexander VIII
1691	Innocent XII
1700	Clement XI
1721	Innocent XIII
1724	Benedict XIII
1730	Clement XII
1740	Benedict XIV
1758	Clement XIII
1769	Clement XIV

POLAND

1674	John Sobieski
1697	Augustus II
1704	Stanislaw Leszczynski
1709	Augustus II (again)
1733	Stanislaw Leszczynski (again)
1734	Augustus III
1764	Stanislaw Poniatowski

PORTUGAL (Braganza dynasty)

1683	Pedro II
1706	John V
1750	Joseph
1777	Pedro III

PRUSSIA (Kings from 1701; prior to 1701, see under Brandenburg)

1701	Frederick I
1713	Frederick William I
1740	Frederick II
1786	Frederick William II

RUSSIA (Romanov dynasty)

1682	Peter I (The Great)
1725	Catherine I
1727	Peter II
1730	Anne
1740	Ivan VI
1741	Elizabeth
1762	Peter III
1762	Catherine II (The Great)
1796	Paul

SAXONY

1680	John George III
1691	John George IV
1694	Frederick Augustus I
1733	Frederick Augustus II

SPAIN

1665	Charles II
1700	Philip V of Anjou
1724	Louis I
1724	Philip V of Anjou
1746	Ferdinand VI
1759	Charles III
1788	Charles IV

SWEDEN

1660	Charles XI
1697	Charles XII
1718	Ulrica Eleonora
1720	Frederick I
1751	Frederick Adolphus
1771	Gustavus III

THE JACOBITE LINE

JAMES II

Born 14 Oct 1633, the son of Charles I and Henrietta Maria. He acceded to the throne on 6 Feb 1685, fled the kingdom on 23 Dec 1688 and died on 6

Sep 1701. He married twice: Anne Hyde, on 3 Sep 1660 (she died 31 Mar 1671), and Mary of Modena, on 30 Sep 1673. The children of James II were as follows:

1.	**Mary**	Born 30 Apr 1662, the daughter of Anne Hyde; married William, Prince of Orange. Proclaimed joint Sovereign with her husband on 13 Feb 1689; died on 28 Dec 1694.
2.	**Anne**	Born on 6 Feb 1665, the daughter of Anne Hyde, acceded to the throne on 8 Mar 1702; died on 1 Aug 1714.
3.	**James Francis Edward**	The 'Old Pretender' or James III; born on 10 June 1688, the son of Mary of Modena. Styled James III in 1701 by Louis XIV; attainted in 1702, he died in Rome on 1 Jan 1766.
4.	**Louisa Maria Theresa**	Born on 28 Jun 1692, the daughter of Mary of Modena; died on 18 Aug 1712.

CHARLES EDWARD STUART

Also known as the 'Young Pretender' or 'Bonnie Prince Charlie', born 31 Dec 1720, the grandson of James II and son of James Francis Edward, the 'Old Pretender'. He landed in Scotland on 25 Jul 1745 to lead the Jacobite forces on behalf of the claims of his father to the throne of Great Britain. Following the decisive defeat of the Jacobite armies at Culloden on 16 Apr 1746, he spent several months as a fugitive in Scotland before escaping to France in September 1746. He died in exile in Rome on 31 Jan 1788.

HENRY BENEDICT MARIA CLEMENT, CARDINAL YORK

Born March 1725, the second son of James, the 'Old Pretender' or James III. He came to England to support his brother Charles Edward in 1745, but on return to Italy became bishop of Ostia and prefect of St. Peter's Rome; Cardinal (1747), archbishop of Corinth (1759), and bishop of Tusculum (1761). Assumed title Henry IX of England, 1788, but accepted gift of money from George III after his residence sacked by the French in 1799. Died at Frascati, August 1807.

2 CHRONOLOGY

THE GLORIOUS REVOLUTION, 1685-1689

1685

6 February   Accession of James II.

16 February   Lawrence Hyde, Earl of Rochester, appointed Lord Treasurer and Lord President of the Council (18 February).

April   Meeting of Scottish Parliament expresses loyalty to James.

11 May   James orders Lord Treasurer to stop recovery of fines from specified 'loyal' recusants.

19 May   Parliament meets; James granted 'for life' the revenues conferred on Charles II. Earl of Danby released from the Tower.

26 May   House of Commons grand committee on religion passes two resolutions pledging them to defend the 'reformed religion' and calling for the enforcement of the laws against all dissenters. After the King displays his anger the Commons rejects the resolutions and accepts the royal pledge to defend the Church of England.

11 June   Outbreak of Monmouth rebellion. Parliament votes new duties on tobacco, sugar, French linen, brandies, calicoes and wrought silks, as well as restoring duties on wine and vinegar which had expired in 1681, against the security of which the King was empowered to raise £400 000.

30 June   Earl of Argyll executed for rising in support of Monmouth.

6 July   Defeat of Monmouth's army at Sedgemoor and capture of Monmouth.

15 July   Monmouth executed at Tower Hill.

September   Judge Jeffreys presides over 'Bloody Assizes' in the West Country.

28 September   Jeffreys appointed Lord Chancellor.

12–19 November   Parliament grants James a further £700 000 on the basis of new duties, but the King's request for Catholic officers to be permitted in the army provokes opposition. James prorogues Parliament (20 November).

4 December   Earl of Sunderland appointed Lord President of the Council.

11

1686

March   Duke of Queensbury removed as Scottish Treasurer and office placed in commission.

June   In the collusive action of Godden v. Hales the Court of King's Bench ruled that James II had the right to dispense with the Test Act for particular cases. James proceeds to introduce further Roman Catholics into the army, and into the universities, Anglican Church, and Privy Council.

14 June   Scottish Parliament prorogued after refusal to grant indulgence to Catholics.

July   James sets up a Court of Ecclesiastical Commission to control the church.

10 December   Earl of Rochester dismissed as Treasurer.

1687

12 February   Declaration of Indulgence issued to Roman Catholics and Quakers in Scotland.

4 April   James II granted extensive indulgence in England to Protestant dissenters and Roman Catholic recusants.

April   James orders Magdalen College, Oxford, to elect Anthony Farmer, a reputed Catholic. When the Fellows refused the College was ordered to set aside their own choice and a visitation of ecclesiastical commissioners was sent to install him.

28 June   Second Declaration of Indulgence in Scotland.

2 July   Parliament, prorogued since 20 November 1685, was dissolved.

3 July   D'Adda publicly received as papal nuncio.

July–August   James begins purge of office-holders, gathering pace in winter of 1687–8. Many Tory Anglicans dismissed from municipal corporations and replaced by nonconformists and Catholics. Many Lord and Deputy Lieutenants removed for showing unwillingness to repeal Test Acts. Scottish burghs ordered to cease elections and await royal nomination.

14 November   Official confirmation of Queen's pregnancy.

1688

3 May   Republication of the Declaration of Indulgence.

4 May   James II orders Anglican clergy to read the Declaration from the pulpit on two consecutive Sundays and Bishops required to see to it that copies distributed.

18 May   Archbishop of Canterbury, Sancroft, and six other Bishops personally petition the King to be excused from reading the Declaration, arousing the King's anger.

8 June   The 'Seven Bishops' are arrested on a charge of seditious libel and committed to the Tower.

10 June   Birth of son to James II and Mary of Modena, providing for a Catholic succession, and alleged by Protestants to be a child smuggled into the palace in a warming pan.

29–30 June   Trial and acquittal of the Seven Bishops.

30 June   Leading Whigs and Tories led by Danby, Shrewsbury, Devonshire, Compton, Sidney, Lumley and Russell invite William of Orange to invade England in defence of 'Liberties'.

30 September   William of Orange accepts invitation to invade England and issues a declaration denouncing the 'evil counsellors' who had subjected the country 'in all things relating to their consciences, liberties and properties to arbitrary government' and calling for 'a free and lawful parliament' to be assembled 'as soon as possible'.

1 November   William and the Dutch invasion fleet successfully set sail for England.

5 November   William of Orange lands at Torbay with 15 000 Dutch troops.

14 November   Earl of Abingdon and Lord Cornbury join William's forces.

15 November   Risings in the North and Midlands in support of William.

19 November   James joins his army at Salisbury.

21 November   William begins march on London.

22 November   Northern and Midland 'rebels' issue a declaration from Nottingham setting forth their 'innumerable grievances' and calling on 'all good protestants and subjects' to support William.

After a Council of War, James decides to retreat with his forces to London. Churchill and Grafton leave James, followed by increasing elements of the royal army.

24 November   James's army begins retreat to London.

26 November   James reaches London and summons a Great Council to meet on the 27th.

27 November   At a Great Council in Whitehall attended by nine bishops and between thirty or forty peers, James is urged to dismiss Catholics from his service, issue a general pardon and call a new Parliament. Writs issued for a new Parliament on 15 January (28th), followed by a Proclamation promising free elections and immunity for all peers and members of the Commons.

29 November   James issues orders for his son to be sent to France.

30 November   *London Gazette* announces that Halifax, Nottingham and Godolphin were to treat with William on the King's behalf.

7–9 December   William meets royal commissioners at Hungerford and terms are arranged for an armistice while Parliament assembled.

10 December   James learns from the commissioners confirmation of William's terms. Meanwhile James secures the Great Seal, burns writs summoning Parliament and annuls those already sent out.

Mary of Modena and the royal heir flee to France.

11 December   James, having disposed of the Great Seal in the Thames, attempts to escape to France but is intercepted at Sheerness and forced to return to London (16th). Widespread anti-Catholic rioting in London and elsewhere. Meeting of peers and bishops at Guildhall issues Guildhall Declaration for a free Parliament to enact 'effectual securities for our religion and laws'. The City of London calls on William to enter London.

12 December   Commander of the fleet, Dartmouth, puts it under William's control. Provisional government under the presidency of Halifax established by the peers in London.

16 December   William summons the fleet to the Nore.

17 December   William summons a meeting of peers at Windsor to advise him on what to do about the King's return. It was decided that the King should go to Ham on the Thames.

18 December   James requests to go to Rochester, upon which William enters London.

20 December   William summons peers to meet him on the 21st to advise on calling 'a free parliament'.

23 December   James leaves for France.

26 December   William summons all those who had sat in Parliament in Charles II's time and a deputation from the City of London to advise him.

28 December   William accepts the invitation of both peers and commons to take charge of the civil administration and to summon a convention.

1689

22 January   Meeting of Convention Parliament.

28 January   The Commons declares that James II had abdicated and that the throne was vacant and against a 'popish prince'.

8 February   Commons approve draft of Declaration of Rights, vesting the throne in William and Mary and the line of succession through Anne.

13 February   Parliament offers the crown to William and Mary who are proclaimed King and Queen for their joint and separate lives, accompanying the offer with a Declaration of Rights. This asserted the 'true, ancient and indubitable rights of the people of this realm' and contained the following provisions: (i) that the making or suspending of law without consent of Parliament is illegal; (ii) that the exercise of the dispensing power is illegal; (iii) that the ecclesiastical commission court and other such like courts are illegal; (iv) that levying money without consent of Parliament is illegal; (v) that it is lawful to petition the sovereign; (vi) that the maintenance of a standing army without the consent of Parliament is illegal; (vii) that it is lawful to keep arms; (viii) that elections of members of Parliament must be free; (ix) that there must be freedom of debate in Parliament; (x) that excessive bail should never be demanded; (xi) that juries should be impanelled and returned in every trial; (xii) that grants of estates as forfeited before conviction of the offender are illegal; (xiii) that parliament should be held frequently.

William and Mary were declared King and Queen for life, the chief administration resting with William; the crown was next settled on William's children by Mary; in default of such issue, on the Princess Anne of Denmark and her children; and in default of these, on the children of William by any other wife.

Parliamentary Committee begins preparation of Declaration into a draft Bill of Rights.

1 March   Oaths of allegiance and supremacy taken to William and Mary, some peers and members of the lower house, as well as six bishops and 400 clergymen refuse, marking the beginning of the non-juror schism.

5 March   Earl of Nottingham made Secretary of State.

12 March   Landing of James II at Kinsale in Ireland opens his campaign to recapture the throne (see p. 155). Meeting of Scottish Convention.

11 April   Coronation of William and Mary.

11 May   William and Mary accept Claim of Right of Scottish Convention Parliament, asserting the constitutional liberties of the Kingdom.

24 May   Toleration Act exempts dissenters who had taken the oaths of allegiance and supremacy from penalties for non-attendance on the services of the established church.

POLITICAL CHRONOLOGY, 1689–1760

1689

January   Meeting of Convention Parliament (22nd). Throne declared vacant (28th) by the Commons.

February   William and Mary proclaimed King and Queen for life (13th). Declaration of Rights drawn up, determining line of succession. Toleration Bill introduced in the Lords (28th).

March   Oaths of allegiance and supremacy (1st), refused by over 400 non-jurors.
             Earl of Nottingham made Secretary of State (5th). Bill of Comprehension introduced in Lords (11th). Landing of James II at Kinsale (12th).

April   Coronation of William and Mary (11th). Scottish Convention passes 'Articles of Grievance' (13th).

May   William and Mary accept crown of Scotland: Toleration Act passed by Parliament (24th); comprehension proposals dropped.

June   Scottish Convention meets as Parliament (5th).

December   Bill of Rights enacted, determining the line of succession and prohibiting a Catholic from succeeding to the throne, as well as reiterating the provisions of the Declaration of February (see p. 15).

1690

February   Convention Parliament dissolved (6th). Sancroft, five Bishops and 400 clergy deprived of their living for refusing to take the oath to William and Mary.

March   Second Parliament of William and Mary meets (20th). Act of recognition affirms the legality of the acts of the Convention Parliament.

May   Act of Grace gives indemnity to all supporters of James II, except those in treasonable correspondence with him (20th). Resignation of Shrewsbury and Halifax. Prorogation of Parliament and appointment of a council of nine to advise Mary during the

King's absence (23rd).

Lords of Articles abolished in Scotland (8th).

June   William leaves for Ireland (14th).

July   Battle of the Boyne (1st), defeat of James and his army.

1691

July   Defeat of French and Irish forces at Aughrim (12th).

August   William offers indemnity to all Highland clans still in rebellion if they will take oath of allegiance by end of year.

October   Treaty of Limerick effectively ends Irish war. Irish soldiers and officers offered free transportation to France; Irish Catholics to retain religious liberties as under Charles II (later repudiated by Irish Parliament).

1692

January   Earl of Marlborough (John Churchill) dismissed for communicating with James II (10th).

February Massacre of Glencoe (13th).

March   Earl of Nottingham becomes sole Secretary of State.

May   Marlborough imprisoned in the Tower but released shortly afterwards.

1693

March   Lord Somers leads Whig 'Junto' as Lord Keeper.

November Dismissal of Earl of Nottingham, Tory Secretary of State.

1694

March   Earl of Shrewsbury, member of Whig Junto, becomes Secretary of State.

May   Removal of leading Tories from government, apart from Danby and Godolphin, leaves power largely in the hands of the Whig Junto, consisting of Somers, Shrewsbury, Wharton, Russell and Montagu.

July   Charter of the Governor and Company of the Bank of England for the raising of a loan of £1 200 000 to finance the siege of Namur.

December   Triennial Act passed (3rd), providing for a new Parliament to be elected every three years; receives royal assent (22nd). Queen Mary dies of smallpox (28th).

Expiration of the licensing act and effective end to press censorship.

1695

May   Duke of Leeds (formerly Earl of Danby) forced to resign as Lord President of Council (6th).

October   Dissolution of Parliament (11th).

November   Meeting of third Parliament of the reign, supported by a large Whig majority.

Recoinage act.

1696

February   Plot to kill the King uncovered led by Sir John Fenwick and Jacobites (14th); Oath of Association to defend William and Protestant succession promulgated throughout England and Wales.

1697

January   Execution of Sir John Fenwick (21st).

April   Lord Somers made Lord Chancellor (22nd); charter of Bank of England renewed.

May   Resignation of Godolphin as First Lord of the Treasury; appointment of Montagu (1st).

September   Treaty of Ryswick signed, ending War of the League of Augsburg.

December   Robert Harley's motion to disband all forces raised since 1680 approved by both houses of Parliament; resignation of Earl of Sunderland. Parliament established a civil list not exceeding £700 000 a year for the support of William himself and the civil administration. William III recognised by Louis XIV as King of England.

1698

August   William III commits England to Partition Treaty with Holland
              (19th), dividing Spanish possessions, without consulting ministers
              or Parliament.

December   Meeting of William's fourth Parliament (6th).

1699

January   Parliament forces William to reduce drastically the size of the
              English army and disband his Dutch guards.

              Act for preventing growth of popery; all persons who refuse
              oaths of allegiance and supremacy to lose estates. Catholic
              school-teachers and priests liable to imprisonment for life.

1700

March   Second Partition Treaty with France and Holland ratified (14th).
              Scottish colonists forced to withdraw from Darien.

April   Parliament prorogued (11th). William forced to dismiss Somers
              as Lord Chancellor (17th).

July   Death of Duke of Gloucester, last of Anne's children.

December   Godolphin rejoins ministry as Treasurer.

1701

February   Parliament resumes sitting (6th); Harley elected Speaker of the
              Commons.

April   Commons begin impeachment proceedings against Whig ministers
              Somers, Orford, and Montagu for failure to consult Parliament
              over Partition Treaties.

June   Act of Settlement passed determining that the Protestant
              succession should pass through the electress Sophia of Hanover,
              granddaughter of James I, next in line after Princess Anne (12th).
              The Act also declares that the sovereigns of Great Britain should
              be Protestant and not leave the kingdom without the consent
              of Parliament; that the country should not be involved in war
              for the defence of the foreign possessions of the sovereigns; that
              no foreigner should receive a grant from the crown or hold office,
              civil or military; that ministers to be responsible for the acts of

their sovereigns; that judges to hold office for life unless guilty of misconduct.

September Death of James II; James Edward proclaimed King of Great Britain and Ireland by Louis XIV.

November Parliament dissolved (11th).

December Sixth Parliament of William III (30th).

1702

February Act for attainder against the Pretender, James Edward Stuart (20th); Act of Abjuration of Pretender, requiring oath of loyalty to King and heirs according to Act of Settlement (24th).

March Death of William III; Queen Anne succeeds to the throne (8th). Marlborough made Captain-General of armed forces (24th).

April Coronation of Queen Anne.

May Declaration of war against France and Spain (4th). Godolphin appointed Lord Treasurer.

June Scottish Parliament proclaims Anne Queen of Scotland and nominates commissioners to treat for Union with England.

October Meeting of Anne's first Parliament (20th).

1703

January Tory bill against occasional conformity defeated in the Lords.

March Queen persuades the Earls of Nottingham and Rochester to dismiss several Whig Lord and Deputy Lieutenants, sheriffs and justices of the peace.

August Scottish Parliament passes Act of Security claiming right to name Protestant successor to Queen Anne and safeguard Scottish Parliament, trade and religion from English domination. Refused royal assent.

November Establishment of Queen Anne's Bounty.

December Second bill against occasional conformity defeated in the Lords after Commons approval (7th).

1704

April Henry St John becomes Secretary at War (20th).

May Robert Harley made Secretary of State (18th).

August Marlborough's victory at Blenheim (13th).

Amended version of Scottish Act of Security given royal assent.

December Further attempt to restrict occasional conformity defeated in Parliament (14–15th).

1705

April Dissolution of Anne's first Parliament (5th).

September Scottish Parliament approves Act for appointment of commissioners to negotiate union with England.

October Second Parliament of Anne's reign meets (25th).

1706

April Scottish commissioners meet English commissioners at Westminster (16th).

May Victory at Ramillies (23rd).

July Articles of Union signed between English and Scottish Commissioners (22nd).

December 3rd Earl of Sunderland appointed Secretary of State (3rd).

1707

January Scottish Parliament ratifies Articles of Union (16th).

March Act of Union joins kingdoms of England and Scotland under name of Great Britain (6th). The Act provides that the princess Sophia of Hanover and her Protestant heirs should succeed to the crown of the United Kingdom; that there would be one Parliament at Westminster to which Scotland should send 16 elective peers and 45 members of the commons; that no more Scottish peers be created; that Scottish law and legal administration remain unchanged; that the Episcopal church in England and Presbyterian in Scotland be unchanged; and for the adoption of a common flag – the Union Jack, a common coinage, and free Anglo-Scottish and colonial trade.

April Final dissolution of Scottish Parliament (28th).

May Union of England and Scotland comes into effect (1st).

October   Second Parliament of Anne reconvenes as first Parliament of Great Britain.

1708

February   Harley and St John dismissed from the Cabinet; Robert Walpole appointed Secretary at War (25th).

March   James Edward, the old Pretender, lands in Scotland; but a French fleet sent to assist him was repulsed by Admiral Byng and he soon returned to France.

July   Battle of Oudenarde (11th).

November   The third Parliament of Queen Anne's reign meets (16th).

1709

September   Battle of Malplaquet (11th).

October   Townshend's Barrier treaty (29th). Copyright Act.

November   Dr Henry Sacheverell preaches a sermon at St Pauls Cathedral, condemning the toleration of nonconformists and praising divine right of monarchy (5th).

December   Dr Sacheverell impeached by House of Commons (13th).

1710

Feb–Mar   Trial of Dr Sacheverell (27 Feb–20 Mar); Dr Sacheverell suspended from preaching for three years (23 Mar); during trial pro-Sacheverell riots occur in which London mobs sack several leading nonconformist meeting houses.

June   Sunderland dismissed as Secretary of State, South (14th).

August   Godolphin and Whig ministry dismissed by the Queen; Robert Harley, as Chancellor of Exchequer, and Henry St John, form Tory ministry (8th).

September   Dissolution of Parliament followed by election (21st).

November   Fourth Parliament of Anne meets with Tory majority (25th).

1711

February   Property Qualification Act passed, county MPs must own property worth £600 and borough MPs property worth £300 per annum.

March   Robert Harley made Lord Treasurer (29th).

May   Harley created Earl of Oxford (23rd).

December   Bill against occasional conformity introduced in the Lords by Nottingham (15th); Duke of Marlborough dismissed as Commander-in-Chief. Duke of Ormond becomes Commander-in-Chief.

1712

January   Anne creates twelve new Tory peers to ensure success of government peace initiative in Lords (1st); Robert Walpole imprisoned in Tower for alleged corruption as Secretary at War.

July   Henry St John created Viscount Bolingbroke.

1713

April   Peace of Utrecht (11th).

August   Anne's fourth Parliament dissolved, followed by elections. Earl of Mar appointed Secretary of State for Scotland (8th).

1714

February   Fifth Parliament of Queen Anne meets (16th)

May   Schism Act passed. No person allowed to keep a school unless a member of the Anglican Church.

July   Henry St John (Bolingbroke) secures dismissal of the Earl of Oxford and begins attempt to pack administration with Jacobite sympathisers. Severe illness of Queen Anne forces calling of Privy Council. Pro-Hanoverian Duke of Shrewsbury appointed Lord Treasurer in place of Oxford (30th).

August   Death of Queen Anne (1st); George I proclaimed King in London and leading cities. Bolingbroke dismissed from office.

September George I arrives in England (18th). *Whig administration formed under Lord Stanhope.* Principal figures: Lord Stanhope (Secretary of State); Lord Halifax (First Lord of the Treasury); Lord Townshend (Secretary of State); Earl of Nottingham (Lord

President of the Council); Lord Sunderland (Lord Lieutenant of Ireland).

October   Coronation of George I (20th).

1715

March   Meeting of first Parliament of George I with large Whig majority (17th).

June   Bolingbroke, Ormond and Oxford impeached. Flight of Bolingbroke and Ormond; Oxford committed to the Tower. Widespread rioting followed by Riot Act strengthening power of magistrates by making many riots a capital offence.

September   Jacobite rising in Scotland under the Earl of Mar.

October   Robert Walpole appointed First Lord of the Treasury.

November   Jacobites defeated at Sheriffmuir and Preston.

December   Pretender (James III) arrives in Scotland (22nd).

1716

February   Pretender flees Scotland after failure of England to rise in support (10th). Impeachment of Jacobite leaders; execution of Derwentwater and Kenmure.

May   Septennial Act extends maximum duration of parliaments to seven years.

December   Lord Townshend dismissed as Secretary of State for opposing French alliance favoured by George I.

1717

January   Triple Alliance formed between England, France and Holland to uphold the Treaty of Utrecht (4th).

February   Convocation of the Church of England ceased to meet regularly.

April   Walpole resigns from administration, succeeded as First Lord by Stanhope. Addison and Sunderland become Secretaries of State.

July   Oxford released from the Tower (1st).

1718

March   Sunderland remodels ministry: Sunderland becomes First Lord of the Treasury, Stanhope Secretary of State, and Aislabie Chancellor of the Exchequer.

August   Quadruple Alliance formed between England, France, the Emperor and Holland.

December   War between England and Spain.

1719

January   Repeal of the Schism and Occasional Conformity Acts.

April   Peerage Bill to fix the number of peers in the House of Lords defeated.

December   Peerage Bill, reintroduced by the Duke of Buckingham, defeated in the Commons.

1720

January   Spain joins Quadruple Alliance, ending hostilities with England.

February   House of Commons accepts South Sea Company's scheme for taking over part of the National Debt in return for exclusive trade in the South Seas.

April   Royal assent given to Act empowering South Seas Company to manage National Debt (7th). Stocks begin a sharp rise.

June   Robert Walpole and Charles Townshend return to office as Paymaster-General and Lord President of the Council respectively.

Oct–Nov   'South Sea Bubble' begins to burst, with panic selling and the ruin of many investors.

December   Walpole begins restoration of public credit. Secret Committee appointed to investigate the affairs of the South Sea Company. The Company's directors are detained and those holding government posts dismissed and expelled from the House of Commons. Aislabie, Chancellor of the Exchequer, and Earl of Sunderland implicated.

1721

February   Death of Stanhope (5th); Townshend becomes Secretary of State in place of Stanhope.

March   House of Commons votes Aislabie guilty of fraud, expels him
             from the House and commits him to the Tower. Sunderland
             acquitted on charges of corruption but eventually resigns.

April   *Walpole administration formed.* Principal figures: Robert Walpole
             (First Lord of the Treasury and Chancellor of the Exchequer);
             Lord Townshend (Secretary of State); Lord Carteret (Secretary
             of State).

1722

April   Death of Sunderland.

May   Atterbury plot by Jacobites uncovered. Leading Jacobite sym-
             pathisers arrested.

October   Meeting of George I's second Parliament (9th). Habeas Corpus
             suspended; penal taxes levied on Catholics and non-jurors;
             Francis Atterbury (Bishop of Rochester) exiled.

1723

May   Lord Bolingbroke pardoned and returns to England in June.

June   System of bonded warehouses established to prevent smuggling
             and increase revenues on tea and coffee.

1724

April   Carteret dismissed as Secretary of State and becomes Lord
             Lieutenant of Ireland; Thomas Pelham Holles, Duke of Newcastle,
             appointed Secretary of State and his brother, Henry Pelham,
             Secretary at War.

1725

April   City Elections Act regulating conduct of elections in London
             increases power of Court of Aldermen and leads to strong
             opposition to Walpole in the City.

July   Riots against malt tax in Scotland.

September Treaty of Hanover between England, France and Prussia.

1726

November   Publication of *The Craftsman*, edited by Bolingbroke and
             Pulteney, attacking Walpole and his foreign policy.

1727

February   Hostilities break out between Britain and Spain.

June   Death of George I; succession of George II. Walpole reappointed First Lord of the Treasury and Chancellor of the Exchequer. Civil List raised to £800 000 per annum.

July   George I's second Parliament formally dissolved.

1729

November   Treaty of Seville with Spain; confirmation of *assiento* treaty allowing limited trade with Spanish colonies; Gibraltar ceded to England.

1730

May   Lord Harrington replaces Townshend as Secretary of State.

1731

March   Treaty of Vienna; Austrian Emperor agrees to disband Ostend East India Company.

1733

March   Widespread opposition to Walpole's Excise Bill.

April   Walpole's majority in House of Commons reduced to 16 on Excise proposals; Walpole offers resignation to the King. Though remaining in office, Walpole postpones discussion of the Bill until June, effectively dropping the scheme.

May   Walpole narrowly staves off defeat in the House of Lords over handling of South Sea Company affairs.

1734

March   Motion to repeal Septennial Act defeated.

April   Dissolution of Parliament, followed by elections (16th).

1735

January   Second Parliament of George II meets (14th), the Walpole administration having lost seats but still commanding a substantial majority.

1736

March	Repeal of Test Act defeated 251 to 123 in Commons. Gin Act passed, taxing spirits and imposing licences for selling them, to come into force on 29 September.
July	Anti-Irish and Gin Act disturbances in London.
September	Porteus Riots in Edinburgh. Fine levied on the city.

1737

September	Frederick, Prince of Wales, quarrels with his father and sides openly with the opposition to Walpole.
November	Death of Queen Caroline (20th).

1738

January	Spanish attacks on British shipping denounced by the opposition in the Commons and the City of London.
March	Examination by Commons Committee of Captain Jenkins who alleged ill-treatment at hands of Spanish Guardas Costas in 1731. Carteret succeeds in passing resolutions in House of Lords condemning Spanish right to search British ships in Spanish American waters.

1739

January	Convention of Pardo agreed between Britain and Spain over trade disputes.
March	Address approving Pardo Convention carried in the Commons by Walpole by only 28 votes against the opposition of William Pitt and the 'Patriots'.
October	Walpole forced to accede to demand for war with Spain – the 'War of Jenkin's Ear'.
November	Capture of Porto Bello by Admiral Vernon.

1740

February   Motion to investigate the Convention of Pardo rejected by 247 votes to 196.

April   Argyll dismissed from his military appointments, because of increasing antipathy to Walpole. Hervey's replacement of Godolphin as Lord Privy Seal offends the Duke of Newcastle who threatens resignation.

June   Death of Sir William Wyndham, chief leader of the Tories.

October   George Dodington loses his post as Commissioner of the Treasury and moves into opposition to Walpole.

1741

February   Motion for Walpole's dismissal defeated by 184 votes.

April   King's Speech invites Parliament to support the Pragmatic Sanction: £300 000 voted in subsidies for Queen Maria Theresa of Austria. Parliament dissolved (25th). In ensuing election Walpole's majority reduced to under 20 seats by defeats in Cornwall and Scotland.

December   Parliament reassembles and Walpole defeated in seven divisions.

1742

February   Walpole decides to resign after defeat over Chippenham election petition (11th). *Carteret administration* formed. Principal figures: John Carteret (Secretary of State); Earl of Wilmington (First Lord of the Treasury).

1743

August   Henry Pelham becomes First Lord of the Treasury in place of Earl of Wilmington.

1744

March   France declares war on Britain.

November   Carteret resigns after increasing disagreement in the Cabinet and Parliament about his foreign policy. *Pelham administration* formed. Principal figures: Henry Pelham (First Lord of the

Treasury); Earl of Harrington (Secretary of State); Duke of Bedford (First Lord of the Admiralty).

1745

May   Battle of Fontenoy. Marshal Saxe defeats Duke of Cumberland.

July   Second Jacobite rebellion. The Young Pretender, Charles Edward Stuart, lands in Scotland and proclaims his father as James VIII of Scotland and James III of England (23rd). Highland clans rise in support.

September The Pretender enters Edinburgh with 2000 men (11th); Jacobite victory at Prestonpans (21st).

December   Pretender reaches Derby, but decides to retreat to Scotland because of lack of support in England (4th).

1746

February   Pelham, Newcastle, Hardwicke and Harrington resign after disagreements with the King over foreign policy. Bath and Granville attempt to form an administration. *Pelham administration* reformed. Principal figures: H. Pelham (First Lord of the Treasury); Earl of Harrington (Secretary of State); Duke of Newcastle (Secretary of State); William Pitt, the Elder (Vice-Treasurer of Ireland).

April   Defeat of Young Pretender and Jacobite forces at battle of Culloden (16th).

May   Pitt becomes Paymaster-General of the forces.

September Flight of the Young Pretender to France.

1748

October   Treaty of Aix-la-Chapelle ends War of Austrian Succession.

1751

May   Act passed for adoption of the reformed (Gregorian) calendar in England and the colonies. Year to begin from January 1 instead of March 25; 11 days to be omitted from the calendar between 3 and 14 September 1752.

1753

June   Jewish Naturalisation Act passed, but repealed the following
             year because of the popular opposition (December 1754).

1754

March   Death of Pelham. *Newcastle administration* formed. Principal
             figures: Duke of Newcastle (First Lord of the Treasury); Earl
             of Holderness (Secretary of State); Henry Fox (Secretary at
             War); William Pitt (Paymaster).

1755

May   Admiral Boscawen fails to prevent French reinforcements
             reaching North America. Subsidy treaties agreed with Hesse-
             Cassel and Russia to provide troops in the event of war.

November   Henry Fox becomes Secretary of State; Pitt dismissed.

1756

January   Treaty between Britain and Prussia (16th).

May   Britain declares war on France (17th).

June   Loss of Minorca after failure of Admiral Byng to defeat French
             invasion fleet.

October   Henry Fox announces intention to resign after severe criticism
             of the conduct of the war in the House of Commons. Newcastle
             resigns; King asks Fox to form an administration, but refuses.
             Devonshire agrees to form an administration with Pitt (29th).

November   *Pitt–Devonshire administration formed.* Principal figures: Duke
             of Devonshire (First Lord of the Treasury); William Pitt
             (Secretary of State).

1757

April   King demands Pitt's resignation after failure to achieve success
             in the war. George Grenville (Treasurer of the Navy) and Legge
             (Chancellor of the Exchequer) resign with Pitt. Widespread
             popular support shown for Pitt.

July   After considerable negotiations *Pitt–Newcastle administration*
             formed. Principal figures: William Pitt (Secretary of State); Duke

of Newcastle (First Lord of the Treasury); Henry Fox (Paymaster).

Militia Act remodels militia with members chosen by ballot; widespread rioting provoked (Aug–Sep).

October   Failure of Rochefort expedition; news of defeats in India and Canada leads to criticism of the conduct of the war in Europe.

November   Victory for Britain's ally, Frederick the Great, at Rossbach.

December   Victory of Frederick at Leuthen.

1758

April   At Second Treaty of Westminster, Prussia and Britain pledged themselves not to make a separate peace. Frederick granted an annual subsidy of £670 000.

July   Capture of Louisburg in North America (26th).

November   Occupation of Fort Duquesne by Colonel Forbes.

1759

May   Capture of Guadeloupe.

June   Capture of Fort Niagara in North America.

July   Bombardment of Le Havre thwarts French plans for invasion of Britain.

August   Boscawen's defeat of French fleet at Lagos (Cape St Vincent).

September Wolfe's victory at Battle of the Plains of Abraham (13th) and capture of Quebec (18th).

November   Defeat of French fleet by Admiral Hawke at Quiberon Bay (20th).

1760

September Surrender of Montreal to the British; virtual loss of Canada by the French.

October   Death of George II (25th); accession of George III.

3 ADMINISTRATIONS AND POLITICAL BIOGRAPHIES

MINISTRIES AND ADMINISTRATIONS*

CHRONOLOGICAL LIST

Date of formation	Name	Years Covered
May 1702	Godolphin–Marlborough	1702–10
Aug 1710	Harley	1710–14
Sep 1714	Stanhope	1714–17
Apr 1717	Stanhope–Sunderland (remodelled 1718)	1717–21
Apr 1721	Walpole	1721–42
Feb 1742	Carteret	1742–4
Nov 1744	Pelham	1744–6
Feb 1746	Bath	1746
Feb 1746	Pelham	1746–54
Mar 1754	Newcastle	1754–6
Nov 1756	Pitt–Devonshire	1756–7
July 1757	Pitt–Newcastle	1757–61

GODOLPHIN–MARLBOROUGH, 1702–10

Ld Treas.	Sidney Godolphin, Ld Godolphin	8 May 02 (dism. 8 Aug 10)
Chanc. Exch.	Henry Boyle	29 Mar 01
	John Smith	11 Feb 08

*Note: The formation of administrations ultimately depended upon the power of appointment to major public offices and to the royal household by the Crown. Although such appointments were made throughout this period, and prior to it, it was only gradually with the development of parliamentary government as a regular feature of political life that wholesale changes in office holders can be identified which relate to changes in royal favour or in the parliamentary situation. While it would be possible to suggest putative titles and dates of administrations prior to 1702, it was with the accession of Anne that the pattern of more readily identifiable ministries and administrations became more clearly evident.

Ld Pres.	Thomas Herbert, E of Pembroke and E of Montgomery	9 July 02
	John Somers, Ld Somers	25 Nov 08
D. Lanc.	Sir John Leveson-Gower	12 May 02
	James Stanley, E of Derby	1 June 06
Master-Gen. of Ordnance	John Churchill, D of Marlborough	1 July 02
Sec. of State (South)	Daniel Finch, E of Nottingham	2 May 02 (vac. c. 22 Apr 1704)
	Sir Charles Hedges	18 May 04 (dism. Dec 06)
	Charles Spencer, E of Sunderland	3 Dec 06 (dism. 13–14 June 10)
	William Legge, Ld Dartmouth	15 June 10 (vac. 6–13 Aug 13)
Sec. of State (North)	Sir Charles Hedges	2 May 02
	Robert Harley	18 May 04 (vac. 13 Feb 08)
	Henry Boyle	13 Feb 08 (vac. Sept 10)
P.S.	John Sheffield, M. of Normanby (D of Buckinghamshire and Normanby, 1703)	27 Apr 02
	John Holles, D of Newcastle-Upon-Tyne (died 15 July 11)	21 Mar 05
B.O.T.	Thomas Thynne, Vt Weymouth	12 June 02
	Thomas Grey, E of Stamford	25 Apr 07
Admir.	Prince George of Denmark	20 May 02
	Queen Anne (Lord High Admiral)	28 Oct 08
	Thomas Herbert, E, of Pembroke	29 Nov 08
	Edward Russell, E of Oxford	8 Nov 09

Sec. at War	George Clarke	3 Mar 92
	Henry St John	20 Apr 04
	Robert Walpole	25 Feb 08
Treas. of the Navy	Sir Thomas Littleton	29 May 99
	Robert Walpole	21 Jan 10
Pay.-Gen.	John Howe	4 Jan 03
	Charles Fox	4 Jan 03
	James Brydges	07

HARLEY, 1710–14 (formed August 1710)

Ld Treas.	John Poulett, Earl Poulett	11 Aug 10
	Robert Harley, E of Oxford	29 Mar 11
	Charles Talbot, D of Shrewsbury (vac. Oct 1714)	30 July 14
Chanc. Exch.	Robert Harley	10 Aug 10
Ld Pres.	Laurence Hyde, E of Rochester	21 Sept 10 (d. 21 May 11)
	John Sheffield, D of Buckinghamshire and of Normanby	14 June 11
D. Lanc.	William Berkeley, Ld Berkeley	21 Sept 10
Master-Gen. of Ordnance	John Churchill, D of Marlborough	1 July 02
	Richard Savage, Earl Rivers	1 Jan 12
	James Douglas, D of Hamilton and Brandon (died 15 Nov 12)	1 July 12
Sec. of State (South)	William Legge, Ld Dartmouth (E of Dartmouth, 1711)	15 June 10 (vac. 6–13 Aug. 1713)
	Henry St John, Vt Bolingbroke	17 Aug 13 (dism. 31 Aug 14)
Sec. of State (North)	Henry St John, Vt Bolingbroke	21 Sept 10
	William Bromley	17 Aug 13 (dism. Sept 14)
P.S.	John Holles, D of Newcastle-Upon-Tyne (died 15 July 11)	21 Mar 05

	John Robinson, Bp of Bristol	31 Aug 11
	William Legge, E of	
	Dartmouth	21 Aug 13
B.O.T.	Thomas Grey, E of Stamford	25 Apr 07
	Charles Finch, E of	
	Winchilsea	12 June 11
	Francis North, Ld Guildford	15 Sept 13
Admir.	Edward Russell, E of Oxford	8 Nov 09
	Sir John Leake	4 Oct 10
	Thomas Wentworth, E of	
	Strafford	30 Sept 12
Sec. at War	George Granville	28 Sept 10
	Sir William Wyndham	28 June 12
	Francis Gwyn	21 Aug 13
Treas. of the Navy	Robert Walpole	21 Jan 10
	Charles Caesar	8 June 11
Pay.-Gen.	James Brydges	…07
	Thomas Moore	…13
	Edward Nicholas	…13

STANHOPE, 1714–17 (formed Sep 1714)

1st Ld Treas.	Charles Montagu, E of	
	Halifax	11 Oct 14
	Charles Howard, E of	
	Carlisle	23 May 15
	Robert Walpole	10 Oct 15
Chanc. Exch.	Richard Onslow	13 Oct 14
	Robert Walpole	12 Oct 15
Ld Pres.	Daniel Finch, E of	
	Nottingham	22 Sept 14
	William Cavendish, D of	
	Devonshire	6 July 16
Ld Chanc.	William Cowper,	
	Lord Cowper	21 Sept 14
P.S.	Thomas Wharton,	
	Earl Wharton	27 Sept 14
	(Seal in commission 30 Apr–	
	2 Sep 15)	

	Charles Spencer, E of	
	Sunderland	2 Sept 15
	Evelyn Pierrepoint, D of	
	Kingston-Upon-Hull	19 Dec 16
D. Lanc.	Heneage Finch, E of	
	Aylesford	4 Nov 14
	Richard Lumley, E of	
	Scarborough	12 Mar 16
Master-Gen. of	John Churchill, D of	
Ordnance	Marlborough	1 Oct 14
Sec. of State (South)	James Stanhope	27 Sept 14
	Paul Methuen	22 June 16
Sec. of State (North)	Charles Townshend,	
	Vt Townshend	17 Sept 14
	James Stanhope	12 Dec 16
Sec. for Scotland	James Graham, D of	
	Montrose	24 Sept 14
	John Ker, D of Roxburghe	13 Dec 16
Pay.-Gen.	Robert Walpole	17 Sept 14
	E of Lincoln	Oct 15
Admir.	Edward Russell, E of Oxford	14 Oct 14
Sec. at War	William Pulteney	Sept 14
B.O.T.	Francis North, Ld Guildford	15 Sept 13
	William Berkeley,	
	Ld Berkeley	13 Dec 14
	Henry Howard, E of Suffolk	12 May 15
Ld Lt of Ireland	Charles Spencer, E of	
	Sunderland	4 Oct 14
	Charles Townshend,	
	Vt Townshend	13 Feb 17

STANHOPE–SUNDERLAND, 1717–18 (formed April 1717)

1st Ld Treas.	James Stanhope,	
	Vt Stanhope	12 Apr 17
Chanc. Exchq.	James Stanhope,	
	Vt Stanhope	15 Apr 17
Ld Pres.	Vacant from 30 Mar 17	

Ld Chanc.	William Cowper, Ld Cowper	21 Sept 14
Sec. of State (South)	Joseph Addison	15–16 Apr 17
Sec. of State (North)	Charles Spencer, E of Sunderland	15–16 Apr 17
Sec. for Scotland	John Ker, D of Roxburghe	13 Dec 16
P.S.	Evelyn Pierrepoint, D of Kingston-Upon-Hull	19 Dec 16
D. Lanc.	Richard Lumley, E of Scarborough	12 Mar 16
	Nicholas Lechmere	19 June 17
Pay.-Gen.	E of Lincoln	Oct 15
Admir.	James Berkeley, E of Berkeley	16 Apr 17
B.O.T.	Henry Howard, E of Suffolk	12 May 15
	Robert Darcy, E of Holdernesse	31 Jan 18
Lt Lt of Ireland	Charles Powlett, D of Bolton	27 Apr 17

RECONSTRUCTED STANHOPE–SUNDERLAND, 1718–21 (March 1718)

1st Ld Treas.	Charles Spencer, E of Sunderland	21 Mar 18
Ld Pres.	Charles Spencer, E of Sunderland	16 Mar 18
	Evelyn Pierrepoint, D of Kingston-Upon-Hull	6 Feb 19
	Charles Townshend, Vt Townshend	11 June 20
Ld Chanc.	Thomas Parker, Ld Macclesfield	12 May 18
Sec. of State (North)	James Stanhope, Earl Stanhope (died 4 Feb 21)	18–21 Mar 18
	Charles Townshend, Vt Townshend	10 Feb 21
Sec. of State (South)	James Craggs (died 16 Feb 21)	16 Mar 18

Chanc. Exch.	John Aislabie	20 Mar 18
P.S.	Evelyn Pierrepoint, D of Kingston-Upon-Hull	19 Dec 16
	Henry Grey, D of Kent	14 Feb 19
	Evelyn Pierrepoint, D of Kingston-Upon-Hull	13 June 20
Pay.-Gen.	Earl of Lincoln	Oct 15
	Robert Walpole	11 June 20
B.O.T.	Robert Darcy, E of Holdernesse	31 Jan 18
	Thomas Fane, E of Westmorland	11 May 19
Ld Lt of Ireland	Charles Pawlett, D of Bolton	27 Apr 17
	Charles, D of Grafton	8 June 20
Sec. of Scotland	John Ker, D of Roxburghe	13 Dec 16
Admir.	James Berkeley, E of Berkeley	16 Apr 17

WALPOLE 1721–42 (formed April 1721)

1st Ld Treas.	Robert Walpole	4 Apr 21
Chanc. Exch.	Robert Walpole	3 Apr 21
Ld Chanc.	Thomas Parker, Ld Macclesfield (Seal in Commission Jan 25)	12 May 18
	Peter King, Ld King	1 June 25
	Charles Talbot, Ld Talbot of Hensol (died 14 Feb 33)	29 Nov 33
	Philip Yorke, Ld Hardwicke	21 Feb 37
Ld Pres.	Charles Townshend, Vt Townshend	11 June 20
	Henry Boyle, Ld Carleton	25 June 21
	William Cavendish, D of Devonshire (died 4 Jun 29)	27 Mar 25
	Thomas Trevor, Ld Trevor of Bromham (died 19 June 30)	8 May 30
	Spencer Compton, E of Wilmington	31 Dec 30

P.S.	Evelyn Pierrepoint, D of Kingston-Upon-Hull (died 5 Mar 26)	13 June 20
	Thomas Trevor, Ld Trevor of Bromham	10 Mar 26
	Spencer Compton, E of Wilmington (Seal in Commission 1 Jan 31)	8 May 30
	William Cavendish, D of Devonshire	12 June 31
	Henry Lowther, Vt Lonsdale	8 May 33
	Francis Godolphin, E of Godolphin	15 May 35
	John Hervey, Ld Hervey of Ickworth	29 Apr 40
Admir.	James Berkeley, E of Berkeley	16 Apr 17
	George Byng, Vt Torrington	29 July 27
	Charles Wager	25 Jan 33
D. Lanc.	Nicholas Lechmere (Ld Lechmere, 1721)	19 June 17
	John Manners, D of Rutland	24 July 27
	George Cholmondeley, E of Cholmondeley	17 May 36
Sec. of State (South)	John Carteret, Ld Carteret	4 Mar 21
	Thomas Pelham-Holles, D of Newcastle	6 Apr 24
Sec. of State (North)	Charles Townshend, Vt Townshend (vacated office 16 May 30)	10 Feb 21
	William Stanhope, Ld Harrington	19 June 30
B.O.T.	Thomas Fane, E of Westmorland	11 May 19
	Benjamin Mildmay, Earl Fitzwalter	14 May 35
	John Monson, Ld Monson	27 June 37
Ld Lt of Ireland	Charles, D of Grafton	8 June 20
	John Carteret, Ld Carteret	6 May 24
	Lionel Cranfield, E of	

	Dorset	23 June 30
	William Cavendish, D of Devonshire	9 Apr 37

CARTERET, 1742–4 (formed Feb 1742)

1st Ld Treas.	Spencer Compton, E of Wilmington	16 Feb 42
	Henry Pelham	27 Aug 43
Chanc. Exch.	Samuel Sandys	12 Feb 42
	Henry Pelham	12 Dec 43
Sec. of State (North)	John Carteret, Ld Carteret	12 Feb 42
Sec. of State (South)	Thomas Pelham-Holles, D of Newcastle-Upon-Tyne	6 Apr 24
Ld Pres.	William Stanhope, E of Harrington	13 Feb 42
Ld Chanc.	Philip Yorke, Ld Hardwicke	21 Feb 37
P.S.	John Hervey, Ld Hervey of Ickworth	29 Apr 40
	John Leveson-Gower, Ld Gower	13 July 42
	George Cholmondeley, E of Cholmondeley	12 Dec 43
D. Lanc.	George Cholmondeley, E of Cholmondeley	17 May 36
	Richard Edgcumbe, Ld Edgcumbe of Mount Edgcumbe	22 Dec 43
B.O.T.	John Monson, Ld Monson	27 June 37
Admir.	Sir Charles Wager	25 Jan 33
	Daniel Finch, E of Winchilsea and E of Nottingham	19 Mar 42
Ld Lt of Ireland	William Cavendish, D of Devonshire	9 Apr 37

PELHAM, 1744–6 (formed Nov 1744)

1st Ld Treas.	Henry Pelham	27 Aug 43

Chanc. Exch.	Henry Pelham	12 Dec 43
Sec. of State (North)	William Stanhope, E of Harrington	24 Nov 44
Sec. of State (South)	Thomas Pelham-Holles, D of Newcastle-Upon-Tyne	6 Apr 24
Ld Pres.	William Stanhope, E of Harrington	13 Feb 42
	Lionel Cranfield Sackville, D of Dorset	3 Jan 45
Ld Chanc.	Philip Yorke, Ld Hardwicke	21 Feb 37
P.S.	George Cholmondeley, E of Cholmondeley	12 Dec 43
	John Leveson-Gower, Ld Gower	26 Dec 44
D. Lanc.	Richard Edgcumbe, Ld Edgcumbe of Mount Edgcumbe	22 Dec 43
B.O.T.	John Monson, Ld Monson	27 June 37
Admir.	Daniel Finch, E of Winchelsea	19 Mar 42
	John Russell, D of Bedford	27 Dec 44
Ld Lt of Ireland	William Cavendish, D of Devonshire	9 Apr 37
	Philip Dormer Stanhope, E of Chesterfield	8 Jan 45

BATH, 1746 (Feb 1746)

On 6 February 1746, George II asked the Earl of Bath (William Pulteney) and Earl Granville (John Carteret) to form a new administration, taking the offices of First Lord of the Treasury and Secretary of State (North) respectively. Henry Pelham, the Duke of Newcastle, the Earl of Harrington and Lord Hardwicke resigned office. Although Bath and Granville took office for a few days, the King was forced to reappoint the previous administration.

PELHAM, 1746–54

1st Ld Treas.	Henry Pelham	14 Feb 46

Chanc. Exch.	Henry Pelham	12 Dec 43
Sec. of State (North)	William Stanhope, E of Harrington (vacated 28 Oct 46)	14 Feb 46
	Philip Dormer Stanhope, E of Chesterfield (vacated 6 Feb 48)	29 Oct 46
	Thomas Pelham-Holles, D of Newcastle-Upon-Tyne	6–12 Feb 48
Sec. of State (South)	Thomas Pelham-Holles, D of Newcastle-Upon-Tyne	14 Feb 46
	John Russell, D of Bedford (vacated 13 June 51)	6–12 Feb 48
	Robert Darcy, E of Holderness	18 June 51
Ld Pres.	Lionel Cranfield Sackville, D of Dorset	3 Jan 51
	John Carteret, E of Granville	17 June 51
P.S.	John Leveson-Gower, Ld Gower	26 Dec 44
D. Lanc.	Richard Edgcumbe, Ld Edgcumbe	22 Dec 43
B.O.T.	John Monson, Ld Monson	27 June 37
	George Montagu, E of Halifax	1 Nov 48
Admir.	John Russell, D of Bedford	27 Dec 44
	John Montagu, E of Sandwich	20 Feb 48
	George Anson, Ld Anson	22 June 51

NEWCASTLE, 1754–6 (formed Mar 1754)

1st Ld Treas.	Thomas Pelham-Holles, D of Newcastle-Upon-Tyne	16 Mar 54
Chanc. Exch.	Sir William Lee	8 Mar 54
	Henry Bilson Legge	6 Apr 54
	Sir George Lyttleton	25 Nov 55

Ld Pres.	John Carteret, E of Granville	17 June 51
P.S.	John Leveson-Gower, Ld Gower (d. 25 Dec 54)	26 Dec 44
	Charles Spencer, D of Marlborough	9 Jan 55
	Granville Leveson-Gower, Earl Gower	22 Dec 55
D. Lanc.	Richard Edgcumbe, Ld Edgcumbe	22 Dec 43
Sec. of State (*North*)	Robert Darcy, E of Holderness	23 Mar 54
Sec. of State (*South*)	Sir Thomas Robinson (vacated Oct 55)	23 Mar 54
	Henry Fox (vacated 13 Nov 56)	14 Nov 55
B.O.T.	George Montagu, E of Halifax	1 Nov 48
Admir.	George Anson, Ld Anson	22 June 51
Ld Lt of Ireland	Lionel Cranfield, D of Dorset	15 Dec 50
	William Cavendish, D of Devonshire	2 Apr 55

PITT–DEVONSHIRE, 1756–7 (formed Nov 1756)

1st Ld Treas.	William Cavendish, D of Devonshire	16 Nov 56
Chanc. Exch.	Henry Bilson Legge	16 Nov 56
	William Murray, Ld Mansfield	13 Apr 57
P.S.	Granville Leveson-Gower, Earl Gower	22 Dec 55
D. Lanc.	Richard Edgcumbe, Ld Edgcumbe	22 Dec 43
Sec. of State (*South*)	William Pitt (Dismissed 6 Apr 57)	4 Dec 56

Sec. of State (North)	Robert Darcy, E of Holderness (vacated 9 Jun 57)	23 Mar 54
B.O.T.	George Montagu, E of Halifax	1 Nov 48
Admir.	Richard Grenville, Earl Temple	19 Nov 56
	Daniel Finch, E of Nottingham	6 Apr 57
Treas. of Navy	George Grenville	25 Nov 56
Ld Lt of Ireland	William Cavendish, D of Devonshire	2 Apr 55
	John Russell, D of Bedford	3 Jan 57

PITT–NEWCASTLE, 1757–61 (formed July 1757)

1st Ld Treas.	Thomas Pelham-Holles, D of Newcastle	29 June 57
Chanc. Exch.	Henry Bilson Legge	2 July 57
	William Wildman Barrington-Shute, Vt Barrington	19 Mar 61
Ld Pres.	John Carteret, E of Granville	17 June 51
P.S.	Richard Grenville-Temple, Earl Temple	5 July 57
Ld Keeper	Sir Richard Henley	30 June 57
D. Lanc.	Richard Edgcumbe, Ld Edgcumbe	22 Dec 43
	Thomas Hay, E of Kinnoull and Ld Hay	24 Jan 58 (renewed 27 Feb 60)
Sec. of State (South)	William Pitt	27 June 57
Sec. of State (North)	Robert Darcy, E of Holderness	23 Mar 54
	John Stuart, E of Bute	25 Mar 61

B.O.T.	George Montagu, E of Halifax	1 Nov 48
Admir.	George Anson, Ld Anson	2 July 57
Treas. of Navy	George Grenville	25 Nov 56
Sec. at War	William Wildman Barrington-Shute, Vt Barrington	14 Nov 55
	Charles Townshend	18 Mar 61
Pay.-Gen.	Henry Fox	July 57
Ld Lt of Ireland	John Russell, D of Bedford	3 Jan 57

MINISTERIAL BIOGRAPHIES

The following names include the major holders of office in the period. Peers are listed under the last title they held, e.g. for Carteret, see Granville. Usually only major offices are included.

ADDISON, JOSEPH (1672–1719)

MP, Lostwithiel 1708; Malmesbury 1709–19. Secretary of State 1717–18; previously Under-Secretary of State 1706; secretary to Wharton when Lord Lieutenant of Ireland, 1709. Distinguished essayist and poet, contributed to Steele's *Tatler* 1709–11, and produced with Steele the *Spectator* 1711–12; contributor to *Guardian* 1713 and revived *Tatler* in 1714.

BATH, E OF   WILLIAM PULTENEY (1684–1764)

MP Hedon 1705–34; Middlesex 1734–42. Secretary at War 1714–17; resigned with Walpole but moved into opposition after failing to secure office under his premiership. Later wrote for *The Craftsman* and joined 'the patriots'. Declined invitation to form administration after the fall of Walpole and refused office, although a member of Cabinet under Wilmington. Created Earl of Bath 1742; failed in attempt to form an administration at behest of George II in 1746.

BEDFORD, 4TH D OF   JOHN RUSSELL (1710–71)

First Lord of the Admiralty 1744–8; Lord Justice of Great Britain 1745,

1748 and 1750; Secretary of State 1748–51; Lord Lieutenant of Ireland 1756–7; Privy Seal 1761–3; Lord President 1763–5.

BOLINGBROKE, 1ST VT   HENRY ST JOHN (1678–1751)

MP, Wooton Bassett 1701–10; Berkshire 1710–12; Secretary at War 1704–8; Secretary of State 1710–13, 1713–14. Took charge of peace negotiations of Utrecht, 1713. Dismissed from office by George I in 1714 for his support for the Pretender. Motion for his impeachment carried, bill of attainder passed against him and name erased from roll of peers, 1714; fled to France and became Secretary of State to the Pretender; dismissed from his service 1716. Pardoned 1723; returned to England 1725. Contributed to *The Craftsman* and author of several political works, notably, *The Idea of a Patriot King*, 1738.

BROMLEY WILLIAM (1664–1732)

MP, Warwickshire 1690–1702; Oxford University 1702–32. Speaker of the House of Commons 1710; Secretary of State 1713–14.

CARLETON, 1ST B   HENRY BOYLE (d. 1725)

MP, Tamworth 1689–90; Cambridge University 1692–1705; Westminster 1705–10. Chancellor of the Exchequer 1701; Lord Treasurer of Ireland 1704–10; Secretary of State 1708–10; Lord President 1721–5.

CARLISLE, 3RD E OF   CHARLES HOWARD (1674–1738)

MP, Morpeth 1690–2; First Lord of the Treasury 1701–2, 1715. Commissioner for Scottish Union.

CHATHAM, 1ST E OF   WILLIAM PITT 'the elder' (1707–78)

MP, Old Sarum 1735–47; Seaford 1747–54; Aldborough 1754–6; Oke-hampton 1756–7; Bath 1757–66. Vice-Treasurer of Ireland 1746; Paymaster-General 1746–55; Secretary of State 1756–7, 1757–61; Privy Seal (Prime Minister) 1766–8. Leader of the House of Commons 1756–61.

CHESTERFIELD, 4TH E OF   PHILIP DORMER STANHOPE (1694–1773)

MP, St Germans 1715–22; Lostwithiel 1722–5. Privy Councillor 1727; Lord Steward 1730–3; Secretary of State 1746–8.

CRAGGS, JAMES (1686-1721)

MP, Tregony 1713-21. Secretary at War 1717-18; Secretary of State 1718-21. Implicated in the South Sea Company scandal.

DARTMOUTH, 1ST E OF   WILLIAM LEGGE (1672-1750)

Privy Councillor 1702; Secretary of State 1710-13; Privy Seal 1713-14.

DEVONSHIRE, 4TH D OF   WILLIAM CAVENDISH (1720-64)

MP, Derbyshire 1741-51. Styled Marquis of Hartington until 1755; Baron Cavendish of Hardwicke, 1751; Duke of Devonshire 1755. Lord Lieutenant of Ireland 1755-6; First Lord of the Treasury (Prime Minister) 1756-7; Lord Chamberlain 1757-62.

GODOLPHIN, 1ST E OF   SIDNEY GODOLPHIN (1645-1712)

MP, Helston 1668-79; St Mawes 1679-81. A Lord of the Treasury, 1679; Secretary of State 1684; Commissioner of the Treasury 1687; head of the Treasury 1690-6. Lord Justice 1695, 1700-1. Lord High Treasurer 1702-10.

GRANTHAM, 1ST B   THOMAS ROBINSON (1695-1770)

MP, Thirsk 1727-34; Christchurch 1748-61. Diplomatist, English representative at Congress of Soissons, 1728-9; ambassador at Vienna 1730-48, joint-plenipotentiary of England in negotiations of Aix-la-Chapelle 1748. Privy Councillor 1750; Secretary of State and leader of the House of Commons 1754-5, joint postmaster-general 1765-6.

GRANVILLE, 1ST E   JOHN CARTERET (1690-1763)

Took seat in House of Lords, 1711. Envoy to Sweden 1719; negotiated peace between the Baltic powers 1719-20. Secretary of State 1742-4; failed to form an administration, 1746; Lord President of the Council 1751-63.

HALIFAX, 1ST E OF   CHARLES MONTAGU (1661-1715)

MP, Maldon 1689-95; Westminster 1695-1700. Clerk of the Privy Council 1689; a Lord of the Treasury 1692. Chancellor of the Exchequer 1694-9; Privy Councillor 1694. Proposed formation of National Debt, 1692; introduced bill establishing Bank of England, 1694; introduced Recoinage Bill 1695. First Lord of the Treasury 1697-9; auditor of the Exchequer, 1699-1714.

Impeached by House of Commons, 1701 for corruption, but charges dismissed. First Lord of the Treasury 1714–15.

HARRINGTON, 1ST E OF   WILLIAM STANHOPE (1690–1756)

MP, Derby 1715–22, 1727–30. Diplomatist and statesman; envoy to Madrid 1717–18; Turin 1718; ambassador in Spain 1719–27. Vice-Chamberlain 1727–30; Privy Councillor 1727–30. Secretary of State 1730–42; Lord President 1742–5; Secretary of State 1744–6, again 1746; Lord Lieutenant of Ireland 1746–51.

HEDGES, SIR CHARLES (d. 1714)

MP, Oxford 1698–1700; Dover 1701; Malmesbury 1701, Calne 1702; West Looe, 1705, 1708, 1710; East Looe, 1713–14. Secretary of State 1700–1; 1702–6.

HOLDERNESS, 4TH E OF   ROBERT D'ARCY (1718–78)

Ambassador to Vienna 1744–6; minister plenipotentiary at the Hague 1749–51. Secretary of State 1751–61; Privy Councillor 1751.

HOLLAND, 1ST B   HENRY FOX (1705–74)

MP, Hindon 1735–41; Windsor 1741–61; Dunwich 1761–3. Lord of the Treasury 1743; Secretary at War 1746–54; Secretary of State 1755–6; Paymaster-General 1757–65; Leader of the House of Commons 1762–3.

LONSDALE, VT   JOHN LOWTHER (1655–1700)

MP, Westmorland 1676–96. Vice Chamberlain 1689–94; Privy Councillor 1689. First Lord of the Treasury 1690–2; Privy Seal 1699–1700. Active supporter of exclusion of Duke of York from the succession and of William III's invasion in 1688.

MANCHESTER, 1ST D OF   CHARLES MONTAGU (1660–1722)

Ambassador extraordinary at Venice 1697; Paris 1699; Venice, again, 1707. Secretary of State 1702.

METHUEN, PAUL (1672–1757)

MP, Devizes 1708–10, Brackley 1713–47. Envoy to the King of Portugal 1697–1705; Minister to Turin 1705; ambassador to Portugal 1706–8. Lord of the Admiralty 1714–17; Secretary of State 1717. Ambassador to Spain and Morocco and Privy Councillor 1714. Comptroller of the Household 1720–5.

NEWCASTLE, 1ST D OF   THOMAS PELHAM-HOLLES (1693–1768)

Lord Chamberlain 1717–24. Secretary of State 1724–46, 1746–54. First Lord of the Treasury 1754–6, 1757–62. Lord Privy Seal, July 1765 to Aug 1766. Created Earl of Clare and Duke of Newcastle 1715.

NOTTINGHAM, 2ND E OF AND 6TH OF WINCHILSEA   DANIEL FINCH (1647–1730)

Privy Councillor 1680; succeeded to his father's title 1682; First Lord of the Admiralty 1681–4; in 1688–9 proposed a regency to fill the gap after the flight of James II. Secretary at War 1688–93; Secretary of State 1702–4; Lord President of the Council 1714–16.

ORFORD, 1ST E OF   ROBERT WALPOLE (1676–1745)

MP, Castle Rising 1700–1; Kings Lynn 1702–12, 1713–42. Secretary at War 1708–11; Paymaster of the Forces 1714–17, 1720–1. Privy Councillor 1714. First Lord of the Treasury and Chancellor of the Exchequer 1715–17, 1721–42. Order of the Bath 1725; Knight of the Garter 1726; Earl of Orford 1742.

OXFORD, 1ST E OF   ROBERT HARLEY (1661–1724)

MP, Tregony 1689–90; New Radnor 1690–1711. Speaker of the House of Commons 1701–5; Secretary of State 1704–8; Chancellor of the Exchequer 1710–1; Lord Treasurer 1711–14. Created Baron Harley, Earl of Oxford and Mortimer 1711; Knight of the Garter 1712. Effective leader of strong Tory administration from 1710; obtained dismissal of Marlborough and helped to force through the peace of Utrecht, but supplanted by Bolingbroke and dismissed from office in 1714. Movement of impeachment against him dismissed, 1717.

PELHAM, HENRY (1695–1754)

MP, Seaford 1717–22; Sussex 1722–54. Secretary at War 1724–30; Paymaster-General 1730–43; First Lord of the Treasury and Chancellor of the Exchequer 1743–54.

PETERBOROUGH, 3RD E OF AND 1ST E OF MONMOUTH CHARLES MORDAUNT (1658–1735)

Privy Councillor 1689; First Lord of the Treasury 1689–90; joint-commander of expeditionary force to Spain 1705; recalled to England 1707 to face enquiry into his conduct. Knight of the Garter 1713; ambassador extraordinary to Italian princes 1713–14.

POULETT, 1ST E   JOHN POULETT (1663–1743)

Privy Councillor 1702; created Earl Poulett 1706. First Lord of the Treasury 1710–11; Knight of the Garter 1713.

ROMNEY, E OF   HENRY SIDNEY OR SYDNEY (1641–1704)

MP, Bramber 1679–81; Tamworth 1689. Envoy to The Hague 1679–81 and General of British regiments in Dutch service 1681–5. Carried invitation to William III and accompanied him to England. Created Privy Councillor and Viscount Sydney 1689. Secretary of State 1690–1; Lord Lieutenant of Ireland 1692–3; Master General of Ordnance 1693–1702. Created an earl 1694; a Lord Justice 1697; Groom of the Stole 1700–2.

SHREWSBURY, 1ST D OF   CHARLES TALBOT (1660–1718)

Accompanied William III to England 1688; Secretary of State 1689–90, 1694–8. Knight of the Garter 1694; accused of complicity in Jacobite intrigues and withdrew temporarily from public affairs. Ambassador to France 1712–13; Lord Lieutenant of Ireland 1713–14. Lord Treasurer 1714 (July–Oct), ensuring Hanoverian succession. Lord Chamberlain 1714–15.

SOMERS, B   JOHN SOMERS (1651–1716)

MP, Worcester 1689–93. Junior Counsel for the Seven Bishops; negotiated with William III preceding his invasion; in Convention Parliament asserted that James II had abdicated; presided over the drafting of the Declaration of Rights. Solicitor-General 1689–93; Lord-Keeper 1693–7; Lord High Chancellor 1697–1700. Created Baron Somers 1697. Impeached in 1700, but acquitted of charges. Lord President 1708–10.

STANHOPE, 1ST E   JAMES STANHOPE (1673–1721)

MP, Newport (I. of Wight) 1715–17. British minister in Spain 1706; appointed commander of British forces in Spain 1708. Secretary of State 1714–17, 1718–21. Took leading part in securing Hanoverian succession; carried impeachment of Ormonde and directed measures for suppressing Jacobite rising of 1715. Lord Treasurer and Chancellor of the Exchequer 1717–18. Defeated on Peerage Bill and compromised by South Sea Bubble question.

SUNDERLAND, 3RD E OF   CHARLES SPENCER (1674–1722)

MP, Tiverton 1695–1702. Envoy extraordinary to Vienna 1705. Secretary of State, 1706–10. Lord Lieutenant of Ireland 1714–17; Lord Privy Seal 1715–16. First Lord of the Treasury 1718–21. Disgraced and forced to resign following South Sea Bubble.

TANKERVILLE, E OF   FORDE GREY (d. 1701)

Succeeded as third Baron Grey 1675. Forced into exile on discovery of Rye House Plot 1683; commanded Monmouth's horse at Sedgemoor, but restored to his title 1685. Supported William III; created Earl of Tankerville 1695; Privy Councillor 1695. Commissioner of Trade 1696; first Commissioner of the Treasury 1699. Lord Privy Seal 1700–1.

TOWNSHEND, 2ND VT   CHARLES TOWNSHEND (1674–1738)

Succeeded to the peerage 1687; negotiator of treaty of union 1706; Privy Councillor 1707; plenipotentiary to Netherlands 1709, but recalled 1711 on change of administration and vote of censure passed against him. Secretary of State 1714–16. Lord Lieutenant of Ireland, 1717; Lord President of the Council 1720–1; Secretary of State, 1721–30. Knight of the Garter, 1724. Resigned following disagreements with Walpole on foreign policy.

TRENCHARD, SIR JOHN (1640–95)

MP, Taunton 1678–81; Dorchester 1688; Thetford 1689–90; Poole 1690–5. Supporter of the Exclusion Bill and implicated in the Rye House Plot; arrested and later fled abroad. Pardoned by James II; knighted 1689. Secretary of State 1692–5.

TRUMBULL, SIR WILLIAM (1639–1716)

MP, East Looe 1685–7; Oxford University 1695–8, knighted 1684; envoy to France 1685; ambassador to Turkey 1686–91; governor of Hudson's Bay and Turkey companies; Lord of the Treasury 1694; Secretary of State, Privy Councillor and Secretary to Lords Justices 1695.

VERNON, JAMES (1646–1727)

MP, Cambridge University 1678–9; Penryn 1695–8; Westminster 1698–1702; Penryn 1705–10. Political agent in Holland 1672; attached to the Paris embassy 1673; secretary to the Duke of Monmouth 1674–8; editor *London Gazette* 1678–89; a commissioner of prizes 1693–1705. Secretary of State 1697–1702; teller of the Exchequer 1702–10.

WILMINGTON, 1ST EARL OF   SPENCER COMPTON (1673–1743)

MP, Eye 1698–1710; East Grinstead 1713–15; Sussex 1715–22; East Grinstead 1722; Sussex 1722–8. Chairman of Committee of Privileges and Elections 1705–10. Speaker of the House of Commons 1715–27; Paymaster-General 1722–30. Knight of the Bath 1725; created Baron Wilmington 1728; and Earl 1730. Lord Privy Seal 1730; Lord President 1730–42; First Lord of the Treasury 1742–3.

4 SELECTED HOLDERS OF MAJOR PUBLIC OFFICE

FIRST LORD OF THE TREASURY

Oct	14	E of Halifax
May	15	E of Carlisle
Oct	15	Robert Walpole
Apr	17	Earl Stanhope
Mar	18	E of Sunderland
Apr	21	Robert Walpole[1]
Feb	42	E of Wilmington
Aug	43	Henry Pelham
Feb	46	E of Bath[2]
Feb	46	Henry Pelham
Mar	54	D of Newcastle
Nov	56	D of Devonshire
Jul	57	D of Newcastle
May	62	E of Bute

LORD CHANCELLOR

1689–93		In commission
Mar	93	Ld Somers
May	00	Sir Nathan Wright (Ld Keeper)
Oct	05	Ld Cowper
Sep	08	In commission
Oct	10	Ld Harcourt
Sep	14	Ld Cowper
May	18	E of Macclesfield
Jan	25	In commission

---

[1] No office of Prime Minister existed in this period, but it is customary to regard Walpole as the first to wield Prime Ministerial authority. It was also to become common for such authority to be combined with the post of First Lord of the Treasury, but not in every case. See the list of administrations (pp. 33–46) for the offices held by the leading politicians in successive administrations.

[2] For the interruption of Henry Pelham's tenure of office in February 1746 see p. 42.

Jun	25	Ld King
Nov	33	Ld Talbot
Feb	37	E of Hardwicke
Nov	56	In commission
Jun	57	E of Northington
Jul	66	Ld Camden

LORD PRESIDENT OF THE COUNCIL

Feb	89	D of Leeds
May	99	E of Pembroke
Jan	02	D of Somerset
Jul	02	E of Pembroke
Nov	08	Ld Somers
Sep	10	E of Rochester
Jun	11	D of Buckinghamshire
Sep	14	E of Nottingham
Jul	16	D of Devonshire
Mar	18	E of Sunderland
Feb	19	D of Kingston
Jun	20	Vt Townshend
Jun	21	Ld Carleton
Mar	25	D of Devonshire
May	30	Ld Trevor
Dec	30	E of Wilmington
Feb	42	E of Harrington
Jan	45	D of Dorset
Jun	51	E of Granville
Sep	63	D of Bedford

LORD PRIVY SEAL

Mar	89	M of Halifax
Feb	90	In commission
Mar	92	E of Montgomery
May	99	Vt Lonsdale
Nov	00	E of Tankerville
Jun	01	In commission
Apr	02	D of Buckinghamshire
Mar	05	D of Newcastle
Aug	11	John Robinson
Aug	13	E of Dartmouth
Sep	14	M of Wharton
Apr	15	In commission

Sep	15	E of Sunderland
Dec	16	D of Kingston
Feb	19	D of Kent
Jun	20	D of Kingston
Mar	26	Ld Trevor
May	30	E of Wilmington
Jan	31	In commission
Jun	31	D of Devonshire
May	33	Vt Lonsdale
May	35	E of Godolphin
Apr	40	Ld Hervey
Jul	42	Ld Gower
Dec	43	E of Cholmondeley
Dec	44	Ld Gower
Jan	55	D of Marlborough
Dec	55	Earl Gower
Jul	57	Earl Temple
Oct	61	In commission

SECRETARY OF STATE FOR THE NORTHERN DEPARTMENT

Oct	88	Vt Preston
Mar	89	E of Nottingham
Dec	90	Vt Sydney
Mar	93	Sir John Trenchard
Mar	94	D of Shrewsbury
May	95	Sir William Trumbull
Dec	97	James Vernon
Nov	00	Sir Charles Hedges
Jan	02	James Vernon
May	04	Sir Charles Hedges
May	04	Robert Harley
Feb	08	Hon Henry Boyle
Sep	10	Henry St John (Vt Bolingbroke)
Aug	13	William Bromley
Sep	14	Vt Townshend
Dec	16	Vt Stanhope
Apr	17	E of Sunderland
Mar	18	Earl Stanhope
Feb	21	Vt Townshend
Jun	30	E of Harrington
Feb	42	Earl Granville
Nov	44	E of Harrington
Feb	46	Earl Granville

Feb	46	E of Harrington
Oct	46	E of Chesterfield
Feb	48	D of Newcastle
Mar	54	E of Holderness
Mar	61	E of Bute

SECRETARY OF STATE FOR THE SOUTHERN DEPARTMENT

Feb	89	E of Shrewsbury
Dec	90	E of Nottingham
Mar	93	E of Nottingham (again)
Mar	94	Sir John Trenchard
Apr	95	D of Shrewsbury
May	99	E of Jersey
Nov	00	James Vernon
Jan	02	E of Manchester
May	04	Sir Charles Hedges
Dec	06	E of Sunderland
Jun	10	Ld (E of) Dartmouth
Aug	13	Vt Bolingbroke
Sep	14	Vt Stanhope
Jun	16	Paul Methuen
Apr	17	Joseph Addison
Mar	18	James Craggs
Mar	21	Ld Carteret
Apr	24	D of Newcastle
Feb	48	D of Bedford
Jun	51	E of Holderness
Mar	54	Sir Thomas Robinson
Nov	55	Henry Fox
Dec	56	William Pitt
Apr	57	E of Holderness
Jun	57	William Pitt
Oct	61	E of Egremont

CHANCELLOR OF THE EXCHEQUER

Apr	89	Ld Delamere
Mar	90	Richard Hampden
May	94	C. Montagu
Jun	99	J. Smith
Mar	01	Hon H. Boyle
Apr	08	J. Smith
Aug	10	Robert Harley

Jun	11	R. Benson
Aug	13	Sir W. Wyndham
Oct	14	Sir Richard Onslow
Oct	15	Robert Walpole
Apr	17	Earl Stanhope
Mar	18	John Aislabie
Feb	21	Sir John Pratt
Apr	21	E of Orford
Feb	42	Ld Sandys
Dec	43	Henry Pelham
Mar	54	Sir William Lee
Apr	54	Henry Bilson Legge
Nov	55	Ld Lyttelton
Nov	56	Henry Bilson Legge
Apr	57	Ld Mansfield
Jul	57	Henry Bilson Legge
Mar	61	Vt Barrington

FIRST LORD OF THE ADMIRALTY

(* = Ld High Admiral)

Feb	89	E of Torrington*
Jan	90	E of Pembroke
Mar	92	Ld Cornwallis
Apr	93	Anthony Carey (Vt of Falkland)
May	94	E of Orford
May	99	E of Bridgwater
Apr	01	E of Pembroke*
May	02	Prince George of Denmark
Oct	08	Queen Anne*
Nov	08	E of Pembroke
Nov	09	E of Orford
Oct	10	Sir John Leake
Sep	12	E of Strafford
Oct	14	E of Orford
Apr	17	E of Berkeley
Jul	27	Vt Torrington
Jan	33	Sir Charles Wager
Mar	42	E of Winchilsea and Nottingham
Dec	44	D of Bedford
Feb	48	E of Sandwich
Jun	51	Ld Anson
Nov	56	Earl Temple
Apr	57	E of Winchilsea and Nottingham

| Jul | 57 | Ld Anson |
| Jun | 62 | E of Halifax |

PRESIDENT OF THE BOARD OF TRADE (since 1696)

May	96	E of Bridgwater
Jun	99	E of Stamford
Jun	02	Vt Weymouth
Apr	07	E of Stamford
Jun	11	E of Winchilsea
Sep	13	Ld Guildford
Dec	14	Ld Berkeley
May	15	E of Suffolk and Bindon
Jan	18	E of Holderness
May	19	E of Westmorland
May	35	Earl Fitzwalter
Jun	37	Ld Monson
Nov	48	E of Halifax
Mar	61	Ld Sandys

CHANCELLOR OF THE DUCHY OF LANCASTER

May	87	Robert Phelipps
Mar	89	D of Ancaster and Kesteven
May	97	E of Stamford
May	02	Ld Gower
Jun	06	E of Derby
Sep	10	Ld Berkeley
Nov	14	E of Aylesford
Mar	16	E of Scarborough
Jun	17	Ld Lechmere
Jul	27	D of Rutland
May	36	E of Cholmondeley
Dec	43	Ld Edgcumbe
Jan	58	E of Kinnoull
Dec	62	Ld Strange

LORD LIEUTENANT OF IRELAND (since 1700)

Dec	00	E of Rochester
Feb	03	D of Ormond
Apr	07	E of Pembroke
Dec	08	E of Wharton
Oct	10	D of Ormond

Sep	13	D of Shrewsbury
Oct	14	E of Sunderland
Feb	17	Vt Townshend
Apr	17	D of Bolton
Jun	20	D of Grafton
May	24	Ld Carteret
Jun	30	D of Dorset
Apr	37	D of Devonshire
Jan	45	E of Chesterfield
Nov	46	E of Harrington
Dec	50	D of Dorset
Apr	55	D of Devonshire
Jan	57	D of Bedford
Apr	61	E of Halifax

CHIEF SECRETARY FOR IRELAND

Feb	88	Patrick Tyrrell
Sep	92	Sir Cyril Wyche
May	95	Sir Richard Aldworth
Dec	00	Francis Gwyn
Feb	03	Edward Southwell
Apr	07	George Dodington
Dec	08	Joseph Addison
Oct	10	Edward Southwell
Sep	13	Sir John Stanley
Oct	14	Joseph Addison
Apr	17	Edward Webster
Jun	20	Horatio Walpole
Aug	21	Edward Hopkins
May	24	Thomas Clutterbuck
Jun	30	Walter Cary
Apr	37	Sir Edward Walpole
May	39	Thomas Townshend
Oct	39	Henry Bilson Legge
Jun	41	Vt Duncannon
Jan	45	Richard Liddell
Jul	46	Sewallis Shirley
Nov	46	Edward Weston
Dec	50	Ld George Sackville
Apr	55	Henry Seymour Conway
Jan	57	Richard Rigby
Apr	61	William Gerard Hamilton

SECRETARY AT WAR

Mar	92	George Clarke
Apr	04	Henry St John (Vt Bolingbroke)
Feb	08	Robert Walpole
Sep	10	Ld Lansdowne
Jun	12	Sir William Wyndham
Aug	13	Francis Gwyn
Sep	14	William Pulteney (E of Bath)
Apr	17	James Craggs
Mar	18	Vt Castlecomer
May	18	Robert Pringle
Dec	18	George Treby
Apr	24	Hon Henry Pelham
May	30	Sir William Strickland
May	35	Sir William Yonge
Jul	46	Henry Fox
Nov	55	Vt Barrington
Mar	61	Hon Charles Townshend
Nov	62	Welbore Ellis

PAYMASTER-GENERAL

	13	Thomas Moore and Edward Nicholas
Sep	14	Robert Walpole
Oct	15	E of Lincoln
Jun	20	Robert Walpole
Apr	21	Ld Cornwallis
	22	Hon Spencer Compton
May	30	Hon Henry Pelham
	43	Sir Thomas Winnington
May	46	William Pitt
Nov	55	{ E of Darlington { Vt Dupplin
Jun	57	Henry Fox

MASTER-GENERAL OF THE ORDNANCE

	81	Ld Dartmouth
	89	D of Schomberg
	93	E of Romney
Jul	02	D of Marlborough
Jan	12	Earl Rivers

Jul	12	D of Hamilton and Brandon (d. Nov 12)
Oct	14	D of Marlborough
Jul	22	Earl Cadogan
Jul	25	D of Argyll and Greenwich
Jul	40	D of Montagu
	42	D of Argyll
	43	D of Montagu
Jan	56	D of Marlborough
Jul	59	Earl Ligonier
Jul	63	D of Rutland

TREASURER OF THE NAVY

Oct	14	John Aislabie
Mar	18	Richard Hampden
Oct	20	Vt Torrington
Apr	24	Hon Pattee Byng
Apr	34	Arthur Onslow
May	42	Hon Thomas Clutterbuck
Dec	42	Sir Charles Wager
Dec	43	Sir John Rushout
Dec	44	George Bubb Dodington (Ld Melcombe)
May	49	Hon Henry Bilson Legge
Apr	54	Hon George Grenville
Jan	56	George Bubb Dodington (Ld Melcombe)
Jun	62	Vt Barrington

MASTER OF THE MINT

	85	Thomas Neale
	99	Isaac Newton (Sir Isaac, 1705) Major Wyvil (York)
	27	John Conduit
	37	Hon Richard Arundel
	44	Hon William Chetwynd (later Vt Chetwynd)

ATTORNEY-GENERAL

Feb	89	Henry Pollexfen
May	89	George Treby
May	92	John Somers
Jun	95	Thomas Trevor
Jun	01	Edward Northey

Apr	07	Simon Harcourt
Oct	08	James Montagu
Sep	10	Simon Harcourt
Oct	10	Sir Edward Northey
Mar	18	Sir Nicholas Lechmere
May	20	Sir Robert Raymond (Ld Raymond)
Feb	24	Sir Philip Yorke (Ld Hardwicke)
Jan	34	Sir John Willes
Jan	37	Sir Dudley Ryder (Ld Ryder)
May	54	Hon William Murray (Ld Mansfield)
Nov	56	Sir Robert Henley (Ld Northington)
Jun	57	Sir Charles Pratt (Earl Camden)
Jan	62	Hon Charles Yorke

SOLICITOR-GENERAL

Feb	89	George Treby
May	89	John Somers
May	92	Thomas Trevor
Jun	95	John Hawles
Jun	02	Simon Harcourt
Apr	07	James Montagu
Oct	08	Robert Eyre
May	10	Robert Raymond
Oct	14	Nicholas Lechmere
Dec	15	John Fortescue Aland
Jan	17	William Thomson
Mar	20	Philip Yorke
Feb	24	Clement Wearg
Apr	26	Charles Talbot
Jan	34	Dudley Ryder
Jan	37	John Strange
	42	William Murray
May	54	Richard Lloyd
Nov	56	Hon Charles Yorke
Jan	62	Fletcher Norton

UNDER SECRETARIES OF STATE FOR THE NORTHERN DEPARTMENT

1692	William Bridgeman
	James Vernon
	Thomas Hopkins (*vice* Vernon)
1697	Thomas Hopkins
	John Ellis (*vice* Bridgeman)

1700	John Ellis
	John Tucker (*vice* Hopkins)
1704	Richard Warr
	Erasmus Lewis
1710	George Tilson
	Horatio Walpole
1717	George Tilson
	Charles Delafaye
1724	George Tilson
	Thomas Townshend
1730	George Tilson
	Edward Weston
1740	Thomas Stanhope (*vice* Tilson)
1742	Edward Weston
	J. A. Balaguier
1745	Edward Weston
	W. R. Chetwynd
1746	W. R. Chetwynd
	John Potter
1748	Andrew Stone
	Thomas Ramsden
1750	Claudius Amyand
	Hugh Valence Jones (*vice* Ramsden)
1751	James Wallis (*vice* Amyand)
	Andrew Stone
1754	James Wallis
	Richard Pottinger (*vice* Stone)
1760	Michael Peter Morin (*vice* Pottinger)
	William Fraser (*vice* Wallis)

UNDER SECRETARIES OF STATE FOR THE SOUTHERN DEPARTMENT

1689	Richard Warr
	John Isham
1699	Robert Yard
	Matthew Prior
1702	Richard Warr
	William Aglionby
1704	John Isham (*vice* Aglionby)
1707	John Tucker
	Joseph Addison
1710	Thomas Hopkins
	Robert Pringle
1714	Robert Pringle (cont.)

	Charles Stanhope
1717	Temple Stanian
	Thomas Tickell
1718	Corbiere
	Charles Delafaye
1724	Charles Delafaye
	Temple Stanian
1735	John Couraud (*vice* Stanian)
	Andrew Stone (*vice* Delafaye)
1743	Thomas Ramsden (*vice* Couraud)
1748	Richard Nevill Aldworth
	John Potter
	Hon Richard Leveson-Gower (*vice* Potter)
1751	Claudius Amyand
	Richard Pottinger
1754	Claudius Amyand
	James Rivers
1755	Claudius Amyand
	James Rivers
	Henry Rivers
1756	Robert Wood
	James Rivers

JUNIOR COMMISSIONERS OF THE TREASURY

Apr	89	Vt Mordaunt
		Ld Delamere
		Ld Godolphin
		Hon Sir H. Capel
		R. Hampden
May	90	Sir J. Lowther
		R. Hampden
		Sir S. Fox
		T. Pelham
Nov	90	Ld Godolphin
		Sir J. Lowther
		R. Hampden
		Sir S. Fox
		T. Pelham
Mar	92	Ld Godolphin
		R. Hampden
		Sir S. Fox

	Sir E. Seymour		T. Pelham
	C. Montagu	Dec 01	E of Carlisle
May 94	Ld Godolphin		Sir S. Fox
	Sir S. Fox		Hon H. Boyle
	C. Montagu		R. Hill
	Sir W. Trumbull		T. Pelham
	J. Smith	Feb 02	E of Carlisle
Nov 95	Ld Godolphin		Sir S. Fox
	Sir S. Fox		Hon H. Boyle
	C. Montagu		R. Hill
	J. Smith		T. Pelham
May 96	Ld Godolphin	May 02	Ld Godolphin
	Sir S. Fox		
	C. Montagu	Jun 07	E of Godolphin
	J. Smith	Aug 10	Earl Poulett
	Sir T. Littleton		R. Harley
May 97	C. Montagu		Hon H. Paget
	Sir S. Fox		Sir T. Mansell
	J. Smith		R. Benson
	Sir T. Littleton	May 11	E of Oxford
	T. Pelham		
		Jul 14	D of Shrewsbury
Jun 99	C. Montagu		
	E of Tankerville	Oct 14	Ld Halifax
	Sir S. Fox		Sir R. Onslow
	J. Smith		Sir W. St Quintin
	Hon H. Boyle		E. Wortley Montagu
			P. Methuen
Nov 99	E of Tankerville		
	Sir S. Fox	May 15	E of Carlisle
	J. Smith		Sir R. Onslow
	Hon H. Boyle		Sir W. St Quintin
	R. Hill		E. Wortley Montagu
			P. Methuen
Dec 00	Ld Godolphin		
	Sir S. Fox	Oct 15	R. Walpole
	J. Smith		Sir W. St Quintin
	Hon H. Boyle		P. Methuen
	R. Hill		Ld Finch
			Hon T. Newport
Mar 01	Ld Godolphin		
	Sir S. Fox	Jun 16	R. Walpole
	Hon H. Boyle		Sir W. St Quintin
	R. Hill		P. Methuen

		Ld Torrington			W. Clayton
		R. Edgcumbe			Sir W. Yonge
Apr	17	J. Stanhope	May	35	Sir R. Walpole
		Ld Torrington			G. Dodington
		J. Wallop			Sir G. Oxenden
		G. Baillie			W. Clayton
		T. Micklethwaite			E of Cholmondeley
Mar	18	E of Sunderland	May	36	Sir R. Walpole
		J. Aislabie			G. Dodington
		J. Wallop			Sir G. Oxenden
		G. Baillie			Ld Sundon
		W. Clayton			T. Winnington
Jun	20	E of Sunderland	Jun	37	Sir R. Walpole
		J. Aislabie			G. Dodington
		G. Baillie			Ld Sundon
		Sir C. Turner			T. Winnington
		R. Edgcumbe			G. Earle
Apr	21	R. Walpole	Oct	40	Sir R. Walpole
		G. Baillie			Ld Sundon
		Sir C. Turner			T. Winnington
		R. Edgcumbe			G. Earle
		Hon H. Pelham			G. Treby
Apr	24	R. Walpole	Apr	41	Sir R. Walpole
		G. Baillie			Ld Sundon
		Sir C. Turner			G. Earle
		W. Yonge			G. Treby
		G. Dodington			T. Clutterbuck
May	25	Sir R. Walpole	Feb	42	E of Wilmington
		Sir C. Turner			S. Sandys
		Sir W. Yonge			Hon G. Compton
		G. Dodington			Sir J. Rushout
		Sir W. Strickland			P. Gybbon
Jul	27	Sir R. Walpole	Aug	43	Hon H. Pelham
		Sir C. Turner			S. Sandys
		G. Dodington			Hon G. Compton
		Sir G. Oxenden			Sir J. Rushout
		W. Clayton			P. Gybbon
May	30	Sir R. Walpole	Dec	43	Hon H. Pelham
		G. Dodington			Hon G. Compton
		Sir G. Oxenden			P. Gybbon

		E of Middlesex			R. Nugent
		H. Fox	Nov	55	D of Newcastle
Dec	44	Hon H. Pelham			E of Darlington
		E of Middlesex			Sir G. Lyttleton
		H. Fox			Vt Dupplin
		Hon R. Arundel			R. Nugent
		G. Lyttleton	Dec	55	D of Newcastle
Jun	46	Hon H. Pelham			Sir G. Lyttleton
		E of Middlesex			R. Nugent
		G. Lyttleton			P. Wyndham O'Brien
		Hon H. Bilson Legge			H. Furnese
		J. Campbell	Nov	56	D of Devonshire
Jun	47	Hon H. Pelham			Hon H. Bilson Legge
		G. Lyttleton			R. Nugent
		Hon H. Bilson Legge			Vt Duncannon
		J. Campbell			Hon J. Grenville
		G. Grenville	Jul	57	D of Newcastle
Apr	49	Hon H. Pelham			Hon H. Bilson Legge
		G. Lyttleton			R. Nugent
		J. Campbell			Vt Duncannon
		G. Grenville			Hon J. Grenville
		Hon H. Vane	Jun	59	D of Newcastle
Mar	54	D of Newcastle			Hon H. Bilson Legge
		Sir G. Lyttleton			R. Nugent
		J. Campbell			Hon J. Grenville
		Hon G. Grenville			Ld North
		Ld Barnard	Dec	59	D of Newcastle
Apr	54	D of Newcastle			Hon H. Bilson Legge
		E of Darlington			Hon J. Grenville
		Hon H. Bilson Legge			Ld North
		Vt Dupplin			J. Oswald

SENIOR (PARLIAMENTARY) SECRETARIES TO THE TREASURY

Apr	89	W. Jephson	Apr	52	J. West
Jun	91	H. Guy	Nov	56	N. Hardinge
Mar	95	W. Lowndes	Apr	58	J. West
Jan	24	J. Scrope	May	62	S. Martin

JUNIOR (FINANCIAL) SECRETARIES TO THE TREASURY (since 1711)

Jun	11	T. Harley	Jul	42	H. Furnese
Nov	14	J. Taylor	Nov	42	J. Jeffreys
Oct	15	H. Walpole	May	46	J. West
Apr	17	C. Stanhope	Apr	52	N. Hardinge
Apr	21	H. Walpole	Nov	56	S. Martin
Jun	30	E. Walpole	Jul	57	J. West
Jun	39	S. Fox	May	58	S. Martin
Apr	41	Hon H. Legge	May	62	J. Dyson

CLERK OF THE TREASURY

		W. Lowndes	Oct	1713	W. Thomas
		S. Langford	Nov	1714	W. Glanville
(by)	1689	R. Squibb	Nov	1714	H. Kelsall
		W. Glanville	Jan	1718	W. Lowndes
		J. Evelyn	Feb	1724	M. Frecker
			Dec	1738	T. Bowen
		W. Shaw	Aug	1742	H. Fane
(by)	1693	R. Aldworth	Nov	1752	P. Leheup
		R. Powys	Jul	1755	C. Lowndes
		J. Taylor	Jul	1757	E. Burnaby
			Jul	1759	J. Postlethwaite
	c.1697	C. Tilson	Jul	1759	R. Yeates

COMMISSIONERS OF CUSTOMS FOR ENGLAND AND WALES

1688	14 Jan	Sir Nicholas Butler
		Sir Dudley North
		Sir John Werden
		Thomas Chudleigh
		William Culliford
1688	28 Feb	Sir Nicholas Butler
		Henry Browne
		Sir Dudley North
		Sir John Werden
		William Culliford
1689	20 Apr	George Booth
		Sir Richard Temple
		Sir John Werden
		Sir Robert Southwell
		Sir Robert Clayton

		Sir Patience Ward
		Thomas Pelham
1691	24 Mar	George Booth
		Sir Richard Temple
		Sir John Werden
		Sir Robert Southwell
		Sir Robert Clayton
		Sir Patience Ward
		Henry Guy
1691	3 Jul	George Booth
		Sir Richard Temple
		Sir John Werden
		Sir Robert Southwell
		Sir Patience Ward
		Sir Robert Clayton
		Charles Godolphin
1694	14 Aug	Sir Robert Clayton
		Sir Patience Ward
		Sir Robert Southwell
		Charles Godolphin
		Sir Walter Young
		James Chadwick
		Samuel Clarke
1696	14 Apr	Sir Robert Clayton
		Sir Patience Ward
		Sir Robert Southwell
		Charles Godolphin
		Sir Walter Young
		James Chadwick
		Samuel Clarke
		Benjamin Overton
1697	21 June	Charles Godolphin
		Sir Walter Young
		Samuel Clarke
		Benjamin Overton
		Sir Henry Hobart
		Sir John Austin
		Robert Henley
1698	22 Nov	Charles Godolphin
		Sir Walter Young
		Samuel Clarke
		Benjamin Overton
		Sir Henry Hobart
		Sir John Austin

		Robert Henley
		Sir William St Quintin
1699	22 Nov	Charles Godolphin
		Sir Walter Young
		Samuel Clarke
		Benjamin Overton
		Robert Henley
		Sir William St Quintin
		Hon Thomas Newport
1701	18 Dec	Charles Godolphin
		Samuel Clarke
		Benjamin Overton
		Robert Henley
		Thomas Newport
		Arthur Maynwaring
		William Culliford
1703	14 Jul	Charles Godolphin
		Samuel Clarke
		Thomas Newport
		Arthur Maynwaring
		William Culliford
		Sir John Werden
		Richard Bretton
1705	15 May	Charles Godolphin
		Samuel Clarke
		Thomas Newport
		William Culliford
		Sir John Werden
		Richard Bretton
		Thomas Hall
1706	6 June	Charles Godolphin
		Samuel Clarke
		Thomas Newport
		William Culliford
		Sir John Werden
		Thomas Hall
		Sir Matthew Dudley
1708	4 May	Charles Godolphin
		Samuel Clarke
		Thomas Newport
		William Culliford
		Sir John Werden
		Sir Matthew Dudley
		Sir John Stanley

1708	23 Dec	Charles Godolphin
		Thomas Newport
		William Culliford
		Sir John Werden
		Sir Matthew Dudley
		Sir John Stanley
		John Shute
1711	25 Jan	Charles Godolphin
		Sir John Werden
		Sir John Stanley
		Matthew Prior
		John Bridges
		Robert Williamson
		Edward Gibbons
1714	17 May	Sir John Werden
		Sir John Stanley
		Matthew Prior
		John Bridges
		Robert Williamson
		Edward Gibbons
		Charles Godolphin
		Sir David Nairne
1714	4 Dec	Sir Walter Young
		Sir Matthew Dudley
		Sir John Stanley
		Robert Williamson
		John Pulteney
		Thomas Walker
		Sir Charles Peers
1715	17 Mar	Sir Walter Young
		Sir Matthew Dudley
		Sir John Stanley
		John Pulteney
		Thomas Walker
		Sir Charles Peers
		Sir Thomas Frankland
1718	2 Jan	Sir Walter Young
		Sir Matthew Dudley
		Sir John Stanley
		John Pulteney
		Thomas Walker
		Sir Charles Peers
		Robert Baylis
1720	1 Oct	Sir Walter Young

		Sir Matthew Dudley
		Sir John Stanley
		John Pulteney
		Thomas Walker
		Sir Charles Peers
		Robert Baylis
1721	4 Sept	Sir Walter Young
		Sir John Stanley
		John Pulteney
		Thomas Walker
		Sir Charles Peers
		Robert Baylis
		Sir John Evelyn
1722	27 Mar	Sir Walter Young
		Sir John Stanley
		Thomas Walker
		Sir Charles Peers
		Robert Baylis
		Sir John Evelyn
		Thomas Maynard

COMMISSIONERS OF CUSTOMS FOR GREAT BRITAIN

Fourteen commissioners were appointed, seven to reside in London, five in Edinburgh, and two to attend the outports.

1723		Sir Walter Young
		Sir John Stanley
		Thomas Walker
		Sir Charles Peers
		Robert Baylis
		Sir John Evelyn
		Thomas Maynard
		Sir James Campbell
		Humphry Brent
		John Campbell
		Brian Fairfax
		Henry Hale
		George Drummond
		John Hill
1727	18 Oct	Sir Walter Young
		Sir John Stanley
		Thomas Walker

Sir Charles Peers
Sir John Evelyn
Thomas Maynard
Sir James Campbell
Humphry Brent
John Campbell
Brian Fairfax
Henry Hale
George Drummond
John Hill
Allan Broderick

1728	19 Jul	Sir Walter Young
		Sir John Stanley
		Thomas Walker
		Sir Charles Peers
		Sir John Evelyn
		Sir James Campbell
		Humphry Brent
		John Campbell
		Brian Fairfax
		Henry Hale
		George Drummond
		John Hill
		Allan Broderick
		Gwynn Vaughan
		Thomas Maynard
1730	21 Sept	Sir Walter Young
		Sir John Stanley
		Thomas Walker
		Sir Charles Peers
		Sir John Evelyn
		Sir James Campbell
		John Campbell
		Brian Fairfax
		Henry Hale
		George Drummond
		John Hill
		Gwynn Vaughan
		George Ross (aft. Ld Ross)
1731	14 May	Sir Walter Young
		Sir John Stanley
		Thomas Walker
		Sir Charles Peers
		Sir John Evelyn

Sir James Campbell
John Campbell
Brian Fairfax
Henry Hale
George Drummond
John Hill
Gwynn Vaughan
George Ross
Wardel George Westby

1731	28 Aug	Sir John Stanley
		Thomas Walker
		Sir Charles Peers
		Sir John Evelyn
		Sir James Campbell
		John Campbell
		Brian Fairfax
		Henry Hale
		George Drummond
		John Hill
		Gwynn Vaughan
		George Ross
		Wardel George Westby
		Sir Robert Baylis
1732	2 Jan	Sir John Stanley
		Sir Charles Peers
		Sir John Evelyn
		Sir James Campbell
		John Campbell
		Brian Fairfax
		Henry Hale
		George Drummond
		John Hill
		Gwynn Vaughan
		George Ross
		Wardel George Westby
		Sir Robert Baylis
		Edward Trelawney
1735	24 May	Sir John Stanley
		Sir Charles Peers
		Sir John Evelyn
		Sir James Campbell
		John Campbell
		Brian Fairfax
		George Drummond

John Hill
Gwynn Vaughan
George Ross
Wardel George Westby
Sir Robert Baylis
Edward Trelawney
Sir Robert Corbett

1737   15 Oct   Sir John Stanley
Sir John Evelyn
John Campbell
Brian Fairfax
John Hill
Gwynn Vaughan
George Ross
Wardel George Westby
Sir Robert Baylis
Sir Robert Corbett
Richard Chandler
Beaumont Hotham
Richard Somers
Colin Campbell

1741   29 June   Sir John Stanley
Sir John Evelyn
John Campbell
Brian Fairfax
John Hill
George Ross (now Ld Ross)
Wardel George Westby
Sir Robert Baylis
Richard Chandler
Beaumont Hotham
Richard Somers
Colin Campbell
Edward Riggs
Isaac Leheup

1742   Sir John Stanley
Sir John Evelyn
John Campbell
Brian Fairfax
John Hill
Wardel George Westby
Sir Robert Baylis
Richard Chandler
Beaumont Hotham

Richard Somers
Colin Campbell
Gwynn Vaughan

At this time, the commission for Great Britain was divided, and nine commissioners were appointed for England and Wales, and five for Scotland.

COMMISSIONERS OF CUSTOMS FOR ENGLAND AND WALES

1742	Sep	Sir John Stanley
		Sir John Evelyn
		Brian Fairfax
		John Hill
		Sir Robert Baylis
		Richard Chandler
		Wardel George Westby
		Beaumont Hotham
		Samuel Mead
1744		Sir John Evelyn
		Brian Fairfax
		John Hill
		Sir Robert Baylis
		Richard Chandler
		Wardel George Westby
		Beaumont Hotham
		Samuel Mead
		Gwynn Vaughan
1747		Sir John Evelyn
		Brian Fairfax
		Sir Robert Baylis
		Richard Chandler
		Wardel George Westby
		Beaumont Hotham
		Samuel Mead
		Gwynn Vaughan
		William Levinz
1748		Sir John Evelyn
		Brian Fairfax
		Richard Cavendish
		Wardel George Westby
		Beaumont Hotham
		Samuel Mead
		Gwynn Vaughan
		William Levinz

	Edward Hooper
1750	Sir John Evelyn
	Sir Miles Stapleton
	Richard Cavendish
	Wardel George Westby
	Beaumont Hotham
	Samuel Mead
	Gwynn Vaughan
	William Levinz
	Edward Hooper
1752	Sir John Evelyn
	Richard Cavendish
	Wardel George Westby
	Beaumont Hotham
	Samuel Mead
	Gwynn Vaughan
	William Levinz
	Edward Hooper
	Thomas Tash
1756	Sir John Evelyn
	Richard Cavendish
	Beaumont Hotham
	Samuel Mead
	Gwynn Vaughan
	William Levinz
	Edward Hooper
	Thomas Tash
	Claudius Amyand
1758	Sir John Evelyn
	Richard Cavendish
	Beaumont Hotham
	Samuel Mead
	William Levinz
	Edward Hooper
	Thomas Tash
	Claudius Amyand
	Henry Pelham
1761	Sir John Evelyn
	Beaumont Hotham
	Samuel Mead
	William Levinz
	Edward Hooper
	Thomas Tash
	Claudius Amyand

Henry Pelham
John Frederick

POSTMASTER-GENERAL

1687   Philip Fowde (for D of York)
1690   Sir Robert Cotton
      Thomas Frankland
1708   Thomas Frankland
      Sir John Evelyn
1715   Ld Cornwallis
      Jason Craggs
1720   Edward Carteret
      Galfridus Walpole
1725   Edward Carteret
      Edward Harrison
1732   Edward Carteret (sole)
1733   Edward Carteret
      Ld Lovel (later Vt Coke and Earl of Leicester)
1739   Sir John Eyles
      Ld Lovel
1744   E of Leicester (sole)
1745   E of Leicester
      Sir Everard Faulkener
1758   E of Leicester (sole)
1759   E of Besborough
      Hon Robert Hampden

SURVEYOR-GENERAL OF THE LAND REVENUES OF THE CROWN

1682	William Harbord	1726	Phillips Gybbon
1692	William Tailer	1730	Exton Sayer
1693	Samuel Travers	1732	Thomas Walker
1710	J. Manley	1750	Vt Galway
1714	Alexander Pendarves	1751	Robert Herbert
1715	H. Chomeley	1769	Peter Burrell
1722	J. Poulteney		

SURVEYOR-GENERAL OF WOODS, FORESTS, PARKS AND CHASES

1688	Philip Riley	1716	Edward Younge
1701	Thomas Hewett	1720	Charles Whithers
1702	Edward Wilcox	1736	Francis Whitworth
1714	Thomas Hewett	1742	Henry Legge

1745	John Phillipson
1756	John Pitt
1763	Sir Edmond Thomas

JUDGE ADVOCATE GENERAL

1684	George Clarke	1734	Sir Henry Hoghton
1705	Thomas Byde	1741	Thomas Morgan
1715	Edward Hughes		

LORD ADVOCATE (SCOTLAND)

1709	Sir David Dalrymple	1742	Robert Craigie
1720	Robert Dundas	1746	William Grant
1725	Duncan Forbes	1754	Robert Dundas
1737	Charles Areskin	1760	Thomas Miller

SECRETARY OF STATE FOR SCOTLAND

Feb	09	D of Queensberry
Sep	13	E of Mar
Sep	14	D of Montrose (dis Aug 15)
Dec	16	D of Roxburghe (dis Aug 25)
Feb	42	M of Tweeddale (res Jan 46)

UNDER SECRETARY OF STATE FOR SCOTLAND*

Feb	09	J. Montgomery	Sep	14	C. Kennedy
Feb	09	N. Rowe	Dec	16	T. Scott
Sep	13	W. Strahan	Feb	42	A. Mitchell

LORD CHANCELLOR: IRELAND

1710	Sir Constantine Phipps
1714	Alan Brodrick (Vt Midleton)
1725	Richard West
1726	Thomas Wyndham (Ld Wyndham)
1739	Robert Jocelyn (Vt Jocelyn)
1757	John Bowes (Ld Bowes)

* Queensberry, the first Secretary of State for the Scottish Department, appointed two Under Secretaries in 1709; his successors, however, employed only one.

ATTORNEY-GENERAL: IRELAND

Dec	86	Sir Richard Nagle
Oct	90	Sir John Temple
May	95	Robert Rochfort
Jun	07	Alan Brodrick
Dec	09	John Forster
Jun	11	Sir Richard Levinge
Nov	14	George Gore
May	20	John Rogerson
May	27	Thomas Marlay
Sep	30	Robert Jocelyn
Sep	39	John Bowes
Dec	41	Stephen George Caulfield
Aug	51	Warden Flood
Jul	60	Philip Tisdall

SOLICITOR-GENERAL: IRELAND

Jul	60	Sir John Temple
Jan	89	Sir Theobald Butler (rem 25 July)
Nov	90	Sir Richard Levinge
May	95	Alan Brodrick
Apr	04	Sir Richard Levinge
Sep	09	John Forster
Dec	09	William Whitsed
Jun	11	Francis Bernard
Nov	14	John Rogerson
Apr	27	Robert Jocelyn
Sep	30	John Bowes
Sep	39	Stephen George Caulfield
Dec	41	Warden Flood
Aug	51	Philip Tisdall
Jul	60	John Gorp

LORD HIGH STEWARD

1689	E of Devonshire (coronation of William III and Mary)
1692	M of Carmarthen (trial of Ld Mohun)
1699	Ld Somers (trials of E of Warwick and Holland, and of Ld Mohun)
1702	D of Devonshire (coronation of Queen Anne)
1714	D of Grafton (coronation of George I)

1716   Ld Cowper (trials of E of Derwentwater, Ld Widdrington, E of Nithsdale, E of Carnwath, Vt Kenmure and Ld Nairne; again in March for trial of E of Wintoun)
1717   Ld Cowper, again (trial of E of Oxford and Earl Mortimer)
1725   Ld King (trial of E of Macclesfield)
1727   D of Dorset (coronation of George II)
1746   Ld Hardwicke (trials of E of Kilmarnock, E of Cromarty and Ld Balmerino)
1747   Ld Hardwicke again (trial of Ld Lovat)
1760   Ld Henley (trial of Earl Ferrers)
1761   Earl Talbot (coronation of George III)

LORD GREAT CHAMBERLAIN

1666   (3rd) E of Lindsey
1701   (4th) E of Lindsey (M of Lindsey, 1707 and D of Ancaster and Kesteven, 1715)
1723   (2nd) D of Ancaster and Kesteven
1742   (3rd) D of Ancaster and Kesteven
1778   (4th) D of Ancaster and Kesteven

LORD STEWARD

1689   E (D) of Devonshire
1707   2nd D of Devonshire
1710   D of Buckinghamshire
1711   Earl Paulet
1714   2nd D of Devonshire (again)
1716   D of Kent
1718   D of Argyll
1725   D of Dorset
1730   E of Chesterfield
1733   3rd D of Devonshire
1737   D of Dorset (again)
1744   3rd D of Devonshire (again)
1749   D of Marlborough
1755   D of Rutland
1761   E of Talbot

LORD CHAMBERLAIN

1689   E of Dorset and Middlesex
1695   E of Sunderland
1699   D of Shrewsbury

1700	E of Jersey
1704	E (M, D) of Kent
1714	D of Shrewsbury
1715	D of Bolton (resigned, Jul 15)
1715–17	vacant
1717	D of Newcastle
1724	D of Grafton
1757	D of Devonshire
1762	D of Marlborough

VICE-CHAMBERLAIN

1689	Sir John Lowther (Vt Lonsdale)
1690	Hon Peregrine Bertie
1706	Thomas Coke (Ld Lovel, E of Leicester)
1727	William Stanhope (E of Harrington)
1730	Ld John Hervey
1740	Ld Sydney Beauclerk
1742	Hon William Finch
1765	George Bussy (Vt Villiers, E of Jersey)

TREASURER OF THE CHAMBER

1689	Sir Rowland Gwin
1692	E of Orford
1702	Vt Fitzharding
1713	Ld De La Warr
1714	E of Radnor
1720	Henry Pelham
1722	Charles Stanhope
1727	Ld Hobart (E of Buckinghamshire)
1744	Sir John Hinde Cotton
1746	Hon Richard Arundel
1747	Ld Sandys
1755	E of Hillsborough
1756	Charles Townshend
1761	Sir Francis Dashwood (Ld Le Despencer)

MASTER OF THE HORSE

1689	Henry de Nassau d'Auverquerque
1702	D of Somerset
1715	Hon Conyers D'Arcy / Francis Negus –Commissioners

1717	Henry Berkeley *vice* D'Arcy. Negus then sole commissioner until 1727.
1727	E of Scarborough
1734	{ Hon James Lumley { Hon Henry Berkeley –Commissioners
1735	D of Richmond
1751	M of Hartington (D of Devonshire)
1755	D of Dorset
1757	Earl Gower
1760	E of Huntingdon
1761	D of Rutland

TREASURER OF THE HOUSEHOLD

1689	Ld Newport (E of Bradford)
1708	E of Cholmondeley
1712	Ld Lansdowne of Bideford
1714	E of Cholmondeley (again)
1725	(Sir) Paul Methuen
1730	Ld Bingley
1731	Ld (E) De La Warr
1737	Earl Fitzwalter
1755	Ld Berkeley of Stratton
1756	Vt Bateman
1757	E of Thomond
1761	E of Powis

COMPTROLLER OF THE HOUSEHOLD

	1689	Hon Thomas Wharton (Ld, E and M of Wharton)
	1702	Sir Edward Seymour
	1704	Sir Thomas Mansell (Ld Mansell)
(May)	1708	E of Cholmondeley
(Oct)	1708	Sir Thomas Felton
(Jun)	1709	Sir John Holland
	1711	Sir Thomas Mansell (again)
	1712	Ld Lansdowne of Bideford
	1713	Sir John Stonehouse
	1714	Hugh Boscawen (Vt Falmouth)
	1720	(Sir) Paul Methuen
	1725	Ld Finch (E of Winchilsea & Nottingham)
	1730	Hon Sir Conyers D'Arcy
	1754	E of Hillsborough

1755   Ld Hobart (E of Buckinghamshire)
1756   Hon Richard Edgcumbe (Ld Edgcumbe)
1761   E of Powis

CAPTAIN OF THE CORPS OF GENTLEMEN PENSIONERS

c. 1689   Ld Lovelace
1693   E (D) of Montagu
1695   D of St Albans
1712   D of Beaufort
1714   D of St Albans (again)
1726   M of Hartington (D of Devonshire)
1731   E of Burlington and Cork
1734   D of Montagu
1740   D of Bolton
1742   Ld (E) Bathurst
1745   Ld Hobart (E of Buckinghamshire)
1756   Ld Berkeley of Stratton
1762   E of Lichfield

CAPTAIN OF THE YEOMEN OF THE GUARD

1702   M of Hartington (D of Devonshire)
1707   Vt Townshend
1714   Ld Paget (E of Uxbridge)
1715   E of Derby
1723   Ld Stanhope (E of Chesterfield)
1725   E of Leicester
1731   Ld (E of) Ashburnham
1733   E of Tankerville
1737   D of Manchester
1739   E of Essex
1743   Ld Berkeley of Stratton
1746   Vt Torrington
1747   Vt Falmouth
1782   D of Dorset

COFFERER OF THE HOUSEHOLD

c. 1688   Ld Herbert of Chirbury
1702   Sir Benjamin Bathurst
1704   Hon Francis Godolphin (E of Godolphin)
1711   Samuel Masham (Ld Masham)
1714   E of Godolphin (again)

1723	William Pulteney (E of Bath)
1725	E of Lincoln
1730	Horace Walpole (Ld Walpole)
1741	Sir William Yonge
1743	Ld Sandys
1744	Edmond Waller
1746	E of Lincoln (D of Newcastle)
1754	Sir George Lyttelton (Ld Lyttelton)
1755	D of Leeds
1761	Hon J. Grenville

LORD HIGH CONSTABLE

(officiated at coronations on dates given below)

11	Apr	1689	D of Ormond
13	Apr	1702	D of Bedford
20	Oct	1714	D of Montagu
11	Oct	1727	D of Richmond, Lennox and Aubigny
22	Sep	1761	D of Bedford

MASTER OF THE GREAT WARDROBE

1685	E of Arran (D of Hamilton)
1689	Ld (E, D of) Montagu
1709	D of Montagu
1750	Sir Thomas Robinson (Ld Grantham)
1754	William Wildman (Vt Barrington)
1755	Ld Grantham (again)
1760	Earl Gower

GROOMS OF THE STOLE

1685	E of Peterborough
1689	E of Portland
1699	E of Romney
1704	Duchess of Marlborough
1710	Duchess of Somerset
1714	E (D) of Dorset and Middlesex
1719	E of Sunderland
1723	E of Godolphin
1735	E of Pembroke
1750	E of Albemarle
1755	E of Rochford

1760   E of Bute
1761   E of Huntingdon

THE ORDERS OF KNIGHTHOOD

KNIGHTS COMPANION OF THE BATH

(from the revival of the Order by George I, May 1725)*

George I (all invested 27 May 1725 and installed 17 June 1725)

Prince William Augustus, D of Cumberland
2nd D of Montagu (Great Master)
6th D of Richmond (not invested)
2nd D of Manchester
E of Burford (D of St Albans)
6th E of Leicester
2nd E of Albermarle
1st E of Delorain
2nd E of Halifax
E of Sussex
1st E of Pomfret
Lord Paulet (son of D of Bolton)
1st Vt Torrington
Vt Malpas (E of Cholmondeley)
Vt Glenorchy (E of Breadalbane)
Ld (1st E) De La Warr
Ld (E) of Clinton
Robert Walpole (2nd E of Orford)
E of Wilmington
William Stanhope
Conyers D'Arcy
Hon Thomas Saunderson (3rd E of Scarborough)
Paul Methuen
Sir Robert Walpole (1st E of Orford)
Robert Sutton
Lt Gen Charles Willis

*The Order is of very ancient origin. After some time in abeyance, it was revived and remodelled by George I by statute dated 18 May 1725. After this date, the Order consisted of the Sovereign, a Great Master and 36 Companions. In 1815, the Order was again remodelled and very much enlarged – partly to reward services in the campaigns against Napoleon.

Sir John Hobart (Ld Hobart, E of Buckinghamshire)
Sir William Gage
Robert Clifton
Michael Newton
William Yonge
Thomas Watson Wentworth (E of Malton, M of Rockingham)
John Monson (Ld Monson)
William Morgan
Thomas Coke (Ld Lovell, Vt Coke, E of Leicester)
4th E of Inchiquin**
Vt Tyrconnell**

**Invested 28 May 1725.

George II

1732	12 Jan	Henry Brydges (M of Carnarvon, 2nd D of Chandos)
		1st Vt Bateman
		Sir George Downing
1732	17 Jan	Charles Gunter Nicol
1742	26 Jun	Sir Thomas Robinson (Ld Grantham)
1743	12 Jul	Lt-Gen Philip Honywood
		Lt-Gen Hon James Campbell
		Lt-Gen John Cope
		Fl Marshal Sir John Ligonier (Earl Ligonier)
1744	28 May	6th Vt Fitzwilliam
		Sir Charles Hanbury Williams
		Henry Calthorpe
		Thomas Whitmore
		Sir William Morden Harbord
1747	29 May	Rear Admiral Peter Warren
1747	14 Nov	Vice-Admiral Edward Hawke (Ld Hawke)
1749	2 May	Lt-Gen Hon Charles Howard
		General Sir John Mordaunt
		Maj-Gen Charles Armand Powlett
		John Savile (Ld Pollington, E of Mexborough)
1752	12 Mar	3rd Ld Onslow
1753	27 Aug	Edward Walpole (son of Robert Walpole)
		Lt-Gen Charles Paulet (5th D of Bolton)
		Edward Montagu (Ld, then Earl, Beaulieu)
		Lt-Gen Hon Richard Lyttelton
1753	12 Dec	Admiral Sir William Rowley
1754	23 Sep	Benjamin Keene
1756	27 Nov	Lt-Gen William Blakeney (Ld Blakeney)

KNIGHTS OF THE GARTER

Creations, 1689–1760

William III

1689	3 Apr	1st D of Schomberg
	14 May	4th E (1st D) of Devonshire
1690	30 Dec	Frederick III, Elector of Brandenburg (King Frederick I of Prussia)
		D of Brunswick and Lüneburg Zell
1692	2 Feb	George IV, Duke of Saxony
		E of Dorset (1st E of Middlesex)
1694	25 Apr	1st D of Shrewsbury
1696	6 Jan	Prince William, D of Gloucester (son of Queen Anne)
1697	19 Feb	1st E of Portland
1698	30 May	D of Newcastle
1700	14 May	8th E of Pembroke (and 5th E of Montgomery)
1701	18 Jun	Elector of Hanover (later King George I of England)
		D of Queensberry (and D of Dover)

Queen Anne

1702	14 Mar	2nd D of Bedford
		E (1st D) of Marlborough
1703	12 Aug	3rd D of Schomberg (and 1st D of Leinster)
1704	6 Jul	1st Ld (1st E of) Godolphin
1706	4 Apr	Elector, Prince of Hanover (King George II of England)
1710	22 Mar	2nd D of Devonshire
		D of Argyll (E, then D, of Greenwich)
1712	25 Oct	4th D of Hamilton (1st D of Brandon)
		D of Kent
		1st Earl Poulett
		21st E of Oxford (and Earl Mortimer)
		3rd E of Strafford
1713	4 Aug	3rd E of Peterborough

George I

1714	16 Oct	2nd D of Bolton
		2nd D of Rutland
		10th E (1st D) of Dorset and Middlesex
		1st E of Halifax

1717	3 Jul	Prince Frederick Lewis (D of Gloucester, D of Edinburgh, Prince of Wales)
		Ernest Augustus (Bp of Osnaburg and D of York)
1718	31 Mar	1st D of St Albans
		2nd D of Montagu
		4th D of Newcastle
		3rd E of Berkeley
1719	29 Apr	1st D of Kingston
		4th E of Sunderland
1721	27 Mar	2nd D of Grafton
		19th E of Lincoln
1722	10 Oct	3rd D of Bolton
		3rd D of Rutland
		1st D of Roxburghe
1724	9 Jul	2nd E of Scarborough
		2nd Vt Townshend
1726	26 May	7th D of Richmond and Lennox
		Sir Robert Walpole (E of Orford)

George II

1730	18 May	William Augustus, D of Cumberland
		5th E of Chesterfield
		3rd E of Burlington and Cork
1733	12 Jun	William of Nassau, Prince of Orange
		3rd D of Devonshire
		E of Wilmington
1738	20 Feb	23rd E of Essex
		1st Earl Waldegrave
1741	20 Mar	Frederick III, Prince (later Landgrave) of Hesse-Cassel
		2nd D of St Albans
		3rd D of Marlborough
		2nd D of Kingston
		2nd D of Portland
1741	2 May	Frederick III, D of Saxe-Gotha
1745	24 Apr	John Adolphus, D of Saxe-Weissenfels
1749	22 Jun	George William Frederick, Pr of Brunswick-Lüneburg (King George III)
		Charles William Frederick, Margrave of Brandenburg-Anspach
		4th D of Leeds
		7th D of Bedford

		14th E of Albemarle
		2nd Earl Granville
1752	13 Mar	Edward Augustus, Pr of Brunswick-Lüneburg
		(D of York and Albany)
		William of Nassau, Prince of Orange
		21st E of Lincoln (2nd D of Newcastle)
		8th E of Winchilsea (E of Nottingham)
		4th E of Cardigan (3rd D of Montagu)
1756	18 Nov	4th D of Devonshire
		7th E of Carlisle
		15th E (3rd D) of Northumberland
		16th E (4th M) of Hertford
1757	30 Jun	2nd E Waldegrave
1759	16 Aug	Ferdinand, Prince of Brunswick-Bevern
1760	4 Feb	2nd M of Rockingham
		Earl Temple

KNIGHTS OF THE THISTLE

*(from the revival and restoration in 1703 to 1760)**

Queen Anne

1704	4 Feb	2nd D of Argyll
1704	7 Feb	1st D of Atholl
		1st M of Annandale
		E of Dalkeith
		6th E of Orkney
		1st E of Seafield (E of Findlater)
1705	30 Oct	2nd M of Lothian
		4th E of Orrery
1706	10 Aug	23rd E of Mar
		3rd E of Loudoun
1710	25 Mar	2nd E of Stair
1713	17 Jan	1st E of Portmore

*On 29 May 1687, James II ordered Letters Patent to be made out for 'reviving and restoring the Order of the Thistle to its full glory, lustre and magnificency'. The earlier history of the Order remains obscure. During the reign of William and Mary the Order remained in abeyance. It was revived again by Anne on 31 December 1703. These 1703 statutes were later modified on 17 February 1715 by George I and on 8 May 1827 by George IV. By this last modification the number of Knights of the Order was extended from 12 to 16.

George I

1716	22 June	1st E of Cadogan
		16th E of Sutherland
1717	1 Mar	6th E of Haddington
1721	28 Mar	2nd E of Tankerville
1725	2 Mar	23rd E of Essex
		E of Dalkeith (2nd D of Buccleuch)
		2nd E of Marchmont
1726	23 Sep	5th D of Hamilton (2nd D of Brandon)

George II

1730	16 May	3rd E of Tankerville
1731	10 Dec	19th E of Moray
1732	2 Jan	2nd E of Portmore
1734	11 Feb	2nd D of Atholl
		3rd M of Lothian
1738	10 Jul	15th E of Morton
		1st E of Hopetoun
		3rd E of Bute
1739	7 Jun	4th E of Berkeley
1741	23 Feb	21st E of Moray
1742	22 Jun	3rd E of Hyndford
1743	29 Mar	4th E of Dysart
1747	10 Feb	3rd D of Gordon
1752	11 Mar	5th E of Dumfries
1753	29 Mar	10th E of Rothes
		1st Earl Brooke (Earl of Warwick)
1755	18 Mar	6th D of Hamilton (and 3rd D of Brandon)

5 PARLIAMENT

HOUSE OF COMMONS

SPEAKERS OF THE HOUSE OF COMMONS, 1688–1760

Date of Election	Name	Constituency
19 May 1685	Sir John Trevor (1637–1717)	Denbigh
22 Jan 1689	Henry Powle (1630–92)	Windsor
20 Mar 1690	Sir John Trevor (1637–1717)	Yarmouth (I. of W.)
14 Mar 1695	Paul Foley (1645–99)	Hereford
6 Dec 1698	Sir Thomas Littleton (1647–1710)	Woodstock
10 Feb 1701	Robert Harley (1661–1724)	New Radnor
25 Oct 1705	John Smith (1655–1723)	Andover
16 Nov 1708	Sir Richard Onslow (1654–1717)	Surrey
25 Nov 1710	William Bromley (1664–1732)	Oxford University
16 Feb 1714	Sir Thomas Hanmer (1677–1746)	Suffolk
17 Mar 1715	Sir Spencer Compton (1673–1743)	Sussex
23 Jan 1728	Arthur Onslow (1691–1768)	Surrey
3 Nov 1761	Sir John Cust (1718–70)	Grantham

CHAIRMEN OF WAYS AND MEANS

28 Mar 1715	William Farrer	
3 Feb 1728	Sir Charles Turner	
9 Feb 1739	Francis Fane	
19 Nov 1754	Job Staunton Charlton	
17 Nov 1761	Marshe Dickinson	

CLERKS OF THE HOUSE

1683	Paul Jodrell
1727	Edward Stables

1732   Nicholas Hardinge
1748   Jeremiah Dyson
1762   Thomas Tyrwhitt

PARLIAMENTARY SESSIONS

Year	Date of assembly	Dates of sessions	Date of dissolution
1689*	22 Jan 1689	22 Jan–20 Aug 1689	
		19 Oct 1689–27 Jan 1690	6 Feb 1690
1690	20 Mar 1690	20 Mar–23 May 1690	
		2 Oct 1690–5 Jan 1691	
		22 Oct 1691–24 Feb 1692	
		4 Nov 1692–14 Mar 1693	
		7 Nov 1693–25 Apr 1694	
		12 Nov 1694–3 May 1695	11 Oct 1695
1695	22 Nov 1695	22 Nov 1695–27 Apr 1696	
		20 Oct 1696–16 Apr 1697	
		3 Dec 1697–5 Jul 1698	7 Jul 1698
1698	24 Aug 1698	6 Dec 1698–4 May 1699	
		16 Nov 1699–11 Apr 1700	19 Dec 1700
1701	6 Feb 1701	6 Feb–24 Jun 1701	11 Nov 1701
1701	30 Dec 1701	30 Dec 1701–23 May 1702	2 Jul 1702
1702	20 Aug 1702	20 Oct 1702–27 Feb 1703	
		9 Nov 1703–3 Apr 1704	
		24 Oct 1704–14 Mar 1705	5 Apr 1705
1705	14 Jun 1705	25 Oct 1705–21 May 1706	
		3 Dec 1706–24 Apr 1707	
		23 Oct 1707–1 Apr 1708	3 Apr 1708
1708	8 Jul 1708	16 Nov 1708–21 Apr 1709	
		15 Nov 1709–5 Apr 1710	21 Sep 1710
1710	25 Nov 1710	25 Nov 1710–12 Jun 1711	
		7 Dec 1711–8 Jul 1712	8 Aug 1713
1713	12 Nov 1713	16 Feb–9 Jul 1714	
		1 Aug–25 Aug 1714	15 Jan 1715

*This was a Convention. The assembly declared itself a Parliament on 20 February 1690 and this declaration received the royal assent on 23 February 1689

1715	17 Mar 1715	17 Mar 1715–26 Jun 1716	
		20 Feb–15 Jul 1717	
		21 Nov 1717–21 Mar 1718	
		11 Nov 1718–18 Apr 1719	
		23 Nov 1719–11 Jun 1720	
		8 Dec 1720–29 Jul 1721	
		31 Jul–10 Aug 1721	
		19 Oct 1721–7 Mar 1722	10 Mar 1722
1722	10 May 1722	9 Oct 1722–27 May 1723	
		9 Jan–24 Apr 1724	
		12 Nov 1724–31 May 1725	
		20 Jan–24 May 1726	
		17 Jan–15 May 1727	
		27 Jun–17 Jul 1727	5 Aug 1727
1727	28 Nov 1727	23 Jan–28 May 1728	
		21 Jan–14 May 1729	
		13 Jan–15 May 1730	
		21 Jan–7 May 1731	
		13 Jan–1 Jun 1732	
		16 Jan–13 Jun 1733	
		17 Jan–16 Apr 1734	17 Apr 1734
1734	13 Jun 1734	14 Jan–15 May 1735	
		15 Jan–20 May 1736	
		1 Feb–21 Jun 1737	
		24 Jan–20 May 1738	
		1 Feb–14 Jun 1739	
		15 Nov 1739–29 Apr 1740	
		18 Nov 1740–25 Apr 1741	27 Apr 1741
1741	25 Jun 1741	1 Dec 1741–15 Jul 1742	
		16 Nov 1742–21 Apr 1743	
		1 Dec 1743–12 May 1744	
		27 Nov 1744–2 May 1745	
		17 Oct 1745–12 Aug 1746	
		18 Nov 1746–17 Jun 1747	18 Jun 1747
1747	13 Aug 1747	10 Nov 1747–13 May 1748	
		29 Nov 1748–13 Jun 1749	
		16 Nov 1749–12 Apr 1750	
		17 Jan–25 Jan 1751	
		14 Nov 1751–26 Mar 1752	
		11 Jan–7 Jun 1753	
		15 Nov 1753–6 Apr 1754	8 Apr 1754

1754   31 May 1754   31 May–5 Jun 1754
                           14 Nov 1754–25 Apr 1755
                           13 Nov 1755–27 May 1756
                            2 Dec 1756–4 Jul 1757
                            1 Dec 1757–20 Jun 1758
                           23 Nov 1758–2 Jun 1759
                           13 Nov 1759–22 May 1760
                           26 Oct 1760–29 Oct 1760
                           18 Nov 1760–19 Mar 1761   20 Mar 1761

COMPOSITION OF THE HOUSE

Period	England	Wales	Scotland	Ireland	County	Borough	Univ.	Total
1688–								
1707	489	24			92	417	4	513
1707–								
1800	489	24	45		122	432	4	558
1801–								
1826	489	24	45	100	186	467	5	658
1826–								
1832	489	24	45	100	188	465	5	658

Prior to 1707, the House of Commons returned 513 members, 489 from England and 24 from Wales. The counties returned 92 members, the boroughs 417 and the ancient universities 4.

During the period 1707–60, after the addition of the Scottish members, the House of Commons returned 558 members, representing 314 constituencies. The detailed breakdown of these figures was as follows:

England, 489 members, 245 constituencies:
- 40   counties, returning 2 members each;
- 196   boroughs, returning 2 members each;
- 2   boroughs (London and the combined constituency of Weymouth and Melcombe Regis), returning 4 members each;
- 5   boroughs (Abingdon, Banbury, Bewdley, Higham Ferrers and Monmouth), returning 1 member each;
- 2   universities (Oxford and Cambridge) returning 2 members each.

Wales, 24 members, 24 constituencies:
- 12   12 counties, returning 1 member each;
- 12   boroughs, returning 1 member each.

Scotland, 45 members, 45 constituencies:
- 27   counties, returning 1 member each;
- 3   pairs of counties, 1 county in each pair alternating with the other in returning 1 member;

1   burgh (Edinburgh), returning 1 member;
14   groups of burghs, each returning 1 member.

This representation remained the same until 1800, when as a result of the Act of Union, total membership of the House of Commons increased to 658, with Ireland returning exactly 100 members.

HOUSE OF LORDS

CLERKS OF THE PARLIAMENTS

| 1660–91 | John Browne | 1716–40 | William Cowper |
| 1691–1716 | Matthew Johnson | 1740–88 | Ashley Cowper |

CLERK ASSISTANT

1660–64	John Throckmorton	1715–23	Matthew Johnson, ju
1664–82	John Walker, sen.	1724–52	James Merest
1682–1715	John Walker, jun.	1753–65	Joseph Wight

GENTLEMAN USHER OF THE BLACK ROD

1683	T. Duppa	1710	Sir W. Oldes
1694	Sir F. Sheppard	1747	Hon H. Bellenden
1698	Sir D. Mitchell	1761	Sir S. Robinson

YEOMAN USHER OF THE BLACK ROD

1660	J. Whynyard	1717	J. Incledon
1690	B. Coling	1754	R. Quarme
1702	J. Phillips	1787	R. Quarme
1709	D. Davis		

SERJEANT-AT-ARMS

1673	{ Sir G. Charnock / R. Charnock	1713	C. Stone
		1747	R. Jephson
1697	R. Persehouse	1789	W. Watson
1713	S. Goatley		

DEPUTY SERJEANT-AT-ARMS

| By 1730 | T. Hollinshead | by 1776 | F. Macklay |

COMPOSITION OF THE HOUSE

Date	Sovereign and regal year	Remarks	Dukes	Marquises	Earls	Viscounts	Barons	Representing Scotland	Archbishops and Bishops	Total
1714	1 George I	After the Union with Scotland in 1707	23	2	74	11	67	16	26	219
1727	1 George II		31	1	71	15	62	16	26	222
1760	1 George III		25	1	81	12	63	16	26	224

SCOTTISH REPRESENTATIVE PEERS

The provisions for electing the Scottish representative peers were contained in the Scottish Union with England Act 1707 (1706, c. 7) and the Union with Scotland Act 1707 (6 Ann c. 78). Later legislation, in 1847 and 1851, introduced certain changes.

There were 16 Scottish representative peers, elected for the period of each Parliament, with by-elections held when necessary to fill such vacancies as occurred. Elections were held in Edinburgh, with peers entitled to vote either in person, or by proxy, or by sending a signed list. The Lord Clerk Register (or the Clerks of Session) acted as Returning Officers.

THE LORD CLERK REGISTER

1705–8	Sir James Murray
1708–14	E of Glasgow
1714–16	E of Ilay
1716	D of Montrose
1716–33	Ld Polwarth (E of Marchmont)
1733–9	E of Selkirk
1739–56	M of Lothian
1756–60	Alexander Hume Campbell
1760–8	E of Morton

ELECTIONS OF SCOTTISH REPRESENTATIVE PEERS

Date			General or by-election	Numbers of peers present
1708	17	Jun	G	57
1710	10	Nov	G	49
1712	14	Aug	B	32
1713	13	Jan	B	25
	8	Oct	G	36
1715	3	Mar	G	43
1716	28	Feb	B	18
1721	1	Jun	B	22
1722	21	Apr	G	42
	15	Aug	B	18
1723	13	Jun	B	13
1727	20	Sep	G	33
1730	17	Nov	B	23
1731	19	Feb	B	17
1732	28	Jan	B	17

1733	21	Sep	B	37
1734	4	Jun	G	60
1736	22	Oct	B	33
1737	14	Apr	B	21
1738	14	Mar	B	21
1739	22	Mar	B	20
1741	13	Jun	G	37
1742	30	Apr	B	24
1744	12	Oct	B	17
1747	1	Aug	G	33
1750	15	Mar	B	25
1752	9	Jul	B	26
	16	Nov	B	23
1754	21	May	G	36

Except for June 1734 (when the place was the Burgh Room) and for June 1741 (when the place was the Court of Exchequer), all elections took place in the Palace of Holyrood House. The Returning Officers were the two Clerks of Sessions.

GROWTH OF THE CONSTITUENCIES

Summary 1509–1707

	Counties	Boroughs	Universities	Progressive total
In existence in 1509	74	222		296
Henry VII Prerogative Charters		14		341
Acts of Parliament		15		
Edward VI Prerogative Charters	16	34		375
Mary I Prerogative Charters		23		398
Elizabeth I Prerogative Charters		62		460
James I Prerogative Charters		11		487
Resolutions of the House of Commons		12	4	
Charles I Resolutions of the House of Commons		20		507
Charles II Acts of Parliament	2	2		513
Prerogative Charters		2		
James II Prerogative Charters				513
Anne Union with Scotland	30	15		558

No further changes occurred until the Union with Ireland in 1800.

THE FRANCHISE

England and Wales By a statute of 1430 (18 Hen. VI c. 7), in the counties the voting qualification was the possession of freehold property valued for the land tax at 40 shillings per annum – the 40s freeholder. In the boroughs various qualifications applied. The main types were:

Scot and Lot (SL)   right of voting vested in inhabitant householders paying poor rate.
Householder (H)   also known as 'potwalloper' franchise. Right of voting vested in all inhabitant householders not receiving alms or poor relief.
Burgage (B)   franchise attached to property in the borough.
Corporation (C)   right of voting confined to the corporation.
Freeman (FM)   right of voting belonged to the freemen of the borough (in the City of London in the livery, rather than in the freemen as a whole).
Freeholder (FH)   right of voting lay with the freeholders.

Scotland In the Scottish counties the franchise belonged to freeholders possessing land valued at 40s 'of old extent' or to owners of land rated at £400 Scots (c. £35 sterling). In Sutherland the vote also extended to tenants of the Earl of Sutherland. The Scottish boroughs, or burghs, were combined in groups for the purpose of electing MPs by a process of indirect election. Voting was vested in the small burgh councils.

CLASSIFICATION OF ENGLISH BOROUGHS, 1760

Electors	SL	H	B	C	FM	FH	Total
Over 5000	1	1			5		7
1001 to 5000	6	2			24	4	36
601 to 1000	7	5			9	1	22
301 to 600	10	1			13		24
101 to 300	8	5	10	1	11	1	36
51 to 100	4		10	2	5		21
50 or fewer	2		15	26	13		56
Total	38	14	35	29	80	6	202

THE CONSTITUENCIES, 1688–1760

ENGLISH COUNTIES

Constituency	MPs	Constituency	MPs
Bedfordshire	2	Lincolnshire	2
Berkshire	2	Middlesex	2
Buckinghamshire	2	Monmouthshire	2
Cambridgeshire	2	Norfolk	2
Cheshire	2	Northamptonshire	2
Cornwall	2	Northumberland	2
Cumberland	2	Nottinghamshire	2
Derbyshire	2	Oxfordshire	2
Devon	2	Rutland	2
Dorset	2	Shropshire	2
Durham	2	Somerset	2
Essex	2	Staffordshire	2
Gloucestershire	2	Suffolk	2
Hampshire	2	Surrey	2
Herefordshire	2	Sussex	2
Hertfordshire	2	Warwickshire	2
Huntingdonshire	2	Westmorland	2
Kent	2	Wiltshire	2
Lancashire	2	Worcestershire	2
Leicestershire	2	Yorkshire	2

ENGLISH BOROUGHS

Constituency	Type of seat	MPs
Abingdon	SL	1
Aldborough	SL	2
Aldeburgh	FM	2
Amersham	SL	2
Andover	C	2
Appleby	B	2
Arundel	SL	2
Ashburton	B	2
Aylesbury	H	2
Banbury	C	1
Barnstaple	FM	2
Bath	C	2

Constituency	Type of seat	MPs
Bedford	FM	2
Bere Alston	B	2
Berwick-on-Tweed	FM	2
Beverley	FM	2
Bewdley	FM	1
Bishop's Castle	FM	2
Bletchingly	B	2
Bodmin	C	2
Boroughbridge	B	2
Bossiney	FM	2
Boston	FM	2
Brackley	C	2
Bramber	B	2
Bridgnorth	FM	2
Bridgwater	SL	2
Bridport	SL	2
Bristol	FM	2
Buckingham	C	2
Bury St Edmunds	C	2
Callington	SL	2
Calne	C	2
Cambridge	FM	2
Camelford	FM	2
Canterbury	FM	2
Carlisle	FM	2
Castle Rising	FM	2
Chester	FM	2
Chichester	SL	2
Chippenham	B	2
Chipping Wycombe	FM	2
Christchurch	C	2
Cirencester	H	2
Clitheroe	B	2
Cockermouth	B	2
Colchester	FM	2
Corfe Castle	SL	2
Coventry	FM	2
Cricklade	FH	2
Dartmouth	FM	2
Derby	FM	2
Devizes	C	2

Constituency	Type of seat	MPs
Dorchester	SL	2
Dover	FM	2
Downton	B	2
Droitwich	C	2
Dunwich	FM	2
Durham	FM	2
East Grinstead	B	2
East Looe	FM	2
East Retford	FM	2
Evesham	FM	2
Exeter	FM	2
Eye	SL	2
Fowey	SL	2
Gatton	SL	2
Gloucester	FM	2
Grampound	FM	2
Grantham	FM	2
Great Bedwyn	B	2
Great Grimsby	FM	2
Great Marlow	SL	2
Great Yarmouth	FM	2
Guildford	FM	2
Harwich	C	2
Haslemere	FH	2
Hastings	FM	2
Hedon	FM	2
Helston	C	2
Hereford	FM	2
Hertford	FM	2
Heytesbury	B	2
Higham Ferrers	FM	1
Hindon	H	2
Honiton	H	2
Horsham	B	2
Huntingdon	FM	2
Hythe	FM	2
Ilchester	H	2
Ipswich	FM	2
King's Lynn	FM	2
Kingston-upon-Hull	FM	2
Knaresborough	B	2

Constituency	Type of seat	MPs
Lancaster	FM	2
Launceston	FM	2
Leicester	FM	2
Leominster	SL	2
Lewes	SL	2
Lichfield	FM	2
Lincoln	FM	2
Liskeard	FM	2
Liverpool	FM	2
London	FM	4
Lostwithiel	C	2
Ludgershall	FH	2
Ludlow	FM	2
Lyme Regis	FM	2
Lymington	FM	2
Maidstone	FM	2
Maldon	FM	2
Malmesbury	C	2
Malton	B	2
Marlborough	C	2
Midhurst	B	2
Milborne Port	SL	2
Minehead	H	2
Mitchell	SL	2
Monmouth	FM	1
Morpeth	FM	2
Newark	SL	2
Newcastle-under-Lyme	FM	2
Newcastle-upon-Tyne	FM	2
Newport	B	2
Newport (I of W)	C	2
New Romney	C	2
New Shoreham	SL	2
Newton	C	2
Newtown (I of W)	B	2
New Windsor	SL	2
New Woodstock	FM	2
Northallerton	B	2
Northampton	H	2
Norwich	FM	2
Nottingham	FM	2

Constituency	Type of seat	MPs
Okehampton	FM	2
Old Sarum	B	2
Orford	FM	2
Oxford	FM	2
Penryn	SL	2
Peterborough	SL	2
Petersfield	B	2
Plymouth	FM	2
Plympton Erle	FM	2
Pontefract	B	2
Poole	FM	2
Portsmouth	FM	2
Preston	H	2
Queensborough	FM	2
Reading	SL	2
Reigate	FH	2
Richmond	B	2
Ripon	B	2
Rochester	FM	2
Rye	FM	2
St Albans	FM	2
St Germans	H	2
St Ives	SL	2
St Mawes	FM	2
Salisbury	C	2
Saltash	C	2
Sandwich	FM	2
Scarborough	C	2
Seaford	SL	2
Shaftesbury	SL	2
Southampton	FM	2
Southwark	SL	2
Stafford	FM	2
Stamford	SL	2
Steyning	SL	2
Stockbridge	SL	2
Sudbury	FM	2
Tamworth	SL	2
Taunton	H	2
Tavistock	FH	2
Tewkesbury	FM	2

Constituency	Type of seat	MPs
Thetford	C	2
Thirsk	B	2
Tiverton	C	2
Totnes	FM	2
Tregony	H	2
Truro	C	2
Wallingford	SL	2
Wareham	SL	2
Warwick	SL	2
Wells	FM	2
Wembley	B	2
Wendover	H	2
Wenlock	FM	2
Westbury	B	2
West Looe	FM	2
Weymouth and Melcombe Regis	FH	4
Whitchurch	B	2
Wigan	FM	2
Wilton	C	2
Winchelsea	FM	2
Winchester	FM	2
Wootton Bassett	SL	2
Worcester	FN	2
Yarmouth (I of W)	C	2
York	FM	2

UNIVERSITIES

	MPs
Cambridge	2
Oxford	2

WELSH COUNTIES

Anglesey	1
Breconshire	1
Cardiganshire	1
Carmarthenshire	1
Carnarvonshire	1

Denbighshire	1
Flintshire	1
Glamorganshire	1
Merionethshire	1
Montgomeryshire	1
Pembrokeshire	1
Radnorshire	1

WELSH BOROUGHS

Constituency	Type of seat	MPs
Beaumaris	C	1
Brecon	FM	1
Cardiff Boroughs	FM	1
Cardigan Boroughs	FM	1
Carmarthen	FM	1
Carnarvon Boroughs	FM	1
Denbigh Boroughs	FM	1
Flint Boroughs	SL	1
Haverfordwest	FM	1
Montgomery	FM	1
New Radnor Boroughs	FM	1
Pembroke Boroughs	FM	1

SCOTTISH COUNTIES

Constituency	MPs	Constituency	MPs
Aberdeenshire	1	Lanarkshire	1
Argyllshire	1	Linlithgowshire	1
Ayrshire	1	Orkney and Shetland	1
Banffshire	1	Peebleshire	1
Berwickshire	1	Perthshire	1
Dumfriesshire	1	Renfrewshire	1
Dunbartonshire	1	Ross-shire	1
Edinburghshire	1	Roxburghshire	1
Elginshire	1	Selkirkshire	1
Fife	1	Stirlingshire	1
Forfarshire	1	Sutherland	1
Haddingtonshire	1	Wigtownshire	1
Inverness-shire	1		
Kincardineshire	1	Buteshire	1
Kirkcudbright Stewartry	1	Caithness*	1

Clackmannanshire ⎱* 1
Kinross-shire ⎰ 1

Nairnshire ⎱* 1
Cromartyshire ⎰ 1

SCOTTISH BURGHS†

Aberdeen Burghs   1
Anstruther Easter Burghs 1
Ayr Burghs   1

Dumfries Burghs   1
Dysart Burghs   1
Edinburgh   1
Elgin Burghs   1
Glasgow Burghs   1
Haddington Burghs   1
Inverness Burghs   1
Linlithgow Burghs   1
Perth Burghs   1
Stirling Burghs   1
Tain Burghs   1
Wigtown Burghs   1

DISBURSEMENT OF SECRET SERVICE MONEY, 1728–60

£

1728	45 744	1745	24 000
1729	57 880	1746	22 000
1730	53 391	1747	41 000
1731	63 918	1748	33 000
1732	73 781	1749	38 000
1733	87 470	1750	29 000
1734	117 140	1751	32 000
1735	66 630	1752	40 000
1736	95 313	1753	35 000
1737	61 999	1754	50 000
1738	72 828	1755	40 000
1739	74 250	1756	38 000
1740	80 116	1757	50 000
1741	80 977	1758	40 000
1742	64 949	1759	30 000
1743	54 300	1760	40 000
1744	34 970		

Source L. B. Namier, *The Structure of Politics at the Accession of George III* (London, 1929), p. 242.

*In alternate Parliaments one of each pair of counties was represented.

†*An indirect system of election operated in all the Scottish burghs except Edinburgh, where the 33 members of the Town Council elected one MP directly. In the other burghs, the Town Councils nominated one delegate each, a majority of electors in each district electing one MP.

6 ELECTIONS

ELECTIONS AND ELECTION RESULTS, 1689–1761

Introduction

An accurate return of election results in this period is fraught with difficulty. It must be noted at the outset that no general election in this period was in fact general, the number of contests ranging from high points such as 1710 and 1722 to the much lower numbers for elections such as 1747 and 1761 (see pp. 118–19). Even at the most heavily contested elections, a very large number of seats remained uncontested. Moreover, in spite of strong party feeling at some points in this period, notably in the reign of Queen Anne, the classification of MPs by party labels is a matter of some contention. Hence, unlike a modern election where almost all seats are contested by candidates standing under a clear party label, this period has both a fluctuating number of contests and uncertain party allegiances. None the less, scholars have attempted to estimate in general terms both the results of the contests that took place at elections and the resulting impact upon representation in the House of Commons. It should be noted that the result of an election was only one factor in determining the composition of the House of Commons: challenges on election petitions subsequent to an election, the allegiance of MPs returned from uncontested seats, and shifts in allegiance at, or shortly following, the sitting of a new Parliament must also be taken into consideration. As a result, allegiance at the opening of a session did not necessarily reflect solely or even primarily the outcome of the last general election. Historians have therefore turned both to contemporary estimates of support and to division lists for estimates of groupings at the opening of a new parliament. Neither source, however, supplies completely reliable indications of allegiance and a degree of imprecision has to be accepted in any estimates so derived. Finally, the role and definition of political groupings and the importance of party allegiance remains a subject of much debate. 'Court and Country' divisions and Namierite analysis of political activity have considerably modified consideration of the importance of party labels for much of this period, although these views have also been subject to criticisms in their turn. The following summary of elections and their results must be viewed in the light of these qualifications.

1689

In the aftermath of the flight of James II, elections were called in January 1689 for the 'Convention Parliament'. Contests took place in nine counties

111

and forty-one boroughs. Although party divisions were not expressed strongly in the mood of national emergency and *de facto* interregnum, Parliament began to divide on partisan issues after the vesting of the throne in William and Mary. One hundred and fifty-one 'hard core' Tories have been identified from the vote against the throne being declared vacant on 5 February 1689, while the 174 members who voted in January 1690 for the Sacheverell clause have been identified as committed Whigs. Nearly 200 members, new and previously elected, can be considered as uncommitted in the Commons as a whole.

1690

The 'Convention Parliament' was prorogued on 27 January 1690 and dissolved ten days later because of William's dissatisfaction with the Whigs' attempt to monopolise office and the Tories' offer of a more favourable settlement of the Revenue. In the absence of division lists for the period 1690–6 a precise delineation of election results is not possible, but there were notable losses by the Whigs and early divisions saw substantial Tory majorities in the Commons, although these were to be eroded in the course of the Parliament with the rise of the Whig 'Junto'.

1695

William's decision to dissolve Parliament was taken before he left England to conduct the military campaigns on the Continent which concluded in the fall of Namur. The election results in the autumn saw significant Tory losses, including six in the City of London and in Westminster, although it was not until early 1696 that the various Whig factions were able to establish a clear majority in the House of Commons.

1698

An election was due in the summer of 1698 under the provisions of the Triennial Act. Parliament was prorogued on 5 July and dissolved two days later, elections taking place in July and August. Analysis of the election results suggests that the Whig 'Junto' lost its majority in the Commons with Tory candidates making significant gains in both county and borough seats.

1700

The instability of the existing Ministry following the election of 1698 led to a major reconstruction of the administration in the autumn of 1700, creating a virtually Tory Ministry with only one Whig remaining in an important office. Dissolution of Parliament did not take place for a further six weeks, partly as a result of the news of the death of Charles II of Spain and its diplomatic repercussions. Eventually Parliament was dissolved on 19

December 1700. The resulting election led to substantial Tory gains with at least thirty former Whigs failing to be returned. Although not in itself sufficient to ensure a Tory majority in the Commons, subsequent divisions showed that the new Parliament contained a significant majority prepared to support the Tories.

1701

As early as September 1701 William III sought to go to the country to obtain a more favourable House of Commons, although the dissolution was not proclaimed until 11 November. In the subsequent election, although the Tories lost seats and some prominent members, the Whig gain was sufficiently small to leave both sides claiming a majority. The Whigs estimated a gain of 30 seats, but modern research has estimated that the new Parliament still contained a nominal Tory majority of 289 Tories to 224 Whigs. After Parliament met, however, the Tory majority was decreased by William's movement towards the Whigs and poor attendance on the part of Tory members. The first divisions were extremely close, the Speakership being carried for the Whigs by only four votes. By the end of February 1702, the Whigs were generally able to obtain a somewhat precarious majority in the divisions with uncommitted members taking the Whig side. Further clarification of the party situation was prevented by the death of William on 8 March 1702.

1702

The formation of a new administration containing many Tories, by Queen Anne, was followed by a general election in the summer, announced by a dissolution on 3 July. The election witnessed at least 87 contests in England and Wales. The election has been estimated at returning a Tory majority of over 130 seats in the new Parliament, reflected in Tory majorities of that order in the divisions of the autumn.

1705

Parliament was prorogued on 14 March 1705 and a dissolution followed shortly under the provisions of the Triennial Act. The election which followed was one of the most bitterly fought of the eighteenth century with over 100 contests in England alone, including 26 counties. According to modern calculations 267 Tories and 246 Whigs were returned, yielding a Whig gain of 60 seats over the previous administration.

1708

The election of 1708 marked the first election for the Parliament of Great Britain following the Act of Union with Scotland, signed the previous year, which entitled 45 Scottish MPs to sit at Westminster. Parliament was prorogued on 1 April and the elections took place in May. It has been suggested that the Whigs gained some 30 seats in England and Wales, producing 291 Whigs and 222 Tories returned. With most of the new Scottish MPs also voting in their favour, the Whigs were able to go on to win most of the votes on election petitions. Sunderland declared it 'the most Whig Parliament [there] has been since the Revolution'.

1710

Following a widespread replacement of the Whig administration in the spring and summer of 1710 with the filling of most of the important ministerial posts by Tories, and a strong tide of anti-Whig feeling in the country, the general election in the autumn produced widespread Tory gains, with contemporary estimates of at least two Tories elected for every Whig returned. Modern estimates suggest that 332 Tories and 181 Whigs were returned for England and Wales, with a Whig majority in Scotland somewhat mitigating the Tory landslide.

1713

The general election which took place in August and September 1713 occurred when both public opinion and the influence of the Court were still predisposed in favour of the Tories, resulting in a large Tory majority in England and Wales only somewhat diminished by a clear Whig majority in Scotland. *The History of Parliament* provides the following breakdown of results:

	Tories	Whigs
England	323	166
Wales	21	3
Scotland	14	31
Total	358	200

Decisions on election petitions, decided overwhelmingly in favour of the Tories, increased the nominal Tory majority to an estimated 372 Tories as opposed to 185 Whigs. This majority, however, proved less conclusive than it appeared as Parliament did not meet to conduct serious business until almost six months later on 2 March 1714, when parliamentary allegiance was beginning to be affected by the question of the Hanoverian succession, much reducing the effective Tory strength in divisions in the House of Commons.

1715

By the time of the death of Queen Anne on 1 August 1714, the Hanoverian succession had been largely secured by pro-Hanoverian appointments to the

Privy Council. Parliament, which had been prorogued on 9 July 1714, met again on 5 August, but was prorogued once more on 25 August awaiting a fresh election, meeting again only to transact the formal business of further prorogation. The dismissal of Bolingbroke at the end of August and George I's arrival in the country on 19 September was followed by the construction of a Whig administration. When Parliament was formally dissolved in January 1715 the election took place in a climate which was flowing strongly against the Tories, who were being widely associated by Whig propaganda as opposing the Protestant succession and as betrayers of British policy interests in the Treaty of Utrecht. The election resulted in an almost complete reversal of party fortunes in 1713. *The History of Parliament* gives the following post-election returns:

	Tories	Whigs
England	195	294
Wales	15	9
Scotland	7	38
Total	217	341

Moreover, as was customary, election petitions were decided in favour of the majority party: of 46 Tory and 41 Whig petitions, no Tory petition was successful but 31 Tories were unseated. As a result, post-petition party strength altered to 372 Whigs to 186 Tories.

1722

Under the provisions of the Septennial Act passed in 1716, an election was due early in 1722 and Parliament was dissolved on 10 March. Against the background of the South Sea scandal and Walpole's increasing supremacy in the House of Commons, the Tories were eclipsed, making the election in some areas, like Scotland, more of a contest between rival groups of Whigs. In all there were more than 150 contests, a larger number than at any other election in the period 1688–1760 and at least 30 more than in 1715. Most of the returns for the English boroughs came in by the end of March, with the results for the English counties, Cornwall, Wales, and Scotland coming in during April.

The results were 379 Whigs returned against 178 Tories, representing a Whig gain of almost 40 seats on the result in 1715. After election petitions had been heard the composition of the House of Commons has been estimated at 389 Whigs to 169 Tories.

1727

The general election which followed the death of George I witnessed 118 contests. Walpole, having secured the continuity of his administration after a brief period of uncertainty, was able to erode further the number of his opponents. Wales which had produced a steady Tory majority hitherto, returned a Whig majority of 14 members, while the English boroughs moved ever more firmly under Whig control. The returns produced 427 Whigs and 131 Tories. Sixty-one petitions followed the elections, 24 of which were heard, resulting in three further Whig gains. The resulting House of Commons therefore consisted of 415 Whig ministerialists, an opposition Whig group of 15 led by Pulteney, and 128 Tories, a nominal majority of 272.

1734

The general election of 1734, called under the provisions of the Septennial Act, took place against the recent background of Walpole's controversial Excise Bill, which he had been forced to withdraw in April of the previous year in the face of bitter opposition and falling majorities. At the dissolution of Parliament in April 1734 the House of Commons has been estimated at containing 342 Whig supporters of the administration, 86 opposition Whigs, and 130 Tories, representing a government majority of 126. The election witnessed 135 contests and was fiercely contested with some Tory successes in the English counties. The election returns were as follows:

Ministerial Whigs	326
Opposition Whigs	83
Tories	149

The government made a further four gains on election petitions, producing a House of Commons consisting of 330 ministerial supporters, 83 opposition Whigs, and 145 Tories.

1741

Parliament was dissolved on 27 April 1741. Following the increasing difficulties of Walpole's administration, the government majority had fallen to around 50 seats, reflecting a considerable defection of ministerial supporters to the ranks of the opposition. The elections witnessed 94 contests but were not fought in a particularly excitable atmosphere. The administration lost seats in two areas of traditional support, Scotland, where the influence of the Duke of Argyll was committed against it, and in Cornwall where the Prince of Wales lent his support to the opposition. As a result, the Ministry lost 21 seats in these two areas alone. The results produced were as follows:

Ministerial Whigs	286
Opposition Whigs	31
Tories	136

Five seats were left unfilled as a result of double returns, leaving a much reduced theoretical majority for the administration of 19.

However, when Parliament met on 1 December 1741, some 23 seats were vacant by death and double returns, reducing the nominal government majority still further to 16 (276 government supporters, 124 opposition Whigs, and 135 Tories). In January and February 1742 the combined opposition sought further to reduce the government majority by contesting election returns. After several close votes, including a number of ministerial defeats, Walpole resigned after losing the determination of the election of Chippenham by 16 votes (241 to 225) on 2 February 1742.

1747

Parliament was dissolved on 18 June 1747. The re-establishment of the Pelham administration, following the unsuccessful attempt by Bath and Granville to form a new administration in February 1746, left a strong government majority of around 160. In a relatively quiet election with only 60 contests, the administration was able to exercise more of the customary influence in places such as Scotland and Cornwall than Walpole had been able to do in 1741. As a result the number of opposition MPs returned for Scotland was reduced from 26 to 10 (out of 45) and in Cornwall from 29 to 19 compared with 1741. Moreover, the seats in the metropolitan area which had often proved a centre of opposition support were largely taken by the ministry. The general election resulted in the following return:

Ministerial Whigs	338
Opposition Whigs	97
Tories	117

Election petitions resulted in the overturn of seven opposition MPs and the government was also successful in six double returns, giving a total when Parliament met of 351 ministerial supporters, 92 opposition Whigs, and 115 Tories, a majority of 144.

1754

Henry Pelham died on 6 March 1754 while preparations were in train for a general election under the provisions of the Septennial Act. At least 62 constituencies went to the poll in 1754 with the influence of the Duke of Newcastle organising the government interest. According to a contemporary listing, the government was estimated to have gained a further 11 seats. The returns were as follows:

Government	368
Opposition Whigs	42
Tories	106
Doubtful	26

1761

Parliament was dissolved on 20 March 1761 and elections were held in circumstances which were somewhat unusual in the eighteenth century, in that there was no organised opposition in the House of Commons and, coming after the accession of George III, under his instructions that no government money should be used to assist the election of the administration's supporters. In the event, the election saw only 53 contests, the lowest number in the period 1688–1761. The election of 113 Tories, including 21 new members, scarcely diminished a substantial government majority.

Sources   The compilation of the above summary owes an enormous debt to the pioneering efforts of the *History of Parliament* project, notably the volumes edited by R. Sedgewick, *The History of Parliament: The House of Commons, 1715–1754* (OUP, 1970) and Sir Lewis Namier and John Brooke, *The History of Parliament: The House of Commons, 1754–1790* (HMSO, 1964). Valuable additional information for the period prior to 1715 has been obtained from W. A. Speck, *Tory and Whig: The Struggle in the Constituencies, 1701–1715* (London, 1970) and B. W. Hill, *The Growth of Parliamentary Parties, 1689–1742* (London, 1976) and *British Parliamentary Parties, 1742–1832* (London, 1985).

GENERAL ELECTIONS, 1701–1761: NUMBER OF CONTESTS

There is no completely reliable return of the number of contests available for this period. In general, this list follows the standard authorities, primarily the volumes of the *History of Parliament* for 1715–54 and 1754–90. Until the volumes dealing with the period prior to 1715 are complete it is not possible to provide an equivalent guide to the period 1688–1715. However, this list is supplemented for 1701 to 1715 by the valuable additional material contained in J. Cannon, *Parliamentary Reform, 1642–1832* (Cambridge, 1973), Appendix 3, and W. A. Speck, *Tory and Whig: The Struggle in the Constituencies* (London, 1970), Appendix E.

	England	Wales	Scotland
1701	89 (18)	2	
1702	85 (18)	2	
1705	108 (26)	2	
1708	92 (14)	5	NA
1710	127 (23)	4	NA
1713	97 (12)	3	NA
1715	111 (17)	8	9

1722	127 (17)	9	20
1727	96 (12)	13	9
1734	107 (13)	8	20
1741	65 (4)	11	18
1747	51 (3)	2	7
1754	60 (5)	4	2[1]
1761	46 (4)	2	6

Notes: figures in brackets denote county contests
[1] Scottish counties only
NA Not Available

7 RELIGION

THE ANGLICAN CHURCH

1688   Archbishop Sancroft and six Bishops protest against James II's Delaration of Indulgence, suspending laws against Catholics and dissenters. Tried for seditious libel, but acquitted.

1689   Toleration Act allows dissenters to worship publicly on taking an oath and permits Quakers to affirm, but excludes Catholics and Unitarians. Attempt to alter the Prayer Book in order to attract the dissenters back to the Church of England fails owing to opposition of Convocation. Archbishop Sancroft, five Bishops and more than 400 clergy, the non-jurors, refuse to take oaths of supremacy and allegiance to William and Mary and are deprived of their livings.

1695   Locke's *Reasonableness of Christianity* published.

1698   The Society for Promoting Christian Knowledge is founded.

1701   Mission branch of the Society for Promoting Christian Knowledge is founded as the Society for the Propagation of the Gospel.

1703   Bill to prevent Occasional Conformity passes the House of Commons but is rejected by the Lords.

1704   Queen Anne's Bounty: Queen Anne surrenders the claim of the throne to first fruits and tenths to endow poorer clergy.

1707   Act of Security of Church of England excludes Presbyterians from holding office in England.

1709   Dr Sacheverell impeached after preaching against toleration of dissenters and denouncing the Whig Ministers as traitors to the Church.

1710   Trial of Dr Sacheverell at Westminster Hall leads to rioting in London and attacks on dissenting chapels. Lords order Sacheverell's sermon to be burnt and silence him for three years.

1711   Occasional Conformity Act passed against Protestant dissenters. Parliament votes £350 000 to build 52 churches in London.

1713   Bishop Gibson produces the *Codex Juris Ecclesiastici Anglicani*, a comprehensive study of the legal rights and duties of the English clergy and of the constitution of the Church.

1714   Schism Act introduced, forbidding nonconformists to teach.

1716   Negotiations between non-jurors and Greek Church for reunion.

1717   Convocation prorogued as a consequence of its censure of Hoadly, Bishop of Bangor, for his sermon declaring against tests of orthodoxy. Convocation does not reassemble again until 1852. Hoadly replies to the censure and 'Bangorian controversy' ensues.

1719   Repeal of Occasional Conformity and Schism Acts.

1723   Francis Atterbury, Bishop of Rochester, exiled for part in pro-Jacobite plot.

1727   First annual Indemnity Act introduced to cover breaches of the Test Act.

1729   John Wesley, junior Fellow of Lincoln College, Oxford, becomes leader of a strict religious society, dubbed Methodists.

1730   Tindal's *Christianity As Old As the Creation* declared that Christ merely confirmed the law revealed by the light of Nature.

1733   Hoadly's *Plain Account of the Lord's Supper*, describing the ceremony as purely memorial, attacked.

1736   Warburton's *Alliance of Church and State* argues for the necessity of an Established church and a test on dissenters.

1739   George Whitefield starts open-air preaching near Bristol.

1745   Many of the non-jurors implicated in the Jacobite rebellion.

1746   SPCK produces Welsh Bible and Prayer Book.

1749   George Whitefield becomes chaplain to Lady Huntingdon.

1753   Lord Hardwick's Marriage Act: clergy to be heavily punished for performing marriage ceremonies without previous publication of banns or production of licence.

1757   Publication of Hume's *Natural History of Religion*.

REVENUES FROM BISHOPRICS, 1760

See	Revenue p.a.
Canterbury	£7000
Durham	£6000
Winchester	£5000
York	£4500

London	£4000
Ely	£3400
Worcester	£3000
Salisbury	£3000
Oxford	£500 (+ £1800)
Norwich	£2000
Bath and Wells	£2000
Bristol	£450 (+ £1150)
Exeter	£1500
Chester	£900 (+ £600)
Rochester	£600 (+ £900)
Lincoln	£1500
Lichfield and Coventry	£1400
St Asaph	£1400
Bangor	£1400
Chichester	£1400
Carlisle	£1300
Hereford	£1200
Peterborough	£1000
Llandaff	£500 (+ £450)
Gloucester	£900 (+ rich Durham prebend)
St Davids	£900 (+ two livings)

Source   A list of the Archbishops, Bishops, Deans and Prebendaries in England and Wales in His Majesty's Gift, with the Reputed Yearly Value of Their Respective Dignities (1762)

ARCHBISHOPS AND BISHOPS

PROVINCE OF CANTERBURY: ENGLAND

Canterbury

1678	William Sancroft	1737	John Potter
1691	John Tillotson	1747	Thomas Herring
1695	Thomas Tenison	1757	Matthew Hutton
1716	William Wake	1758	Thomas Secker

London

1676	Henry Compton	1723	Edmund Gibson
1714	John Robinson	1748	Thomas Sherlock

Winchester

1684	Peter Mew(s)	1723	Richard Willis
1707	Jonathan Trelawney	1734	Benjamin Hoadly
1721	Charles Trimnell		

Bath and Wells

1685	Thomas Ken(n)	1727	John Wayne
1691	Richard Kidder	1743	Edward Willes
1704	George Hooper		

Bristol

1685	Jonathan Trelawney	1733	Charles Cecil
1689	Gilbert Ironside	1735	Thomas Secker
1691	John Hall	1737	Thomas Gooch
1710	John Robinson	1738	Joseph Butler
1714	George Smalridge	1750	John Conybeare
1719	Hugh Boulter	1756	John Hume
1724	William Bradshaw	1758	Philip Yonge

Chichester

1685	John Lake	1722	Thomas Bowers
1689	Simon Patrick	1724	Edward Waddington
1691	Robert Grove	1731	Francis Hare
1696	John Williams	1740	Matthias Mawson
1709	Thomas Manningham	1754	William Ashburnham

Ely

1684	Francis Turner	1723	Thomas Greene
1691	Simon Patrick	1738	Robert Butts
1707	John Moore	1748	Thomas Gooch
1714	William Fleetwood	1754	Matthias Mawson

Exeter

1689	Jonathan Trelawney	1724	Stephen Weston
1708	Offspring Blackall	1742	Nicholas Claget
1717	Lancelot Blackburn	1747	George Lavington

Gloucester

1681	Robert Frampton	1731	Elias Sydall
1691	Edward Fowler	1735	Martin Benson
1715	Richard Willis	1752	James Johnson
1721	Joseph Wilcocks	1760	Williams Warburton

Hereford

1662	Herbert Croft	1721	Benjamin Hoadly
1691	Gilbert Ironside	1724	Henry Egerton
1701	Humphrey Humphries	1746	James Beauclerk
1713	Philip Bisse		

Lichfield

1671	Thomas Wood	1717	Edward Chandler
1692	William Lloyd	1731	Richard Smalbroke
1699	John Hough	1750	Frederick Cornwallis

Lincoln

1675	Thomas Barlow	1716	Edmund Gibson
1692	Thomas Tenison	1723	Richard Reynolds
1695	James Gardiner	1744	John Thomas
1705	William Wake		

Norwich

1685	William Lloyd	1727	William Baker
1691	John Moore	1733	Robert Butts
1708	Charles Trimnell	1738	Thomas Gooch
1721	Thomas Green	1748	Samuel Lisle
1723	John Leng	1749	Thomas Hayter

Oxford

1688	Timothy Hall	1715	John Potter
1690	John Hough	1737	Thomas Secker
1699	William Talbot	1758	John Hume

Peterborough

1685	Thomas White	1729	Robert Clavering
1691	Richard Cumberland	1747	John Thomas
1718	White Kennett	1757	Richard Terrick

Rochester

1684	Thomas Sprat	1731	Joseph Wilcocks
1713	Francis Atterbury	1756	Zachary Pearce
1723	Samuel Bradford		

Salisbury

1667	Seth Ward	1723	Benjamin Hoadly
1689	Gilbert Burnet	1734	Thomas Sherlock
1715	William Talbot	1748	John Gilbert
1721	Richard Willis	1757	John Thomas

Worcester

1683	William Thomas	1717	John Hough
1689	Edward Stillingfleet	1743	Isaac Maddox
1699	William Lloyd	1759	James Johnson

PROVINCE OF CANTERBURY: WALES

Bangor

1673	Humphrey Lloyd	1723	William Baker
1689	Humphrey Humphries	1728	Thomas Sherlock
1702	John Evans	1734	Charles Cecil
1716	Benjamin Hoadly	1738	Thomas Herring
1722	Richard Reynolds	1743	Matthew Hutton

1748   Zachary Pearce
1756   John Egerton

Llandaff

1679	William Beaw	1739	Matthias Mawson
1706	John Tyler	1740	John Gilbert
1724	Robert Clavering	1749	Edward Cressett
1729	John Harris	1755	Richard Newcome

St Asaph

1680   William Lloyd
1692   Edward Jones
1703   George Hooper
1704   William Beveridge
1708   William Fleetwood
1715   John Wynne
1727   Francis Hare
1732   Thomas Tanner
1736   Isaac Maddox
1743   John Thomas (elected December 1743 but translated before
        consecration)
1744   Samuel Lisle
1748   Robert Hay Drummond

St David's

1687	Thomas Watson	1731	Elias Sydall
	[vacant 1699–1705]	1732	Nicholas Claggett
1705	George Bull	1743	Edward Willes
1710	Philip Bisse	1744	Richard Trevor
1713	Adam Ottley	1753	Anthony Ellis
1724	Richard Smallbrooke		

PROVINCE OF YORK

York

1688	Thomas Lamplugh	1743	Thomas Herring
1691	John Sharp	1747	Matthew Hutton
1714	William Dawes	1757	John Gilbert
1724	Lancelot Blackburn		

Durham

1674	Nathaniel Crew	1750	Joseph Butler
1721	William Talbot	1752	Richard Trevor
1730	Edward Chandler		

Carlisle

1684	Thomas Smith	1723	John Waugh
1702	William Nicolson	1735	George Fleming
1718	Samuel Bradford	1747	Richard Osbaldeston

Chester

1686	Thomas Cartwright	1714	Francis Gastrell
1689	Nicholas Stratford	1726	Samuel Peploe
1708	William Dawes	1752	Edmund Keene

Sodor and Man

1684	Baptist Levinz
1698	Thomas Wilson
1755	Mark Kildesley

SCOTLAND

(Although episcopal government in the Church of Scotland was abolished in 1689, some bishops continued to exercise their functions; dates of the death of Bishops are given in parentheses).

Aberdeen
1682   George Haliburton (d. 1715)

Argyll
1688   Alexander Monro (not consecrated; d. 1698)

Brechin
1684   James Drummond (d. 1695)

Caithness
1680   Andrew Wood (d. 1695)

Dunblane
1684   Robert Douglas (d. 1716)

Dunkeld
1686   John Hamilton (d. 1689)

Edinburgh
1687   Alexander Rose (d. 1720)

Galloway
1688   John Gordon (d. 1726)

Glasgow
1687   John Paterson (d. 1708)

The Isles
1680   Archibald Graham (or MacIlvernock), (d. 1702)

Moray
1688   William Hay (d. 1707)

Orkney
1688   Andrew Bruce (d. 1699)

Ross
1696   James Ramsay (d. 1696)

St Andrews
1684   Arthur Rose (d. 1704)

Note: dates given are those of consecration or, in the case of translation from another see, confirmation of new appointment.

SCOTLAND

1688   News of William III's landing leads to the beginning of restoration of Presbyterianism.

1689   Episcopal clergy ejected and Presbyterianism restored. All acts supporting episcopacy rescinded and episcopacy abolished, though some of the Scottish Bishops perpetuate themselves and are still strongly supported in the east and north-east.

1690   Lay patronage abolished and Act of Supremacy rescinded. Ejected ministers restored and General Assembly meets.

1695   First Catholic Bishop appointed for Scotland.

1698   Aikenhead executed for blasphemy at Edinburgh.

1700   Estimate that out of 900 parishes, ministers in 165 adhered to the Episcopal Church.

1707   Act of Union gives full rights to the Presbyterian Church of Scotland.

1711   Greenshields, an Episcopalian, is condemned by the Court of Session for using the English liturgy in Edinburgh, but the decision reversed by the House of Lords.

1712   Toleration Act for Scotland. Right of nominating ministers restored to laymen, unless Roman Catholics, thereby depriving kirk sessions of the right of electing ministers. Strict Presbyterians refuse to recognise the Act restoring lay patronage.

1725   'Holy Bounty' granted to protestantise the Highlands.

1730   Glas attacks the civil establishment of the Church and forms the Glassite Sect, later developed by his son-in-law Sandeman.

1733   Secession from Church of Scotland led by Ebenezer Erskine in protest at lay patronage, the growth of toleration, and the threatened abolition of penal statutes against witchcraft.

1746   Following the Jacobite rebellion, the Scottish episcopal clergy are persecuted. Meetings of more than five are forbidden; public services are banned and made illegal to have churches or chapels. Some clergy resign their orders and others go into exile.

1747   Erskine's secession Church splits into Burghers, led by Erskine, and anti-Burghers.

1752   A compromise reached on lay patronage; presbytery could satisfy itself on life, learning and doctrine of patron's nominee.

PROTESTANT DISSENTERS

1688   James II orders a Declaration of Indulgence, suspending laws against Catholics and dissenters, to be read in all churches.

1689   Toleration Act allows dissenters to worship publicly on taking an oath, and permits Quakers to affirm, but excludes both Catholics and Unitarians. Protestant dissenters allowed to build chapels. Attempts to alter the Prayer Book to attract the dissenters back to the Church fails owing to opposition of Convocation.

1694   George Fox's *Journal* published.

1696   Toland's *Christianity not Mysterious* founding the Deist movement in England is burnt by the public hangman.

1697   Lord Mayor of London, a dissenter, openly practices Occasional Conformity.

1702   Defoe's *Short Way with Dissenters* satirises the sentiments of extreme High Churchmen.

1703   A bill to prevent Occasional Conformity passes the House of Commons but defeated in the Lords by the opposition of Whig peers.

1709   Dr Sacheverell preaches against toleration of dissenters.

1710   Trial of Dr Sacheverell leads to attacks on dissenting chapels in London.

1711   Occasional Conformity Act passed.

1714   Bolingbroke introduces the Schism Act, forbidding nonconformists to teach.

1715   Widespread attacks on dissenting meeting houses especially in London, the North-West and the Midlands.

1716   Dr Williams founds the Dr Williams Library.

1718   Act of quieting and establishing corporations. Dissenters could retain seat without taking sacrament if not challenged within six months.

1719   Repeal of Schism and Occasional Conformity Acts. Meeting of Presbyterians at Salters Hall protests against the need to subscribe to a belief in the Trinity by the clergy, beginning a major shift towards Unitarianism.

1727   Walpole introduces the first annual bill of indemnity for neglect of the Test and Corporation Acts, enabling dissenters to take the sacrament after, not before election.

        Ministers of Presbyterian, Independent and Baptist congregations around London form General Body of Protestant Dissenting Ministers.

1728   Moravian mission established in England.

1729   Doddridge establishes a Presbyterian Academy at Market Harborough.

1732   Organisation of Protestant dissenting deputies to act as pressure group for dissenters.

1736   Attempt to relieve Quakers from tithes fails.

DISSENTERS' PLACES OF WORSHIP, 1691–1760
(all denominations)

	Permanent	Temporary
1691–1700	32	1247
1701–10	41	1219
1711–20	21	875
1721–30	27	448
1731–40	24	424
1741–50	27	502
1751–60	55	703

Source A. D. Gilbert, Religion and Society in Industrial England: Church, Chapel and Social Change, 1740–1914 (London: Longman, 1976), p. 34.

THE METHODIST MOVEMENT

1729   John Wesley, junior Fellow of Lincoln College, Oxford, becomes leader of a strict religious society formed by his brother Charles Wesley and dubbed 'Methodists'.

1738   John Wesley returns from America, falls under the influence of Peter Böhler, a Moravian, and is converted in Aldersgate on 24 May. George Whitefield undertakes missionary work in America.

1739   George Whitefield starts open-air preaching at Kingswood, Bristol. John Wesley follows Whitefield's example of preaching in the open air. Methodist Society meets in Old Foundry, Moorfields, London.

1740   Wesley severs his connection with the Moravians. He begins to employ lay preachers and build chapels. Wesley and Whitefield agree to differ over the doctrine of predestination.

1743   Methodists produce rules for 'classes'. Welsh Calvinistic Methodist body founded by Whitefield. Serious anti-Methodist rioting in Wednesbury.

1744   First Methodist Conference held at Foundry Chapel, London, consisting of John and Charles Wesley, four clergy and four lay preachers. Resolves that Bishops are to be obeyed 'in all things indifferent', canons to be observed 'as far as can be done with a safe conscience' and 'societies to be formed where the preachers go'.

1747   Methodist societies grouped into circuits. First of John Wesley's visits to Ireland.

1749   Calvinists under Whitefield desert Wesley; Whitefield becomes chaplain to Lady Huntingdon.

1756   Wesley's *Twelve Reasons Against a Separation from the Church* attempts to restrain breakaway tendencies among his followers.

1760   Wesley's lay preachers take out licences as dissenting teachers; some begin to administer the sacraments.

ROMAN CATHOLICISM

In 1685, England was divided into four districts by the Papacy – London, Midland, Western, Northern – in each of which a papal vicar exercised the authority normally possessed by the ordinary (bishop). In law Roman Catholic priests faced the penalties of high treason for saying Mass; unlicensed teachers could be fined 40s a day; laymen refusing to take an oath denying the spiritual authority of the Pope, were guilty of recusancy. This meant they could not hold any office, keep arms, go to Italy, travel more than five miles without licence, or be executor, guardian, doctor or lawyer. They could not sit in Parliament nor on corporations. The nearest protestant kin could claim lands from a Roman Catholic heir. Roman Catholics were also subject to double land tax.

In practice the treatment of Roman Catholics was not so severe as the laws allowed: few were punished for saying or hearing Mass and magistrates seldom tendered the recusancy oath except in times of national emergency.

1688	James II orders a Declaration of Indulgence to be read in all churches, suspending laws against both Catholics and dissenters. Widespread attacks on Catholic property in London, York, Norwich, Newcastle, Cambridge, Oxford, Bristol and elsewhere (continuing into January 1689), following on the birth of James II's heir. Flight of James II effectively ends his attempt to reimpose Catholicism in England.
1689	Roman Catholics excluded from terms of Toleration Act.
1695	Act passed 'for preventing growth of popery'. Priests forbidden to exercise their functions and Catholics prevented from inheriting or buying land or sending their children abroad, unless they abjured their religion.
1714	Ultramontane Roman Catholics refuse to abandon claims of Pope Sixtus V to release subjects of a heretic monarch from oath of fealty.
1716	Recusancy laws enforced in many counties as a consequence of the Jacobite rising.
1717	Pope burning processions held in London and Oxford to celebrate George I's return from Hanover.
1723	Levy of £100 000 placed on Roman Catholics as a result of Atterbury plot.
1746	Attacks on Catholic chapels in Liverpool and Sunderland following Jacobite rising.
1747	Duke of York, the brother of Charles Edward Stuart, created a cardinal (d. 1805).
1760	Pitt obtains from the Theological Faculties of the Sorbonne, Louvain and other universities, a declaration that the Pope has no civil authority in England, that he cannot absolve from the Oath of Allegiance, and that faith must be kept with heretics.

8 TREATIES AND DIPLOMACY

PRINCIPAL TREATIES 1688–1760

Date signed		Place Signed
1689		
Apr 20	Treaty with the Netherlands concerning the fitting out of a fleet	Whitehall
Aug 15	Treaty with Denmark	Copenhagen
Aug 22	Convention with the Netherlands concerning prohibition of commerce with France	London
Aug 24	Treaty of friendship and alliance with the Netherlands	Whitehall
Oct 22	Treaty with the Netherlands concerning ships taken from the enemy	Whitehall
Dec 9	Accession of Great Britain to Grand Alliance between the Emperor and the Netherlands (12 May 1689)	—
1690		
May 16	Treaty of alliance with Elector of Brandenburg	Westminster
Nov 3	Treaty of defensive alliance with Denmark and the Netherlands	Copenhagen
1691		
Jun 30	Convention with Denmark and the Netherlands touching the commerce in France	Copenhagen
Oct 22	Treaty with the Netherlands concerning vessels captured and recaptured	Whitehall
1692		
Oct 31	Convention with Spain and the Netherlands for the fleet in the Mediterranean	The Hague
Dec 22	Subsidy treaty with the Netherlands and Elector of Hanover	The Hague
1693		
Feb 20	Treaty of subsidy with Elector of Saxony	Dresden

132

Mar	2	Instrument of England and the Netherlands for payment of 150 000 dollars to Elector of Saxony	Dresden

1694

May	23	Treaty of subsidy with the Netherlands and Elector of Saxony	Dresden
Oct	11	Additional articles with Tripoli	Tripoli

1695

Mar	18	Convention with the Emperor, the Netherlands and Bishop of Munster	The Hague
Apr	5	Renewal of articles of peace with Algiers of 1686	Algiers

1696

Dec	3	Treaty with Denmark and the Netherlands	The Hague

1697

Sep	20	Articles of peace with France	Ryswick

1698

May	14	Convention with Sweden and the Netherlands for entering into a defensive triple league	The Hague
Jun	28	Renewal of articles of peace with Algiers of 1686	Algiers
Sep	24/Oct 11	Treaty with France and the Netherlands concerning settlement of succession of Spain on the Electoral Prince of Bavaria (First Partition Treaty)	Loo/The Hague

1699

May	16	Articles of peace with Tunis	Tunis

1700

Jan	16	Treaty with Sweden	London
Jan	23–30	Treaty of alliance with Sweden and the Netherlands	The Hague/London
Mar	3–25	Treaty with France and the Netherlands for settling succession of Crown of Spain (Second Partition Treaty)	London/The Hague
Aug	17	Treaty of peace and commerce with Algiers	Algiers

1701

Jan	20	Treaty of Alliance with Denmark and the Netherlands	Odensee

Jun 15	Treaty between Denmark and Britain, and the Netherlands	Copenhagen
Aug 10	Additional articles with Algiers	Algiers
Sep 7	Treaty with the Emperor and the Netherlands (Accessions: Prussia 18 Feb 1702; Wolfenbuttel 21 Apr 1702; Treves 22 Jun 1702; Elector of Mainz and Margrave of Brandenburg in the name of the Circle of Franconia 24 Jun 1702; the Bishop of Constance and Duke of Württemburg in the name of the Circle of Suabia 4 Aug 1702; Elector of Mainz in his own name and that of the Circle of the Rhine Sep 1702; the Bishop of Munster 18 Mar 1703; Mecklenburg 14 Sep 1703; Savoy by Treaty with Britain 4 Aug 1704; the Bishop of Munster and Paderborn 1 Mar 1710)	The Hague
Oct 7	Convention between Britain and the Netherlands, and Sweden confirming previous treaties	The Hague
Nov 11	Particular and perpetual alliance with the Netherlands	The Hague

1702

30 Dec 1701– 20 Jan 1702	Treaty of alliance with Prussia and the Netherlands	The Hague/London
30 Dec 1701– 20 Jan 1702	Treaty of subsidy between Britain and the Netherlands, and Prussia	The Hague/London
Feb 7/13	Convention with the Netherlands and Landgrave of Hesse-Cassel	The Hague/London
Apr 12	Articles with the Netherlands concerning the Pretender	The Hague
Apr 18	Agreement with the Empire and the Netherlands for declaring war with France and Spain on the same day	The Hague
May 8	Convention with the Netherlands and Elector of Treves	The Hague
May 6–17	Convention with the Netherlands and Elector of Treves	The Hague/London
Jun 21	Convention with Brunswick Luneburg for a supply of 10000 men	The Hague
Nov 16	Convention with Brunswick Luneburg (with separate article 12 Dec 1702–2 Jan 1703)	The Hague

1703

Mar 13	Convention with the Netherlands and Bishop of Munster	The Hague

Mar	15	Convention with the Netherlands and Duke of Holstein	The Hague
Mar	15	Convention with the Netherlands to employ 20 000 additional troops in 1703	The Hague
Mar	27	Convention with the Netherlands and Duke of Saxe-Gotha	The Hague
Mar	31	Convention with the Netherlands and Landgrave of Hesse-Cassel	The Hague
Apr	11	Treaty with the Emperor and the Netherlands prohibiting commerce with France	The Hague
May	16	Treaty of defensive alliance between Britain, the Empire and the Netherlands, and Portugal	Lisbon
May	17	Convention with the Netherlands and Elector Palatine	The Hague
Jun	20	Treaty with the Netherlands for renewal of former treaties	Westminster
Aug	16	Treaty of stricter alliance and for the tranquillity of Europe with Sweden and the Netherlands	The Hague
Oct	28	Treaty of peace and commerce with Algiers	Algiers
Nov	20–Dec 24	Convention with Elector of Brunswick	London/The Hague
Dec	27	Treaty of commerce with Portugal	Lisbon

1704

Aug	4	Treaty with Savoy (with separate article Nov 18)	Turin
Nov	28	Treaty with King of Prussia	Berlin
Dec	30	Convention with Elector of Brunswick and Duke of Zell	London

1705

Feb	20	Treaty with Portugal concerning post office	London
Jun	20	Treaty of alliance with Principality of Catalonia	Genoa
Dec	3	Treaty with Prussia renewing treaty of 1704	Berlin
Dec	8	Convention with Elector of Hanover	Hanover

1706

May	20	Convention with the Netherlands and Landgrave of Hesse-Cassel (further treaty 25–27 Mar 1701)	Cassel

May 26	Convention with the Netherlands and Elector Palatine	The Hague
Oct 22	Treaty of commerce with Danzig	Danzig
Nov 18	Convention with Elector of Brunswick Lüneburg	The Hague
Nov 24	Treaty with Prussia (further treaty 19 Apr 1708)	The Hague
	Treaty with the Netherlands for securing Protestant succession	

1707

| Jul 10 | Treaty of peace and commerce with Spain | Barcelona |

1708

Apr 14	Convention with the Emperor for 4000 Imperialists to be sent from Italy to Catalonia	The Hague
Apr 14	Convention with Elector of Hanover	The Hague
Mar 10–Apr 17	Convention with the Netherlands and Landgrave of Hesse-Cassel	Brussels/The Hague

1709

Jan 14	Convention with Elector of Brunswick	The Hague
Feb 22	Convention with the Netherlands and Elector of Saxony (renewed 7 May 1710 and 24 Mar 1711)	The Hague
Mar 31	Treaty with the Netherlands and Prussia	The Hague
Apr 12	Treaty with Prussia	The Hague
May 28	Articles preliminary to the treaties of a general peace (of 1713) between Britain, the Empire and the Netherlands, and France	The Hague
Oct 29	Treaty with the Netherlands for securing the succession to the Crown of Great Britain, and for settling a barrier for the Netherlands against France	The Hague
Nov 7	Convention with Elector of Treves	The Hague
Nov 8	Convention with Elector of Brunswick	The Hague

1710

| Mar 31 | Convention with the Netherlands and the Emperor concerning Imperial neutrality (renewed Aug 4) | |
| May 30 | Treaty with Poland for two battalions | Camp before Douay |

Oct 29	Military convention between Marlborough and Prince Eugene	The Hague
Oct 15	Convention with Elector of Brunswick	The Hague
Nov 30	Convention with Elector of Treves	The Hague
Dec 7	Military convention between Marlborough and Prince Eugene	The Hague

1711

May 27	Military treaty between Marlborough and Prince Eugene	The camp at Warde
Sep 27	Preliminary articles for a treaty of peace with France	London
Dec 22	Confirmation of treaties with the Netherlands	London
Dec 28	Convention with Elector of Brunswick	London

1712

Jan 14	Convention with Elector of Treves	The Hague
Jan 25	Convention with the Netherlands and Elector of Brunswick	The Hague
Mar 24	Convention with Elector of Saxony	The Hague
Aug 19	Treaty of suspension of arms with France (prolonged Dec 7–14)	Paris

1713

Jan 29–30	Treaty with the Netherlands guaranteeing Protestant succession to Crown of Great Britain and the barrier of the Netherlands	Utrecht
Mar 8	Declaration of commerce and navigation with the Two Sicilies	Utrecht
Mar 14	Convention with the Emperor for evacuating Catalonia	Utrecht
Mar 14	Convention with France for evacuating Catalonia	Utrecht
Mar 26	The Asiento with Spain for supplying slaves to the Spanish West Indies	Madrid
Mar 27	Preliminary treaty of peace with Spain	Madrid
Apr 11	Treaty of peace and friendship with France	Utrecht
Apr 11	Treaty of navigation and commerce with France (additional articles 9 May)	Utrecht
Jul 13	Treaty of peace and friendship with Spain	Utrecht
Jul 26	Provisional regulation of trade in the Spanish Low Countries between Britain and the Netherlands	Utrecht

| Dec | 9 | Treaty of navigation and commerce with Spain | Utrecht |

1714

| Jul | 22 | Treaty of peace, friendship and commerce with Morocco | Tehuan |

1715

Jul	26	Convention with Austrian Netherlands concerning import of British woollen cloths	London
Nov	15	Treaty with United Provinces and Charles VI for restoration of Austrian Netherlands, to Charles, except for the barrier given to the United Provinces (Barrier Treaty)	Antwerp
Dec	14	Treaty of commerce with Spain	Madrid

1716

Feb	6	Treaty with the Netherlands (with Separate Article Apr 3)	London
May	25	Treaty of alliance with Emperor (Additional Article 1 Sep 1717)	London
May	26	Convention with Philip V of Spain for explaining the articles of the Assiento (1713)	Madrid
Jul	19	Treaty of peace with Tripoli	Tripoli
Aug	30	Treaty of peace and commerce with Tunis	Tunis
Oct	29	Treaty of peace and commerce with Algiers	Algiers

1717

| Jan | 4 | Treaty of alliance with France and the Netherlands | The Hague |

1718

Jul	18	Convention with France for bringing about peace between the Emperor and the Kings of Spain and Sicily	Paris
Jul	18	Convention with France for settling separate and secret articles of Quadruple Alliance	Paris
Aug	2	Quadruple Alliance with Charles VI, France and the Netherlands (Accession: King of Sardinia Nov 8)	London
Dec	22	Convention with Charles VI and the Netherlands concerning the Barrier Treaty of 1715	The Hague

1719

Feb	8	Convention with Hamburg concerning the herring trade	Hamburg
Apr	14	Capitulation for the Dutch troops	The Hague
Aug	4	Treaty with Prussia	Berlin
Aug	29	Preliminary convention with Sweden	Stockholm
Oct	27	Convention between Sweden and Denmark (signed by Lord Carteret and the Swedish Minister)	Stockholm
Oct	30	Convention with Denmark	Copenhagen
Nov	18	Convention with Emperor and France, excluding sons of Philip of Spain and Elizabeth Farnese from succession to Tuscany, Parma and Piacenza	The Hague

1720

Jan	21	Treaty with Sweden	—
Feb	16	Accession of Spain to convention between France and Britain of 18 Jul 1718	The Hague
Feb	17	Accession of Spain to Treaty of London of 2 Aug 1718	The Hague
Feb	29	Convention for armistice by sea with France and Spain	The Hague
Mar	18	Instrument of admission of King of Sardinia to Act of Accession of King of Spain to Treaty of London, signed by Britain, France, Spain, Sardinia and the Empire	The Hague
Apr	2	Convention for suspension of arms by sea with France, Spain, Sardinia and the Empire	The Hague

1721

Jan	23	Treaty of peace and commerce with Morocco	Fez
Jun	13	Treaty with Spain	Madrid
Jun	13	Treaty of defensive alliance with France and Spain	Madrid
Sep	27	Act of guarantee with France concerning the renunciations by the Emperor and the King of Spain	Paris

1722

Aug	27	Act of guarantee with France of the Kingdom of Sardinia	Versailles

1723

Oct	10	Treaty with Prussia	Charlottenbourg

1724

Jan	24	Act of guarantee with France	Cambrai

1725

Sep	3	Defensive treaty of alliance with France and Prussia	Hanover

1726

Aug	9	Act of accession of the Netherlands to Treaty of Hanover	The Hague

1727

Mar	12	Convention with Hesse-Cassel	London
Mar	14	Accession of Sweden to Treaty of Hanover	Stockholm
Apr	16	Treaty of alliance with France and Denmark	Copenhagen
May	31	Preliminary articles between the Emperor and the Allies of Hanover	Paris
Nov	25	Treaty with Duke of Wolfenbuttel	London

1728

Jan	14	Articles of peace and commerce with Morocco (Additional Articles Jul 1729)	Mequinez
Mar	6	Convention with the Emperor, Spain and the Netherlands concerning the execution of the Preliminaries of 31 May 1727	The Pardo
May	27	Renewal of former treaties with the Netherlands	London

1729

Mar	18	Treaty of peace with Algiers	Algiers
Sep	6/8	Convention agreeing to mediation over differences with Prussia	Berlin
Nov	9	Treaty of peace and friendship with France and Spain	Seville
Nov	21	Accession of the Netherlands to treaty of Nov 9	Seville

1730

Mar	31	Articles of peace and commerce with Tripoli	Tripoli

1731

Mar	16	Treaty of peace and alliance with the Emperor, in which the Netherlands are included	Vienna
Jul	22	Treaty with Spain and the Emperor (Accession: Tuscany Sep 21)	Vienna

Oct	17	Convention with Bremen concerning the herring trade	Bremen
Oct	31	Regulation signed by plenipotentiaries of Britain and Spain for introduction of Spanish garrisons into Tuscany	Leghorn

1732

Feb	20	Act of concurrence of the Netherlands to the Treaty of Vienna of 16 Mar 1731	The Hague
Feb	20	Article with the Netherlands concerning the East India Company at Ostend	The Hague

1734

Sep	30	Treaty and secret articles with Denmark	London
Dec	2	Treaty of commerce with Russia	St Petersburg
Dec	15	Treaty of peace with Morocco	—

1738

Sep	9	Convention with Spain	London

1739

Jan	14	Convention with Spain	The Pardo
Mar	14	Treaty with Denmark	Copenhagen

1740

May	9	Treaty with King of Sweden, as Landgrave of Hesse-Cassel	London

1741

Apr	3	Treaty with Russia	St Petersburg
Jun	24	Convention with Queen of Hungary	Hanover

1742

Feb	23	Cartel for exchange of prisoners with Spain	Paris
Jun	25	Convention with Queen of Hungary	London
Nov	18	Treaty of defensive alliance with Prussia	London
Dec	11	Treaty with Russia	Moscow

1743

Feb	15	Treaty with Austria-Hungary	London
Sep	13	Definitive treaty of peace, union, friendship and mutual defence with Hungary and Sardinia	Worms

1744

Feb	10	Convention with Austria-Hungary	London

Apr 27	Treaty of alliance with Elector of Cologne	London
May	Treaty of alliance with Elector of Mainz (prolonged Jun 1747)	—
Jul 4	Treaty with the Netherlands and the Elector of Cologne	The Hague
Aug 11	Treaty with Queen of Austria-Hungary	London
Sep 18	Convention with the Netherlands	London

1745

Jan 8	Treaty of alliance with Queen of Hungary, Poland and the Netherlands	Warsaw
Apr 2	Treaty with Queen of Hungary	London
May 21	Treaty granting £60 000 to Sardinia	London
Jun 1	Convention with Queen of Hungary	At the quarters of General de Lapines
Jun 8	Convention with Queen of Hungary	Hanover
Jun 16	Treaty with King of Sweden, as Landgrave of Hesse-Cassel	Hanover
Aug 26	Preliminary convention with Prussia (with further declaration signed in London 12 Sep)	Hanover

1746

Jun 10	Convention with Queen of Hungary	London
Jun 10	Treaty with Sardinia	London
Jul 21	Subsidiary treaty with the Netherlands and Bavaria	Munich
Aug 30	Provisional convention of subsidy between Britain and the Netherlands, and Queen of Hungary	The Hague

1747

Jan 12	Convention for the campaign of 1747 with Austria-Hungary, the Netherlands and Sardinia	The Hague
Jun 12	Convention with Russia	St Petersburg
Nov 19	Convention between Britain and the Netherlands, and Russia for passage of Russian troops across Germany	St Petersburg
Nov 27	Convention with Russia	St Petersburg

1748

Jan 26	Convention for the campaign of 1748 with Austria-Hungary, the Netherlands and Sardinia (Additional Convention May 3)	The Hague

Feb	1	Subsidiary convention with the Netherlands and Duke of Wolfenbuttel	The Hague
Apr	30	Preliminary articles of peace with France and the Netherlands	Aix-la-Chapelle
Oct	18	Treaty of Aix-la-Chapelle with France and the Netherlands (Accessions: Spain Oct 20; Austria-Hungary Oct 23; Modena Oct 25; Genoa Oct 28; Sardinia Nov 7)	Aix-la-Chapelle

1750

Jan	15	Treaty of peace with Morocco (Additional Articles Feb 1751)	Fez
Aug	22	Alliance with Austria-Hungary and Bavaria	Hanover
Aug	22	Alliance with the Netherlands and Bavaria	Hanover
Oct	5	Treaty of commerce with Spain	Madrid
Oct	30	Alliance with Russia and Austria-Hungary	St Petersburg

1751

Jun	3	Additional article with Algiers	Algiers
Sep	13	Alliance with the Netherlands and Poland	Dresden
Sep	19	Treaty of peace and commerce with Tripoli	Tripoli
Oct	19	Treaty of peace and commerce with Tunis	Bardo

1753

| May | 11 | Alliance with the Empire, Hungary and Modena | Vienna |

1755

| Jun | 18 | Treaty with Landgrave of Hesse-Cassel | Hanover |
| Sep | 30 | Treaty with Russia | St Petersburg |

1756

| Jan | 16 | Treaty with Prussia | London |

1758

| Apr | 11 | Treaty with Prussia | London |
| Dec | 7 | Convention with Prussia | London |

1759

| Jan | 17 | Convention with Landgrave of Hesse-Cassel | London |
| Nov | 9 | Convention with Prussia | — |

1760

| Jan | 14 | Treaty with Duke of Brunswick | Marburg |

Apr	1	Convention with Hesse-Cassel	London
Jul	28	Treaty of peace and commerce with Morocco	Fez
Dec	12	Convention with Prussia	—

1761

Jan	28	Renewal of peace with Tripoli	Tripoli
Mar	3	Protocol with Hesse	London
Aug	10	Convention with Brunswick for troops	Brunswick

PRINCIPAL BRITISH DIPLOMATIC REPRESENTATIVES,* 1688–1760

Abbreviations of Diplomatic Rank: Amb: Ambassador; Env: Envoy; Ex: Extraordinary; In Ch of Aff: In Charge of Affairs; Mil: Military; Min: Minister; Miss: Mission; Plen: Plenipotentiary; Res: Resident; Sec: Secretary; Spec: Special.

BAVARIA

George Stepney	1704	No special rank
Seigneur de St Saphorin	1725	No special rank
Isaac Leheup	1726	No special rank
Sir Thomas Robinson (Baron Grantham)	1745	Env Ex + Plen
Onslow Burrish	1746–58	Min
Fulke Greville	1764–70	Env Ex

DENMARK

Robert Molesworth (Vt Molesworth)	1689–92	Env Ex
Hugh Greg	1692–1701	In Ch of Aff
	1701–2	Min Res
Robert Sutton (Baron Lexington)	1693	Env Ex
James Cressett	1699–1700	Env Ex
James Vernon	1702–6	Env Ex
Daniel Pulteney	1706–15	Env Ex
Lord Polwarth	1716–20	Env Ex
	1720–1	Amb Ex
Baron Glenorchy	1720–31	Env Ex
Adm. Sir John Norris	1727	Env Ex
Brig. Richard Sutton, MP	1729	Spec Mil Miss

* *British Diplomatic Representatives, 1689–1789*, D. B. Horn, Camden 3rd Series, vol. *XLVI*, 1932, London.

Walter Titley	1729–30	Sec in Ch of Aff
	1731–9	Min Res
	1739–68	Env Ex

THE EMPIRE

Baron Paget	1689–92	Env Ex
George Stepney	1693	Sec or Agent
Baron Lexington	1694–7	Env Ex
Robert Sutton	1697–1700	Sec, later Res
George Stepney	1701–5	Env Ex
	1705–6	Env Ex + Plen
Charles Whitworth (Baron Whitworth)	1703–6	In Ch of Aff
Earl of Sunderland	1705	Env Ex
Duke of Marlborough	1705	No special rank
Baron Raby (Earl of Strafford)	1706	Env Ex + Plen
Earl of Manchester	1707	No special rank
Sir Philip Meadowe	1707–9	Env Ex
Maj-Gen. Francis Palmes	1707–8	Env Ex
	1709–11	Env Ex
Earl of Peterborough	1711	No special rank
Abraham Stanyan	1712–13	No special rank
James Stanhope (Earl Stanhope)	1714	No special rank
Baron Cobham	1714–15	Env Ex + Plen
Maj-Gen. William Cadogan (later Earl Cadogan)	1715	rank unknown
Abraham Stanyan, MP	1716–18	Env Ex + Plen
Seigneur de St Saphorin	1718–21	rank unknown
	1721–7	Env Ex + Plen
Earl Cadogan	1719–20	Amb Ex + Plen
Charles Harrison	1724–5	Min
Lord (Earl 1729) Waldegrave	1727–31	Amb Ex + Plen
Thomas Robinson, MP	1730	Min
	1730–50	Min Plen
Thomas Villiers	1742–3	Min Plen
Robert Keith	1748–53	Min
	1753–7	Min Plen

FLANDERS

John Eckhart	1689–92	Res
Robert Wolseley	1692–6	Env Ex
Richard Hill	1696–9	Env Ex
Marmande	1699–1701	Sec

George Stepney	1706–7	Env Ex + Plen
John Lawes	1707–8	In Ch of Aff
Lt-Gen. William Cadogan	1707–11	Env Ex + Plen
Earl of Orrery	1711–12	Env Ex
	1712–13	Env Ex + Plen
John Lawes	1712–14	Act Min Plen
Lt-Gen. William Cadogan	1714–15	Env Ex + Plen
William Leathes	1715–17	Sec at Brussels
	c. 1718–24	Res
Robert Daniel	1722–45	In Ch of Aff
Onslow Burrish	1742–4	Sec
	1744	Res
Solomon Dayrolle	1752–7	Min

Diplomatic relations suspended 1757–63

FRANCE

Earl of Portland	1697–8	Env + Amb Ex
Matthew Prior	1698–9	Sec
Earl of Jersey	1698–9	Amb Ex
Earl (Duke) of Manchester	1699–1701	Amb Ex

1701–13 Rupture of diplomatic relations

Matthew Prior	1712–15	Plen
Duke of Shrewsbury	1712–13	Amb Ex
Earl of Peterborough	1713–14	Amb Ex
General Charles Ross	1714	Env Ex
Earl of Stair	1714–15	Min
Earl of Stair	1715	Env Ex
Earl of Stair	1715–20	Amb Ex
Col William Stanhope, MP	1719	Plen
Sir Robert Sutton	1720–1	Amb + Plen
Sir Luke Schaub	1721–4	Amb
Thomas Crawford	1722–4	Res
Horatio Walpole	1723	No special rank
	1724	Env Ex
	1724–7	Amb Ex
	1727–30	Amb Ex + Plen
Lord Waldegrave	1725	Env Ex
	1727–8	No special rank
	1730–40	Amb Ex + Plen
Anthony Thompson	1740–4	In Ch of Aff

Diplomatic relations suspended 1744–8

| Earl of Albemarle | 1749–54 | Amb Ex + Plen |

Diplomatic Relations suspended 1755–63

GERMANY *see under* THE EMPIRE

NETHERLANDS *see under* UNITED PROVINCES OF THE NETHERLANDS

OTTOMAN EMPIRE *see under* TURKEY

POLAND

George Stepney	1698	No special rank
Sir William Browne	1700	Res
Rev John Robinson	1702–7	Env Ex
Earl of Stair	1709–10	Env Ex
George Mackenzie	1710–14	Sec in Ch of Aff
Charles Whitworth (Baron Whitworth)	1711	Amb Ex + Plen
James Scott	1711–15	Env Ex
Sir Richard Vernon	1715–18	Env Ex
Lt-Gen. Francis Palmes	1718–19	Env Ex + Plen
James Scott	1719–22	Min, later Env Ex
Edward Finch	1725–7	Min Plen
George Woodward	1728–31	Res
Sir Luke Schaub	1730–1	Spec Miss
George Woodward	1732–5	Env Ex
Denton Boate	1735–8	Sec in Ch of Aff
Thomas Villiers	1738–43	Env Ex
Edward Finch	1740	Min Plen
Sir Thomas Villiers	1744–6	Env Ex + Plen
Sir Charles Hanbury Williams, MP	1747–9	Env Ex
	1750	Min
	1751–5	Env Ex + Plen
Viscount Stormont	1756–63	Env Ex

PORTUGAL

John Methuen	1692–7	Env Ex
Paul Methuen	1697–1706	Env Ex (In Ch of Aff, 1694–6)
John Methuen	1703–6	Amb Ex + Plen
John Milner	1706	In Ch of Aff
Paul Methuen	1706–8	Amb Ex
Earl of Galway	1707–10	Amb Ex + Plen
George Delaval	1710–14	Env Ex
Henry Worsley	1713–19	Env Ex

Henry Worsley	1719–22	Env Ex + Plen
Thomas Lumley (Sir Thomas	1722–4	Env Ex
Saunderson, KB from 1723)	1724–5	Env Ex + Plen
Brig. James Dormer	1725–7	Env Ex
Baron Tyrawly	1728–41	Env Ex
Adm. Sir John Norris	1735–7	Min Plen
Hon Charles Compton	1741–2	In Ch of Aff
	1742–5	Env Ex
Benjamin Keene	1745–50	Env Ex + Plen
Abraham Castres	1749–57	Env Ex
Baron Tyrawly	1752	Min Plen
Hon Edward Hay	1757–62	Env Ex

PRUSSIA

Baron Lexington	1689	Env Ex
James Johnston	1690–2	Env Ex
George Stepney	1692	In Ch of Aff
George Stepney	1698–9	Env Ex
Philip Plantamour	1699–1703	In Ch of Aff
Count von Friesen	1700	Env Ex (appt cancelled)
James Cressett	1700	Env Ex
Baron Raby	1701	rank uncertain
	1703–5	Env Ex
	1705–11	Amb Ex
Charles Whitworth (Baron)	1711	no spec rank
Brig. William Breton	1712–14	Env Ex
Earl of Forfar	1715	Env Ex
Baron Polwarth	1716	Env Ex + Plen
Charles Whitworth (Baron)	1716–17	Env Ex + Plen
	1719–22	Min Plen
James Scott	1722–4	Min
Col (Brig 1727) Charles du Bourgay	1724–30	Env Ex
Captain Melchior Guy Dickens	1730–40	Sec
	1740–1	Min
Thomas Robinson	1741	Spec Miss
Earl of Hyndford	1741–4	Env Ex + Plen
Thomas Villiers	1746	Min Plen
Henry Bilson Legge, MP	1748	Env Ex + Plen
Sir Charles Hanbury Williams, KB	1750–1	Env Ex + Plen
Andrew Mitchell	1756–60	Min

RUSSIA

Charles Goodfellow	1699–1712	Min + Con-Gen
Charles Whitworth (Baron)	1704–9	Env
Charles Whitworth (Baron)	1709–11	Amb Ex
Charles Whitworth (Baron)	1711–12	Amb Ex + Plen
George Mackenzie	1714–15	Min Res
James Haldane	1716–17	Min Res
Adm. Sir John Norris	1717	Env Ex + Plen
Charles Whitworth	1717	No special rank
Capt. James Jefferyes	1718–21	Min Res
Diplomatic relations suspended 1719–30		
Thomas Ward	1728–30	Consul-General
	1730–1	Min Res
Claudius Rondeau	1730–1	Consul-General
	1731–9	Min Res
Lord Forbes	1733–4	Min Plen
Edward Finch, MP	1740–2	Env Ex + Plen
Sir Cyril Wich, Bart	1741–2	Env Ex
	1742–4	Env Ex + Plen
Baron Tyrawly	1743–5	Env Ex + Plen
Earl of Hyndford	1744–5	Min Plen
	1745–9	Amb Ex + Plen
Lt-Col Melchior Guy Dickens	1749–55	Env Ex + Plen
Baron Jakob Wolff	1744–50	Consul-General
	1750–9	Min Res
Sir Charles Hanbury Williams, KB, MP	1755–7	Amb + Plen
Robert Keith	1757–62	Env Ex + Plen

SARDINIA AND SAVOY

Edmund Poley	1691–3	Env Ex
William Aglionby	1693–4	Env Ex
Earl of Galway	1693–6	Env Ex
Richard Hill	1699	Env Ex
Richard Hill	1703–6	Env Ex
John Chetwynd (Vt)	1705–6	No special rank
Paul Methuen	1706	Env Ex
John Chetwynd (Vt)	1706–13	Env Ex
Maj-Gen. Francis Palmes	1708–10	Env Ex
Earl of Peterborough	1710–11	No special rank
Abraham Stanyan	1712–13	Spec Mission
Earl of Peterborough	1712	Min Plen
Earl of Peterborough	1713	Amb + Ex Plen

George St John	1714	Env Ex
John Molesworth (Vt 1725)	1720–5	Env Ex + Plen
John Hedges	1726–7	Env Ex
Earl of Essex	1731–2	Min Plen
	1732–6	Amb
Arthur Villettes	1734–41	Sec
	1741–9	Res
Lt-Gen. Thomas Wentworth	1747	No special rank
Lt-Gen. James St Clair	1748	No special rank
Earl of Rochford	1749–55	Env Ex + Plen
Earl of Bristol	1755–8	Env Ex
James Stewart Mackenzie	1758–60	Env Ex

SPAIN

Alexander Stanhope	1689–99	Env Ex
Francis Schonenberg	1690–1702	Env Ex
William Aglionby	1692 & 1700–1	No special rank
Col Mitford Crowe	1705–6	No special rank
Col Mitford Crowe	1706	Env Ex + Plen
Paul Methuen	1705–6	Env Ex
Brig (Earl) Stanhope	1706	Env Ex
Brig (Earl) Stanhope	1706–7	Env Ex + Plen
Brig (Earl) Stanhope	1708–10	Env Ex + Plen
Earl of Peterborough	1706–7	Amb Ex + Plen
Henry Worsley, MP	1708	Env Ex
James Craggs	1708–11	Res Env Ex
Duke of Argyll	1711	Amb Ex + Plen
Baron Lexington	1712–13	Amb Ex + Plen
Baron Bingley	1714	Amb Ex
Paul Methuen, MP	1715	Amb Ex + Min Plen
George Bubb	1715–17	Env Ex + Plen
Col William Stanhope	1717–18	Env Ex + Plen
Earl Stanhope	1718	No special rank

Diplomatic relations suspended 1718–20

Col William Stanhope	1720–1	Env Ex + Plen
	1721–7 & 1729	Amb Ex + Plen
Benjamin Keene	1727–34	Min Plen
	1734–9	Env Ex + Plen
Abraham Castres	1739	Plen

Diplomatic relations suspended 1739–46

Sir Benjamin Keene (KB 1754)	1746–57	Amb Ex + Plen
Earl of Bristol	1758–61	Amb Ex + Plen

SWEDEN

William Duncombe	1689–92	Env Ex
Rev. John Robinson	1692–6	In Ch of Aff/Agent
Rev. John Robinson	1696–1702	Min Res
Rev. John Robinson	1702–9	Env Ex
George Stepney	1702	Env Ex
Robert Jackson	1710–17	Min Res
Robert Jackson	1719–29	Min Res
Capt. James Jefferyes	1711–15	Res or Min
Lord Carteret	1719–20	Amb Ex + Plen
William Finch, MP	1720–4	Env Ex
Adm. Sir John Norris	1720	Plen
Stephen Poyntz	1724–7	Env Ex + Plen
	1727	Amb Ex
Vice-Adm. Sir Charles Wager	1726	Plen
Isaac Leheup, MP	1727	Env Ex + Plen
Edward Finch, MP	1728–39	Env Ex
Lt-Col Melchior Guy Dickens	1742–8	Min

Diplomatic relations suspended 1748–1763 apart from abortive mission in 1757

SWITZERLAND (including Geneva and the Grison Leagues)

Thomas Coxe	1689–92	Env Ex
Baron de Heunniguen	1689–90	Env Ex
	1692–1702	Env Ex
Marquis d'Arsellières	1695–1710	'generally employed'
William Aglionby	1702–5	Env Ex
Abraham Stanyan	1705–14	Env Ex (& to the Grisons from 1707)
Francis Manning	1708–9	In Ch of Aff
	1709–13	Sec to the Grisons
Francis Manning	1716–22	Res
James Dayrolle	1710 & 1715–17	Res at Geneva
Comte de Marsay	1717–34 &	In Ch of Aff, or
	1734–9	Min Res to Helvetic Republic & to the Grison Leagues
	1739–62	Min at Geneva
John Burnaby	1743–50	Min
Jérôme de Salis	1743–50	Env Ex to Grison Leagues
Arthur Villettes	1749–62	Min

TURKEY

Sir William Trumbull	1687–91	Amb
Sir William Hussey	1690–1	Amb
Thomas Coke	1691–3	In Ch of Aff
William Harbord	1691–2	Amb
William Paget (Baron)	1692–1702	Amb
Sir James Rushout	1697–8	Amb
George Berkeley (Earl)	1698–9	Amb
Sir Robert Sutton	1700–17 & 1718	Amb
Edward Wortley-Montagu	1716–18	Amb
Abraham Stanyan	1717–30	Amb
Earl of Kinoull	1729–36	Amb
Sir Everard Fawkener	1735–46	Amb
James Porter	1746–62	Amb

UNITED PROVINCES OF THE NETHERLANDS

Earl of Pembroke	1689	Amb Ex
Vt Dursley	1689–94	Env Ex
William Harbord	1690	Amb
Matthew Prior	1694–7	Sec
Vt Villiers (Earl of Jersey)	1695–7	Env Ex (+ Plen)
Sir Joseph Williamson	1697–9	Amb Ex
Alexander Stanhope	1700–6	Env Ex
Earl (Duke) of Marlborough	1701	Amb Ex + Plen
	1702–12	Amb Ex + Plen
James Dayrolle	1706–12	Res
George Stepney	1706–7	Env Ex + Plen
Lt-Gen. William Cadogan	1707–11	Env Ex + Plen
Charles Townsend (Vt)	1709–11	Amb Ex + Plen
Horatio Walpole (Baron)	1709–11	Sec of Embassy
Earl of Orrery	1711	Env Ex + Plen
Baron Raby (E of Strafford)	1711–14	Amb Ex + Plen
Lt-Gen. William Cadogan	1714–16	Env Ex + Plen
(Baron 1716, Earl 1718)	1716–21	Amb Ex + Plen
Horatio Walpole	1715 & 1715–16	Min & Plen
William Leathes	1717	Res
Charles Whitworth (Baron Whitworth 1721)	1717	Env Ex
	1717–21	Min Plen
James Dayrolle	1717–39	Res
Horatio Walpole	1722	Min Plen

William Finch	1724–8	Env Ex + Plen
Earl of Chesterfield	1728–32	Amb Ex + Plen
William Finch	1733–4	Min Plen
Horatio Walpole	1734	Min
	1734–7 & 1739	Amb Ex + Plen
Robert Trevor	1736–9	Sec
	1739–41	Env Ex
	1741–7	Env Ex + Plen
Earl of Stair	1742–3	Amb Ex + Plen
Earl of Chesterfield	1745	Amb Ex + Plen
Earl of Sandwich	1746–9	Min Plen
Solomon Dayrolle	1747–52	Res
Earl of Holderness	1749–51	Min Plen
Sir Joseph Yorke, KB	1751–61	Min Plen

9 THE ARMED FORCES

OUTLINES OF BRITISH CAMPAIGNS*

WAR OF THE GRAND ALLIANCE 1688–1697

1688	Sep 25	Louis XIV invaded the Palatinate.
1689	May 12	Treaty between the Emperor and the Netherlands signed at Vienna; the accession of England (on 9 Dec), Spain, Savoy, Brandenburg, Saxony, Hanover and Bavaria established the Grand Alliance.
	Aug 25	Battle of Walcourt – Prince George Frederick of Waldeck, with an English contingent of 8000 men under Marlborough, defeated the French.
1690	Jul 1	Battle of **Fleurus** – French under Duc de Luxembourg defeated the allies.
	Jul 10	Battle of **Beachy Head** – Admiral de Tourville with 78 ships defeated Torrington's Anglo-Dutch fleet of 73.
1691	Apr 8	Mons fell to the French.
	Sep 20	Waldeck defeated at the battle of Leuze.
1692	May 29– Jun 3	Battle of **La Hogue** – Admirals Russell and Rooke led an Anglo-Dutch fleet of 96 ships to victory over de Tourville with 44.
	Aug 3	Battle of Steenkerke – William III attacked Luxembourg's strong defensive position; he was repulsed, but the French were unable to pursue.
1693	Jun 27–28	Battle of **Lagos** – de Tourville attacked a Smyrna convoy, and, after beating off Rooke's escorting squadron, he destroyed 100 ships.
	Jul 29	William sent 20 000 men to relieve Liège, and stood with the rest of his army at **Neerwinden**, where he was attacked and defeated by Luxembourg.
	Oct 11	French captured Charleroi.

*Where the name of a battle is given in bold type further details can be found in the section Principal Battles 1688–1763'.

1695	Jan	Luxembourg dies, and was replaced by the Duc de Villeroi.
	Sep 1	Namur surrendered to William.
1696	Jun 8	Assault on Brest a failure.
1697	Sep 20	Treaty of Ryswick – Louis XIV restored his conquests, and recognised William III as King of England.

REVOLUTION OF 1688 AND THE WARS IN SCOTLAND AND IRELAND 1688–1691

1688	Nov 5	William of Orange landed at Torbay and advanced on London; James II fled to France (see pp. 13–16).
1689	Feb 13	William and Mary proclaimed joint sovereigns of England.
	Mar 22	James II landed in Ireland at Kinsale with 5000 French soldiers. He marched with the Jacobite Earl of Tyrconnel to the north, where the Protestants had declared for William III.
	Apr 29	Londonderry besieged. An English naval force under Capt Leake raised the siege on 9–10 Aug. After local forces under Col Wolseley defeated the Jacobites the siege of Enniskillen was lifted, and William's army overran the whole of Ulster.
	Jul 17	In Scotland a Royalist army was routed at **Killiecrankie** by Jacobites led by Viscount Graham of Claverhouse and Dundee. He was killed in the battle, however, and the rising collapsed.
1690	Jun 14	William landed in Ireland and advanced on Dublin.
	Jul 1	James was defeated at the battle of the **Boyne**, and fled to France.
	Sep–Oct	Marlborough took Cork and Kinsale.
1691	Jul 12	Jacobites defeated at the battle of **Aughrim.**
	Oct 13	Limerick surrendered on the signing of a treaty bringing the Irish war to a close.

WAR OF THE SPANISH SUCCESSION, 1701–1713

(a) **Flanders**

| 1700 | Nov | Death of Charles II of Spain; Louis XIV's grandson becomes Philip V. |

1701	Sep 7	Treaty between England, the Netherlands and the Emperor.
1702	Mar 8	Death of William III.
	May 15	England declared war on France.
	Jun–Jul	Marlborough advanced into the Spanish Netherlands, but the Dutch deputies vetoed plans to bring the French to battle.
	Sep–Oct	Marlborough besieged the Meuse fortresses and captured Venlo, Roermond and Liège.
1703	May	Marlborough invaded the electorate of Cologne and took Bonn, but failed in his plan to seize Antwerp.
1704		Marlborough's intention was to concentrate the allied forces in the Danube Valley to save Vienna, drive the French out of Germany and eliminate Bavaria from the war.
	May	Marlborough began the march to the Danube.
	Jun	Marlborough met Prince Eugène and Louis of Baden at Mondelsheim, continuing with Louis to the Danube.
	Jul 2	Marlborough captured **Donauwörth**, forcing the French to retreat southwards.
	Aug 6	Marlborough and Eugène joined forces, while Louis of Baden was sent to besiege Ingolstadt.
	Aug 13	As the French and Bavarians advanced, Marlborough and Eugène attacked and decisively defeated them at **Blenheim**.
1705		Stalemate in the Low Countries. Marlborough pierced the French lines at Tirlemont on 18 Jul, but Dutch caution prevented him from exploiting this.
1706	May 23	Villeroi, marching towards Liège, was heavily defeated by Marlborough at **Ramillies,** and driven back to Courtrai.
	Jun–Oct	Marlborough captured Antwerp, Dunkirk, Menin, Dendermonde and Ath, firmly establishing his hold on the Spanish Netherlands.
1707		Vendôme, who had replaced Villeroi, held the Flanders front.
1708	Jul 4–5	French army took the offensive, and captured Ghent and Bruges.
	Jul 11	Marlborough defeated Vendôme at **Oudenarde**.
	Jul 12	Vendôme checked the pursuing Allies at Ghent.

Marlborough's plan for the invasion of France was not accepted. Instead Lille was besieged and fell on 22 Oct.

1709	Jan	Ghent and Bruges fell to the Allies.
	Jul 29	Allies captured Tournai, and besieged Mons. Villars was ordered to defend Mons, so advanced and entrenched at Malplaquet threatening the besiegers.
	Sep 11	Marlborough and Eugène defeated the French at **Malplaquet**, but suffered very heavy casualties.
	Oct 26	Mons surrendered.
1710		Marlborough captured Douai on 10 Jun and Béthune on 30 Aug.
1711		Marlborough succeeded in breaking the French 'ne plus ultra' defensive lines in Aug, but was dismissed from his command on 31 Dec.
1712	Jul 24	After the English contingent had been withdrawn, Eugène was defeated by Villars at **Denain**.
1713	Apr 11	Treaty of Utrecht – The French ceded Newfoundland, Nova Scotia, St Kitts and the Hudson Bay territory to England, and undertook to demolish the fortifications at Dunkirk. They also recognised the Protestant Succession, and agreed not to help the Stuarts.

(b) Spain and the Mediterranean

1702	Aug–Sep	Anglo-Dutch force of 50 ships and 15 000 men under Admiral Rooke and the Duke of Ormonde repulsed at Cadiz.
	Oct 12	Rooke destroyed the Spanish treasure fleet in Vigo Bay.
1703	May 16	Portugal joined the alliance.
1704	Feb	Rooke landed the Archduke Charles with 2000 English and Dutch troops at Lisbon.
	Aug 4	Rooke captured Gibraltar.
	Aug 24	French navy under the Count of Toulouse defeated by Rooke in battle of **Malaga**.
1705	Mar 10	Admiral Sir John Leake defeated a French squadron under Admiral de Pointis in battle of Marbella, and the siege of Gibraltar was lifted.

	Jun	Allied troops under Admiral Sir Cloudesley Shovell and Lord Peterborough landed in Catalonia.
	Oct 3	Allies captured Barcelona, but were besieged by the French.
1706	Apr 30	French lifted the siege of Barcelona when Lord Henry Galway led an invasion of Spain from Portugal.
	Jun 26	Galway captured Madrid, but the French retook it in Oct.
	Jun–Sep	English fleet under Leake captured Cartagena, Alicante and the Balearic Islands of Mallorca and Ibiza.
1707	Apr 25	Galway's advance on Madrid was halted by the French under the Duke of Berwick at the battle of **Almanza**.
	Jul–Aug	Prince Eugène besieged Toulon, with the support of the allied fleet under Shovell, but was unsuccessful, although the French had scuttled 50 ships in the harbour in case the city fell.
1708	Aug	Admiral Leake captured Sardinia.
	Sep	General James Stanhope captured Minorca.
1710	May	Stanhope advanced on Madrid, but had to retreat, pursued by Vendôme.
	Dec 10	Stanhope was defeated and captured at **Brihuega**.
1714	Sep 11	French captured Barcelona.
1715	Feb	Spain and Portugal made peace by the treaty of Madrid.

JACOBITE REBELLIONS, 1715 & 1745 (see p. 155 for Scotland in 1688–9)

1. 'The Fifteen'

| 1715 | Sep 6 | Earl of Mar raised Stuart standard at Braemar. A Jacobite army advanced to Preston, but was forced to surrender there on 13 Nov. On the same day Mar fought an inconclusive battle with government troops led by the Duke of Argyll at **Sheriffmuir**. |
| | Dec 22 | James Edward, the Pretender, landed at Peterhead, but returned to France Feb 1716, as Jacobites dispersed before advancing government forces. Attempts by the Duke of Ormonde to land in Devon Oct–Dec 1715 found no support. |

2. 'The Forty-Five'

1745   Jul 23   Charles Edward, the Young Pretender, landed in Scotland.

His army of Highlanders entered Edinburgh Sep 17, and routed an English army under Sir John Cope at **Prestonpans** Sep 21.

Dec 4   Jacobite army reached Derby, but then began to retreat, pursued by the Duke of Cumberland. Jacobites won battles of Penrith, 18 Dec, and Falkirk 17 Jan 1746, but were decisively defeated at **Culloden** 16 Apr.

1746   Sep   Charles Edward escaped to France.

WAR OF THE QUADRUPLE ALLIANCE, 1718–1720

1717   Jan 4   England, France and Holland formed Triple Alliance to oppose Spanish ambitions in France and Italy. Spain occupied Sardinia Nov 1717, and Sicily Jul 1718.

1718   Aug 2   Austria joined the Triple Alliance, and an English fleet landed Austrian troops near Messina, which surrendered Oct 1719.

Aug 11   Admiral Byng destroyed Spanish fleet off **Cape Passaro.**

1719   Failure of Spanish expedition to Scotland. French army invaded Spain, and British amphibious forces captured Vigo and Pontevedra.

Dec 5   Spanish prime minister, Alberoni, dismissed.

1720   Feb 17   Treaty of The Hague concluded the war. The succession to Tuscany, Parma and Piacenza was assured to Charles, eldest son of Philip of Spain and Elizabeth Farnese, while Philip renounced his claims in France and Italy. Sardinia was given to Victor Amadeus of Savoy in place of Sicily, which was made over to Austria.

A further conflict broke out in 1727, when England and France sought to prevent Charles from taking over the Italian Duchies. After brief hostilities, negotiations were opened, and peace was made at the Treaty of Seville 9 Nov 1729, in which Charles' claims were recognised.

WAR OF THE AUSTRIAN SUCCESSION, 1739–1748

1739	Oct 19	England declared war on Spain after prolonged commercial disputes (War of Jenkins' Ear).
		Admiral Vernon captured Porto Bello Nov 1739. But attacks on Cartagena, Cuba and Panama failed, and Vernon and General Wentworth were recalled in 1742.
		1740–4 Anson carried out his circumnavigation, raiding Spanish South American possessions.
1740	Oct	The death of Emperor Charles VI, the succession of Maria Theresa, and Frederick the Great's invasion of Silesia in December brought on the general European conflict, the War of the Austrian Succession.
1741	Sep	George II concluded a treaty with France neutralising Hanover.
1742		After Walpole's resignation in Feb, Carteret persuaded George II to end Hanover's neutrality, and sent an army of English, Hanoverians and Hessians (Pragmatic Army) under Lord Stair to the Low Countries.
1743		Joined by Dutch and Austrian troops, led by George II, the Pragmatic Army advanced and defeated the French at **Dettingen** 27 Jun. Attempts to invade France were unsuccessful.
1744	Mar	France formally declared war on England, and a French army led by Marshal de Saxe invaded the Low Countries.
		A Franco-Spanish plan for an invasion of England came to nothing. A drawn naval engagement took place off Toulon in Feb.
1745		Saxe besieged Tournai, and defeated a relieving army at **Fontenoy** 11 May. Tournai fell 22 May.
	Jun 16	In North America an expedition captured Louisburg from the French.
1746		Saxe completed the conquest of the Austrian Netherlands, taking Brussels in Feb, Antwerp in Jun, and defeating the allies at **Roucoux** 11 Oct.
1747		Saxe invaded Holland, and defeated Cumberland at **Lauffeld** 2 Jul.

Admirals Anson and Hawke won decisive naval victories off **Cape Finisterre** in May and Oct.

1748   Oct 18   Treaty of Aix-la-Chapelle concluded the war. The main points were that Prussia retained Silesia and Glatz. Parma, Piacenza and Guastalla were ceded to Don Philip of Spain. France evacuated the Austrian Netherlands, restored the barrier fortresses to the Dutch and recognised the Hanoverian succession in England. Louisburg was exchanged for Madras, captured by the French in 1746.

SEVEN YEARS' WAR, 1756–1763

(a) **Europe**

1756   Aug 29   Frederick the Great's invasion of Saxony began the conflict in Europe (Britain and France had been at war since May 1756).

1757   Jul   A French army invaded Hanover. Cumberland was defeated at **Hastenbeck,** and signed the Convention of Kloster-Seven 8 Sep, disbanding his army.

        Nov 5   Frederick the Great's victory at Rossbach. The Convention was repudiated, and Ferdinand of Brunswick was given command of the allied army.

1758   Apr   British subsidies to Frederick by the Treaty of London. Ferdinand launched an offensive against the French, pushing them across the Rhine 27 Mar, and defeating them at Krefeld 23 Jun. The French replied by invading Hesse.

1759   Apr 13   Ferdinand defeated by Broglie at **Bergen.**

        Aug 1   Ferdinand defeated the French at **Minden**; they retreated from Hesse.

1760   Broglie was victorious at Korbach 10 Jul, but this was offset by Ferdinand's victory at **Warburg** 31 Jul. Hanover was saved, but a diversion on the lower Rhine was defeated by the French at **Kloster Kamp** 16 Oct.

1761   Ferdinand's advance from Westphalia was defeated by Broglie near Grünberg 21 Mar. A French counter-thrust was defeated at **Vellinghausen** 15 Jul.

	Oct 5	Pitt resigned, and Bute refused to renew the subsidy treaty with Frederick.
1762	Jan 5	Death of Empress Elizabeth of Russia.
	May 5	Treaty of St Petersburg – peace between Prussia and Russia.
	May 22	Peace between Prussia and Sweden.
1763	Feb 15	Treaty of Hubertusburg signed by Prussia, Austria and Saxony, restoring the *status quo ante bellum*.

(b) North America

1754	Jul 3	A Virginian force led by George Washington was forced to surrender to the French at Fort Necessity.
1755	Jul 9	Braddock's expedition to attack Fort Duquesne was destroyed at the **Monongahela River**.
1756	Aug	Montcalm captured Forts Oswego and George, and built Fort Ticonderoga.
1757	Jun–Sep	British expedition to attack Louisburg led by Lord Loudoun failed.
1758		A fourfold attack on the French planned.
	Jul	Fort Duquesne and Louisburg captured by Amherst; but Abercromby's attack on Fort Ticonderoga failed.
	Sep	Forts Frontenac, Oswego and Duquesne taken from the French.
1759	Jul	Fort Niagara fell to British expedition.
	Aug	Ticonderoga and Champlain captured.
	Jun–Sep	Attack on Quebec by Wolfe and Saunders. The French led by Montcalm were defeated in battle before **Quebec** 13 Sep, after Wolfe had scaled the Heights of Abraham. Quebec surrendered 18 Sep.
1760	Sep 8	Marquis de Vaudreuil surrendered Montreal, and with it French Canada.

(c) Naval and Minor Operations

| 1755 | Jun 8 | Boscawen captured two French ships carrying reinforce- |

ments to Canada, although the rest escaped. There was a general attack on French shipping.

1756	Jun 28	Minorca fell to the French. Admiral Byng, who had failed to relieve it after an inconclusive naval battle 20 May, was executed.
1757	Sep	Failure of a raid on Rochefort.
1758	Feb	Commodore Holmes captured Emden.
		Attacks on the French coast: Cherbourg taken in Jun, but expedition against St Malo repulsed in Sep.
		All French factories on the West African coast captured.
1759	May	Guadeloupe taken from the French.
	Aug 18	Boscawen defeated the French Mediterranean fleet off Lagos.
	Nov 20	Hawke destroyed Brest squadron in battle of **Quiberon Bay.**
1760	Feb	French expedition to Ireland surrendered at Kinsale.
1761	Jun	Dominica and Belle Île captured from French.
1762	Jan 4	England declared war on Spain, and seized Havana in Aug, and Manila in Oct. A British army led by Lord Tyrawley helped the Portuguese to resist a Spanish invasion.
		Rodney forced the surrender of Martinique, Grenada, St Vincent and St Lucia.
		St John's, Newfoundland was lost to the French.

(d) Treaty of Paris, 10 Feb 1763

Signed by Britain, France, Spain and Portugal. Principal points:

France ceded to Britain Canada, Nova Scotia, Cape Breton and all lands east of the Mississippi, except New Orleans; she retained fishing rights on the Newfoundland banks.

England restored to France the islands of Guadeloupe, Martinique, St Lucia and Maria Galante. France evacuated territories of Hanover, Hesse, Brunswick and Prussia. Minorca exchanged for Belle Île.

Britain restored Havana to Spain, in exchange for Florida. Spain had been compensated for this in the secret Treaty of San Ildefonso 3 Nov 1762 by receiving from France New Orleans and all Louisiana west of the Mississippi. Spain recovered Manila, and evacuated Portugal and Portuguese colonies.

In Africa, Britain kept Senegal and restored Goree to France.

INDIA

1746	Sep	Madras fell to the French, led by Dupleix and Admiral de la Bourdonnais, who had driven off Commodore Peyton in a naval engagement at Negapatam in Jul.
	Nov	French began unsuccessful siege of Fort St George; ended on arrival of Admiral Boscawen in Apr 1748.
1748	Aug–Oct	Dupleix successfully defended Pondicherry against Boscawen.
	Oct	At the Treaty of Aix-la-Chapelle Madras was restored to Britain, in exchange for Louisburg.
1751		Chanda Sahib, Nawab of the Carnatic, besieged British garrison at Trichinopoly. As a diversion Robert Clive captured Chanda Sahib's capital, Arcot, and withstood a 50-day siege Sep–Nov.
		Clive then defeated the French and their allies at Arni in Nov 1751 and **Covrepauk** in Feb 1752.
1754	Aug	Dupleix relieved of his post. His successor, Godeheu, made peace with the British in the Carnatic.
1756	Jun 20	Surajah Dowlah, Nawab of Bengal, captured Calcutta, and imprisoned 146 Europeans in the 'Black Hole', where 123 died.
1757	Jan 2	Robert Clive and Admiral Watson recaptured Calcutta.
	Jun 23	Clive routed Surajah Dowlah at **Plassey**.
1758		French force under Comte de Lally-Tollendal reached Pondicherry, and captured Fort St David in Jun.
Dec 1758–Feb 1759		Lally unsuccessfully besieged Madras.
1760	Jan 22	Eyre Coote defeated Lally at **Wandiwash**.
1761	Jan 15	Lally's surrender at Pondicherry marked the end of the French bid for power in India.

PRINCIPAL BATTLES, 1688–1763

I Land

Battle	Date	Campaign	Combatants	Strength of armies	Commanders	Casualties
ALMANZA	25 Apr 1707	War of the Spanish Succession	French and Spanish	25 000	Marshal Berwick	4000
			British, Portuguese, Dutch and Germans	15 000	Lord Galway and Marqués das Minas	
AUGHRIM	12 Jul 1691	War of the English Succession	British and allies	25 000	General de Ginkel	700
			French and Irish		General St Ruth	7000
BAHUR	26 Aug 1752	British Conquest of India	British	2500	Major Lawrence	80 out of 400 British
			French	2500	M. Kirjean	
BERGEN	13 Apr 1759	Seven Years' War – Germany	French	30 000	Duc de Broglie	1800
			Allies	24 000	Ferdinand of Brunswick	2500
BLENHEIM	13 Aug 1704	War of Spanish Succession	Allies	56 000	Marlborough and Eugène	12 000
			French and Bavarians	60 000	Marshals Tallard and Marsin, and Elector of Bavaria	29 000 (+ 11 000 prisoners)
BOYNE	11 Jul 1690	War of English Succession	English	36 000	William III	500
			Irish	25 000	James II	1500
BRIHUEGA	10 Dec 1710	War of Spanish Succession	French	20 000	Duc de Vendôme	1800
			British	2500	Earl of Stanhope	500 (+ 2000 prisoners)

Battle	Date	Campaign	Combatants	Strength of armies	Commanders	Casualties
COVREPAUK	14 Feb 1752	British Conquest of India	British	1700	Robert Clive	70
			French	2400	Joseph Dupleix	350
CULLODEN	16 Apr 1746	Jacobite Rebellion	Royalists	9000	Duke of Cumberland	250
			Jacobites	5000	Prince Charles Edward	1000
DENAIN	24 Jul 1712	War of Spanish Succession	French	24000	Marshal Villars	500
			Allies	10500	Earl of Albermarle and Prince Eugène	8000
DETTINGEN	27 Jun 1743	War of Austrian Succession	Allies	40000	George II	2500
			French	60000	Marshal the Duc de Noailles	6000
DONAUWÖRTH	2 Jul 1704	War of Spanish Succession	British and Imperialists	50000	Marlborough	5374
			French and Bavarians	12000	Count D'Arco	—
FLEURUS	1 Jul 1690	War of the Grand Alliance	French	45000	Marshal Luxembourg	2500
			British, Spanish, German	37000	Prince of Waldeck	6000 (+ 8000 prisoners)
FONTENOY	11 May 1745	War of Austrian Succession	French	52000	Marshal de Saxe	7000
			Allies	46000	Duke of Cumberland	7000
HASTENBECK	26 Jul 1757	Seven Years' War – Germany	French	60000	Marshal d'Estrées	2350
			Allies	36000	Duke of Cumberland	1300

Battle	Date	War	Side	Strength	Commander	Casualties
KILLIECRANKIE	17 Jul 1689	Jacobite Rebellion	Jacobites	2500	Dundee	900
			Royalists	3400	General Mackay	2500
KLOSTER KAMP	23 Jun 1758	Seven Years' War – Germany	Allies	7500	Erbprinz of Hesse-Cassel	1600
			French	7000	Marquis de Castries	3000
LAUFFELD	2 Jul 1747	War of Austrian Succession	French	120000	Marshal de Saxe	14000
			Allies	90000	Duke of Cumberland	5600
MALPLAQUET	11 Sep 1709	War of Spanish Succession	Allies	90000	Marlborough and Eugène	20000
			French	90000	Marshal Villars	12000 (+500 prisoners)
MINDEN	1 Aug 1759	Seven Years' War – Germany	Allies	42500	Ferdinand of Brunswick	2700
			French	54000	Marquis de Contades	4900
MONONGAHELA RIVER	9 Jul 1755	Anglo-French struggle for North America	French, Indians	900	Captains Beaujeu and Dumas	65
			British, Virginians	1400	General Braddock	900
NEERWINDEN	29 Jul 1693	War of the Grand Alliance	French	80000	Marshal Luxembourg	9000
			English	50000	William III	19000
OUDENARDE	11 Jul 1708	War of Spanish Succession	Allies	80000	Marlborough and Eugène	7000
			French	85000	Duke of Burgundy and Vendôme	6000 (+9000 prisoners)
PLASSEY	23 Jun 1757	Seven Years' War – India	British	3000	Robert Clive	65
			Bengal	60000	Surajah Dowlah	500

Battle	Date	Campaign	Combatants	Strength of armies	Commanders	Casualties
PRESTONPANS	21 Sep 1745	Jacobite Rebellion	Jacobites Royalists	2500 2300	Prince Charles Edward Sir John Cope	140 400
QUEBEC	13 Sep 1759	Seven Years' War – Canada	British French	5000 4500	General Wolfe Marquis de Montcalm	660 1400
RAMILLIES	23 May 1706	War of Spanish Succession	Allies French	60000 60000	Marlborough Marshal Villeroi	5000 8000 (+ 7000 prisoners)
ROUCOUX	11 Oct 1746	War of Austrian Succession	French Allies	120000 80000	Marshal de Saxe Prince Charles of Lorraine	5000 5000
SHERIFFMUIR	13 Nov 1715	Jacobite Rebellion	Royalists Jacobites	4000 9000	Duke of Argyll Earl of Mar	600 500
VELLINGHAUSEN	15–16 Jul 1761	Seven Years' War – Germany	Allies French	65000 92000	Ferdinand of Brunswick Prince de Soubise and the Duc de Broglie	1400 5000
WANDIWASH	22 Jan 1760	Seven Years' War – India	British French	4400 3600	Colonel Coote Comte de Lally-Tollendal	190 out of 1900 Europeans 600 out of 2300 Europeans
WARBURG	31 Jul 1760	Seven Years' War – Germany	Allies French	35000	Ferdinand of Brunswick Chevalier du Muy	1200 2000

II Sea

Battle	Date	Campaign	Combatants	Number of ships engaged	Commanders	Ships lost
BEACHY HEAD	30 Jun – 10 Jul 1690	War of the Grand Alliance	French	78	Admiral de la Jonquière	
			British and Dutch	73	Lord Torrington	7
CAPE FINISTERRE	3 May 1747	War of Austrian Succession	British	16	Admiral Anson	
			French	9	Admiral de la Jonquiere	10
CAPE FINISTERRE	14 Oct 1747	War of Austrian Succession	British	14	Admiral Hawke	
			French	9	Admiral de l'Etanduere	4
CAPE PASSARO	11 Aug 1718	War of the Quadruple Alliance	British	21	Admiral Byng	
			Spanish	22	Don Antonio Castañeta	15
LAGOS	27– 28 Jun 1693	War of the Grand Alliance	French	71	Admiral de Tourville	
			Dutch and British	23 (+ 400 convoy ships)	Sir George Rooke	3 (+ 100 merchant ships)
LA HOGUE	29 May– 3 Jun 1692	War of the Grand Alliance	Dutch and British	96	Admirals Russell and Almonde	
			French	44	Admiral de Tourville	15
MALAGA	24 Aug 1704	War of Spanish Succession	British and Dutch	45	Sir George Rooke	0
			French	53	Admiral Comte de Toulouse	0
QUIBERON BAY	20 Nov 1759	Seven Years' War	British	23	Admiral Hawke	2
			French	21	Marshal de Conflans	5

STRENGTH AND COST OF THE BRITISH ARMY, 1689–1763

	Total supplies granted for the Army (£)	Subsidies and pay of foreign troops (£)	Numbers of men voted	Numbers of officers and men in army according to Mutiny Act
1689	2 244 610			
1690	2 413 384			
1691	2 380 698		69 636	
1692	1 825 015		64 924	
1693	1 879 791	162 738	54 562	
1694	2 319 808		83 121	
1695	2 357 076	159 429	87 702	
1696	2 297 109		87 440	
1697	2 297 109		87 440	
1698	1 803 014		35 875	
1699	1 350 000		12 725	
1700	365 000		12 725	
1701	562 033		22 725	
1702	1 261 517	194 517	52 396	
1703	1 590 778	237 464	63 396	
1704	2 115 381	504 190	70 475	
1705	2 456 669	611 166	71 411	
1706	2 694 584	712 797	77 345	
1707	3 054 156	863 547	94 130	
1708	3 030 894	683 462	91 188	
1709	4 016 025	860 669	102 642	
1710	4 002 908	874 619	113 268	
1711	2 864 812	785 730	138 882	
1712	3 397 078	798 958	144 650	
1713	1 146 553	9301	24 400	
1714	1 153 060		16 347	
1715	1 274 907		18 851	
1716	1 520 083		Not stated	
1717	1 523 911	250 000	Not stated	
1718	919 731		16 347	
1719	809 637		17 866	
1720	926 644		19 500	14 294 (home) 5546 (abroad)
1721	904 174	72 000	19 840	12 434
1722	844 472		19 840	16 449
1723	941 990		23 840	16 449
1724	923 300		23 810	16 449
1725	912 968		23 810	16 087
1726	976 034	75 000	23 772	24 013
1727	1 391 730	270 000	32 058	22 950
1728	1 370 184	305 924	28 501	22 955
1729	1 352 099	316 259	28 882	17 709
1730	1 195 712	266 259	23 836	17 709
1731	1 196 060	247 509	23 756	17 709
1732	934 381	22 694	23 756	17 709
1733	907 593		23 756	17 704
1734	980 887		25 634	25 744
1735	1 149 228	56 250	34 354	17 704
1736	1 004 020	56 250	26 314	17 704
1737	1 039 199	42 187	26 314	17 704
1738	961 743		26 896	17 704

	Total supplies granted for the Army (£)	Subsidies and pay of foreign troops (£)	Numbers of men voted	Numbers of officers and men in army according to Mutiny Act
1739	1 021 494	70 583	26 896	35 963
1740	1 268 429	58 333	40 859	46 288
1741	1 703 195	295 752	53 395	46 284
1742	1 809 145	293 263	51 044	51 519
1743	2 546 487	265 195	51 696	51 936
1744	3 071 907	585 200	53 358	55 425
1745	3 028 535	933 219	53 128	74 187
1746	3 354 635	1 266 402	77 664	59 776
1747	3 191 432	1 364 707	61 471	61 489
1748	3 997 326	1 743 316	64 966	18 857
1749	1 730 477	213 991	28 399	18 857
1750	1 238 707	60 985	29 194	18 857
1751	1 077 345	30 000	29 132	18 857
1752	1 041 554	52 000	29 132	18 857
1753	1 069 235	52 000	29 132	18 857
1754	1 068 185	52 000	29 132	18 857
1755	1 139 548	52 000	31 422	34 263
1756	2 174 540	468 946	47 488	49 749
1757	2 516 119	355 639	68 791	53 777
1758	4 173 890	1 475 897	88 370	52 543
1759	4 882 444	1 968 178	91 446	57 294
1760	6 926 490	1 844 487	99 044	64 971
1761	8 615 293	2 091 659	105 221	67 776
1762	7 810 539	1 023 583	120 633	17 536
1763	4 877 139	321 907	120 419	17 532

Source   Parliamentary Papers, 1868–69, vol. XXXV, pp. 693–703; C. M. Clode, *The Military Forces of the Crown*, vol I, pp. 398–9.

ANNUAL PARLIAMENTARY VOTES FOR THE NAVY, 1689–1763

	Number of seamen and marines voted	Numbers borne (inc marines on shore)	Total grant £
1689	21 695	22 322	1 198 648
1690	27 814	31 971	1 612 976
1691	29 970	35 317	1 791 694
1692	30 000	40 274	1 575 890
1693	33 010	43 827	1 926 516
1694	40 000	47 710	2 500 000
1695	40 000	48 514	2 382 712
1696	40 000	47 677	2 516 972
1697	40 000	44 743	2 372 197
1698	10 000	22 519	1 539 122
1699	15 000	15 834	1 296 383
1700	7 000	7 754	956 342

	Number of seamen and marines voted	Numbers borne (inc marines on shore)	Total grant £
1701	30 000	22 869	1 380 000
1702	45 000	33 363	2 209 314
1703	45 000	40 805	2 209 314
1704	45 000	40 433	2 080 000
1705	48 000	43 081	2 230 000
1706	48 000	46 125	2 234 711
1707	48 000	45 055	2 210 000
1708	48 000	44 529	2 210 000
1709	48 000	47 647	2 200 000
1710	48 000	46 493	2 200 000
1711	48 000	46 735	2 200 000
1712	48 000	38 106	2 260 000
1713	20 000	21 636	1 200 000
1714	10 000	13 098	1 068 700
1715	8000*	13 475	1 146 748
1716	10 000*	13 827	984 473
1717	10 000*	13 086	947 560
1718	10 000*	15 268	910 174
1719	13 500*	19 611	1 003 133
1720	13 500*	21 188	1 397 734
1721	10 000*	16 746	789 250
1722	7000*	10 122	1 607 894
1723	10 000*	8078	736 389
1724	10 000*	7037	734 623
1725	10 000*	6298	547 096
1726	10 000*	16 872	732 181
1727	20 000*	20 697	1 239 071
1728	15 000*	14 917	1 495 561
1729	15 000*	14 859	996 026
1730	10 000*	9686	863 787
1731	10 000*	11 133	742 034
1732	8000*	8360	698 885
1733	8000*	9682	748 283
1734	20 000	23 247	2 452 670
1735	30 000	28 819	1 768 914
1736	15 000*	17 010	1 037 436
1737	10 000*	9858	799 201
1738	20 000*	17 668	1 292 886
1739	16 890	23 604	856 689
1740	41 930	37 181	2 157 688
1741	46 550	47 121	2 718 786

	Number of seamen and marines voted	Numbers borne (inc marines on shore)	Total grant £
1742	51 550	44 283	2 765 574
1743	51 550	49 865	2 653 764
1744	51 550	53 754	2 521 085
1745	51 550	53 498	2 567 084
1746	51 550	58 021	2 661 535
1747	51 550	58 508	3 780 911
1748	51 550	50 596	3 640 352
1749	17 000*	18 602	5 179 878
1750	10 000*	12 040	1 021 521
1751	8000*	9972	1 056 559
1752	10 000*	9771	1 794 561
1753	10 000*	8346	810 207
1754	10 000*	10 149	910 889
1755	22 000*	33 612	1 714 289
1756	50 000*	52 809	3 349 021
1757	66 419	63 259	3 503 939
1758	74 845	70 694	3 874 421
1759	84 845	84 464	5 236 263
1760	88 355	86 626	5 609 708
1761	88 355	80 954	5 594 790
1762	89 061	84 797	5 954 252
1763	34 287	38 350	5 128 977

*No marines voted in these years.
Source   Parliamentary Papers 1868–69, vol XXXV, pp. 693–5.

COMMANDERS 1688–1763

AMHERST, JEFFREY AMHERST, BARON 1717–97

Ensign in the Guards 1731. ADC to Ligonier and Cumberland in Austrian Succession. Maj-Gen 1758, and given command of expedition against French in Canada. Chief command in America Sep 1758 after capture of Louisburg, and led attack on Ticonderoga 1759. Governor-General of British North America 1760–3. Privy Councillor and Lt-Gen of the Ordnance 1772. C-in-C of the army 1772–95 (except 1782–3). Baron 1776. General 1778. Field Marshal 1796.

ANSON, GEORGE ANSON, BARON 1697–1762

Entered navy 1712. Captain 1724. Given command of Pacific squadron, and carried out circumnavigation 1740–4. Rear-Admiral 1744. Promoted to

Board of Admiralty 1745. Vice-Admiral, and command of Channel Fleet 1746. Defeated French off Cape Finisterre May 1747, and created Baron. First Lord of the Admiralty 1751-6 and 1757-62, carrying out important administrative reforms. Admiral of the Fleet 1761.

BOSCAWEN, EDWARD 1711-61

Entered navy 1726. Took part in attacks on Porto Bello 1739 and Cartagena 1741. MP for Truro 1741. Fought in battle off Cape Finisterre May 1747. Made C-in-C of forces in East Indies 1747. Vice-Admiral 1755. Second-in-command of fleet under Hawke 1757. Admiral 1758, and cooperated with Amherst and Wolfe in capture of Louisburg. Privy Councillor, and command of Mediterranean fleet 1759. In the battle of 18 Aug off Lagos he disrupted French plans for invading Britain. General of Marines 1760.

BRADDOCK, EDWARD 1695-1755

Ensign in Coldstream Guards 1710. Served in Holland at siege of Bergen-op-Zoom 1747. Maj-Gen 1754, and appointed to command in North America. He mounted an expedition to attack Fort Duquesne, but his force was destroyed in an ambush after crossing the Monongahela 9 Jul 1755. He himself was wounded, and died 13 Jul.

BURGOYNE, JOHN 1723-92

Cornet in 13th Light Dragoons 1740. Took part in raids on Cherbourg 1758, and St Malo 1759. Raised a light cavalry regiment and commanded it in Portugal 1762. MP for Midhurst 1761, and for Preston 1768. Maj-Gen 1772. Sent to Boston 1774, then to Canada as second-in-command to Carleton. Led an expedition from Canada 1777, but was forced to surrender his whole force at Saratoga 17 Oct. C-in-C in Ireland 1782-3.

CLIVE, ROBERT CLIVE, BARON 1725-74

Sent to Madras in service of East India Company 1743. Fought a duel and twice attempted suicide. Taken prisoner when Madras fell in 1746, but escaped to Fort St David. In Sep 1751 he seized Arcot to distract Chanda Sahib from the siege of Trichinopoly, and followed this with victories at Arni and Covrepauk. In England 1753-5. Returning to Madras, he led the expedition which retook Calcutta Jan 1757, and defeated Surajah Dowlah at Plassey in June. Governor of Bengal 1757-60. Returned to England 1760. Baron in Irish peerage 1762. Knighted 1764. MP for Shrewsbury 1761-74. During his second period as Governor and C-in-C of Bengal 1765-7 he carried out important administrative reforms. Acquitted of corruption in India before Parliamentary Committees 1772-3. Committed suicide 22 Nov 1774.

COOTE, SIR EYRE 1726–83

Entered army at an early age, and served in Germany in Austrian Succession and against Jacobites 1745. In India 1754–62. Played important part in victory at Plassey 1757. Defeated French at Wandiwash 1760. In the following year he captured Pondicherry, and was given command of East India Company forces in Bengal. MP for Leicester 1768. Made C-in-C in Madras Presidency 1769, but quarrelled with the Governor and returned to England 1770. Knighted 1771. Maj-Gen 1775. Lt-Gen 1777. Returned to India as C-in-C 1779, and defeated Hyder Ali. Died at Madras 28 Apr 1783.

CUMBERLAND, WILLIAM AUGUSTUS, DUKE OF   1721–65

Second surviving son of George II. Colonel of Coldstream Guards 1740. Maj-Gen 1742. Lt-Gen 1743. Wounded at Dettingen 1743. C-in-C of the allied army 1745; defeated at Fontenoy. Recalled to put down the Jacobite Rebellion; defeated the rebels at Culloden 1746 and earned the nickname 'Butcher'. Returned to Flanders 1747, and defeated by Saxe at Lauffeld. On outbreak of Seven Years' War he was defeated at Hastenbeck Jul 1757, and signed the Convention of Kloster-Seven for the evacuation of Hanover. As a result he resigned in disgrace Oct 1757.

GAGE, THOMAS 1721–87

Lieutenant in 48th Foot 1741. Fought in Flanders in Austrian Succession, and at Culloden. Sent to America 1754, and wounded in Braddock's expedition 1755. Organised a Light Infantry Regiment (80th) 1758, and commanded light infantry in attack on Ticonderoga. Governor of Montreal 1760. Maj-Gen 1761. Lt-Gen 1770. C-in-C in North America 1763–72. Governor of Massachusetts Bay 1774. Sent force to seize arms at Concord, and fought battle of Bunker Hill 1775. Appointed C-in-C in North America Aug 1775, but resigned Oct. General 1782.

GRANBY, JOHN MANNERS, MARQUIS OF   1721–70

Eldest son of Duke of Rutland. MP for Grantham 1741–54 and Cambridgeshire 1754–70. Colonel of a Regiment raised in 1745 to suppress Jacobites; served as a volunteer on Cumberland's staff. Served in Flanders 1747. Maj-Gen 1755. Colonel of Royal Horse Guards 1758. Lt-Gen 1759. Succeeded Sackville in command of British forces 1759, and defeated French at Warburg 1760. Master-General of the Ordnance 1763. C-in-C of the Army 1766–70.

HAWKE, EDWARD HAWKE, BARON 1705–81

Entered navy 1720. Captain 1734. Took part in action at Toulon 1744. Rear-Admiral and second-in-command of Channel Fleet 1747, commanding it from Sep due to Sir Peter Warren's ill-health. He defeated French off Cape Finisterre Oct 1747, and was knighted. MP for Portsmouth 1747–76. Vice-Admiral 1748. Succeeded to Warren's command 1748–52. Command of western squadron 1755. Sent to relieve Byng in the Mediterranean 1756. Admiral 1757, and led naval force in unsuccessful expedition to Rochefort. Command of western squadron 1759; defeated French at Quiberon Bay 20 Nov. First Lord of the Admiralty 1766–71. Admiral and C-in-C of the Fleet 1768. Baron 1776.

HOWE, RICHARD HOWE, EARL 1726–99

Entered navy 1739. Post Captain 1746. MP for Dartmouth 1757–82. Succeeded as viscount in Irish peerage 1758. Commanded ships in raids on French coast 1758, and played important part in battle of Quiberon Bay 1759. A Lord of the Admiralty 1763–5. Treasurer of Navy 1765–70. Rear-Admiral 1770. Vice-Admiral 1775. Command of North America Station 1776–8. Admiral, viscount and command of Channel Fleet Apr 1782; relieved Gibraltar in autumn. First Lord of the Admiralty Jan–Apr 1783, and Dec 1783–Aug 1788. Baron and Earl 1788. Command of Channel Fleet May–Dec 1790, and 1793–7; defeated French off Ushant 1794. Admiral of the Fleet and General of Marines 1796. Helped pacify mutineers at Spithead 1797.

HOWE, WILLIAM HOWE, VISCOUNT 1729–1814

Cornet in Cumberland's Light Dragoons 1746. MP for Nottingham 1758–80. Commanded 58th Foot Regiment at siege of Louisburg 1758, and leading a newly formed light infantry battalion, took part in capture of Quebec 1759 and Montreal 1760. Maj-Gen 1772. Lt-Gen 1775. Sent to Boston as second-in-command and led left wing in battle of Bunker Hill. Succeeded Gage in supreme command Oct 1775. Resigned 1778. Lt-Gen of the Ordnance 1782–1803. General 1793. Held home commands 1793 and 1795. Succeeded to viscountcy on death of his brother Admiral Lord Howe 1799. Governor of Plymouth 1805.

LIGONIER, JOHN LIGONIER, EARL 1680–1770

Born at Castres in France of Huguenot parents who took refuge in Ireland 1697. Served under Marlborough 1702–11. Lt-Governor of Fort St Philip, Minorca 1712. Colonel of 7th Dragoon Guards 1720. Maj-Gen 1739. Lt-Gen 1743. Staff officer to George II; commanded second division at Dettingen and the Foot at Fontenoy. C-in-C in Netherlands 1746–7. MP for Bath 1748. Lt-Gen of the Ordnance 1748–56. Viscount in Irish peerage 1757. C-in-C of the army 1757–9, and military adviser to Pitt. Master-General of the Ordnance 1759–62. Baron 1763. Field Marshal and Earl 1766.

MARLBOROUGH, JOHN CHURCHILL, 1ST DUKE OF 1650–1722

Born at Ashe in Devon. Commission in Foot Guards 1667. Served in Tangier garrison 1668–70. Captain 1672. Fought at battle of Sole Bay 28 May 1672, then joined English contingent fighting with the French against the Dutch. Baron Churchill in Scottish peerage 1682 (English peerage 1685). Colonel of the 1st Royal Dragoons 1683. Second-in-command under Lord Feversham of army which defeated Monmouth at Sedgemoor 1685. His defection to William of Orange ensured James II's downfall in 1688. Created Earl of Marlborough and given command of expeditions in Flanders and Ireland. Losing royal favour, he was sent to the Tower suspected of treason in 1692. He was released but did not return to Court until 1695. On accession of Queen Anne, an intimate friend of the Marlboroughs, in 1702, Marlborough was made Captain-General of the Forces and Master-General of the Ordnance. He went to Holland on 15 May 1702 and in the next seven years defeated the French in four great battles: Blenheim 1704, Ramillies 1706, Oudenarde 1708 and Malplaquet 1709. In 1711 he was recalled by the Tory government and relieved of his commands.

RODNEY, GEORGE BRYDGES RODNEY, BARON 1718–92

Entered navy 1732. Post Captain 1742. Took part in Hawke's victory off Cape Finisterre Oct 1747. Governor and C-in-C of Newfoundland 1749–52. MP for Saltash 1751, and for Northampton 1768. Served in expedition against Rochefort 1757, and at capture of Louisburg 1758. Rear-Admiral 1759. Raided transport ships on French coast 1759–60. C-in-C of Leeward Islands station 1761–3. Vice-Admiral 1762. Baronet 1764. Governor of Greenwich Hospital 1765–70. Jamaica command 1771–4. Admiral 1778. C-in-C of Leeward Islands 1779–82. Ordered to relieve Gibraltar on his way to the West Indies, he defeated the Spanish and captured a convoy Jan 1780. Defeated French at the battle of the Saints 1782, and created a baron.

SACKVILLE, GEORGE SACKVILLE, VISCOUNT 1716–85

Known from 1720–70 as Lord George Sackville, and from 1770–82 as Lord George Germain.

Third son of Duke of Dorset. Captain in 6th Dragoon Guards 1737. Distinguished service in Austrian Succession; wounded at Fontenoy. MP for Dover 1741–61, Kent 1761–8, and East Grinstead 1768–82. Involved in Irish affairs 1750–6. Maj-Gen 1755. Lt-Gen of the Ordnance 1757–9. Took part in attack on Saint Malo 1758. Given command of British contingent in Germany Oct 1758. Court-martialled for refusing to charge at Minden 1759. Colonial Secretary 1775–82. Viscount 1782.

WOLFE, JAMES 1727–59

Second lieutenant in Marines 1741. Transferred as Ensign to 12th Foot 1742. Fought at Dettingen 1743, against Jacobites at Falkirk and Culloden 1745–6, and was wounded at Lauffeld 1747. Garrison duty in Scotland and England 1749–57. Quartermaster-general in attack on Rochefort 1757. Served under Amherst in expedition against Cape Breton 1758, and was largely responsible for capture of Louisburg. Given command as a Major-General of expedition against Quebec; killed in battle of Heights of Abraham 13 Sep 1759 which led to the capture of the city.

10 THE COLONIES

MAIN TERRITORIES UNDER BRITISH RULE BY 1763

Territory	Original entry into British rule and status in 1763
Antigua	Colony (1663)
Bahamas	First settled 1646: colony (1783)
Barbados	First settled 1627: colony (1662)
Bengal	Ceded by France (1763)
Bermuda	First settled 1609; colony (1684)
Bombay	Ceded by France (1763)
British Honduras	First settled 1638
Canada	Ceded colonies from 1713 onwards.
Cayman, Turks and Caicos Islands	Ceded (1670)
Connecticut	Permanently settled 1635
Delaware	Permanently settled 1683
Dominica	Colony (1763)
Gambia	Settlement began 1618
Georgia	First settled 1733
Gibraltar	Ceded colony (1713)
Gold Coast	Settlement began 1750
Grenada	Ceded colony (1763)
Hudson's Bay Company	Ceded by France (1713)
India	Settlement began 1601
Jamaica	Colony (seized 1655 and ceded 1670)
Madras	Ceded by France (1763)
Maryland	First settled 1634
Massachusetts	First settled 1620
Minorca	Seized from Spain 1708
Montserrat	First settled (1642) as colony
Newfoundland	Settlement began 1623
New Hampshire	First settled 1623
New Jersey	First settled 1664

179

New York	First settled 1614
North Carolina	First settled 1650
Nova Scotia	Ceded by France (1713)
Pennsylvania	First settled 1682
Quebec	Ceded by France (1713)
Rhode Island	First settled 1636
St Christopher (St Kitts) and Nevis	Colony (1625)
St Helena	Administered by E. India Co. 1673
St Vincent	Ceded colony (1763)
South Carolina	First settled 1670
Virginia	First settled 1607
Virgin Islands	Colonies (1666)
Windward Isles	Colonies (1763)

CHRONOLOGY OF BRITISH COLONIAL EXPANSION, 1688–1760

1689   William and Mary recognise old Charters of colonies.

1690   East India Company makes peace with Mogul Empire; factory at Calcutta established.

1691   Revolution settlement of the New England colonies; new charter granted to Massachusetts; Governor and other officials to be appointed by the Crown.

1693   Carolina divided into North and South Carolina.

1695   Formation of Company of Scotland for trade with Africa and the Indies.

1696   Establishment of Board of Trade and Plantations.

1697   Under Treaty of Ryswick, Hudson's Bay company reduced to only one factory (Fort Albany). Publication of Dampier's *New Voyage Round the World*.

1698   Major attack on old East India Company in new legislation with Act creating New East India Company. Erection of Fort William to protect Calcutta; first Darien expedition by Company of Scotland.

1699   Second Darien expedition also fails.

1702   Delaware becomes separate Crown Colony; French portion of St

Kitts captured at outbreak of the War of the Spanish Succession; merger agreed of rival East India Companies.

1703   Methuen Treaty with Portugal.

1704   English capture Gibraltar.

1708   Capture of Minorca.

1709   Fusion of rival East India Companies completed. New body entitled United Company of Merchants of England trading to the East Indies.

1710   Capture of Nova Scotia.

1711   Formation of South Sea Company.

1713   Treaty of Utrecht signed. France ceded whole of Hudson's Bay, French St Kitts, the Newfoundland settlements and Nova Scotia (except for Cape Breton Island). Spain ceded Gibraltar and Minorca. The Asiento (the monopoly of supplying slaves to Spanish American colonies) also abandoned (granted to the South Sea Company).

1729   Dispute over government of Carolina resolved and divided into North and South Carolina by Act of Parliament.

1732   Proprietary grant to General James Oglethorpe of Georgia.

1733   New colony of Savannah founded by Oglethorpe.

1739   War of Jenkins' Ear; capture of Porto Bello by Admiral Vernon.

1740   Expedition of Commodore George Anson to attack Spanish colonies on Pacific coast of South America. Oglethorpe from Georgia makes unsuccessful attack on Florida.

1741   Attack on Cartagena by Vernon and Wentworth; Dupleix appointed Governor of Pondicherry.

1742   Unsuccessful attack on Cuba.

1744   Capture of Annapolis (in Nova Scotia) by the French marks beginning of Anglo-French struggle over the colonies.

1745   British capture Louisburg; William Shirley (the Governor of Massachusetts) and William Pepperell, leader of the force, both received baronetcies.

1746   French capture of Madras by La Bourdonnais.

1747   Decisive naval victories by Anson at Cape Finisterre and Hawke at Belle Île. Unsuccessful French attacks on Fort St David (Cuddalore).

1748   Peace of Aix-la-Chapelle; mutual restoration of colonies. Four disputed islands (St Lucia, Dominica, St Vincent and Tobago) declared neutral. Formation of the Ohio Company (followed by the Loyal Company and Greenbriar Company).

1749   Dupleix's unauthorised war in India; Chanda Sahib adopted by Dupleix as Nawab of the Carnatic; Chanda Sahib victorious at Battle of Ambur. Marquis de Bussy power behind the throne in the Deccan; foundation of Halifax in Nova Scotia.

1750   British settlement begins on Gold Coast.

1751   British support for Mohammed Ali; Clive successfully attacked Arcot (capital of the Carnatic). Subsequent victory for Clive at Battle of Arni.

1752   Georgia becomes a Crown Colony; relief of siege of Trichinopoly; Mohammed Ali now the effective Nawab.

1753   Dupleix recalled (he received the order in 1754). French in effective control of Ohio, establishment of Fort Duquesne.

1755   Defeat of General Edward Braddock's march to attack Fort Duquesne. Deportation of 6000 French ('Arcadians') from Nova Scotia. Construction of Fort Edward on the east of the Hudson.

1756   Outbreak of Seven Years' War. Initial French successes included fall of Minorca (Admiral Byng subsequently shot) and advances by Montcalm in Canada. Nabob of Bengal imprisons British in 'Black Hole' of Calcutta.

1757   Further French successes in Canada; fall of Fort William Henry to Montcalm. British forced back to upper waters of the Hudson. Battle of Plassey gives Clive mastery of Bengal.

1758   Repulse of Abercrombie before Ticonderoga; capture of Louisburg. Capture of Forts Duquesne and Frontenac.

1759   Capture of Forts Niagara and Ticonderoga. General Wolfe captures Quebec after battle of the Heights of Abraham.

1760   Surrender of Montreal and Canada to British. Battle of Wandiwash breaks French power in India.

IRELAND, 1688-1760

1688   Irish troops dispatched to England (Oct). Londonderry refuses to accept Catholic garrison (Dec).

1689   Landing of James II at Kinsale in Ireland (12 Mar); joined by
          Tyrconnell and enters Dublin (24 Mar). Siege of Protestants at
          Londonderry opens (20 Apr). Irish Parliament issues an Attainder,
          confiscating the land of 2000 of William's adherents (May). Siege
          of Londonderry lifted (28 Jul) by Kirke and defeat of Catholic
          forces at Newton Butler (28 Jul). William III sends Marshal
          Schomberg with 10 000 troops to Belfast (August).

1690   7000 French troops arrive at Kinsale to support James (Mar).
          William lands in Ireland (14 Jun). William defeats James's forces
          at Battle of the Boyne (1 Jul) and James flees to France while his
          forces retreat to the west. First siege of Limerick repulsed (Aug);
          Cork and Kinsale taken by William's forces.

1691   Fall of Athlone (30 Jun) and defeat of James's forces at Battle of
          Aughrim by Ginkel (12 Jul). Second siege of Limerick which
          surrenders on 3 October. Treaty, or pacification of Limerick offers
          free transportation to all Irish officers and soldiers desiring to go
          to France. Irish Catholics to have same religious liberties as enjoyed
          under Charles II and the right to carry arms and practise their
          professions. 1 000 000 acres of 'rebel' estates confiscated.

1692   Meeting of Irish Parliament (Oct). William and Mary recognised
          as rulers. Catholics prevented from sitting in Parliament and laws
          passed to limit their worship, ownership of property and education
          in defiance of Treaty of Limerick. Parliament prorogued for refusing
          to pass money bill (Nov).

1693   Irish Parliament dissolved (Jun).

1695   Irish Parliament passes bills prohibiting Catholics from sending
          children abroad to be educated and preventing them bearing arms.

1697   Irish Parliament banishes all Roman Catholic bishops and monastic
          clergy. Treaty of Limerick ratified but modified to incorporate penal
          laws against Catholics.

1699   Irish export woollen trade restricted.

1703   Act passed determining conditions of Catholic worship; priests
          required to register name and parish in order to celebrate mass or
          face imprisonment or execution.

1704   Act prevents land being passed on to Catholics. Protestant dissenters
          excluded from office.

1709   Catholic clergy required to take Oath of Abjuration of Stuart
          pretender. Refused by 1000 Catholic priests.

1710   Linen Board set up to supervise linen industry.

1713   Duke of Shrewsbury appointed Lord Lieutenant.

1714   Schism Act extended to Ireland.

1719   Law-suit of Sherlock v. Annesley leads to Act for better securing of the dependency of the Kingdom of Ireland upon the Crown of Great Britain, declaring that the British Parliament had full authority to make laws 'of sufficient force and validity to bind the kingdom and people of Ireland' and denying the status of the Irish House of Lords as a Court of Appeal. Act of Toleration granted religious freedom to Protestant dissenters, but Test Acts retained.

1720   Irish cotton industry restricted by British Parliament. Jonathan Swift publishes anonymously a pamphlet supporting Irish manufacturers against British.

1721   Duke of Grafton appointed Lord Lieutenant.

1722   Grant to William Wood, a Wolverhampton ironmaster, of a patent to coin money for Ireland (Jul) arouses controversy.

1723   Irish Parliament protests against 'Wood's halfpence' (Sep) and refuses to transact further business.

1724   Lord Carteret replaces Grafton as Lord Lieutenant. Swift publishes first of *Drapier's Letters* (Feb), attacking the new coinage and the constitutional relationship between Britain and Ireland.

1725   British government reduces amount of currency to be issued by Wood from £108 000 to £40 000. Attempt to prosecute printer of *Drapier's Letters* fails and government withdraws Wood's patent completely.

1727   Irish Catholics deprived of the vote.

1727–30 Series of poor harvests leads to widespread famine.

1731   Duke of Dorset becomes Lord Lieutenant. Dublin Society set up to encourage agriculture and the arts.

1740–1 Serious famine leads to between 80 000 and 400 000 deaths.

1745   Earl Chesterfield becomes Lord Lieutenant and begins suspension of penal laws against Catholics.

1746   Irish forbidden to export glassware.

1747   Charles Lucas begins to publish the *Citizen's Journal*. John Wesley makes first of 42 visits to Ireland; first Methodist church established in Dublin.

1750   Roman Catholics admitted to lower grades of the army.

1753   Irish Parliament defeats money bill to dispose of Irish budget
        surplus to defray English national debt. Henry Boyle, Speaker of
        Irish Commons, dismissed as Chancellor of Exchequer. Widespread
        rejoicing in Dublin. Parliament prorogued.

1755   Marquess of Hartington appointed Lord Lieutenant to secure
        compromise on money bill. Boyle given earldom and other officials
        reinstated.

1759   Crowds invade Parliament on rumour of union with England.
        Henry Flood enters Parliament and leads 'patriots'. Restrictions
        on export of Irish cattle to England lifted.

NORTH AMERICA, 1688-1760

1689   On news of 'Glorious Revolution' in England, James II's appointee
        as president of New England, Sir Edmund Andros, seized and
        imprisoned in Boston (18 Apr). Assembly of representatives meets
        at Boston. Proclamation of William and Mary.

        King William's War sees operation of French with Indian support
        against the colonists.

1690   Sir William Phipps captures Port Royal (Apr) but fails in attack on
        Quebec.

1692   New charter issued for Massachusetts and appointment of Sir
        William Phipps as governor. The charter of the colony included the
        provinces of Maine, Nova Scotia and all land north of the
        St Lawrence. The Crown to appoint the governor and vested in
        him the right of calling, proroguing and dissolving the general
        court, appointing military officers and law officers and of vetoing
        acts of the legislature and appointments made by it. The electoral
        franchise was extended to all freeholders with a yearly income of
        40 shillings and all inhabitants having personal property to the
        amount of £40. Religious liberty granted to Roman Catholics.
        Beginning of the Salem witch craze (Feb). Twenty persons executed
        by October.
        Construction of Fort William Henry in Maine.
        College of William and Mary in Virginia.

1693   Penn dismissed from government of Pennsylvania.

1696   French capture fort at Pemaquid.

1697   At Peace of Ryswick both sides restore each others' conquests.

1699   French settle Louisiana.

            First Scottish settlement at Darien.

1701   William Penn obtained a new charter for Pennsylvania.

            Yale College founded at New Haven, Connecticut.

1702   War of Spanish Succession leads to renewed fighting between France and Britain.

1703   Pennsylvania divided into the province and the territories with separate assemblies.

1704   French with Indian support defeat Deerfield, but Colonel Church leads expedition on the French settlements in New England.

1706   French and Spanish invade Carolina but repulsed.

1710   English fleet captures Port Royal and renamed Annapolis.

1711   Tuscaroras and other tribes attack colonists in Carolina, but eventually crushed by Barnwell.

1713   Treaty of Utrecht results in cession of Hudson Bay and Straits of Nova Scotia, Newfoundland, and St Christopher to England.

            Treaty with eastern Indians at Portsmouth. Rectification of the boundary between Massachusetts and Connecticut.

1715   Yamassees and allied tribes attack Carolina, but repulsed.

1718   Captain Wood Rogers, governor of New Providence, suppressed the buccaneers in the West Indies and extirpates the pirates on the coast of Carolina.

1719   Beginning of discontent of colonists against the proprietary government in Carolina. The colonists' assembly refused to be dissolved and elected a new governor, resisting the old governor with arms.

1720   Prohibition of trade between Indians and French in New York.

1721   Royal Council declares Charter of Proprietors of Carolina forfeit and establishes a provisional royal government.

1722   In New York, governor Burnet opens negotiations with the Iroquois confederacy at Albany and establishes a trading-house at Oswego.

1724   Indian hostilities in New England with Abinakis.

1725   Yamassees assault English colonists in Carolina from Spanish Florida.

1726	Governor of Massachusetts, Shute, obtains from the Crown the power to suppress debate and limited power of adjournment by the representatives.
	In New York, a treaty brings new Indian tribes under English protection.
1728	Boundary between Virginia and North Carolina surveyed and settled.
1729	Agreement reached with proprietors of Carolina. Seven sold their titles and property, an eighth retained his property but lost his proprietary power. The Crown assumed the right of nominating governors and councils. The province was divided into North and South Carolina.
1731	Settlement of boundary between New York and Connecticut.
1733	Settlement of Georgia under James Oglethorpe and 20 other trustees for the Crown. Liberty of worship granted to all except Roman Catholics. First settlement established at Savannah.
1738	Foundation of Princeton College, New Jersey.
1739–48	War between Britain and Spain.
1740	Oglethorpe leads unsuccessful expedition against Florida.
	Expedition against Cartagena fails.
1741	Colonists attack Cuba.
1742	Spanish expedition against Georgia repulsed.
1744–8	War with France.
1745	Siege and capture of French fort of Louisburg on Cape Breton Island by colonial troops under William Pepperell.
1746	Projected attack on Canada by the colonists frustrated by the arrival of a French fleet, under D'Anville.
1747	Rioting in Boston against impressment of sailors.
1748	Treaty of Aix-la-Chapelle between England, France and Spain leads to reciprocal surrender of conquests in North America.
	Formation of the Ohio Company under a charter from the English Crown.
1750	Disputes between French and English over boundaries of Arcadia.
1751	Governor Clinton, of New York, in association with South Carolina,

Massachusetts and Connecticut concludes a peace with the 'Six Nations' Indian confederacy.

1752   Trustees of Georgia give up their Charter and Georgia is placed on the same footing as the other royal colonies. Introduction of Gregorian calendar in the colonies.

1753   George Washington despatched from Virginia to remonstrate with the French on the Allegheny and the Ohio for encroachments on Virginian territory.

1754   Virginia sends a force to the Ohio, part commanded by Washington, but he is captured and forced to withdraw. Conference of colonial delegates at Albany with the Six Nations. Benjamin Franklin draws up a plan for the union of all the colonies under a president appointed by the crown, with an elected grand council of delegates, with a right of legislation subject to the veto of the president and the approval of the crown. Connecticut, objecting to the veto power, refused to sign the proposal, which was later rejected both by the colonies and the crown.

1756–63 War between England and France. Braddock sent from England to command forces in North America. Colonial governors and Braddock decide to mount three expeditions: against Fort Duquesne; against the fort at Niagara; and against Crown Point in New York. Meanwhile, 3000 troops from Massachusetts captured forts Beausejour and Gaspereaux in Nova Scotia (June).
For the further events of the Seven Years' War in North America, see p. 162.

PRINCIPAL COLONIAL GOVERNORS

ANTIGUA

1682	Nathaniel Johnson
1689	General Codrington
1698	Colonel John Yeamans (Lieut-Gov)
1698	Christopher Codrington
1704	Sir William Matthew
1706	Colonel Parke
1710	Col John Yeamans (Lieut-Gov)
1710	Gen Hamilton
1711	Walter Douglas
1715	General Hamilton
1721	John Hart

1728   Lord Londonderry
1730   William Matthew
1752   Sir George Thomas

BAHAMAS

1687	Bridges	1717	Woodes Rogers
1690	Cadwallader Jones	1721	George Phenny
1694	Trott	1728	Woodes Rogers
1694	Nicholas Webb	1733	Richard Fitzwilliam
1700	Elias Hasket	1738	John Tinker
1700	Ellis Lightfoot	1759	William Shirley
1704	Birch		

BARBADOS

1685	Edwin Stede (Deputy)	1720	Samuel Cox (President)
1690	James Kendall	1722	Henry Worsley
1694	Francis Russell	1731	Samuel Barwick (President)
1696	Francis Bond (President)	1733	James Dotin (President)
1698	Ralph Grey	1733	Lord (Viscount) Scroop Hov
1701	John Farmer (President)	1735	James Dotin (President)
1703	Sir Bevill Granville	1739	Hon Robert Bing
1706	William Sharpe (President)	1740	James Dotin (President)
1707	Metford Crowe	1742	Sir Thomas Robinson
1710	George Willington (President)	1747	Hon Henry Grenville
1711	Robert Lowther	1753	Ralph Weeks (President)
1720	John Frere (President)	1756	Charles Pinfold

BENGAL (Presidents)

1700   Sir Charles Eyre
1701   John Beard
1705–10   Vacant: members of council presided in rotation
1710   Anthony Weltden
1711   John Russell
1713   Robert Hedges
1718   Samuel Feake
1723   John Deane
1726   Henry Frankland
1728   John Deane
1732   John Stackhouse
1739   Thomas Braddyll
1746   John Forster
1748   William Barwell

1749	Adam Dawson	1760	John Z. Holwell
1752	William Fytche	1760	Henry Vansittart
1752	Roger Drake	1764	John Spencer
1758	Col Robert Clive		

BERMUDA

1687	Sir R. Robinson	1721	Sir J. Bruce Hope
1691	Isaac Richier	1727	Capt J. Pitt
1692	Capt Goddard	1737	Alured Popple
1698	Samuel Day	1745	William Popple
1700	Capt Bennett	1764	G. J. Bruere
1713	Henry Pullein		

BOMBAY (Governors)

1681	Sir John Child	1729	Robert Cowan
1690	Bartholomew Harris	1734	John Horne
1694	Sir John Gayer	1739	Stephen Law
1704	Sir Nicholas Waite	1742	William Wake
1708	William Aislabie	1750	Richard Bourchier
1715	Charles Boone	1760	Charles Crommelin
1722	William Phipps		

CONNECTICUT

1683	Robert Treat	1742	Jonathan Law
1698	FitzJohn Winthrop	1751	Roger Wolcott
1708	Gordon Saltonstall	1754	Thomas Fitch
1725	Joseph Talcott		

GEORGIA

1733	James Edward Oglethorpe	1754	John Reynolds
1750	William Stephens	1757	Henry Ellis
1750	Henry Parker		

GIBRALTAR

1704–6	Georg von Hessen-Darmstadt
1707–11	Roger Elliott
1711–13	Thomas Stanwix
1713–20	E of Portmore
1720–7	Richard Kane
1727–30	Jasper Clayton
1730–8	Joseph Sabine

1738–9	Francis Columbine
1739–49	William Hargrave
1749–52	Humphry Bland
1752–6	Thomas Fowke
1756	E of Tyrawley
1756–8	E of Panmure
1758–61	Earl Home

HUDSON'S BAY COMPANY

1670	Prince Rupert	1700	Stephen Evance
1683	James Stuart	1712	Bibye Lake
1685	John Churchill	1743	Benjamin Pitt
1691	Stephen Evance	1746	Thomas Knapp
1696	William Trumbull	1750	Atwell Lake

JAMAICA

1687	D of Albemarle	1722	D of Portland
1690	E of Inchiquin	1728	Maj-Gen Hunter
1702	William Selwyn	1735	H. Cunningham
1710	Ld A. Hamilton	1738	G. Trelawney
1716	Peter Heywood	1752	Charles Knowles
1718	Sir N. Lawes	1758	George Haldane

MADRAS (Governors)

1687	Elihu Yale	1725	James Macrae
1692	Nathaniel Higginson	1730	George Morton Pitt
1698	Thomas Pitt	1735	Richard Benyon
1709	Gulston Addison	1744	Nicholas Morse
1709	Edmund Montague (Acting)	1746	John Hinde
1709	William Fraser (Acting)	1747	Charles Floyer
1711	Edward Harrison	1750	Thomas Saunders
1717	Joseph Collet	1755	George Pigot
1720	Francis Hastings (Acting)	1763	Robert Palk
1721	Nathaniel Elwick		

MARYLAND

1684	William Joseph	1709	Edward Lloyd
1691	Lionel Copley	1714	John Hart
1693	Thomas Lawrence	1720	Charles Calvert
1694	Francis Nicholson	1726	Benedict Leonard Calvert
1698	Nathaniel Blackistone	1731	Samuel Ogle
1703	John Seymour	1732	Charles Calvert

1735	Samuel Ogle	1752	Benjamin Taskar
1742	Thomas Bladen	1753	Horatio Sharpe
1747	Samuel Ogle		

MASSACHUSETTS

1686	Edmund Andros	1728	William Burnett
1689	Simon Bradstreet	1729	William Dummer
1692	William Phipps	1730	William Tailer
1694	William Stoughton	1730	Jonathan Belcher
1699	E of Bellomont	1741	William Shirley
1700	William Stoughton	1749	Spencer Phips
1702	Joseph Dudley	1753	William Shirley
1715	William Tailer	1756	Spencer Phips
1716	Samuel Shute	1757	Thomas Downal
1723	William Dummer		

MINORCA

Governors (since seizure from Spain, 1708)

1708	James Stanhope	1718	George Forbes
1711	Duke of Argyll	1730	Richard Kane
1713	Earl of Peterborough	1737	Earl of Hertford
1714	Duke of Argyll (again)	1742	Earl of Stair
1716	George Carpenter	1747	Earl of Tyrawley (to 1756)

NEWFOUNDLAND

Governors

1729	Capt Osborne	1750	Capt Drake
1737	Capt Vanburgh	1753	Capt Bonfoy
1740	Lord G. Graham	1755	Capt Dorril
1741	Hon J. Byng	1757	Capt Edwards
1744	Sir C. Hardy	1760	Capt Webb
1749	Lord Rodney		

NEW HAMPSHIRE

*Governors**

1692	John Usher	1715	George Vaughan
1697	William Partridge	1717	John Wentworth
1699	office vacant until 1703	1730	David Dunbar
1703	John Usher (again)	1741	Benning Wentworth

*Up to 1692, known as Presidents of the Council, from 1692 to 1741 as Lieutenant-Governors, then Governors.

NEW JERSEY*

Governors

1703	Baron Cornbury	1732	William Cosby
1708	John Lovelace	1736	John Hamilton
1709	Richard Ingoldsby	1738	Lewis Morris (third term)
1710	Robert Hunter	1746	John Hamilton (again)
1719	Lewis Morris	1747	Jonathan Belcher
1720	William Burnet	1757	Thomas Pownall
1728	John Montgomerie	1757	John Reading
1731	Lewis Morris (again)	1758	Francis Bernard

*Prior to 1703, divided into East Jersey and West Jersey

NEW PLYMOUTH*

1686   Edmond Andros
1689–92 Thomas Hinckley

*See under Massachusetts after 1692

NORTH CAROLINA

1689	Philip Ludwell	1714	Charles Eden
1691	Thomas Jarvis	1722	Thomas Pollock (again)
1694	John Archdale	1722	William Reed
1696	John Harvey	1724	George Burrington
1699	Henderson Walker	1725	Richard Everard
1704	Robert Daniel	1731	George Burrington (again)
1705	Thomas Cary	1734	Gabriel Johnston
1706	William Glover	1752	Nathaniel Rice
1708	Thomas Cary (again)	1753	Matthew Rowan
1711	Edward Hye	1754	Arthur Dobbs
1712	Thomas Pollock		

NOVA SCOTIA

1749	Hon E. Cornwallis	1754	C. Lawrence
1752	V. Hopson	1756	A. Moulton

PENNSYLVANIA

1688	John Blackwell	1703	Edward Shippen
1690	Thomas Lloyd	1704	John Evans
1693	William Markham	1709	Charles Gookin
1699	William Penn	1717	William Keith
1701	Andrew Hamilton	1726	Patrick Gordon

194

BRITISH HISTORICAL FACTS, 1688 1760

1736	James Logan	1754	Robert Hunter Morris
1738	George Thomas	1756	William Denny
1747	Anthony Palmer	1759	James Hamilton
1748	James Hamilton		

RHODE ISLAND

1686	Edmond Andros	1740	Richard Ward
1689	John Coggeshall	1743	William Greene
1690	Henry Bull	1745	Gideon Wanton
1690	John Easton	1746	William Greene
1695	Caleb Carr	1747	Gideon Wanton
1696	Walter Clarke	1748	William Greene
1698	Samuel Cranston	1755	Stephen Hopkins
1727	Joseph Jencks	1757	William Greene
1732	William Wanton	1758	Stephen Hopkins
1734	John Wanton		

SOUTH CAROLINA

1686	James Colleton	1711	Charles Craven
1690	Seth Sothel	1717	Robert Johnson
1692	Philip Ludwell	1719	James Moore
1693	Thomas Smith	1721	Francis Nicholson
1694	Joseph Blake	1724	Arthur Middleton
1695	John Archdale	1729	Robert Johnson
1696	Joseph Blake	1735	Thomas Broughton
1700	James Moore	1737	William Bull
1703	Nathaniel Johnson	1743	James Glen
1709	Edward Tynte	1756	William Henry Lyttelton
1710	Robert Gibbes		

11 LAW AND ORDER

LEGAL OFFICE HOLDERS

CHIEF JUSTICES (KING'S BENCH)

1689	Sir John Holt
1710	Sir Thomas Parker (Ld Macclesfield)
1718	Sir John Pratt
1725	Sir Robert Raymond (Ld Raymond)
1733	Sir Philip Yorke (Ld Hardwicke)
1737	Sir William Lee
1754	Sir Dudley Ryder (Ld Ryder)
1756	Lord Mansfield

CHIEF JUSTICES (COMMON PLEAS)

1689	Sir Henry Pollexfen (died, June 1690)
1692	Sir George Treby
1701	Lord Trevor (removed, October 1714)
1714	Sir Peter King
1725	Sir Robert Eyre
1736	Sir Thomas Reeve
1737	Sir John Willes
1762	Sir Charles Pratt (Ld Camden)

CHIEF BARONS OF THE EXCHEQUER

1686	Sir Edward Atkyns (resigned October 1694)
1695	Sir Edward Ward
1714	Sir Samuel Dodd
1716	Sir Thomas Bury
1722	Sir James Montague
1723	Sir Robert Eyre
1725	Sir Geoffrey Gilbert
1726	Sir Thomas Pengelly
1730	Sir James Reynolds
1738	Sir John Comyns
1740	Sir Edmund Probyn
1742	Sir Thomas Parker

MASTER OF THE ROLLS

1689	Sir Henry Powle
1693	Sir John Trevor
1717	Sir Joseph Jekyll
1738	Hon John Verney
1741	William Fortescue
1750	Sir John Strange
1754	Sir Thomas Clarke

MAJOR DEVELOPMENTS IN PUBLIC ORDER

THE GAME LAWS

The taking of game by all except propertied landowners was forbidden by a succession of statutes at least from 1 James I, c. 27, and the property qualification for taking game was further increased by 7 James I, c. 11. Under 22 and 23 Car. II, c. 25 only persons who possessed freehold estate of at least £100 per annum or a leasehold estate of at least £150 a year, or were the son or heir-apparent of an esquire or person of higher degree were entitled to take game. The game laws also exposed crops to the damage of hunters and hounds during the hunting season. Further restrictions were introduced under 4 W. and M., c. 23, while the 'Black Act' of 1723 made into felonies a large number of poaching and related offences which had hitherto been considered misdemeanours. The severity of the law was further increased by Acts subsequent to 1760, notably in 1770, 1800 and 1816.

THE RIOT ACT, 1715

The Riot Act (1 Geo. I, st. 2, c. 5) was passed in June 1715 in the wake of serious rioting following the accession of George I. The statute *supplemented* the existing Common Law offence of riot committed when three or more assembled together to achieve a common purpose by violence or tumult, by making more serious riots automatically a felony when previously they would normally be considered as misdemeanours. Earlier statutes such as I Mar. st. 2 c. 12 (1553) and I Eliz. c. 16 had taken steps in a similar direction, but only for the duration of the reign. The Act of 1715 made it a felony for twelve or more persons riotously to assemble and not to disperse within an hour after the proclamation requiring them to disperse; to oppose the making of such a proclamation and not to disperse within an hour after the making of the proclamation had been opposed; unlawfully to assemble to the disturbance of the public peace and when so assembled unlawfully and with force to demolish or pull down any church, chapel or other building for religious worship, or any dwelling-house, barn, stable or outhouse. It also empowered magistrates to call on the assistance of all able-bodied persons to put down riots and indemnified them for any injuries caused.

The Riot Act greatly strengthened the law against rioters by automatically making it a felony to remain assembled an hour after the reading of the Act, even if no further violent action was taken. By making such offences a felony, it provided for capital punishment in the case of serious riots, and permitted the use of lethal force to disperse them. However, there was a common misapprehension that an hour should be allowed to elapse before any action was taken against rioters whereas, in fact, reasonable force could be employed to disperse rioters at any time under the existing common law of riotous offences. The hesitancy of both magistrates and military to act was demonstrated on a number of occasions, notably in the case of the Gordon Riots of 1780.

WESTMINSTER WATCH ACT, 1735

An Act was passed enabling the householders of Westminster to pay for their own regular watchmen by means of a regular rate. Other metropolitan parishes adopted a similar system in subsequent years to provide a more reliable and responsible system of street patrols, often recruited from fit, army veterans of good character.

THE BOW STREET POLICE OFFICE, 1739

Sir Thomas De Veil, a former army colonel, was the first of a line of distinguished and active magistrates in Westminster. In 1739 he moved to a house in Bow Street from which he conducted business as a magistrate until 1746. In 1749 Henry Fielding took over his position, followed in 1754 by his blind half-brother John. These magistrates dispensed justice daily from the office and were noted for their lack of corruption. In 1753 Henry Fielding proposed, and had accepted by the Duke of Newcastle, a group of paid thief-takers to work under his direction. The 'Bow Street Constables' continued to be used throughout the century and were called in by provincial magistrates to assist with serious crimes.

LONDON HORSE PATROLS, 1752

In 1752 Henry Fielding organised a system of horse patrols to protect travellers on the roads surrounding the metropolis, but its expense led to it being discontinued by 1754. From 1756 a more limited system of patrol was organised by John Fielding. It was later supplemented (c. 1763) by a Foot Patrol financed by £4000 from the Civil List.

THE MILITIA ACT, 1757

The Elizabethan militia was a much decayed and little-used force by the mid-eighteenth century. The crisis of the Seven Years' War and the need to counter a possible invasion threat and replace the regular forces of the crown while they guarded the coasts or went abroad led, in 1757, to the creation of a militia for England and Wales (it did not apply to Scotland). The Militia Act envisaged a body of 60 000 men organised on a county basis, the bulk of whom were to be found by quotas levied on each county and filled by a ballot of all able-bodied men between 18 and 50 years of age. Militia service was for three years, although it was permitted to find a substitute or pay a fine of £10. The force was to train every Sunday between February and October and drill for a few days at Whitweek. When embodied it was to receive army pay and come under normal army discipline. Officers were selected according to property qualifications. Service overseas was not envisaged, although it could involve any part of the British Isles.

The introduction of the Act led to widespread rioting because of misplaced fears of service overseas and resentment that the rich could escape the ballot by paying the fine or buying a substitute. Although the full complement of militia took some time to embody, in the half century after 1757 it was to become, with supplementary legislation, an important domestic peace-keeping force.

POPULAR DISTURBANCES IN BRITAIN
(excluding Ireland)

1688	Sep–Nov	Attacks on Catholic property in London, York, Newcastle, Bristol, Norwich, Cambridge and Oxford.
	Dec	Following the flight of James II from London further attacks on Catholic property in London and upon the embassies of Catholic powers. Similar attacks in the country and in Edinburgh a crowd sacks Holyrood Chapel.
1693–5		Food riots in the Severn Valley, Thames Valley, Northamptonshire, Essex and Suffolk.
1695		Election riots at Oxford, Exeter, Westminster and elsewhere.
1697	June	Anti-enclosure riots at Epsworth, Lincolnshire.
1698		Election riots at Westminster.
1699		Drainage works destroyed by crowds at Deeping Fen, Lincolnshire.

1702		Attacks on dissenting meeting houses at New-castle-under-Lyme.
1703–4	Dec–Feb	Anti-prelate and anti-government riots in Edinburgh.
1705		Election riots at Coventry, Chester, Salisbury and Honiton.
1707		Riots at Edinburgh and Dumfries against the Act of Union.
1709		Food disturbances at Kingswood, Tyneside, Essex and North Wales.
1710	Mar	Pro-Sacheverell disturbances at Oxford, Exeter, Hereford, Barnstaple, Gainsborough, Frome, Cirencester, Sherborne, Walsall, West Bromwich, Ely, Bridgnorth, York, Canterbury, Norwich, Nottingham, Northampton, Taunton, Liverpool, Chester, Northwich, Marlow, Whitchurch, Coventry, Chippenham, Newark and London.
		Framebreaking in London by Spitalfields weavers.
1713		Bristol election riot.
1714	Sep	Pro-Hanoverian disturbances in Bristol.
1715	Jun–Aug	Attacks upon dissenting meeting houses in over 30 towns, especially in Manchester and the Midlands.
1716	May	Political disturbances in Cambridge.
	Jul	'Mug-house' riots in London between Whigs and Tories. Five rioters hanged.
1717		Disturbances amongst the cloth workers in Taunton and Exeter during industrial dispute.
1719	May	Disturbances during keelmen's strike in Newcastle.
	Jun	Weavers' disturbances in Norwich and Colchester.
		Attacks on women wearing calicoes in London by Spitalfields weavers.
1720	May	Further silk-weavers disturbances in London.
		Riots in Tiverton against imported Irish worsted.

1722	Jul	Pro-Jacobite disturbance at Leicester.
1723		Widespread poaching and other disturbances in Windsor Forest led to the Black Act.
1725		Anti-malt tax riots in Edinburgh.
		Weavers' riots in Crediton.
1726		Riots in Lincoln because of work on the cathedral towers.
	Nov	Riots in Wiltshire and Somerset by woollen workers.
1727		Anti-turnpike riots near Bristol.
1727–9		Food riots in Cornwall and North Wales.
1731		Anti-turnpike riots in Gloucestershire.
1732	Apr–Oct	Riots at the Mayoral elections in Chester.
1734	Mar–Apr	Widespread election riots.
1735		Anti-enclosure riots in Forest of Dean.
1736	Jul–Aug	Disturbances in London against the Gin Act and against Irish workmen.
	Sep	Porters riot in Edinburgh.
1737		Food riot in Penryn.
1738–40		Riots in West Country during dispute in woollen industry.
1740–1	Apr–Jan	Extensive food riots in England and Wales; Newcastle Guildhall sacked.
1743	May & Oct	Attacks upon Methodists in Wednesbury.
1744	Apr	Attacks upon Methodists at St Ives, Cornwall.
1746	Apr–May	Attacks on Catholic chapels in Liverpool. Also attacks on Catholic property in Bath and Sunderland.
	Oct	Attacks on the houses of Jacobites in Manchester.
1749	Jul–Aug	Turnpikes demolished around Bristol.
1750	Mar–May	Disturbances during keelmen's strike in the north-east.

1751	May	Two suspected witches killed by mob at Tring.
1754		Disturbances at the Oxford election. Election and anti-enclosure riots at Leicester.
1756–7	Aug–Dec	Over 140 food riots in England and Wales.
1757	Aug–Sep	Widespread riots against the operation of the Militia Act, especially in Yorkshire, Lincolnshire, Nottinghamshire, Bedfordshire, Hertfordshire, Cambridgeshire, Norfolk and Huntingdonshire.
1758	Jun	Anti-enclosure riots at Shaw Hill, Wiltshire.
1759		Anti-militia riots in Huntingdonshire.

12 SOCIAL DEVELOPMENTS

ESTIMATES OF THE POPULATION OF ENGLAND AND WALES, 1700–1760
(*in millions*)

	Rickman[1]	Finlaison[2]	Farr[3]	Brownlee[4]	Griffith[5]	Tranter[6]
1700–1	5.5	5.1	6.1	5.8	5.8	5.8
1710–11	5.2	5.1	6.3	6.0	6.0	6.0
1720–1	5.6	5.4	6.3	6.0	6.1	6.0
1730–1	5.8	5.7	6.2	6.0	6.0	6.1
1740–1	6.1	5.8	6.2	6.0	6.0	6.2
1750–1	6.5	6.0	6.3	6.1	6.3	6.5
1760–1	6.7	6.5	6.7	6.6	6.7	6.7

Sources:

[1] J. Rickman, *Observations on the Results of the Population Act, 41 Geo. III*, p. 9 (in *State Papers*, 1802, vii).
[2] J. Finlaison – 1831 census, *Enumeration Abstract*, P. x/v.
[3] W. Farr – 1861 census, *General Report*, p. 22.
[4] J. Brownlee, 'History of the birth and death rates in England and Wales', in *Public Health* (June and July, 1916).
[5] G. Talbot Griffith, *Population Problems in the Age of Malthus* (Cambridge, 1926), p. 18.
[6] N. L. Tranter, *Population since the Industrial Revolution: the case of England and Wales* (London, 1973), p. 41.

ESTIMATES OF THE POPULATION OF IRELAND, 1687–1767
(*in thousands*)

1687	2167	1725	3042	1754	3191
1712	2791	1726	3031	1767	3480
1718	2894	1732	3018		

Source K. H. Connell, *The Population of Ireland, 1750–1845* (Oxford, 1950), p. 25.

ESTIMATES OF THE POPULATION OF SCOTLAND, 1650–1800

| 1650 | 1 000 000 | 1725 | 1 100 000 | 1775 | 1 375 000 |
| 1700 | 1 040 000 | 1750 | 1 250 000 | 1800 | 1 500 000 |

Source J. Babuscio and R. Minta Dunn, *European Political Facts, 1648–1789*, (London, 1985), p. 340.

PRINCIPAL URBAN POPULATIONS

ENGLISH CITIES

Cities	1650	1700	1750
London	400 000	550 000	675 000
Liverpool	1500	5500	22 000
Manchester	4500	8000	18 000
Birmingham	3500	7000	23 500
Bristol	15 000	20 000	40 000
Plymouth	5000	7000	14 000
Norwich	20 000	30 000	36 000
Sheffield	2500	3500	12 000
Bath	1000	2500	6500
Portsmouth	3000	5000	10 000
Leeds	4000	6000	11 000
Nottingham	5000	7000	12 000
Newcastle	12 000	15 000	25 000
Hull	3500	6000	11 000
Sunderland	3000	5000	9000
Leicester	3500	5500	9000
Exeter	12 000	14 000	15 000
York	10 000	10 500	12 000
Coventry	7000	7000	12 000
Chester	7500	9000	11 000
Yarmouth	10 000	11 000	12 000
Oxford	8500	9000	10 000
Worcester	8000	8500	9500
Colchester	9500	10 000	9500
Cambridge	8500	9000	9500
Canterbury	7000	7500	8000
Salisbury	7000	7000	7000
Edinburgh	25 000	35 000	57 000 (1755)
Glasgow		12 000	25 000

Source *European Political Facts, 1648–1789, op. cit.*, p. 341.

MAJOR SOCIAL LEGISLATION

1691   Register of parishioners in receipt of poor relief to be kept.

1694   Wartime tax on births, marriages, and deaths, at 2s, 2s 6d, and 4s respectively. Higher duties for the wealthy.

1697   Settlement Act. Strangers were allowed to enter a parish provided that they possessed a settlement certificate showing that they would be taken by their old parish if they required poor relief. Paupers and their families were to wear a capital 'P' on their clothing. Punishment for disobeying the instruction could be loss of relief, imprisonment, hard labour and whipping.

1722–3 Parishes encouraged to build or rent workhouses and allowed to contract out their maintenance and supervision. Parishes allowed to form unions to set up viable workhouses.

1736   Gin Act. Required retailers to take out a licence of £50 and pay a duty of £1 on every gallon sold.

1747   Master and servant. Disputes between master and servant might be referred to the Justices. Apprentices' indentures could be cancelled in cases of ill-treatment.

1752   Gregorian Calendar introduced. Eleven days, 3–13 September, were removed from the calendar in order to bring the existing calendar in conformity with the Gregorian. Year to start from 1 January instead of from March.

1754   Hardwicke's Marriage Act. This declared that marriages could only be solomnised after the publication of banns which were to be recorded in the marriage register or in a separate book.

SOCIAL STRUCTURE OF THE POPULATION

GREGORY KING'S ESTIMATE OF THE POPULATION AND WEALTH OF ENGLAND AND WALES, CALCULATED FOR 1696

Rank	Number of families	Persons	Yearly income per family £	Yearly expenditure per family £	Total income of group £
Temporal Lords	160	6400	2800	2400	448 000
Spiritual Lords	26	520	1300	1100	33 800
Baronets	800	12 800	880	816	704 000
Knights	600	7800	650	498	39 000

Esquires	3000	30 000	450	420	1 350 000
Gentlemen	12 000	96 000	280	268	3 360 000
Clergy, superior	2000	12 000	60	54	120 000
Clergy, inferior	8000	40 000	45	40	360 000
Persons in the Law	10 000	70 000	140	119	1 400 000
Sciences and Liberal Arts	16 000	80 000	60	57.10s.	960 000
Persons in Offices (higher)	5000	40 000	240	216	1 200 000
Persons in Offices (lower)	5000	30 000	120	108	600 000
Naval Officers	5000	20 000	80	72	400 000
Military Officers	4000	16 000	60	56	240 000
Common Soldiers	35 000	70 000	14	15	490 000
Freeholders (better sort)	40 000	280 000	84	77	3 360 000
Freeholders (lesser)	140 000	700 000	50	45.10s.	7 000 000
Farmers	150 000	750 000	44	42.15s.	6 600 000
Labouring people and servants	364 000	1 275 000	15	15.5s.	5 460 000
Cottagers and Paupers	400 000	1 300 000	6.10s.	7.6.3d.	2 600 000
Artizans, Handicrafts	60 000	240 000	40	38	2 400 000
Merchants by sea	2000	16 000	400	320	800 000
Merchants by land	8000	48 000	200	170	1 600 000
Shopkeepers, Tradesmen	40 000	180 000	45	42.15s.	1 800 000
Common Seamen	50 000	150 000	20	21.10s.	1 000 000
Vagrants		30 000	2	3	60 000

HOSPITAL FOUNDATIONS, 1688–1760

1696   St Peter's, Bristol

1708   French Protestant

1713   Bethel (Norwich)

1720   Westminster

1726   Guy's

1734   St George's, London

1738   Bath General

1739   Queen Charlotte's

1740   London Hospital

1745   Durham, Newcastle-upon-Tyne and Northumberland Infirmary

1745   Gloucester Infirmary

1745   Liverpool Royal Infirmary

1745   Middlesex

1745   Shrewsbury Infirmary

1746   Middlesex County

1746   Worcester Royal Infirmary

1746   London Lock

1750   City of London Maternity

1751   St Luke's, London

1752   Manchester Royal Infirmary

1753   Devon and Exeter

1758   Magdalen

EDUCATION

1690   Haberdashers Askes school founded.

1697   Appleby Parva school (Leics) founded.

1698   The Society for the Propagation of Christian Knowledge begins to set up schools for the poor.

1700   Battersea Grammar School founded.

1702   Chair of Organic Chemistry created at Cambridge.

1704   Watford Grammar School founded.
        Chairs of Astronomy and Experimental Philosophy created at Cambridge.

1705   Dame Allan's School, Newcastle.

1707   Chair of Anatomy set up at Cambridge.

1714   Worcester College, Oxford founded.
        Radcliffe Library, Oxford founded.

1716   Building of Codrington Library, All Souls, Oxford, commenced (completed 1756).

1724   Regius Chair of Modern History created at Cambridge.

1725   Allan Ramsay starts Edinburgh Circulating Library.

1728   Chair of Botany founded at Cambridge.

1729   Doddridge founds dissenting academy. Dr Williams Library founded in Cripplegate, London.

1732   Portsmouth Grammar School founded.

1733   Bayley's School, Warwickshire, founded.

1737   Bancroft's School, Woodford Green, founded.

1740   Circulating Library established in the Strand. Cawthorn and Hutt's
        'British Library' a circulating library, is founded.
        Hertford College, Oxford founded.

1748   Kingwood School, Somerset founded.
        Thomlinson Library, Newcastle, founded.

1749   St Edmund's School, Canterbury, founded.
        St Olave's School, Orpington, founded.
        Chairs of Astronomy and Geometry founded at Cambridge.

1753   Library of Sir Hans Sloane purchased for the nation and forms
        basis of the British Museum. Harleian Collection purchased by the
        British Museum.

1755   Signet Library, Edinburgh, founded.

1757   Circulating Library opened in Birmingham.

1758   Liverpool Lyceum founded.

1759   British Museum opened at Montague House, London.

1760   Warrington Library founded.

NEWSPAPERS

Foundation Dates of Newspapers and Periodicals, 1688–1760

1690   Worcester Journal

1695   Stamford Mercury

1702   Bristol Post Boy

1702   Daily Courant

1708   Norwich Postman

1710–11 Nottingham Guardian (Journal)

1711   North Mail
          Newcastle Journal

1712   Norwich Gazette
          Liverpool Courant

1714   Exeter Mercury

1720   Northampton Mercury

1726   Weekly Lloyd's List

1734   Daily Lloyd's List

1737   Belfast Newsletter

1739   Gentleman's Magazine
       The Scot's Magazine

1741   Coventry Standard
       Birmingham Gazette

1748   Aberdeen Press and Journal

1754   Yorkshire Post

1759   Public Ledger (London)

13 ECONOMY AND FINANCE

PRICE OF WHEAT, 1688–1760
(*Shillings per Winchester quarter*)

	Exeter	Eton College	Winchester College
1688	20.50	20.17	18.95
1689	24.36	28.47	29.30
1690	28.01	26.58	23.40
1691	39.65	33.47	37.18
1692	43.29	42.67	45.92
1693	43.46	61.51	57.67
1694	24.56	34.36	34.59
1695	38.69	56.78	53.98
1696	57.68	44.33	49.24
1697	55.29	54.00	56.74
1698	41.25	55.04	55.55
1699	36.67	39.49	37.53
1700	33.40	30.59	32.59
1701	27.20	25.52	24.87
1702	24.90	23.76	26.52
1703	27.97	40.25	38.49
1704	N.A.	26.89	26.52
1705	25.79	21.75	22.29
1706	28.01	20.92	23.03
1707	32.93	24.70	26.91
1708	55.27	47.00	48.36
1709	59.47	74.10	69.52
1710	38.63	45.92	44.98
1711	34.12	45.39	40.81
1712	37.02	30.60	35.26
1713	45.40	50.76	48.89
1714	30.29	30.07	31.11
1715	34.35	39.50	43.56
1716	32.08	37.46	38.07
1717	29.60	35.41	34.96
1718	27.80	27.57	25.04
1719	39.12	29.53	31.55

1720	36.39	31.42	31.55
1721	29.36	28.56	25.81
1722	30.69	27.94	28.77
1723	29.05	29.00	27.99
1724	34.57	32.25	36.15
1725	41.04	43.13	38.07
1726	30.72	31.03	29.55
1727	46.78	41.18	44.37
1728	N.A.	42.08	44.22
1729	N.A.	32.64	30.22
1730	N.A.	28.16	29.96
1731	20.00	23.87	22.74
1732	24.46	22.06	22.94
1733	29.22	24.70	24.68
1734	36.53	33.01	31.10
1735	34.67	34.41	33.19
1736	28.50	32.42	26.91
1737	27.68	29.83	25.94
1738	28.50	27.94	26.50
1739	40.84	34.73	36.39
1740	50.74	48.73	50.20
1741	29.34	28.16	26.64
1742	24.11	22.74	20.92
1743	22.00	19.49	18.13
1744	22.50	20.16	18.55
1745	28.97	28.77	26.22
1746	33.16	29.38	28.03
1747	29.45	27.64	26.98
1748	29.08	29.83	28.58
1749	29.80	27.80	26.78
1750	31.92	26.96	27.61
1751	37.84	37.76	34.93
1752	36.75	35.20	34.59
1753	31.15	32.70	33.19
1754	28.69	25.52	25.94
1755	36.39	29.23	30.40
1756	51.91	49.17	42.12
1757	36.77	43.52	42.12
1758	30.39	34.67	31.24
1759	29.40	29.17	29.00
1760	34.12	27.41	28.59

Source   B. R. Mitchell and P. Deane, *Abstract of British Historical Statistics*, 2nd edn (Cambridge, 1971), pp. 486–7.

OVERSEAS TRADE – ENGLAND AND WALES, 1697–1760
(£000)

	Imports	Exports	Re-exports
1697	3344	2295	1096
1698	4608	3582	1608
1699	5621	3655	1570
1700	5840	3731	2081
1701	5796	4049	2192
1702	4088	3130	1144
1703	4450	3888	1622
1704	5329	3723	1804
1705			
1706	4064	4142	1447
1707	4267	4173	1602
1708	4699	4404	1495
1709	4511	4406	1507
1710	4011	4729	1566
1711	4686	4088	1875
1712			
1713	5811	4490	2402
1714	5929	5564	2440
1715	5641	5015	1908
1716	5800	4807	2243
1717	6347	5384	2613
1718	6669	4381	1980
1719	5367	4514	2321
1720	6090	4611	2300
1721	5908	4512	2689
1722	6378	5293	2972
1723	6506	4725	2671
1724	7394	5107	2494
1725	7095	5667	2814
1726	6678	5001	2692
1727	6799	4605	2670
1728	7569	4910	3797
1729	7541	4940	3299
1730	7780	5326	3223
1731	6992	5081	2782
1732	7088	5675	3196
1733	8017	5823	3015
1734	7096	5403	2897
1735	8160	5927	3402

1736	7308	6118	3585
1737	7074	6668	3414
1738	7439	6982	3214
1739	7829	5572	3272
1740	6704	5111	3086
1741	7936	5995	3575
1742	6867	6095	3480
1743	7802	6868	4442
1744	6363	5411	3780
1745	7847	5739	3333
1746	6206	7201	3566
1747	7117	6744	3031
1748	8136	7317	3824
1749	7918	9081	3598
1750	7772	9474	3225
1751	7943	8775	3644
1752	7889	8226	3469
1753	8625	8732	3511
1754	8093	8318	3470
1755	8773	7915	3150
1756	8962	8632	3089
1757	9253	8584	3755
1758	8415	8763	3855
1759	8923	10079	3869
1760	9833	10981	3714

Source   B. R. Mitchell and P. Deane, *Abstract of British Historical Statistics* 2nd edn (Cambridge, 1971), pp. 279–80.

THE COAL TRADE, 1668–1760

	Shipped coastwise from Newcastle (thousands of Newcastle chaldrons, 1 chaldron = 53 cwt)	Shipped coastwise from Sunderland	Imported into London (thousands of London chaldrons, 1 chaldron = 25½ cwt)
1688	231		
1689	168		
1690	137		
1691	177		
1692	156		
1693	180		

1694	160	
1695	171	
1696	151	
1697	181	
1698	211	
1699	221	
1700	205	335
1701	245	400
1702	153	243
1703	170	301
1704	198	
1705	182	
1706	163	
1707	151	
1708	193	361
1709	211	
1710	168	328
1711		
1712		
1713		346
1714		414
1715		388
1716		412
1717		440
1718		412
1719		420
1720		425
1721		459
1722		460
1723	262	458
1724	253	451
1725	266	471
1726	286	508
1727	276	496
1728	247	453
1729	293	494
1730	277	455
1731	311	475
1732	269	451
1733	291	496
1734	274	448
1735	282	503
1736	297	512
1737	276	476

1738	271		491
1739	288		442
1740	321		563
1741	263		453
1742	270		457
1743	298		478
1744	273		468
1745	295		471
1746	303		487
1747	259		469
1748	271	147	450
1749	299	135	504
1750	288	162	458
1751	343	129	539
1752	308	177	508
1753	301	167	508
1754	305	166	527
1755	294	174	479
1756	311	175	550
1757	274	179	503
1758	240	187	452
1759	302	187	552
1760	285	180	499

Source   B. R. Mitchell and P. Deane, *Abstract of British Historical Statistics* (Cambridge, 1971), pp. 108–10, 122.

OUTPUT OF WOOLLEN CLOTH IN THE WEST RIDING, 1726–60
(*thousand pieces*)

	Broad cloth	Narrow cloth
1727	29.0	
1728	25.2	
1729	29.6	
1730	31.6	
1731	35.6	
1732	35.5	
1733	34.6	
1734	31.1	
1735	31.7	

1736	38.9	
1737	42.3	
1738	42.4	
1739	43.1	58.8
1740	41.4	58.6
1741	46.4	61.2
1742	45.0	62.8
1743	45.2	63.5
1744	54.6	63.1
1745	50.5	63.4
1746	56.6	68.8
1747	62.5	68.4
1748	60.8	681.
1749	60.7	68.9
1750	60.4	78.1
1751	61.0	74.0
1752	60.7	72.4
1753	58.4	71.6
1754	56.1	72.4
1755	57.1	763.
1756	33.6	79.3
1757	55.8	77.1
1758	60.4	66.4
1759	51.9	65.5
1760	49.4	69.6

Source   Report of the Select Committee on the Woolen Manufacture, State Papers, 1806, p. 25.

OUTPUT OF SILK, CALICOES AND LINENS, 1713–60
(*in thousand yards*)

1713	2028	1723	3064	1733	2925
1714	2580	1724	2886	1734	2793
1715	1840	1725	2760	1735	3005
1716	2503	1726	2898	1736	2630
1717	2654	1727	2861	1737	3057
1718	2689	1728	2216	1738	3150
1719	2841	1729	2684	1739	3224
1720	1699	1730	2279	1740	3125
1721	1048	1731	2123	1741	3027
1722	1535	1732	2427	1742	2766

1743	3064	1749	3997	1755	4932
1744	3037	1750	4417	1756	4206
1745	2629	1751	4224	1757	4184
1746	2729	1752	4208	1758	5134
1747	3527	1753	4230	1759	5698
1748	3220	1754	4388	1760	6359

[z] Silks, Linens, Calicoes and stuffs charged with duty.

Source   B. R. Mitchell and P. Deane, *Abstract of British Historical Statistics*, 2nd edn (Cambridge, 1971), p. 184.

EXPORTS OF SILK AND LINEN FROM ENGLAND AND WALES, 1697–1760

	Silk (thousands of lb)	Linen (thousands of yards)
1697	41	145
1698	55	285
1699	48	245
1700	38	181
1701	39	141
1702	28	138
1703	33	145
1704	32	147
1705		
1706	42	139
1707	44	171
1708	52	323
1709	57	348
1710	54	304
1711	46	427
1712		
1713	44	287
1714	52	293
1715	58	363
1716	47	324
1717	62	381
1718	71	576
1719	40	448

1720	41	412
1721	38	497
1722	43	601
1723	44	451
1724	49	471
1725	86	672
1726	50	575
1727	37	632
1728	45	742
1729	43	810
1730	58	741
1731	42	748
1732	47	707
1733	45	610
1734	36	645
1735	45	955
1736	47	1040
1737	46	778
1738	47	1176
1739	49	1238
1740	40	1523
1741	58	2201
1742	62	2120
1743	71	1690
1744	46	1354
1745	40	1423
1746	50	3031
1747	56	2667
1748	54	2990
1749	60	4068
1750	63	4068
1751	23	3868
1752	92	4025
1753	90	5004
1754	85	4802
1755	91	3324
1756	89	4528
1757	93	5982
1758	118	7116
1759	173	8389
1760	198	10494

Source B. R. Mitchell and P. Deane, *Abstract of British Historical Statistics*, 2nd edn (Cambridge, 1971), pp. 201, 209.

RAW COTTON IMPORTS AND RE-EXPORTS, 1697–1760
(*in 1000 lbs*)

	Imports	*Re-exports*			
1697–8	1266	404	1730	1545	77
1699	1349	60	1731	1473	172
1700	1396	313	1732	1605	199
1701	1976	208	1733	1918	134
1702	1505	125	1734	1478	170
1703	757	173	1735	2198	168
1704	1446	420	1736	2296	460
1705			1737	1679	153
1706	461	95	1738	2537	169
1707	499	27	1739	2246	82
1708	2800	16	1740	1546	82
1709	907	35	1741	1680	109
1710	714	51	1742	1933	169
1711	675	62	1743	1268	65
1712			1744	2032	17
1713	1798	849	1745	1635	86
1714	1755	471	1746	2408	33
1715	1762	101	1747	2325	35
1716	2161	205	1748	5258	385
1717	2034	320	1749	1837	357
1718	2082	125	1750	2318	64
1719	1489	147	1751	2977	74
1720	1968	159	1752	3496	86
1721	1513	71	1753	4278	176
1722	2103	98	1754	3181	145
1723	2144	102	1755	3820	155
1724	977	76	1756	3089	375
1725	1841	103	1757	2706	888
1726	1523	115	1758	2225	237
1727			1759	2552	343
1728	1561	87	1760	2359	618
1729	1182	94			

Source   B. R. Mitchell and P. Deane, *Abstract of British Historical Statistics*, 2nd edn (Cambridge, 1971), p. 177.

OUTPUT OF TIN AND COPPER, 1688–1760

	White tin[1] (in thousand tons)	Copper ore[2] (in thousand tons)
1688	1.4	
1689	1.5	
1690	1.3	
1691	1.3	
1692	1.2	
1693	1.3	
1694	1.2	
1695	1.3	
1696	1.2	
1697	1.1	
1698	1.3	
1699	1.4	
1700	1.4	
1701	1.4	
1702	1.1	
1703	1.6	
1704	1.5	
1705	1.4	
1706	1.5	
1707	1.5	
1708	1.5	
1709	1.4	
1710	2.2	
1711	1.4	
1712	1.4	
1713	1.4	
1714	1.1	
1715	1.2	
1716	1.1	
1717	1.7	
1718	1.6	
1719		
1720	1.5	
1721	1.2	
1722	1.4	
1723	1.4	
1724	1.6	
1725	1.7	

1726	1.5	5.0
1727	1.6	6.7
1728	1.5	6.8
1729	1.6	6.9
1730	1.6	6.9
1731		7.0
1732	1.9	7.3
1733	1.6	7.0
1734	1.8	6.0
1735	1.8	5.2
1736	1.6	8.0
1737	1.7	9.0
1738	1.4	10.0
1739	1.8	11.0
1740	1.7	5.0
1741	1.6	5.5
1742	1.8	6.1
1743	1.9	7.0
1744	1.9	7.2
1745	1.7	6.7
1746	1.9	7.0
1747	1.8	4.9
1748	2.0	6.0
1749	1.1	7.2
1750	2.9	9.4
1751	2.3	11.0
1752	2.6	12.1
1753	2.5	13.0
1754	2.7	14.0
1755	2.8	14.2
1756	2.8	16.0
1757	2.8	17.0
1758	2.7	15.0
1759	2.6	16.7
1760	2.7	15.8

[1] Tin paying coinage dues.
[2] Copper ore sold at public ticketings in Cornwall and Devon.

Source   B. R. Mitchell and P. Deane, *Abstract of British Historical Statistics*, 2nd edn (Cambridge, 1971), pp. 153–4, 156.

EXPORTS OF TIN, COPPER AND LEAD, 1697–1760

	Tin blocks (thousand tons)	Copper and brass (tons)	Lead and shot (thousand tons)
1697	0.9	72	8.0
1698	1.3	130	13.2
1699	1.2	130	11.6
1700	1.4	169	11.6
1701	1.3	137	12.9
1702	0.9	97	9.2
1703	1.0	98	11.1
1704	0.9	75	10.2
1705			
1706	1.2	62	13.0
1707	0.9	60	14.7
1708	1.4	186	14.1
1709	1.1	70	10.6
1710	3.4	100	12.9
1711	0.5	96	14.1
1712	0.5	96	14.1
1713	0.7	166	11.6
1714	1.2	209	17.6
1715	1.3	207	10.8
1716	0.7	213	12.1
1717	1.1	236	13.6
1718	1.1	179	8.3
1719	1.8	182	10.7
1720	1.0	158	7.4
1721	1.0	155	10.0
1722	0.9	174	10.6
1723	1.3	207	9.1
1724	1.2	227	9.9
1725	0.8	269	9.4
1726	1.3	243	10.2
1727	1.4	239	12.5
1728	1.2	320	10.6
1729	1.3	372	12.3
1730	1.4	436	11.4
1731	1.2	429	12.5
1732	1.5	404	15.1
1733	1.3	404	15.1

1734	1.4	344	11.7
1735	1.6	442	12.7
1736	1.1	505	11.8
1737	1.5	535	12.0
1738	1.4	688	12.1
1739	1.4	584	13.4
1740	1.4	502	14.5
1741	1.5	678	14.0
1742	1.5	769	11.8
1743	1.2	930	16.2
1744	1.4	794	9.7
1745	1.5	626	11.9
1746	1.8	817	12.8
1747	1.6	786	11.0
1748	1.5	953	11.2
1749	1.6	1206	12.6
1750	1.8	1378	14.0
1751	1.8	1094	13.6
1752	1.9	1051	10.9
1753	1.6	1462	15.8
1754	1.8	1281	13.6
1755	1.7	1086	12.4
1756	1.6	1165	14.9
1757	1.6	1150	13.0
1758	1.6	1128	12.0
1759	1.7	1287	12.3
1760	1.9	1570	12.0

Source   B. R. Mitchell and P. Deane, *Abstract of British Historical Statistics*, 2nd edn (Cambridge, 1971), pp. 161, 164, 169.

PUBLIC INCOME AND EXPENDITURE IN GREAT BRITAIN, 1688–1760

	Total net income (£,000)	Total net expenditure (£,000)
1688–91[1]	8613	11543
1692[2]	4111	4255
1693	3783	5576
1694	4004	5602

1695	4134	6220
1696	4823	7998
1697	3298	7915
1698	4578	4127
1699	5164	4691
1700	4344	3201
1701	3769	3442
1702	4869	5010
1703	5561	5313
1704	5394	5527
1705	5292	5873
1706	5284	6692
1707	5471	8747
1708	5208	7742
1709	5206	9160
1710	5248	9772
1711	5179	15 142[3]
1712	5748	7864
1713	5780	6362
1714	5361	6185
1715	5547	6228
1716	5582	7076
1717	6514	5885
1718	6090	6534
1719	6026	6152
1720	6323	6002
1721	5954	5873
1722	6150	6978
1723	5993	5671
1724	5773	5438
1725	5960	5516
1726	5518	5543
1727	6103	5860
1728	6741	6504
1729	6294	5711
1730	6265	5574
1731	6080	5347
1732	5803	4974
1733	5522	4595
1734	5448	6360
1735	5652	5852
1736	5762	5793
1737	6077	5129
1738	5716	4725

1739	5820	5210
1740	5745	6161
1741	6244	7388
1742	6416	8533
1743	6567	8979
1744	6576	9398
1745	6451	8920
1746	6249	9804
1747	6961	1145[3]
1748	7199	1194[3]
1749	7494	12 544[3]
1750	7467	7185
1751	7097	6425
1752	6992	7037
1753	7338	5952
1754	6827	6030
1755	6938	7119
1756	7006	9589
1757	7969	11 214
1758	7946	13 200
1759	8155	15 382
1760	9207	17 993

[1] 5 November 1688 to 29 September 1691.
[2] Years to 1752 ending 29 September, thereafter 10 October.
[3] Contains debt items consolidated from previous years.

Source   B. R. Mitchell and P. Deane, *Abstract of British Historical Statistics* 2nd edn (Cambridge, 1971), pp. 386–7, 389–80.

NATIONAL DEBT, 1691–1760
(£000 000)

1691	3.1[1]	1702	14.1	1711	22.4
1692	3.3	1703	13.6	1712	34.9
1693	5.9	1704	13.4	1713	34.7
1694	6.1	1705	13.0	1714	36.2
1695	8.4	1706	13.0	1715	37.4
1696	10.6	1707	14.5	1716	37.9
1697	16.7	1708	15.2	1717	39.3
1700	14.2	1709	19.1	1718	39.7
1701	14.1	1710	21.4	1719	41.6

1720	54.0	1735	49.3	1748	76.1
1721	54.9	1736	49.7	1749	77.8
1722	52.7	1737	48.5	1750	78.0
1723	53.6	1738	47.5	1751	78.1
1724	53.8	1739	46.9	1752	76.9
1725	52.7	1740	47.4	1753	75.0
1726	52.9	1741	48.8	1754	72.2
1729	52.1	1742	51.3	1755	72.5
1730	51.4	1743	53.5	1756	74.6
1731	51.7	1744	57.1	1757	77.8
1732	50.1	1745	60.1	1758	82.1
1733	50.0	1746	64.9	1759	91.3
1734	49.1	1747	69.4	1760	101.7

[1] Year ending 29 September to 1752, thereafter 10 October.

Source   B. R. Mitchell and P. Deane, *Abstract of British Historical Statistics* 2nd edn (Cambridge, 1971), pp. 401–2.

COMPANY FOUNDATIONS, 1688–1760

1688   Cooke, Troughton & Simms, London (Scientific instruments)
         Lloyd's, London (Insurance)
         A. Mackintosh, Cambridge (Ironmongers)

1690   *Berrow's Worcester Journal*, Worcester (Newspapers)
         Merryweather & Sons, London (Fire-engineering)

1692   Coutt's Bank, London (Banking)

1694   Bank of England, London (Banking)

1695   Richard Austie, Devizes (Tobacco)
         Bank of Scotland, Edinburgh (Banking)
         Henekeys, London (Wine merchants)
         H. Tiffin & Son, London (Pest control)
         Stamford Mercury, Stamford (Newspapers)

1696   Hand-in-Hand Fire Office, London (Insurance)
         Lloyd's News, London (Newspapers)

1697   *Old Moore's Almanack*, London (Almanacs)

1698   Society for the Promotion of Christian Knowledge, London
         (Printing and charity work)

1699   Berry Brothers & Rudd, London (Wine merchants)

1700   Englefields, London (Pewterers)
          D. & S. Radford, London (Tobacco)
          Charlie Richards & Company, London (Wine merchants)

1702   *Bristol Post Boy*, Bristol (Newspapers)
          Daily Courant, London (Newspapers)
          Silk Hill, Derby (Silk Manufacture)

1703   Norman Society, London (Friendly Society)
          Society for the Mutual Help of Swiss in London, (Friendly Society)

1704   Bristol City Line of Steamships (Shipping)

1706   Crosse & Blackwell, London (Food manufacturing)
          R. Twining & Co., London and Andover (Tea merchants)

1707   Fortnum and Mason, London (Food retailing)
          W. B. Gurney & Son, London (Shorthand writers)

1708   *Norwich Postman*, Norwich (Newspapers)

1709   Coalbrookdale Company, Coalbrookdale, Shropshire (Iron manu-
          facture and engineering)

1710   William Dalton & Sons, London (Pest Control)
          Nottingham Guardian-Journal, Nottingham (Newspapers)
          Perrotts (Nicol & Peyton), London (Textiles)
          Sun Insurance Company, London (Insurance).

1711   *Newcastle Journal*, Newcastle (Newspapers)
          Nottingham Journal, Nottingham (Newspapers)
          C. & J. Rivington, London (Printing)
          Scotts' Shipbuilding & Engineering Company, Greenock (Ship-
          building)

1712   *Liverpool Courant*, Liverpool (Newspapers)
          Norwich Gazette, Norwich (Newspapers)
          Portals, Haverstock, Hampshire (Papermaking)

1714   *Exeter Mercury*, Exeter (Newspapers)
          Union, or Double Hand-in-Hand, Fire Office, London (Insurance)

1715   Allen & Hanburys, London (manufacturing Chemists)

1717   Austin & McAslan, Glasgow (Seeds)
          Drummonds Bank, London (Banking)
          Westminster Fire Office, London (Insurance)

1718   Joseph Bryant, Bristol (Ropes)
          Cooke, Troughton & Simms, York (Scientific instruments)

1719   Pike, Spicer & Company's Brewery, Portsmouth (Brewing)
         York Mercury, York (Newspapers)

1720   Brock's Fireworks, Sanophar, Scotland (Fireworks)
         Fribourg & Treyer, London (Tobacco)
         London Assistance (Insurance)
         Northampton Mercury, Northampton (Newspapers)
         Royal Exchange Assurance (Insurance)

1722   Thomas Andrews, Comber, Northern Ireland (Flour-milling)

1723   Tollemach & Cobbold, Ipswich (Brewing)
         Stephen Mitchell and Son, Linlithgow, Scotland (Tobacco)

1724   Longmans, Green & Company, London (Printing and publishing)

1725   Charles Davis (Hatters)
         Dring & Fage, London (Scientific Instruments)
         Drivers Jonas, London (Auctioneers)
         Mary Tuke (later Rowntrees), York (Cocoa)

1727   Royal Bank of Scotland (Banking)

1728   John Broadwood & Sons, London (Musical instruments)
         Ellis's bookshop, London (Booksellers)
         J. S. Fry & Sons, Bristol (Cocoa)

1730   Floris, London (Perfume)
         Taylor, Walker & Company, London (Brewing)

1731   Royal Dublin Society, Dublin (Agricultural Shows)

1733   Epworth Press, London (Printing and publishing)

1734   *Lloyd's List*, London (Newspapers)

1736   Gourock Ropework Company, Glasgow (Ropes)

1739   J. R. Phillips & Company, Bristol (Wine merchants)
         Scots Magazine (Newspapers)

1740   E. & W. Austie, Devizes (Tobacco)
         Booth's Distilleries, London (Gin distilling)
         Thwaites & Reed, London (Clockmaking)

1741   *Birmingham Gazette*, Birmingham (Newspapers)
         Coventry Standard, Coventry (Newspapers)
         Stephen Mitchell's Snuff-mill, Waukmilton, Scotland (Tobacco)

1742   Lagavulin Distillery, Islay, Scotland (Whisky)
         Whitbreads Brewery, London (Brewing)

1743   Bushmill's Distillery, Bushmills, Northern Ireland (Whisky)

1744   Cluttons, London (Auctioneers)
          King & Company, Kingston-upon-Hull (Ironmongers)
          Sotheby's, London (Auctioneers)
          Worthington, Burton-on-Trent (Brewing)

1746   British Linen Bank, Edinburgh (Banking)
          Glenochil Distillery, Stirling, Scotland (Whisky)

1747   Bottesford Friendly Society, Leicestershire (Friendly Society)
          J. &. N. Phillips & Company, Manchester (Cotton)

1748   Joseph Gardner & Sons, Liverpool (Timber)
          Press and Journal, Aberdeen (Newspapers)

1749   Finney's, Newcastle (Seeds)
          Justerini & Brooks, London (Wine merchants)
          William Younger & Company, Edinburgh (Brewing)

1750   Alloa Glass Works, Alloa, Scotland (Glass-making)
          Benskin's Cannon Brewery, Watford (Brewing)
          Bouchard Aine, London (Wine merchants)
          Brusna Distillery, Kilbeggan, Ireland (Whisky)
          Coalport China Company, Stoke-on-Trent (Pottery)
          Crosses & Heatons, Bolton (Cotton)
          Dollond & Aitchinson, London (Opticians)
          Eaden Lilley, Cambridge (Retailing)
          Harrison & Sons, London (Painting)
          Parker Gallery, London (Art dealers)
          Arthur Reader, London (Art dealers)
          Royal Crown Derby Porcelain Company, Derby (Pottery)
          C. Shippan, Chichester (Food manufacturing)
          Woodhouse, Carey & Browne, London (Sugar-brokers)

1751   Beatson, Clark & Company, Rotherham (Glassmaking)
          Culter Mills Paper Company, Aberdeenshire (Papermaking)
          Vacher & Son, London (Printing)
          Worcester Royal Porcelain Company, Worcester (Pottery)

1752   Clokie & Company, Castleford (Pottery)
          George Waterson & Sons, Edinburgh (Stationers)

1753   Glyn Mills, London (Banking)

1754   Royal Society of Arts, London (Agricultural shows)
          Yorkshire Post, Leeds (Newspapers)

1755   Brecknockshire Agricultural Society (Agricultural shows)

| 1756 | Bradford & Sons, Yeovil (Timber) |
| | James Latham, London (Timber) |

| 1757 | Charrington's Anchor Brewery, London (Brewing) |
| | Thomas Street Distillery, Dublin (Whisky) |

| 1758 | Fawcett Preston & Company, Liverpool (Engineering) |
| | Showerings, Shepton Mallet, Somerset (Cider) |

1759	Carron Company, Falkirk, Scotland (Iron manufacture and engineering)
	Dreweatt, Watson & Barton, Newbury, Berkshire (Auctioneers)
	Guinness Brewery, Dublin (Brewing)
	James Lock & Company, London (Hatters)
	William Playne & Company, Minchinhampton, Gloucestershire (Woollen manufacture)
	Public Ledger, London (Newspapers)
	Wedgwood, Barlaston, Staffordshire (Pottery)

1760	Baxter, Payne & Lepper, Beckenham, Kent (Auctioneers)
	John Burgess & Son, London (Food manufacture)
	W. Drummond & Sons, Stirling (Seeds)
	Zachary & Company, Cirencester (Wine merchants)

PARLIAMENTARY ENCLOSURE ACTS, 1688 to 1760 (BY COUNTY)

County	Place	Area enclosed (acres)
Bedford		
1742	Sutton	2200
1760	Aspley Guise	na
Berkshire		
1724	Sunninghill	1190
1743	Aston Tirrold	423
1746	Inkpen	na
1758	Upton	1800
Buckinghamshire		
1738	Ashenden	1300
1742	Wotton Underwood	1668
1744	Shipton	640

Derbyshire

1727	Scarcliffe and Palterton	970
1756	Weston cum Membris and Sawley	na
1760	Mackworth	na

Dorset

1733	Buckland Newton	1600
1736	West Stafford	600

Gloucester

1726	Little Rissington	na
1727	Cherrington	2200
1729	Wich Risington	2000
1731	Prestury	na
1731	Upper and Lower Slaughter	2845
1739	Shipton, Moyle and Dovel	800
1744	Westonbirt	350
1753	Eastlechmartin	1863
1753	Quennington	3000
1755	Hawling	881
1759	Little Barrington	1860
	Preston upon Stower	900

Hampshire

1740	Andover	na
1741	Chawton	na
1743	Dunmer	1760
1749	East Woodhay and Hollington	1300
1757	Barton Stacey	2507
1757	Earlstone	488
1759	Bishop's Waltham	205
1760	Folkesworth	510
1760	Fletton	na

Huntingdon

1727	Overton, Longville and Botolph's Bridge	1515

Leicester

1730	Horninghole	916
1734	Little and Great Claybrooke	430

1744	Langton	na
1749	Norton juxta Twycross	1744
1752	Narborough	1050
1755	Knighton	1680
1757	Wymeswold	1440
1758	Great Glen	1000
1759	Breedon	1336
1759	Belgrave	1000
1759	Desford and Peckleton	1010
1759	Evington and Stoughton	1000
1759	Hoton	1100
1759	Loughborough	na
1759	Oadby	1800
1759	Sileby	2200
1760	Barrow upon Soar	2250
1760	Frisby upon the Wreake	1500
1760	Hoby	1000
1760	Hinckley	2000
1760	Melton Mowbray	2000
1760	Somerby	1400
1760	Seagrave	na

Lincoln

1731	Biscathorpe	na
1734	Wollesthorpe	240
1736	Stallingborough	3642
1751	Dunsly (Dunsby)	1500
1752	Wytham on the Hill	1370
1754	Normanton	3000
1757	Baumber (Banborough)	2048
1757	Stragglethorpe	287
1758	Hareby	451
1759	Coleby	na
1759	Fillingham	2800
1759	Harmston	2528

Norfolk

1755	Brancaster	2350
1755	Swanton, Morley and Worthing	1400
1760	Litcham	600

Northampton

1727	Grafton	318
1733	Chipping Warden	1964
1743	Great Brington	4000
1745	Faxton	1170
1749	Wakerly and Wittering	na
1750	Nether Hoyford, Stow with Nine Churches and Bingbrooke	1365
1751	Farthingstone	1662
1752	Drayton	1487
1753	Hinton	1050
1754	Welton	2520
1755	Norton by Daventry	901
1756	Boughton and Pitford	2993
1758	Upper and Lower Boddington	3000
1758	Helmdon	1550
1758	Woodford	1067
1759	Ecton	3605
1759	Slapton	1330
1760	Blakesley	2000
1760	West Garndon	700
1760	Marston St Lawrence	1680
1760	Sulgrave	2485

Northumberland

1740	Gunnerton Ingrounds	2300
1757	West Matfen	300

Nottingham

1759	Barton and Clifton	1500
1759	Everton	2000
1759	Staunton	na
1760	Costock or Corthingstoke	710
1760	Broughton Sulney	2000
1760	Coddington	1780
1760	Clifton	na
1760	Hawksworth	na
1760	Hayton	1260
1760	Nusson	3760

Oxford

1730	Mixbury	2400

1757	Burchester	1200
1757	Piddington	1060
1758	Northleigh	2160
1759	Neithrop and Wickham	2109

Rutland

1756	Egleton or Edgeton	844
	Tinwell	1013
1758	Edith Weston	1200
1759	Thistleton	1380

Suffolk

| 1736 | Ixworth | 1300 |

Warwickshire

1726	Bobenhull	1000
1730	Lillington	na
1730	Welsbourne Hastings	na
1731	Bishop's Tachbroke	688
	Nuneaton and Attleborough	2670
1732	Little Kinneton	1617
1733	Barston	400
	Westbourne Hastings and	
	Newbold Pacy	1400
1739	Pailton	900
1740	Stichall	600
1741	Brinklow	1700
1742	Aston Cantlow	4067
1744	Wolfamcoat	1690
1753	Kilmorton	569
1755	Churchover	1120
1755	Great Harbarow	945
1755	Kenilworth	1100
1756	Clifton upon Dunsmore	700
1756	Radway	1277
1756	Sow	1400
1757	Loxley	647
1757	Morton Morrell	1225
1757	Prior's Hardwicke	770
1757	Prior's Marston	3800
1757	Wolfamcoat	1800
1758	Geydon	1470

1758	Wilmcote	na
1759	Honington	1365
1759	Willoughby	1500
1760	Barford	1733
1760	Southam	2200

Wiltshire

1726	Compton Bassett	na
1732	Staunton	800
1741	Sherston Magna	1000
1748	Badbury	na
1749	Broad Blumsden	700

Worcester

| 1733 | Aston Magna | na |
| 1736 | Alderminster | na |

Yorkshire, West Riding

1729	Thurnscoe	500
1757	Bishopsthorpe	1000
1759	Bolton upon Dearne	1000
1760	Adwicke in the Street	1000
1760	Calton	na

Yorkshire, East Riding

1731	Catwicke	1760
1740	Bewholm	1600
1741	Great and Little Driffield	3800
1746	Kelfield	600
1755	Nunburnholme	na
	Stillingfleet	800
1757	Fulford	780
1757	Pocklington	na
1758	Ottringham	2400
1758	Skirpenbeck	1980

Yorkshire, North Riding

1748	Faceby in Cleveland	1600
1755	Marsk and Redcar	1400
1755	Slingsby	na
1756	Sutton in the Forest	3000

1756	Warthill	800
1758	Brompton and Sawden	na
1759	East Cotham	800

Adapted from G. Slater, *The English Peasantry and the Enclosure of Common Fields* (London, 1907), Appendix B.

RIVER AND CANAL IMPROVEMENTS

1705 (*c.*)   Yorkshire Derwent navigation opened.

1710   River Itchen navigation opened.

1714 (*c.*)   River Nene navigation opened.

1717   River Tone navigation opened.

1723   River Kennet navigation opened.

1727   Bristol Avon navigation opened.

1732   River Weaver navigation opened.

1736   Mersey and Irwell navigation opened.

1742   River Douglas navigation opened. Newry Canal (Ulster) opened.

1750   Upper Medway navigation opened.

1751   River Don navigation opened.

1757 (*c.*)   River Blyth navigation opened.

1757   St Helens Canal, the Sankey navigation, opened.

14 LOCAL GOVERNMENT

THE COUNTY

ADMINISTRATIVE DIVISIONS

County for the purposes of administration England and Wales were divided into 52 counties (40 and 12 respectively), two of which, Lincolnshire and Yorkshire were subdivided into 'parts' or 'ridings'. Scotland was divided into 33 counties.

County Corporate By 1689 there were 19 cities and boroughs styled 'counties in themselves' by royal charter (viz. Bristol, Canterbury, Carmarthen, Chester, Coventry, Exeter, Gloucester, Haverford West, Hull, Lichfield, Lincoln, London, Newcastle, Norwich, Nottingham, Poole, Southampton, Worcester, York). These were exempt from control by the county sheriff, but most remained within the military jurisdiction of the Lord Lieutenant.

County Palatine By 1689, those counties in which the prerogatives exercised by the Crown had been claimed by a great earl or a Bishop (Lancashire, Cheshire, Durham and the Isle of Ely) largely conformed to the more general county organisation of England and Wales. Elements of Palatinate prerogative, largely formal in character, were to remain until the nineteenth century in Durham and Lancashire.

Hundred (or Wapentake, Ward, Lathe, Rape) an administrative subdivision of the county under a group of justices and a High Constable for matters of law, order and rate collection.

Parish (see also p. 241) smallest administrative unit, into which hundreds were subdivided; under a Petty Constable for matters of law, order and rate collection.

COUNTY ADMINISTRATION

Function designed to enable central government to extract from the county its service to the State – not to encourage establishment of local self-government; but a large proportion of adult males, all unpaid, were involved in the structure of local government as jurymen or officials at parish level.

CONTROLS EXERCISED BY CENTRAL GOVERNMENT

(1) All major officers (except coroners) appointed and dismissed by the monarch.

(2) The Court of King's Bench could overrule the justices of the peace by taking cases out of their hands or quashing their verdicts if a mistake had been made.

(3) All civil officers required to present themselves at the Assizes before the King's judges to give an account of the maintenance of law and order within the county.

(4) The Privy Council could issue orders at any time for immediate implementation of statutes and common law.

SERVICES DEMANDED BY CENTRAL GOVERNMENT AND EXECUTED BY COUNTY OFFICIALS

(1) Military service: either the *posse comitatus* (against internal rebellion) or the *militia* (for national defence).

(2) Taxes: aids, subsidies, land tax, ship money, etc.

(3) Maintenance of the peace.

(4) Upkeep of main bridges and gaols.

COUNTY OFFICERS

Lord Lieutenant office dated from mid-sixteenth century; its holder was normally chosen from among the greatest noblemen and appointed for life; he presided over the whole county. One man could hold office for more than one county. From 1689 the office was often combined with that of Custos Rotulorum (Keeper of the Rolls of the Peace). Responsible for organising the county militia and nominating justices of the peace; frequently a member of Privy Council.

Deputy Lieutenants controlled the militia during absences of the Lord Lieutenant; normally nominated by the latter (subject to royal approval) from amongst the ranks of the lesser nobility or greater gentry.

Custos Rotulorum a civil officer, keeper of the county rolls; from the sixteenth century the office was increasingly combined with that of Lord Lieutenant.

High Sheriff appointed for one year, normally from amongst the minor nobility; service was obligatory. The office had declined in importance since the Middle Ages. Responsible for the County Court, control of Parliamentary elections, nomination of jurymen and ceremonial duties for judges of Assize.

Under Sheriff a professional appointed for one year by the High Sheriff to undertake all but his ceremonial duties; responsible for execution of all writs and processes of law, for suppression of riots and rebellions, and for holding the County Court.

High Bailiff appointed by the High Sheriff to execute his instructions in the hundred.

Foot Bailiff (or Bound Bailiff) appointed by the High Sheriff or Under Sheriff to carry messages or search our individuals for the execution of justice.

Clerk of the Peace a professional officer receiving fees for his services to individuals; appointed for life by the Custos Rotulorum. *Duties*: to draft formal resolutions of the justices at Quarter Sessions and to advise them on matters of law. Duties often performed by a Deputy Clerk (a leading solicitor in the county town).

Coroner a professional officer earning fees from his service; between two and 12 elected for life by freeholders of the county from amongst their own number (in certain liberties the traditional right of appointment held by an individual or group – e.g. the Dean of York in the Liberty of St Peter, York; holders of office then known as **franchise coroners**). *Duties*: to hold inquests on (1) suspicious deaths, committing to trial anyone whom the Coroner's Jury find guilty of murder; (2) treasure trove, pronouncing on rightful ownership.

High Constable appointed normally for one year by Quarter Sessions; service was obligatory; assisted by petty constables in each parish. *Duties* to execute instructions of the justices in the hundred; towards the end of the seventeenth century also responsible for collecting the county rate assessed at Quarter Sessions and for repair of bridges and gaols.

Justices of the Peace gradually, under the Tudors and Stuarts, took over from the great officers the government of the county, both judicial and administrative, executing statutes issued from central government. *Qualifications for office* had to be a £20 freeholder resident in the county; to receive the sacraments in accordance with the Anglican rite; to have sworn the oaths of allegiance and supremacy; and to have (in theory) some knowledge of law and administration. The Justices Qualification Act of 1744 laid down that each justice had to have an estate or freehold, copy hold, or customary tenure of the value of £100. Nominated by the Lord Lieutenant and appointed by the monarch, normally for life, from amongst the noblemen and gentry. *Duties* 'to keep and cause to be kept all ordinance and statutes for the good of our peace' and 'to chastise and punish all persons that offend' against such statutes. Commission revised in 1590 to enable justices to act in three ways: individually; jointly, with colleagues in a division; collectively, as a General Sessions of the County

Court of Quarter Sessions   a General Sessions of the Peace for the whole county to be held four times a year; all justices of the peace summoned to attend under the theoretical chairmanship of the Custos Rotulorum; also summoned were the Sheriff, high bailiffs, high constables, coroners and petty constables, who were required to report offences from within their areas. *Juries in attendenace*: one Jury of Inquiry from each hundred; a Grand Jury and petty juries from the county at large.

Functions

(1)   to try private individuals for breaches of the law;
(2)   to hear presentments against parishes or hundreds (or against individual officers) for failure to carry out their duties;
(3)   to carry out routine administration – e.g. licensing of traders, maintenance of gaols and bridges, regulation of wages and prices, supervision of houses of correction, etc; and
(4)   to hear appeals against decisions by local justices.

Private or Special Sessions   Divisional Sessions, usually based on the hundred and meeting in many cases at monthly intervals. *Summoned to attend*: justices from the division; local parish and hundred officials. Empowered by Privy Council Order (1605) to deal with all matters not requiring juries (e.g. vagrancy, poor relief, etc.).

Petty Sessions   various legislation empowered any two justices sitting together to appoint local overseers of the poor and surveyors of the highways, to supervise accounts of parochial officials, to make rates, to license alehouses, to make orders for maintenance of illegitimate children and removal of paupers, to try and punish certain categories of offenders (e.g. poachers, unlicensed ale-keepers, rioters, etc.) and to hear and commit to Quarter Sessions more serious cases (e.g. larceny, assault, etc.).

The Quorum Clause   the Commission required that, where only two justices were sitting, one should be a justice who had been 'named' in the Commission (i.e. who possessed real knowledge of the law). By the end of the seventeenth century, this clause was scarcely valid, because all justices were named as the quorum.

Justices acting individually   each justice had the power

(1)   to commit suspects to the county gaol to await trial;

(2)   to require a person by summons to appear at the next Quarter Sessions;

(3)   to punish by fine or stocks those guilty of profane oaths, drunkenness, non-attendance at church, breaking the Sabbath, rick-burning or vagrancy; and

(4)   to present at Quarter Sessions any parishes or parish officers failing in their responsibilities for highway maintenance and poor relief.

County Court   although by the seventeenth century most of its dealings had been taken over by Quarter Sessions, etc., it still met under the High Sheriff (or, in practice, the Under Sheriff).

Functions

(1)   to recover civil debts under 40s;

(2)   to witness the High Sheriff's return of the writs requiring election of a Coroner and of two knights of the shire to represent the county in Parliament and

(3)   to assess, with the help of a jury, matters of compensation (for road-widening etc.).

Grand Jury (or Grand Inquest)   composed of between 12 and 24 men, usually drawn from landowners, merchants, manufacturers, clergy and other professional people. An Act of 1692 laid down that a juror should possess freehold, copyhold or life tenure land worth at least £10 per year. An Act of 1730 added leaseholders of £20 a year. An Act of 1696 provided for lists of jurors to be compiled by constables and presented to Quarter Sessions. Summoned by the High Sheriff to attend for one or two days at Quarter Sessions or Assizes; verdicts and presentments valid if at least twelve members agreed.

Functions

(1)   to consider criminal bills of indictment; then as 'true bills' (if a *prima facie* case had been established) or to reject them with the endorsement 'ignoramus';

(2)   to consider presentments of parishes and hundreds (or individual officers) for neglect of their duty, and to return a 'true bill' (as above) if case established;

(3)   to make a formal presentment for repair of the county gaol, county hall, bridges or houses of correction before county funds were released for these purposes by the justices; and

(4)   to express county opinion on matters of common concern in petitions to Parliament or presentments at Quarter Sessions or Assizes (e.g. over unlawful assemblies, vagrancy, etc.)

Hundred Jury (or Petty Jury or Inquiry)   each hundred and borough would have its own Petty Jury, composed of between 12 and 24 men and summoned by the High Sheriff through the high bailiffs. Unanimity not required in verdicts or presentments, if at least 12 members agreed. *Functions*: to make a presentment at Quarter Sessions of any public nuisances (especially concerning rivers, bridges, roads) or any local officials neglectful of duties. By the end of the seventeenth century these juries were falling into disuse: tasks taken over by high constables and petty constables.

Traverse or Felons' Juries   formed from a panel of petty jurymen summoned by the High Sheriff from the county as a whole; used to decide issues of fact in criminal trials.

THE PARISH

ADMINISTRATIVE FUNCTION

By the seventeenth century the parish was both the ecclesiastical division (in which a priest performed his duties to the inhabitants) and a unit of local government within the larger area of a hundred. By employing unpaid amateurs as parish officers, supervised by justices of the peace, the central government succeeded in collecting its dues and enforcing its statutes even at the remotest local level.

NATURE OF PARISH OFFICE

Terms of Office   service unpaid, compulsory, one year's duration (or until a replacement appointed).

Qualification for Office   no property or religious qualification: in some parishes all males serviced in rotation, in others holders of certain units of land served in rotation.

Exemptions from Office   peers, clergy, Members of Parliament, barristers, justices of the peace, revenue officers, members of the Royal College of Physicians, aldermen of the City of London; exemption could also be gained by paying a fine or finding a substitute.

Responsibilities   officer personally responsible to the justices or to the Bishop (in the case of churchwardens), not to the parish, duties were arduous, time-consuming and often unpopular.

PARISH OFFICERS

Churchwardens usually between two and four appointed annually. Method of appointment varied considerably: by methods described above, by election at an open or close meeting of the Vestry, by nomination of retiring churchwardens, by appointment by the incumbent – or by a combination of these. Sworn in by the Archdeacon. Responsible for

(1)   maintenance and repair of church fabric;
(2)   provision of materials required for services;
(3)   allocation of seats in church;
(4)   maintenance of churchyard;
(5)   annual report to the Bishop on the progress of the incumbent, condition of the fabric and moral state of the parish;
(6)   assistance to the Constable and surveyors of highways in civil duties within the parish;
(7)   assistance to overseers of the poor in relief of poverty, lodging of the impotent poor, apprenticing of children; and
(8)   levying a church rate on all parishioners when required for poor-law purposes, and maintaining proper accounts.

Constable established in office by two justices (or, occasionally, by surviving manorial Court Leet): responsible to justices of the peace, working under High Constable for the hundred; expenses paid by a 'constable's rate' on the parish or by fees for specific duties. Duties:

(1)   to deal with grants according to the law;
(2)   to supervise alehouses;
(3)   to call parish meetings as required;
(4)   to apprehend felons;
(5)   to place minor trouble-makers in the stocks;
(6)   to attend the justices in Petty and Quarter Sessions, making presentments on law-breakers, etc; and
(7)   to levy the county rate in the parish.

Surveyor of the Highways established by statute in 1555; formally appointed by the Constable and churchwardens after consultation with other parishioners; responsible to the justices of the peace for giving a regular report on state of the roads, for receiving instructions on work to be done and for rendering his accounts.

Duties

(1)   to direct 'statute labour' as required on local roads (wealthier inhabitants to send men, oxen and horses; ordinary parishioners to offer six days' personal labour);

(2)   to collect fines from defaulters and commutation fees from those who bought exemption;

(3)   to order the removal of obstructions from the highways (e.g. overgrown hedges and trees, undrained ditches, etc); and

(4)   to collect a highway rate, if authorised at Quarter Sessions, and any fines imposed on the parish for failure to maintain its highways.

In 1691 the law was altered whereby the justices chose a surveyor from a list of those eligible provided by the inhabitants. The surveyor was obliged to survey the highways three times a year and organise the statute labour provided by landowners to repair the roads or collect money in lieu.

Overseers of the Poor   established by statute in 1597; between two and four appointed for each parish by the justices to whom they were responsible. *Duties* (in co-operation with churchwardens):

(1)   to relieve destitute people;
(2)   to remove paupers without settlement rights to their former parish;
(3)   to make provision for illegitimate children;
(4)   to apprentice destitute children;
(5)   to assess and collect the poor rate;
(6)   to prepare accounts for the justices.

MINOR PAID OFFICES

Parish Clerk	Hogwarden
Sexton	Pinder
Bellringer	Beadle
Scavenger	Dog Whipper
Town Crier (or Bellman)	Vestry Clerk
Hayward	

Parish Vestry   a parish meeting held in church at Easter, and at other times if necessary.

Functions

(1)   to elect usually one churchwarden;
(2)   to decide on a church rate to defray the churchwarden's expenses and to cover repairs to the fabric;
(3)   to make any new by-laws for the parish; and
(4)   to administer the pound and common pasture.

MUNICIPAL CORPORATIONS

By 1689 there were approximately 200 boroughs in England and Wales which had received the privilege of incorporation through royal charter and possessed some or all of the powers listed below.

POWERS OF THE CORPORATION

(1)   To own, administer and sell property and land.
(2)   To administer the common meadow and wasteland.
(3)   To control trade; to hold markets and fairs.
(4)   To return burgesses to sit in Parliament.
(5)   To create a magistracy for the purpose of holding borough Petty Sessions and borough Quarter Sessions.
(6)   To formulate by-laws.
(7)   To levy local taxes and tolls.

OBLIGATIONS OF THE CORPORATION

(1)   To collect the King's revenue and to execute his writs.
(2)   To maintain the King's peace; to enforce his laws; to organise the nightly watch.
(3)   To support financially the borough's burgesses in Parliament.
(4)   To repair walls, bridges and streets.
(5)   To administer charitable trusts for schools, hospitals, poor people, etc.

MEMBERSHIP OF THE CORPORATION

Method of gaining membership, seldom stipulated in the Charter, varied considerably. Qualifications required for gaining 'freedom' included at least one of the following:

(1)   ownership of freehold within the borough (in some cases only the owners of certain specified burgages would qualify);
(2)   working an apprenticeship under a freeman of the borough (usually for seven years);
(3)   birth (i.e. sons of freeman) or marriage (i.e. husbands of freeman's widow or daughter);
(4)   membership of local guilds or trade companies;
(5)   co-option by gift, redemption or purchase;
(6)   membership of the Governing Council (i.e. no freemen outside). Freemen were normally admitted to membership by formal presentment of a local jury. Freemen could also be disfranchised for breach of duty, misdemeanour, etc.

MINOR OFFICIALS OF THE CORPORATION

Responsible to the chief officers; often salaried or collecting fees; possessing uniform or staff of office.

Agricultural Officials haymakers, pound-keepers, woodwards, pasture-masters, common-keepers, mole-catchers, swineherds, etc.

Market Officials bread-weighers, butter-searchers, ale-tasters, searchers and scalers of leather, searchers of the market, fish and flesh searchers, coalmeters, cornprizers, etc.

Order and Maintenance Officials water bailiffs, bridge-keepers, Serjeant-at-Mace or Beadle. Town Crier or Bellman, Scavenger or Street Warden, Cleaner of the Castle Walks. Cleaner of the Water Grates, Sweeper of Streets, Weeder of Footpaths, etc.

CHIEF OFFICERS OF THE CORPORATION

Mayor (or Bailiff, Portreeve, Alderman, Warden) named in the charter as head of the Corporation; with wide powers. Presided at all meetings of the Council; responsible for the management of Corporate estates; always a justice of the peace, presided at the borough Quarter Sessions; responsible for courts under the Corporation's jurisdictions; usually acted as Coroner and Clerk of Market; sometimes acted as Keeper of Borough Gaol and Examiner of Weights and Measures; appointed minor officials.

Bailiffs status varied considerably – in 40 boroughs they were heads of the Corporation, in about 100 they were minor officials, in about 30 they were chief officers. Normally two bailiffs. As chief officers, responsible for summoning juries, accounting for fines, collection of rents, etc; sometimes acted also as Treasurer, Coroner, Keeper of Borough Gaol, Clerk of Market; often, as justices of the peace, sat as judges on borough courts; occasionally undertook duties of Sheriff within the borough. Usually elected by the Council.

Recorder a lawyer; legal adviser to the Corporation. President at some of the borough courts, administered oath of office to Mayor; as a justice of the peace, sat at the Borough Court of Quarter Sessions; usually received an attendance fee or nominal stipend.

Chamberlain (or Treasurer, Receiver) the treasurer of the Corporation, usually appointed by the Council.

Town Clerk   usually appointed by the Council, but not a member of it. Responsible for a wide range of administration; often Clerk of the Peace, Clerk of the Magistrates and clerk of all the borough courts; sometimes Coroner, Keeper of the Records, Deputy Recorder, president of the borough court.

Aldermen

Known usually as the Mayor's Brethren, sometimes responsible for ensuring that by-laws were enforced in a particular ward of the borough; but principally a permanent and select consultative council (always part of the Common Council). Also collectively performed some judicial functions (licensing alehouses, making rates, appointing constables, etc.); tenure was normally for life.

Councillors

Usually 12, 24 or 48 in number; had no specific functions other than to form the Court of Common Council (together with the aldermen and chief officers).

COURTS OF THE CORPORATION

Court of Record (or Three Weeks' Court, Court of Pleas or Mayor's Court)   a court of civil jurisdiction consisting of one or more of the specified judges (usually, Mayor, Bailiff, Recorder, Town Clerk, aldermen, etc.); often met every three weeks. Jurisdiction limited to suits arising within the borough; usually personal actions for debt or concerning land.

Court Leet   right to hold court normally granted in the Charter; responsible for minor criminal jurisdiction, making of by-laws, control of commons and wastes, appointment of officers and admission of new tenants and freeholders. Administrative functions gradually taken over by the administrative courts during the latter part of the seventeenth century.

Borough Court of Quarter Sessions   gradually took over criminal jurisdiction from the Court Leet; normally only six justices of the peace, all of whom held particular positions (e.g. Mayor, Recorder, High Steward, Common Clerk, Coroner, etc.); often sat monthly or even weekly to hear a great variety of offences and complaints and to pass administrative orders.

Court of Pie Powder   held by Mayor or deputy to deal summarily with offenders at the market or fair.

Court of Orphans held by Mayor or deputy to administer estates of minors.

Court of Conservancy held by Mayor or deputy to enforce rules concerning the river.

Court of Admiralty held by Mayor or deputy to deal with matters concerning harbours, fishing or shipping.

Court of Common Council an administrative court consisting of aldermen, councillors and chief officers; members fined for absence, sworn to secrecy and obliged to wear their gowns of office; committees appointed to deal with particular functions; by the seventeenth century had acquired wide powers of administration.

LORD LIEUTENANTS OF COUNTIES*

Cheshire

	1727	Vt Malpas (3rd E of Cholmondeley)
	1771	4th E (1st M) of Cholmondeley

Cornwall

	1740	Hon Richard Edgcumbe (1st Ld)
	1761	Ld Edgcumbe (Vt later E of Mount-Edgcumbe)

Cumberland

	1759	Sir James Lowther (later E of Lonsdale) (until 1802)

Derbyshire

	1756	4th D of Devonshire
	1764	M of Granby

Devonshire

	1751	D of Bedford
	1771	Earl Poulett

Dorset

	1733	4th E of Shaftesbury
	1771	Ld (E) Digby

* In the absence of definitive lists of the Lords Lieutenants this table is not comprehensive. It also uses some sources whose accuracy could not be checked.

Durham

1689	E of Scarborough
1712	Ld Crewe (Bp of Durham)
1715	E of Scarborough
1721	William Talbot (Bp of Durham)
1754	1st E of Darlington
1758	2nd E of Darlington
1792	3rd E of Darlington (D of Cleveland)

Essex

1675	D of Albemarle
1714	E of Suffolk and Bindon
1719	E of Suffolk
n.a.	E of Thomond
1741	Earl Fitzwalter
1756	E of Rochford
1781	Earl Waldegrave

Gloucestershire

1754	Ld Ducie
1761	Ld Chudworth

Herefordshire

1690	E (D) of Shrewsbury
1704	E (D) of Kent
1715	Ld Coningsby
1727	D of Chandos
1741	Charles Hanbury Williams
1747	Vt Bateman
1802	E of Essex

Hertfordshire

1689	E of Shrewsbury (during minority of E of Essex)
1691	E of Essex
1711	E of Salisbury
1714	Earl Cowper
1764	E of Essex

Huntingdonshire

1739	D of Manchester
1762	4th D of Manchester

Kent

1687	Ld Tenham
1692	E of Westmoreland and Vt Sidney (jointly)
1702	E of Nottingham and Winchilsea
1705	1st E of Rockingham
1724	E of Leicester
1737	2nd E of Rockingham
1746	3rd E of Rockingham
1746	1st D of Dorset
1766	2nd D of Dorset

Leicestershire

1721	3rd D of Rutland
1779	4th D of Rutland

Lincolnshire

1742	3rd D of Ancaster and Kesteven
1778	4th D of Ancaster and Kesteven

Middlesex

1714	D of Newcastle
1762	E (D) of Northumberland

Monmouthshire

1715	John Morgan
1720	William Morgan
1728	Sir William Morgan
1732	Thomas Morgan
1771	D of Beaufort

Norfolk

1757	E of Orford
1792	Marquess Townshend

Northamptonshire

1749	E of Halifax
1771	E of Northampton

Northumberland

1753	E (3rd D) of Northumberland
1786	4th D of Northumberland

Nottinghamshire

1763	D of Kingston

Oxfordshire

1760	4th D of Marlborough

Rutland

1751	9th E of Exeter
1779	E of Winchilsea and Nottingham

Shropshire

1761	E of Bath

Somerset

1711	1st Earl Poulett
1744	2nd Earl Poulett
1764	E of Thomond

Staffordshire

1755	Earl Gower (M of Stafford)

Suffolk

1763	Ld (Vt) Maynard

Sussex

1677	E of Dorset
1705	D of Somerset
1754	E of Ashburnham
1757	E of Abergavenny
1759	In commission
1762	E of Egremont

Westmorland

1758	Sir James Lowther (E of Lonsdale) (until 1802)

Worcestershire

    1751   6th E of Coventry (until 1808)

Yorkshire

    1740   E of Holderness
    1751   M of Rockingham

LORD MAYORS OF LONDON, 1688–1760
(*Years ending 9 November*)

1688	Sir John Shorter (d.)	1718	Sir William Lewen
	Sir John Eyles	1719	Sir John Ward
1689	Sir John Chapman	1720	Sir George Thorold
	Sir Thomas Pilkington	1721	Sir John Fryer
1690	Sir Thomas Pilkington	1722	Sir William Stewart
1691	Sir Thomas Pilkington	1723	Sir Gerard Conyers
1692	Sir Thomas Stamp	1724	Sir Peter Delme
1693	Sir John Fleet	1725	Sir George Mertins (or Martyns)
1694	Sir William Ashurst	1726	Sir Francis Forbes
1695	Sir Thomas Lane	1727	Sir John Eyles
1696	Sir John Houblon	1728	Sir Edward Beecher
1697	Sir Edward Clarke	1729	Sir Robert Baylis
1698	Sir Humphrey Edwin	1730	Sir Richard Brocas
1699	Sir Francis Child	1731	Sir Humphrey Parsons
1700	Sir Richard Levett	1732	Sir Francis Child
1701	Sir Thomas Abney	1733	John Barber
1702	Sir William Gore	1734	Sir William Billers
1703	Sir William Dashwood	1735	Sir Edward Bellamy
1704	Sir John Parsons	1736	Sir John Williams
1705	Sir Owen Buckingham	1737	Sir John Thompson
1706	Sir Thomas Rawlinson	1738	Sir John Barnard
1707	Sir Robert Bedingfield	1739	Micajah Perry
1708	Sir William Withers	1740	Sir John Salter
1709	Sir Charles Duncombe	1741	Sir Humphrey Parsons (d.)
1710	Sir Samuel Garrard, bt		Daniel Lambert
1711	Sir Gilbert Heathcote	1742	Sir Robert Godschal (d.)
1712	Sir Robert Beachcroft		George Heathcote
1713	Sir Richard Hoare	1743	Robert Willimot (or Willmot)
1714	Sir Samuel Stanier	1744	Sir Robert Westley
1715	Sir William Humphreys	1745	Sir Henry Marshall
1716	Sir Charles Peers	1746	Sir Richard Hoare
1717	Sir James Bateman	1747	William Benn

1748	Sir Robert Ladbroke	1754	Edward Ironside (d.)
1749	Sir William Calvert		Thomas Rawlinson
1750	Sir Samuel Pennant (d.)	1755	Stephen Theodore Jansen
	John Blachford	1756	Slingsby Bethell
1751	Francis Cockayne	1757	Marshe Dickinson
1752	Thomas Winterbottom (d.)	1758	Sir Charles Asgill
	Robert Alsop	1759	Sir Richard Glyn, bt
1753	Sir Crispe Gascoyne	1760	Sir Thomas Chitty

Roadmaps and Revelations

Roadmaps and Revelations

Finding the Road to Business Succeess on Route 101

Paul R. Niven

WILEY

John Wiley & Sons, Inc.

For general information on our other products and services, or technical support, please contact our Customer Care Department within the United States at 800-762-2974, outside the United States at 317-572-3993 or fax 317-572-4002.

Wiley also publishes its books in a variety of electronic formats. Some content that appears in print may not be available in electronic books.

For more information about Wiley products, visit our Web site at http://www.wiley.com.

Library of Congress Cataloging-in-Publication Data:

Niven, Paul R.
    Roadmaps and revelations : finding the road to business success on Rte 101 / Paul R. Niven.
       p.   cm.
    Includes bibliographical references and index.
    ISBN 978-0-470-18001-3 (cloth)
       1. Success in business.   2. Organizational effectiveness.   3. Strategic planning.   I. Title.
    HF5386.N48   2009
    658.4'09—dc22

                                                                            2008052146

Printed in the United States of America
10 9 8 7 6 5 4 3 2 1

Contents

Introduction

For over a dozen years I have been blissfully immersed in the world of the Balanced Scorecard, helping organizations of all types and sizes effectively implement this powerful tool. The Scorecard system was developed in the early 1990s by Robert Kaplan and David Norton as a tool for executing strategy. In fact, the subtitle of their first book on the subject, *The Balanced Scorecard*, is "Translating Strategy Into Action." The assumption accompanying the Balanced Scorecard is that organizations wishing to use the framework have already developed a strategy and wish to execute it using this proven methodology.

But is it a valid assumption that organizations pursuing the Balanced Scorecard have a strategy currently in place? My experience tells me it is not. One of the first questions I ask when beginning my work with a new client is: "May I see your strategic plan?" This simple and straightforward query has yielded a multitude of responses over the years, from eye rolling that says between the lines, "You've got to be kidding!" to "Well, we really don't have a strategy per se, more like a mission," to the most troubling,

"Strategy? We don't have one, that's why we're developing a Balanced Scorecard." This last response is most troubling because, as I said, the Balanced Scorecard was designed to assist in strategy execution, not formulation.

For those precious few organizations that do possess a strategic plan, the word strategic seems conspicuously absent from the actual product they show me. Quite frequently the plan is more reminiscent of what Peter Drucker once labeled, "A hero sandwich of good intentions," in other words, a wish list of all the organization dreams of accomplishing. The matter of choice, of prioritizing among competing alternatives, which is inherent in the proper crafting of a strategy, is sadly missing from these documents. At the other end of the strategy spectrum is the plan containing vague and generic language, empty platitudes, and popular buzzwords typically associated with poorly constructed mission statements.

Is it possible that the planning *process* followed in boardrooms and conference rooms around the globe is to blame for the sorry end results achieved? Research and experience into this matter suggest that is very likely the case. McKinsey recently reported that just 45 percent of 800 surveyed executives were satisfied with the strategic planning process. And just 23 percent indicated that major strategic decisions were made within its borders. An earlier study on the subject discovered something even more toxic, albeit comical. It seems that some managers so detest the annual planning process, useless being a word that springs from their lips, that they propose folding their business into other strategic business units (SBUs) for planning purposes, so that they might avoid the entire exercise. Perhaps their reluctance to participate may be traced to the fact that, for many organizations, strategic planning has morphed from a penetrating and insightful analytical exercise to a haze-inducing number-crunching extravaganza.

The lack of true strategic plans, and invigorating planning processes led me to write this book. Of course, I'm hardly the first to spill ink over this subject, in fact in its relatively short history, the field has spawned thousands of books, articles, theories, seminars, white papers, blogs, you name it. I owe a tremendous debt to the likes of Michael Porter, Henry Mintzberg, Michael Raynor, W. Chan Kim, Renée Mauborgne, and many more who have studied the field, cataloged their immense knowledge, and shared their findings to our great benefit. The researchers above, and many others, have done a good job presenting strategy from an academic and conceptual angle, but I feel a new and simpler approach is necessary to reach a broad audience eager to learn more about this traditionally vexing and intimidating topic.

Roadmaps and Revelations is the fictional, yet realistic, tale of a man faced with the challenge of developing a strategic plan for his organization. I chose to use a story to impart the lessons contained in the book because stories communicate in a way that other genres simply cannot. You can lose yourself in a story, empathize with the characters, recognize the situations in which they find themselves embroiled, and most important, many of us can remember and learn more effectively from a story. The book concludes with a section summarizing the key principles outlined during the fable and an overview of the process.

I am sometimes asked, "What's hot in business right now? What's on the cutting edge?" If the sheer volume of books, articles, and other media are correct, then the answer is execution. Although it may be ubiquitous at the moment, and rightly so given the economic climate we face, execution is a timeless principle, one that has been, and will always be, pursued relentlessly by outstanding organizations. But to pass through the gates of execution you must first possess something to actually execute. That something is strategy. Without a concise strategy, one that is easy to understand and act upon, you're left rudderless, unable to steer your organization in a meaningful and decisive way, and ultimately at the mercy of whatever fickle winds may be blowing the business world at the time. This book will ensure you know how to develop a simple yet powerful strategy you can use to set your course to success. I wish you the best of luck and encourage you to share your own strategic stories with me.

Taking it Further

I invite you to visit www.roadmapstrategy.com for additional resources, including a series of guided exercises to help you create your own strategy. There you'll find tools and resources that facilitate your journey by working through the Roadmap Strategy process, and allowing you to chart your progress along the way. In addition, there are links to other helpful sites you can visit as you embark on creating and executing your strategy.

Roadmaps and Revelations

1

Emergency Meeting

"**D**id you have a pleasant stay?" The perky front desk clerk of the Arm of Gold Resort and Spa, one of Napa's finest according to the brochure, seemed to demand this information more than inquire. Rory Angus Newman, head down and eyes fixed on the bill in front of him returned an amiable enough, "Yes, it was fine." As he signed a copy he felt a presence bearing down on him. He wheeled apprehensively, and collided with the oncoming dervish that was Brian Rettenauer. "Emergency meeting in the Merlot Room in five minutes," Brian panted as he continued his sprint through the hotel in search of other members of the Kitteridge Company's executive ranks.

Rory shrugged his shoulders, gathered his belongings, and headed straight for the coffee machine. So close to a quick and quiet getaway, he thought. Across the lobby, clicking along at a confident pace, strode Mark Alston, who picked up speed as he spied Rory filling a 16-ounce cup at the French vanilla

1

station. Rory kept his head down but to no avail; Mark was on him in seconds. "This doesn't look good for you Newman," Mark boomed, drawing the attention of a smattering of hotel patrons filling up on their free breakfast buffet. Rory took a sip of his coffee, faced his longtime foe and said flatly, "What was that Mark?"

"I said it doesn't look good for you."

"What doesn't look good?" Rory was slightly irritated now.

Mark took a step closer. His cropped red hair and sharp features glowed in the light from the heat lamp warming this morning's selection of waffles and pancakes.

"The sale, that's what the meeting's about. Old man Kitteridge is finally giving up the goods, selling the kingdom to Olivenhain Enterprises. And you know they aren't going to put up with what passes for planning around here." He paused for effect, like an anchorman delivering the six o'clock news, then added: "I'd polish up that resume if I was you buddy boy."

"It's *were you*. If I *were* you. They didn't teach you that in grad school?"

"Whatever, smart guy. Bottom line is your days are numbered around here."

His job done, Mark smiled like the Grinch who stole Christmas and slinked away. Rory paused, then glanced around the country-kitchen-themed room. At least a dozen people were staring at him now, most likely thrilled at what they'd overheard; a juicy anecdote of corporate shenanigans they could share with their own coworkers. He put a lid on his coffee, grabbed his bags, and followed the signs to the Merlot Room.

2

The Challenge

L ike many a hotel conference venue, the Merlot Room was decked out in bold-patterned but slightly worn carpet, beige walls that had been assaulted by thousands of pushpins and torn pieces of masking tape over the years, and tables arranged in a U shape, each covered by an off-white cloth. The whole space exuded a slightly eerie quality thanks to the overhead cove lighting.

Rory settled into a chair next to his good friend and coworker Melville Bell, whose oversized horn-rimmed glasses and bald head shimmering in the soft light gave him the look of a cute and harmless troll.

"Morning Mel, what's this all about, anyway? And who's that guy beside Carson?" Rory tipped his chin toward the quintessential "suit" seated next to Carson Kitteridge, the company's venerable founder and president. Carson and the suit studied a stack of papers and made occasional notations, seemingly oblivious to the group sitting with rapt attention before them.

Melville looked up from his water glass as if it were a crystal ball and said, "My prognostication is big change around the corner. I mean prodigious."

The rest of the team assembled around the table and Carson rose slowly, then began to speak.

"Good morning everyone, sorry for the short notice on this. I know a lot of you had other business today and were anxious to get back to the office, so I . . ." He stammered slightly and looked down at the suit. "*We* will keep this brief, but of course you'll be hearing a lot more in the days ahead. We've been here at this beautiful resort for the past two days discussing our plans for the upcoming year, and I'm sure you've noticed that I've been absent from a lot of what I understand were excellent discussions. And I'm also certain you're aware of some of the rumors circulating about the company." He paused, as if to compose himself.

"Well, the rumors are true. Last night I agreed to sell the Kitteridge Company to Olivenhain Enterprises." With that revelation looks were exchanged around the table and a number of gasps were heard. "We all want the company to grow and Olivenhain's international presence and proven track record of successful acquisitions convinced me this was the right decision for all of us."

Mark's eyes darted toward Rory and a smile crept across his face. As Carson droned on about the synergies of joining the Olivenhain "family," Rory's attention drifted.

He had joined Kitteridge as an accounting clerk straight out of college 15 years earlier. The company, which manufactured and sold high-end aerobic equipment (treadmills, stair climbers, and elliptical machines) to upscale clubs and hotels, meshed with his love of physical fitness. Rory was all-state in track and field during high school, and to the envy of many had maintained his boyish looks and runner's physique over the years. He jumped at the job offer when it was presented after just one informal interview during which the head of personnel, as it was then known, stated proudly that Kitteridge was the Cadillac of the market. Even back then the metaphor had seemed a bit outdated.

By the time Rory joined the company, Kitteridge was an established name in the industry. From their base of operations in the San Francisco area they supplied equipment across the country. Growth was slow but steady, and it seemed the entire company was run based on the intuition of its charismatic founder, Carson Kitteridge. No fancy spreadsheets or analysis for Carson, thank you very much. He was more comfortable holding a metaphorical finger to the wind, gauging the economic environment, and making decisions based almost entirely on gut instinct.

Rory rose steadily through the ranks and by his 10th year had assumed the title of director of planning, with responsibility for the family-run company's "planning" function, which consisted primarily of compiling the annual budget and monitoring it on an ongoing basis. He was good at his job, liked his coworkers, and felt quite content working for a company that took the idea of work-life balance very seriously. Vacations were generous and encouraged, ongoing education was always a priority, and not a week went by that he wasn't able to squeeze in at least a couple of three-mile runs followed by a soothing shower in the company's state-of-the-art on-site gym. The company had also graciously extended an offer of paid leave once Rory and his wife Hannah completed their adoption of a baby from Russia, a process they had recently begun.

Things began to change at Kitteridge around 2005. Growth slowed and the turbulent business environment, whose influences Kitteridge once appeared immune to, began to take its toll. In an attempt to modernize, Carson hired Mark Alston, the son of a fellow patron he knew from his many evenings spent at the San Francisco opera. Mark possessed the type of pedigree that was foreign to most of Kitteridge's longtime employees. Raised in the Northeast, prep school, then off to an elite and leafy Ivy League campus, and finally an MBA from a prestigious school in the Midwest. Before appearing as the savior of Kitteridge, Mark had spent several years at a boutique consulting firm. He was dripping with the enthusiasm and slightly arrogant savvy his education and experience had provided, which made the denizens of Kitteridge both apprehensive and hopeful as Mark stepped on board their quiet train. He was driven and ambitious and it wasn't long before rumors of his cutthroat past began to fill the halls.

Drawing on his promise of free rein from Carson and from his library of business best sellers, Mark attempted to shake things up at Kitteridge through sophisticated planning and human resource techniques, but Carson, while interested, typically deferred to his homespun methods. He seemed to like the fresh air of modern ideas but relied on his time-tested techniques like a comfortable old sweater when the time for actual decisions arose. Unable to lash out at Carson, Mark directed the bulk of his frustration toward Rory who he viewed as dangerously out of touch and behind the times, despite the fact that they were the same age, and in fact born just two days apart. Their heated exchanges had become the stuff of legend at Kitteridge, where it was not uncommon to hear the fiery debates echoing through the hallways at any time during the day. Mark wanted drastic change and expected the planning department to carry out his recommendations with complete and unquestioned compliance. Rory, on the other hand, felt Mark's methods were downright dangerous and bordering on unethical. The chasm between the two left little room for compromise and over time lines were drawn, and it appeared Mark especially took the division personally, viewing Rory as the ultimate barrier to his success.

"And I would like to thank Rory for his outstanding efforts over these past several years." Melville jabbed Rory in the side as discreetly as possible to break him from his reverie. Rory smiled timidly and Carson continued.

"Of course change, as we all know, is accompanied by both opportunity and challenge. The days ahead, while bright with promise, may prove difficult for some of us as we adjust to the Olivenhain style of management and operations. With me here today is Jim Tobin, executive vice president of operations for Olivenhain Global. Jim, would you like to say a few words?" Jim, whose necktie was so tight you might worry he could develop glaucoma, jumped up and shook Carson's hand then turned to the group.

"On behalf of everyone at Olivenhain Enterprises, I'm thrilled to welcome you to our family of companies. Over the days ahead you'll be learning much, much more about our exciting plans for Kitteridge—and the first thing you should know is that we're retaining the name." He stopped as if awaiting applause for this consolation, but none was forthcoming so he hastily continued with an obviously scripted Olivenhain commercial he'd delivered countless times before. Of course no one around the table was hearing a single word as every brain cell in the room was focused on the question, "What does this mean for me?" Rory would be the first to discover.

As the meeting came to a close and the astonishing news began to settle upon the stunned group, Carson summoned Rory to a corner of the room where he was huddled, in what seemed a menacing fashion to Rory, with Jim Tobin and Mark. As Rory reached the trio Jim's hand extended as if on a spring.

"Jim Tobin. Glad to meet you Rory, we're excited to have you on board with us." Before Rory could say a word the hypersuit continued.

"Carson and Mark have filled me in on the planning function, and we're anxious to give you a significant increase in profile around here by ramping up the process substantially. We purchased Kitteridge based on the reputation of the product and its strong brand image, but we know there's a ton of untapped potential here." He paused again as he had done when addressing the group. Was he expecting validation or a cheer of enthusiasm, Rory wondered.

"Rory, we've got a major opportunity for you." Another pause for applause—did this guy major in drama?

"We need a strategic plan to guide this ship and we're confident you're the man to deliver it. Now let me clarify. We don't expect you to develop the plan. What we need right away is a 'plan to plan' if you catch my drift. We know the company hasn't been big on formal planning in the past." He cast an accusatory peek at Carson before continuing: "Of course, we've got our methods at corporate, but we want something new, something fresh . . . something that works. Did you know the vast majority of strategic plans are never executed?" His eyes penetrated Rory's. Once again, however, before Rory could answer Hurricane Jim was back in action. "It's true, and we believe a big factor is complexity. We want you to lay the groundwork for a simple process. What are the elements of a strategic plan that are robust, will set us up for success in execution, but are relatively simple?"

Jim drew a breath allowing Mark to interject: "I personally recommended you to Jim for this Rory, went out on a limb for you buddy. I'm sure you won't let the team down." Jim and Carson beamed at this announcement while Rory shot a scowl Mark's way. "I'm sure you did Mark," he thought. Jim put his arm around Rory, who shifted slightly at the touch, and then the frenzied suit began anew.

"Okay Rory, down to brass tacks. We need your report on how to develop a winning strategic plan in five days. I know it's fast but that's the way things are going to be from now on, you're going from a Model T to a Ferrari my friend. Can you deliver?"

Six wide eyes peered at Rory; he was surrounded. His head was spinning—so many thoughts: "Yes, I can do it . . . What, of course I can't do it . . . It's a great opportunity . . . What's a strategic plan anyway? . . . Five days, did he say five days? And, I've got the reunion . . ."

Carson then put his hands on Rory's shoulders like a trusted uncle, which he found reassuring. Finally a voice of calm in this suddenly turbulent sea, he thought. Rory leaned in for what were sure to be words of sage counsel and warm encouragement. Carson inhaled and whispered, "Don't embarrass me." As Rory attempted to absorb that blow the ring of his phone pierced the air. He looked down quickly to see a text message from Hannah: "Call me ASAP."

3

Change of Plans

The past 12 months had been challenging for Hannah and Rory. Hannah was particularly close to her parents, as is often the case in small families. Her mother was part of an earlier generation, the now near-extinct stay-at-home mom, who excelled at all things domestic. Need a recipe for leftover potatoes? Call Mom. Red wine on a tablecloth? No problem, Mom has the remedy. Pantry an overstuffed mess? Mom can straighten it up in a jiffy. Accompanying the master's degree in household management was a teeming reservoir of energy that would make an Olympian envious.

Her mother began to slow down a few years ago, and at first the changes were minor and seemingly inconsequential: difficulty maneuvering a key in a lock or dropping a shirt she was ironing. Later, the problems compounded and she began to experience soreness in her limbs and an uncontrollable twitching. Convinced there was something amiss, Hannah and her father insisted on a visit to their doctor. Then began a battery of tests, "to rule things out" the doctor said reassuringly. The process of elimination, however, ultimately led to the devastating diagnosis of ALS, more commonly known in the United States as "Lou Gehrig's Disease." The horrific disease robbed her of virtually everything we take for granted: standing, walking, getting in and out of bed, the mundane things that taken together form the fabric of our lives. Within three years she was gone.

It's an over-used word in the modern times we live in, but her mother truly was Hannah's hero in every way. To lose her at the relatively young age of 61 seemed a criminal offense for which no recourse or worldly explanation could ever suffice.

An already stressful time was burdened further when Rory and Hannah learned their application for the adoption of a child from Russia had finally been approved. The agency found a beautiful healthy baby girl, although at this point Rory and Hannah had only heard descriptions and not seen a single photograph of their future daughter. They were thrilled, naturally, but deeply saddened with the timing, knowing Hannah's mother would never witness the joy of their impending union. She would never know the joy of holding the baby, showering her with love, and spoiling her the way she had warned she would. Additionally, the paperwork and miles of red tape associated with an international adoption, not to mention the cost, added taxing challenges most unwelcome during the present circumstances.

Hannah had always been friendly but never close to her many aunts, uncles, and cousins spread across the country. Her father was a career military man, so a nomadic existence for the tight-knit family unit saw them setting up housekeeping in all points north, south, east, and west. Extended family visits were confined to the major events in life: weddings, milestone anniversaries, births, and sadly, deaths. So it was that her family gathered in San Francisco for her mother's funeral. Amidst the abundant tears those few days were also a wealth of laughs, sharing of old family lore, and promises to stay much closer in the days ahead. Often such promises are vacant, prompted by the emotional purity of the moment, but in this case they held fast. Just two months after the funeral, Hannah's Uncle Frank suggested a family reunion at his place in San Diego, bringing together the entire clan for a "celebration of life" as he put it. Planning began immediately, providing a wonderful diversion for Hannah and her father, and a touchstone event for everyone in the family.

Orchestrating national political conventions cannot be much more difficult than a family reunion. From a brainstormed list of five or six items, the tally of duties soon numbered in the dozens: accommodations for more than 50 people ranging in age from 2 to 82, food acquisition and preparation, transportation—both getting people to San Diego and then shuttling them around one of the country's largest counties, and of course creating a slate of activities pleasing to all ages and tastes. After much deliberation it was decided the reunion would feature a "great outdoors" theme with guided nature hikes in some of San Diego's many backcountry treasures, parasailing at Torrey Pines for the intrepid among them, and even skeet shooting, which, it was determined, would be new to every member of the family. The threat of injury from this last pursuit was a constant source of anxiety for Hannah's Great-Aunt Kathryn. "Someone will lose an eye, you mark my words," she warned.

Hannah had left San Francisco for San Diego several days earlier to help her father and uncle with the bevy of last-minute details. Rory was attending a Kitteridge off-site meeting in the Napa Valley and would make the close to 500-mile journey on his own. He was looking forward to the solitary drive and planned to travel the 101 with its spectacular mix of stunning ocean vistas, golden valleys, and rolling, oak-dotted hills.

Still somewhat stunned by the events of the early morning meeting, Rory dazedly shook the hands of Jim Tobin, Carson, and even the mischievous Mark, then made his way to the resort's tree-lined parking lot. His head was spinning from the strategic planning responsibility so suddenly thrust upon him just moments ago. He reached his car, opened the back door and placed his bags on the seat. He drew a deep breath and pressed the preset key on his phone for Hannah. She picked up on the first ring.

"Where are you? I've been calling all morning." she said.

"Yeah, sorry, they called an emergency meeting."

She interrupted quickly: "Emergency meeting—is everything okay?"

Rory paused; was everything okay? He didn't know at this point.

"Carson sold the company."

"What! To who? Why?"

"Olivenhain Enterprises. They're big, global . . . I guess he finally wanted to cash out."

"What's wrong? You sound funny, what's going on?" Hannah could always tell when something wasn't right with her husband, a skill she had cultivated over years of interpreting cryptic verbal and nonverbal messages from her partner.

"Nothing. Nothing."

Silence.

"Come on Rory, I've got a million things going on down here, don't play ga . . ."

"*You've* got a million things going on?" Rory snapped. "I just found out I've got five days to figure out how to develop a strategic plan for a company that to this point has relied on the whims of the boss. Our so-called strategic plans have been nothing but visions in Carson's head and now I've got less than a week to formalize a real process. And I'm playing games!"

"I'm sorry." She paused for a beat and then continued. "Big companies like to cut people, right? Do you think you're safe? We've got that payment to the adoption agency next week; it's a lot of money. Should we cancel?"

"Don't panic. I'll figure it out. I've got nine hours in the car by myself, that'll give me a head start on where to go with this."

Once again the line was quiet. Finally, Hannah broke the silence.

"Speaking of the drive."

"What about it?"

"I just got a call from a second-cousin named Sydney Wise."

"Who?"

"Syd-ney Wise!" She accentuated each syllable, clearly frustrated now. "I only met him once, when I was about nine. I think he lived in Europe for a while, I'm not sure. Anyway, he leaves me a voice mail at 5 A.M. saying he's coming. I don't know how he even got an invitation, I mean he's pretty far out on the family tree."

Rory dropped his chin on the car roof and exhaled deeply as Hannah continued.

"I called him back and he tells me he was supposed to have a meeting in San Francisco but it was cancelled, but he'd already booked the ticket and the time so he decided to come to the reunion. He's getting into San Francisco at nine-thirty and he asked if there was anyone driving down today."

"You didn't." Rory snapped. "The car is my bubble Hannah, you know that, and today of all days."

"What choice did I have Rory? Let him take a bus and then find out tomorrow night that you drove right past him? It's a fam-i-ly reunion Rory," she said, again with the syllables. Rory groaned to himself. He realized there was no point in debating this, no possible outcome that would have him in that car alone. The die was cast.

"All right. Where and when?"

"He'll be outside at door C1 on the arrivals level at 10 o'clock."

"What does he look like?"

Now it was Hannah's turn to emit a frustrated sigh.

"Well, let's see, I think he was wearing a Fonzie T-shirt, with white shorts, blue and red striped socks, and Adidas Tobacco sneakers . . . when he was nine! How should I know what he looks like?"

The sting of sarcasm was not well received. Rory took the phone from his ear, stared at it, and feigned throwing it into the nearby bushes. He managed to compose himself a moment later, and returned it to his ear.

"Okay, I'll find him. I gotta go then." His eyes darted to the Swatch watch he bought 10 years ago and couldn't bear to part with despite the scratched face. "Call him back and tell him I'll be late; it's already after nine and at least 60 miles to the airport from here."

"Thanks, Sweetie. Love you," Hannah replied as a conciliatory wave washed over the conversation.

"I love you, too. I'll call you later when the eagle has landed." They both managed a fairly anemic chuckle at this and hung up.

Rory fell into the driver's seat of his Capri blue Mercedes C230 and sped out of the sun-soaked parking lot, bound for San Francisco International Airport. He traveled along Silverado Trail through the picturesque village of Napa with its many wine tasting bars and quaint restaurants, then joined the Napa Vallejo Highway, and eventually found himself zipping along Interstate 80 West.

Whether it was a defense mechanism against the tumultuous events of the past hours he couldn't say, but all his mind could settle on was how much he enjoyed being in the car, alone. This car particularly. The C230 was by most estimations a starter Mercedes, but Rory treasured his leased sanctuary and treated it with the reverence typically accorded a Maserati or Aston Martin. Weekly baths with luxurious soaps, applied and caressed with a lamb's wool glove, were lavished on the entry-level vehicle, and nary a speck of dust or debris—either inside or out—was to be tolerated. Rory's father didn't provide many of the customary lessons a father passes on—the birds and the bees for example—but he did implore his son to follow two simple rules of living: Always have polished shoes and a clean car. Rory adhered to both without question.

And so it was in this frame of mind, cherishing the solitude of his one true private and personal space, that Rory found himself when turning on Route 101's exit number 423A toward San Francisco International Airport. Traffic slowed to a crawl as he approached the arrivals level, with its mix of taxis, limos, courtesy vehicles, and families and friends all prepared to rescue the weary travelers at curbside. Rory scanned the periphery slowly and carefully. Soon door C1 came into view and beneath it a shadowy figure emerged.

4

The Red Zone Is for Immediate Loading and Unloading Only

Rory maneuvered the Mercedes into the far right lane, positioning himself inches behind a white Prius, and inches in front of a metallic red Prius—this was San Francisco after all. With C1 directly to his right he pulled the car to the curb, put it in park and stared out the passenger side window at the figure beneath the door. Still nothing but a shadow, but then he followed the dying glow of a cigarette as it fell to the ground and was extinguished under a heavy looking calf-high leather boot. The boot twisted from side to side and then led the entire figure out of the darkness and into the pale light of the sidewalk. This had to be Sydney Wise.

Over the years Rory had met many of Hannah's relatives and found them to be a fairly pedestrian lot. Sure, a few of them had their eccentricities, like Uncle Duke who took to wearing pajama bottoms in public because, as he put it: "The Chinese do it." But most of the family fell comfortably under the label of normal; raised in good homes, off to college, pursuing careers, living their lives. The figure approaching the car, lugging and then abruptly dropping a hockey-gear-sized duffel bag, didn't fit the mental brush Rory had used to paint Hannah's family.

Rory jumped from the car to meet Sydney at the curb but before he could utter any form of greeting his ears were assaulted with a booming "You Rory?" Taken slightly aback Rory offered a tentative nod of the head and extended his hand, which Sydney clutched with great vigor, squeezing it so hard Rory felt it might be crushed with another second at the mercy of the vice-like grip.

"Don't shake hands like a fish," Sydney grumbled.

Rory produced a tentative chuckle and reached for Sydney's enormous bag. "I got it," Sydney said, picking it up as if it were as weightless as a dollop of freshly fallen snow.

Sydney trudged toward the back of the car and Rory, ever the accommodating host, pressed the trunk button on his fob in preparation. A second later, just as Sydney reached for the handle, the trunk flew up catching him square in the chin with an audible thud.

"What the #*%$!"

More muffled expletives and an accusatory glance were directed toward a somewhat rattled Rory, still absorbing the presence before him. Of course it wasn't just Sydney's seemingly crude manner that put Rory slightly off—"Couth of a gladiator" was his initial thought—but his commanding physical presence as well. Sydney's red corkscrew curls, dangling beneath a bright orange bandana, hovered at least six feet five inches above the ground. He wore faded khaki cargo shorts held up with a rhinestone-studded leather belt and stained below the right pocket, which was stuffed with who knows what. Contrasting with the worn shorts was a jet black, freshly pressed, short-sleeved Tommy Bahama shirt of woven silk emblazoned with a scantily clad lady and a pair of tumbling dice.

No words were exchanged as the two proceeded to their respective doors and took their places inside the car. Rory started the engine, looked in the rearview mirror and spotted a sudden parting of the sea of cars approaching from the rear. He hit the accelerator sending the car jerking forward, vaulting Sydney, who had yet to fasten his seat belt, into the dash. Before Rory could apologize for the latest offense, he spotted a Hertz bus bearing down on his left and slammed the brakes. The G force propelled Sydney back into his seat, and sent his long arms flying, the left one smacking Rory across the chest.

"Sorry," Rory offered feebly.

Sydney produced a glare but nothing else. Rory, his heart now ticking faster than a Timex on speed, steadied the ship and followed the exit signs that would lead back to the 101.

Moments later they emerged from under the cavernous tunnels and subterranean lanes of the airport terminal into the bright California sun. Sydney was fidgeting like a caged animal, attempting to fit his leviathan proportions into a seat that had been positioned for Hannah's modest frame. At one point he twisted his torso to reach the recline adjuster at the base of his seat and while doing so swung his left hand across his body, with his fingers coming to rest on the passenger side window. Rory snuck a glance at this display just as Sydney lifted his huge digit from the window, leaving a greasy fingerprint right in the middle of the pristine glass. Rory was aghast. It was all he could do to keep the car steady.

Knowing he had to get his mind off this criminal transgression against his beloved car, Rory decided the time was right for some small talk, and turned to Sydney with the most innocuous query he could imagine.

"So, how was your flight?"

Sydney paused, clearly not about to defer to the typical response of "fine," or "got here safely, that's the main thing." After an awkwardly long period of silence, he rubbed his stubbly chin and began.

"Let me tell you what it's like to fly the friendly skies these days. I get to the security line in Denver and there's this official behind a little table with a bunch of banned stuff on it. You know, water bottles, large shampoo containers, and other grooming products, some food. But he's also got this giant family-sized vat of chocolate syrup. So I'm wondering, how desperate a chocoholic do you have to be to carry a jug of chocolate syrup with you wherever you go? Is the plan to drizzle it over the delicacies they give you on the plane these days? Ummm, chocolate-covered stale mini pretzels. So when I get to the guy and he starts droning on with the speech I stop him and say, 'Fortunately for all of us I left my chocolate syrup at home today.'"

"Okay, semi-bizarre," Rory thought, but hey, everybody has airport stories, and he could empathize, as could anyone who has been in an airport the last seven years. Rory decided this was a good opportunity for some early road trip bonding and drew a breath in anticipation of regaling Sydney with a few travel tales of his own. Before he could get the first word out, however, Sydney launched in with renewed vehemence.

"So then I get on the plane. It's full, of course, but I end up getting the whole last row to myself. I'm just getting comfortable, thinking about a little snooze when I hear the flight attendants, who are sitting right behind me in the galley. I guess there was one deadheading the flight, not working but sitting back there. Apparently, she had never met the other two before, a guy and a woman but they seemed to hit it off pretty well, especially the deadheader and the guy. A little chitchat between them and then *boom!* They start bashing the corporate hierarchy. One of them says, 'The corporate office has boneheads in it,' which got a ringing endorsement from the other. Then the guy says, 'My boss is the worst, she can't manage for shit.' The lambasting was interrupted because the two working the flight had to do the safety announcement. They get back a minute later and the deadhead says, 'That's the way to do it, short and sweet. Ours is long and boring.' And I'm thinking, they wonder why people don't like airlines. Even the employees hate them."

With that Sydney paused once more, and Rory wondered if now was the time to interject, but again, after a short break, Sydney continued.

"It's clear to me there was no alignment in that operation. Those 'corporate boneheads' as they put it, need to develop a simple strategy and communicate it to each and every employee, so they don't get this kind of attitude from their people. With a concise strategy, they can all get behind a few simple ideas and be on the same page."

Rory swiveled his head toward Sydney, causing the car to veer into the next lane and forcing the driver of a FedEx truck to blare his horn in protest. Did his ears deceive him? This guy, who looks like Rambo on a Vegas vacation, goes from spitting vitriol to sounding like a business guru? And did he say "strategy"?

5

Who Is this Guy?

With San Jose now in their sights, the two continued in the noiseless bubble of the Mercedes. Rory felt tempted to ask Sydney more about his reference to strategy, but after silently assessing the gruff giant next to him he concluded the only strategy Sydney Wise was capable of concocting would be how to win a knife fight that broke out at a no-limit Texas Hold 'em game.

The 101 momentarily narrowed to two lanes in each direction causing traffic to thicken and leaving Rory stuck behind a slow moving Buick Lacrosse. He checked his blind spot to go around the Buick but as he pressed the left arrow signal the Buick beat him to the punch and slid gently into the outside lane in front of him. Rory followed, expecting to be around the dark brown sedan in a matter of seconds, when he noticed "it" in the back window. A Kleenex box adorned with a hand-crafted crochet cover: the telltale signature of a driver north of 65 and never good news if you're in a hurry.

"Great, a TP," Rory muttered under his breath.

"What's that?" Sydney, who at this point had tolerated only a handful of words from Rory, at last seemed somewhat aware of his chauffeur's existence. "What's toilet paper got to do with anything?"

"Not toilet paper, tentative passer, TP," Rory returned. "You know, someone who gets out in the fast lane and just hovers there like they're being pulled by a slow magnetic force. TP."

For whatever reason Sydney found this description humorous and let out a hearty chuckle that took Rory somewhat off guard but pleased him nonetheless. The laugh seemed to take a bit of the rough edge off Sydney as well.

"So you're Hannah's husband, right?"

"That's right, Rory Newman."

"Don't you mean Rory Angus Newman?" Sydney countered.

"How'd you know that?" Rory asked.

"Saw it on the reunion web site."

Rory squinted, "There's a web site for the reunion?"

"How'd you get a name like that anyway? You don't look Scottish to me."

"My mother is Scottish actually, a MacIntosh. I've got six brothers and sisters and every one of them have pretty mainstream names—Will, Dan, Pete, Betsy, Jake, and the slightly exotic Mary Margaret. By the time they got to me, I'm the youngest, my mother had to pay tribute to the heritage I guess. In high school everybody called me RAN, when the Flock of Seagulls had 'I Ran' on the radio."

"So what do you do when you're not rally drivin' at the airport, RAN?" Sydney asked.

"I'm director of planning at Kitteridge, we make—"

"Fitness equipment," Sydney interrupted.

"Right."

"And what specifically do you do as the director of planning?"

Rory drew a deep breath and was about to answer when his phone rang through the car's audio system. The display identified the caller as Mark Alston. Rory sighed, then slapped the phone button on his steering wheel.

"Hi Mark, what can I do for you?"

"Hello Newman." Mark's voice crackled over the speaker. He was trying to imitate Jerry Seinfeld's famous greeting whenever he encountered Kramer's buddy, and his nemesis in the show, Newman, but with his nasal voice and strange East Coast accent, it sounded more like a pathetic attempt at impersonating John Cleese.

"What is it Mark?"

"Just a little reminder my friend, 4 days, 21 hours, and 35 minutes. I personally, can't wait to see your report. What a bright future you have at Olivenhain," Mark cackled sarcastically.

"Is that all, Mark?"

"That's it."

"Good-bye." Rory pounded the phone's END button as if squishing an unwelcome insect on the dinner table.

"What was that?" Sydney inquired.

With office towers gleaming on either side as they rolled through San Jose, Rory explained his situation to Sydney: his history at Kitteridge, their historical lack of formal planning, the hiring of Mark to turn things around, and the sudden sale announced just this morning.

The tale was interrupted at this point by an odd sight at the side of the road. Outside a classic Volkswagen Vanagan, a young man was on his knees with hands extended to a waif-like girl in a white cotton dress. Both Rory and Sydney wondered whether he was asking for her hand in marriage or begging forgiveness. An odd place for either endeavor they thought.

As the Vanagan receded into the rearview mirror, Rory reached the climax of his Kitteridge life story by outlining the challenge that had been awarded him of creating a "plan to plan" in the next five days.

Sydney contemplated things for a moment and declared, "Why doesn't that Mark character do it? He's supposed to shake things up, right?"

"You want to know why Mark doesn't do it?" Rory asked. "Everyone thinks Mark is this big hotshot, Ivy League magician going to save our bacon right? But you know why he didn't last in consulting?" Rory turned to Sydney expecting the obligatory reply but none was forthcoming so he continued.

"He didn't have the chops," Rory paused, wondering where this line, better suited to a 1950s film noir, had come from. Sydney raised his eyebrows a touch, adding to Rory's slight embarrassment at his verbal flourish.

"When push came to shove I heard he let all his clients down, never achieved any real results. A big talker, that's all. And there's more." With this last line he had transitioned from a noir actor to an infomercial host.

"Big-time ethical issues. My buddy at work, Mel, told me he had it on good account that Mark would do anything to win a contract. One time they were putting together a team for a job and the client insisted on this one guy they thought was really talented. Turns out the poor guy had died a couple of weeks earlier. You think that stopped Mark? He went ahead and sent the client a letter assuring him this guy would lead the team. Can you believe that?"

Sydney absorbed this revelation quietly, much to the chagrin of Rory who was hoping for a more enthusiastic and sympathetic response. As Rory was about to politely inquire whether or not his story reached the other side of the car, the shrill sounds of "My Sharona" filled the air. The 1979 debut single by The Knack served as Sydney's ringtone and he seemed to delight in the tinny rendition, letting it play to the equivalent of at least four rings before answering.

"Wise . . . umm . . . hmmm . . . yeah . . ."

Rory never felt comfortable in the presence of someone on his mobile phone, especially in the car. What if it was a personal conversation? It's not like he could leave the room. Should he pull over? Fortunately, in this case, Sydney appeared completely oblivious to Rory's presence as he mulled over the words of the caller at the other end of the line before speaking again.

"Yeah, but if China does revalue the yuan, and if it rises in value—which it probably will—Japanese products will instantly become cheaper vis a vis their Chinese counterparts. And if that happens, the increased competitiveness will expand Japanese exports and benefit the yen against the euro and the dollar. I say we stay put for now."

With nary a good-bye, see you later, or take care, Sydney ended the call and tossed the phone in the car's cup holder.

If the road stretching out in front of them suddenly turned from asphalt to Jell-O, Rory couldn't have been more surprised. "Who is this guy?" he wondered. The curiosity was too much to bear. Adopting the most casual tone he could muster, he asked, "So, what do you do Sydney?" Without missing a beat Sydney replied: "As little as possible, amigo." "Great," Rory thought, "That's very helpful."

As Rory dreamt up ways to reframe his question, the gas light on his display interrupted his reverie. The "reserve fuel" message flashed for about five seconds then receded into a small icon in the left corner of the display. The light served as a terrific annoyance to Rory. He hated interrupting the rhythm of a road trip to pump gas and made it a habit to always gas up the night before embarking. But last night there had been a Kitteridge dinner and before he knew it, the sweet Napa claret flowing freely around the table rendered driving, even to the corner for gas, out of the question.

Of course, there wasn't much rhythm in this trip, and maybe a pit stop was just what the doctor ordered to jolt things into some kind of harmony. Yes, a break was exactly what they needed. His inner dialogue, rich with contentment over this decision, was interrupted by Sydney's gravelly baritone.

"I guess you could call me a serial entrepreneur."

"Huh?" Rory replied, returning to the car's orbit.

"Over the last 20 years, I've started, built up, then sold at least a half dozen companies across this great land of ours—God bless it." This last portion was intoned with the reverence of a fervent patriot.

Rory felt conflicted. He was anxious to dig deeper into the treasure that Sydney had just laid out in front of him, but the red glow of the gas light was causing mild palpitations that had to be exorcised immediately. About 500 feet ahead was the Monterey Street exit for the town of Gilroy. Rory steered the Benz to the right lane and hit the exit at a smooth 65 miles per hour.

"Garlic capital of the world," Sydney noted as he took in the surroundings.

Rory spotted a gas station just north of the exit and steered the car into the entrance a few seconds later. He pulled up to a vacant row of pumps and slid the gear shift into park. Sydney quickly extricated himself from his seat belt and said, "I gotta hit the head." He unfolded himself from the seat and headed for the station while Rory proceeded to the pump.

As Sydney disappeared through the decal-covered door, Rory reached into his pocket and pulled out his phone. He pecked at the keys with the speed and dexterity of a texting-crazed teenager reaching out to her BFF and waited for the results. Within three seconds he had his response, and once again it shocked him. "Sydney Wise: Colorado Entrepreneur of the Year" screamed the hyperlinked text on his tiny browser window. Below that another eye-opener: "Wise sells stake in Pastiche Holdings for $25 million." Sydney's life story was rolling out before Rory's eyes and it was spellbinding: his rise from humble beginnings, his untold entrepreneurial successes, his management prowess, and his recent philanthropic pursuits, which he preferred remain under the radar.

Rory was swirling in a tidal wave of confusion. This guy, this Rambo in a silk shirt, was a business guru, a genius. "How could all this have stayed a secret? Why didn't Hannah know about him?" Still marveling at his discovery, he put the phone on the roof of the car and pulled the lever, which began the flow of overpriced supreme gasoline.

As Rory pumped, a mid-1980s red Camaro pulled up to the station's air machine. Out vamped what many would consider an appropriate occupant for such a conveyance, a woman of early 40s vintage in painted-on jeans, high heels, and a black tank top. Filling the tire wasn't a rote chore for her, it resembled something more akin to performance art. Rory, still smiling from what his sleuthing had uncovered, had barely noticed her but did catch her gaze for the briefest of moments. This casual contact between the two strangers caused the passenger door of the Camaro to fly open. A blur in black leather made a beeline for Rory. He was thin and wiry and a ball of fury as he opened his frothy mouth to speak.

"Wha choo starin' at, son?" he demanded. Rory was frightened, but interestingly his first thought was, "These two are not from California."

"Nothing . . . I wasn't staring at anything," he replied.

"You best not be lookin' at my lady," Mister Leather spat, as he took a menacing stride toward Rory.

Rory took an instinctive step back, which produced the unintended effect of dislodging the handle from his tank, sending a torrent of gas at his feet, and streaming under the car toward Mister Leather, who screamed: "You tryin' to light me on fire, fool?"

"No . . . no . . ." Rory juggled the slippery gasoline handle but managed to get it back in place at the pump ending the pungent flood. Then the potential gravity of the situation hit him with all the wallop of a punch in the face, a punch he felt he was likely to be on the business end of in a second or two.

Just then, Sydney emerged from the station, polishing off the last bite of a Twinkie. Without uttering a word he took a circuitous route around the brewing altercation; his square cut head turning slowly as he surveyed the landscape, his gaze finally settling on the front of the old Camaro.

Mister Leather was oblivious to Sydney's presence and began a slow stealthy, cat-like crawl toward Rory. He spread his bony fingers then formed them into fists so tight the backs of his palms turned white. "You gonna' get it now fool," he hissed as his step quickened through the puddled gasoline. He cocked his small hard fist, drawing his arm back like a bow and was about to unleash his fury when Sydney grabbed his shoulder, stopping him cold.

"Just curious, what else have you got in the car besides that . . . lady?" Sydney asked with a degree of calm considerably out of whack for the volatile situation.

"Get your hand off me ya stupid ape!" Mister Leather writhed under Sydney's powerful grip. "It's none a your concern what I got in my car."

With a single hand and in a motion so fluid it was worthy of a ballroom champion, Sydney spun Mister Leather in a pirouette that ended with him facing the front of the Camaro.

"I'm sure the local police would be interested in that," Sydney pointed to the car's license plate. It was old and bent and encased in mud, but if you looked hard enough you could see the car's registration was two years out of date.

Mister Leather squirmed and snapped free of Sydney but then stood fixed as a statue. Finally he looked slowly at the car, then at Sydney and Rory, and once again at the car. He stepped backward, awkwardly and slightly off balance until he reached the car. He motioned for his companion to get in, which she did and they sped off, sending a cloud of dust spiraling from the ground.

His composure slowly returning, Rory turned to Sydney and said, "What was that all about?"

"What do you mean?" Sydney returned.

"I mean that I was sure that guy was real trouble, and I was equally certain one of the three of us was going to end up in a heap on the ground, covered in four-dollar-a-gallon gas." Sydney moved closer, the sun perched directly over his right shoulder, causing Rory to squint. With the solemnity of someone under oath he said, "If you're observant, you can *think* your way out of anything, Newman."

With Rory quietly observing his every step, Sydney walked casually to the other side of the car. As he opened his door he noticed Rory's phone sitting on the roof. Using his ample wingspan he grabbed the device, which was still on. Looking down he eyed the text: "Sydney Wise: Colorado Entrepreneur of the Year." He tossed it at Rory who had assumed his position behind the wheel, and was busy massaging hand sanitizer into his fingers.

"Here, you forgot this."

Rory looked at the browser window, and then stared at Sydney. Finally, he said, "Can you help me?"

Sydney adjusted his flaming orange bandanna, straightened the collar of his shirt, but never broke his forward gaze when he said, "It looks like you need all the help you can get."

They shared a laugh as the car lunged forward, sending a final wave of gasoline spraying across the spot where the old Camaro had sat just moments before.

6

What Is Strategy, Anyway?

Rory's adrenaline reserves were as full as the gas tank as the two made their way back to the 101 and continued south. "What an adventure." The notion rushed through his head with the fury of a roller coaster. He already had an anecdote for life, and they'd only been in the car for a little over an hour. He stole a glance Sydney's way, and thought to himself, "Not a bad guy, after all." Just when the full effects of the warm fuzzies were descending on him, Sydney ripped the Velcro fastener on the left pocket of his shorts and fished out a king-sized pack of Marlboros. "Mind if I smoke?" he asked, but it looked as though he'd assumed a positive response because the cigarette was dangling from his mouth before Rory could open his.

The air in an operating room couldn't be purer than that in Rory's car. He wouldn't even let the family's beloved Golden Retriever, Jock, ride along, for fear his malodorous dog breath would pollute the pristine environment. Fast food? Don't even think about it. The thought of toxic cigarette smoke, the vilest offender he could imagine, started a chain reaction in his mind that eventually manifested itself in his face, which was now contorted like a slinky. Sydney caught the bizarre sight from the corner of his eye, harrumphed slightly and stuffed the cigarette back in its package.

"I take it you're not a smoker?" he asked.

"No, never. Well, there was that one time when I was 12, my friends and I stole a pack from my mother's purse. . . ."

Sensing a long story, Sydney decided to redirect.

"So, let's talk about this challenge you've got."

Rory, perfectly content to embrace the change of subject, said: "Okay. Simply put, I've got five days to tell my company how we go about developing a strategic plan."

"Strategic plan." Sydney rubbed the coarse whiskers on his chin and repeated the phrase.

"Yup, strategic plan."

"So tell me," Sydney glared at Rory, "Just exactly what is strategy?"

Rory's mouth opened immediately but to his surprise nothing came out. His lips quivered again, as if trying to shake loose some invisible tape prohibiting any words from escaping, but still nothing. How could this word, one he'd been accustomed to hearing since his college days, a word uttered practically non-stop by business gurus, and used frequently at Kitteridge, not elicit an immediate definition?

Finally, he said: "Well, I guess strategy is a set of tactics to support the budget."

"So the budget comes first?" Sydney inquired.

Rory thought about this. Most of his career had been spent compiling budgets, tracking budgets, and analyzing budget trends. Over the years the terms budget and strategy had become inseparable. Before he could compose a reply, Sydney broke the silence that had descended over the car.

"Let's get another opinion. Call someone at your company right now, could be anyone from the janitor to the CEO, I don't care, and ask them what strategy is."

"What?" Rory mumbled.

"You heard me," Sydney returned.

"Well, I only have a few people on speed dial, it's not a representative sample of the company or anything."

"Just do it," Sydney snapped.

Rory pressed the phone icon on the car's display, then the phone book symbol and scrolled through until he found Melville Bell. He tapped the call button. It took three rings to produce a response.

"Bell here," Melville sputtered as if his mouth were completely full.

"Mel, it's Rory, did I catch you at a bad time?"

"Rory, no. I was just finishing my kefir. Did I tell you the line descends from Mohammed?"

"It's a cultured milk drink," Rory whispered to Sydney whose eyebrows were now interrupting his forehead. "He's hooked on it."

"Mel, how would you define the word strategy?" Rory asked.

Melville Bell was not one to offer snap answers. Although his title at Kitteridge reflected operations management, he was widely regarded as the company intellectual, comfortable opining on any topic from shareholder value to Voltaire. After a considerable silence, he answered.

"Strategy is a sophisticated and systematic plan of action."

Rory turned his head to Sydney, seeking his approval. Was this the answer he was looking for? Sydney simply stared out the window as the car whizzed by a sign announcing the San Juan Batista Mission, established in 1797.

"Rory, are you still there?" Melville asked.

"Yeah, Mel." He looked at Sydney again. Still no response. "That was it, I'll talk to you later." Before Melville could reciprocate the good-bye, Rory ended the call.

"Well?" Rory asked.

"Call someone else."

Rory sighed but tapped the display once again. This time he landed on his chief accountant, Kimberley Patel. He cast a suspicious look Sydney's way while pressing the call button.

"This is Kimberley."

"Kim, it's Rory. Just a quick question, how would you define strategy?"

"Huh?"

"Strategy."

"What's this about Rory?" Kim appeared less enthusiastic about participating in the impromptu survey than Melville had.

"Strategy Kim, how would you define it?"

"Did you get that variance report I e-mailed last night?" Kim asked.

"Yes, and—" Before Rory could say another word he felt Sydney's glare like a laser piercing the space between them. "Strategy Kim," he commanded through the speaker.

"Well, if you must know, I'd say strategy equals goals. Happy now?"

"Ecstatic. Thanks Kim, talk to you later." As with Melville, Kim was quickly dispatched.

Before Rory could turn to Sydney, eager to glean his opinion on the short interrogations, it hit him. "We all said different things." He was still considering the ramifications of this, when Sydney said: "Did you notice that sign back there for the mission?"

"San Juan Batista? Yeah, I saw it."

"It's been around for a long time, since 1797," Sydney mused. "Some things stand the test of time. Reminds me of a quote from Karl von Clausewitz some years later."

The wheels in Rory's brain were spinning frantically, with every brain cell directed at determining who in the world Karl von Clausewitz is, or was. An entertainer? Sports star? Politician? Business pundit? Instead of conceding to a pure guess, Rory opted to nod his head knowingly.

"As you know," Sydney emphasized, "von Clausewitz was a German general who said back in 1832 that the first task of any theory is to clarify terms and concepts that are confused. Only after agreement has been reached regarding terms and concepts can we hope to consider the issues easily and clearly and expect others to share the same viewpoint." Sydney paused, allowing the full weight of von Clausewitz's words to register with Rory, then continued. "Did you notice anything about the three definitions of strategy you and your colleagues came up with?"

Rory nodded in the affirmative. "Yeah, they were all different."

"Which means?" Sydney asked.

"Which means it's going to be next to impossible to develop a plan when we're all not even speaking the same language."

"Exactly." Sydney was staring intently at Rory now. "The first thing you have to do *before* developing a strategic plan is come to agreement on what strategy is, and just as important, what it isn't." He shifted his glance back to the arrow straight road spread out in front of them, then continued.

"I gave a speech in Moscow once, and they used simultaneous translation, you know, like they do at the UN. I was going along gangbusters with my talk on entrepreneurship; I saw lots of heads nodding, laughs in all the right places. Everything was peachy. Then all of a sudden, I look out and see a wall of blank faces. I didn't know it but the transmission to their earphones had been stopped and they couldn't hear the translation, just me blabbering on in English. We literally weren't speaking the same language, and the communication hit a brick wall.

It's the same in business. Everyone has to be on the same page with what you mean by common terms like strategy and mission. Then, and only then do you have a chance to execute."

"So what is strategy then?" Rory asked.

Sydney didn't hesitate. "I define strategy as the broad priorities adopted by an organization in recognition of its operating environment and in pursuit of its mission."

While Rory was still absorbing this, attempting desperately to commit it to memory, Sydney continued.

"But getting to those priorities ain't easy. It means a lot of soul searching and answering some fundamental questions about your business. That's the process part of the equation. And maybe if we have time," he squinted at the speedometer, which registered a swift 79 miles per hour, "I can tell you a bit about that."

Rory's foot tended to get a bit heavy when he was absorbed in thought. Given all he had to learn before they hit San Diego the next day, he wondered if a collection of speeding tickets wasn't in his immediate future.

7

Ask a Silly Question

The two continued south with the Diablo Range shining brightly on their left. The sun-soaked rolling hills, dotted with chaparral and California oaks, momentarily distracted Rory. "Such simple yet captivating beauty," he thought.

He reflected upon the scene and began to draw a parallel with strategic planning. "Maybe strategic planning is simple, too. Maybe I'm just overcomplicating it," he thought. Then he challenged himself to describe in his head the scene stretching out before them, rationalizing that if he could do that, then perhaps he'd be able to create a simple description of the planning process as well. He dwelt on the subject at considerable length, sucking his lip to Sydney's dismay, and tapping his fingers relentlessly on the steering wheel. At long last the best he could conjure up was that the scene reminded him of the background picture you see on the boot up screen of Windows. "Pathetic," he thought, realizing that if this little experiment was any kind of harbinger, he had his work cut out for him.

Desperate to change the song repeating in his head: "This is going to be impossible . . . This is going to be impossible," he blurted out to Sydney, "You know, we do have a planning process." Sydney cast an incredulous look and replied, "Why don't you tell me about it."

"Well." Rory began. "We get together at least once a year, if we can align everyone's calendar that is, usually go to a nice resort for a few days, and we talk about things."

"Things?" Sydney countered.

"Yes, things," Rory shot back as if perturbed that he must defend such an obvious statement. "You know, the market, customers, the economy, what happened last year, all of that."

"And what do you do with this information?" Sydney inquired.

Rory jerked forward as if to begin his response with a grand gesture, but stopped suddenly and slumped back in his seat. After a few moments he said, "We create budgets and goals."

"How many?" Sydney snapped turning toward Rory.

"How many what?"

"Goals. How many goals do you create?" Sydney's voice rifled through the car.

"Oh, lots!" Rory offered confidently.

"I thought so." Sydney puffed as he crossed his massive arms. He inhaled a massive breath and went on. "You know what Kissinger said about planning at most organizations?"

Rory's mood brightened immediately at the mention of a name he at least recognized, although he was still somewhat confused by the reference to the former statesman. Before he could reply, Sydney continued.

"Kissinger said that what passes for planning is frequently the projection of the familiar into the future. In other words, you look back at what you already know and you hope that information will serve you well in the future. Then, you brainstorm a bunch of goals, or what Peter Drucker, who is really the father of management thinking, calls a hero sandwich of good intentions. We'll do this, and we'll do that, and we'll do this, all the while ignoring what's actually going on around you."

Pleased with this monologue, Sydney sat back and glanced at Rory who continued to stare straight ahead, trying desperately to keep up with the running spiel. He was a good two beats behind and just now getting to the Drucker reference. Once he was back in real time he felt a defense of his company's tactics was in order.

"These meetings are hard work you know. We don't just sit around drinking coffee and eating cookies."

"It's gettin' a little warm in here," Sydney said.

Rory wasn't sure if his passenger's opinion was metaphorical or literal and eventually settled on it being a bit of both. He reached for the air-conditioning button and tapped it lightly, sending a cool breeze wafting though the car.

"Better?"

"Thanks. Listen, I didn't mean to say you don't work up a little intellectual sweat at your meetings, but strategic planning is tough, and people know it's tough. You're basically trying to look into an unknowable future, choose from a dense forest of possibilities, and craft a winning response to what you see in your crystal ball. That's tough stuff, and it's probably the reason why so many companies don't do it correctly."

"But experts can get a glimpse of what to expect in the future, can't they?" Rory asked while gesturing toward the sky outside the windshield.

An audible "hmpphh" made its way to Rory's ears as Sydney began. "Back in 1984, *The Economist* conducted an interesting study. They asked four finance ministers, four chairmen of multinational companies, four Oxford economics students, and four London garbage collectors to generate 10-year forecasts on a number of key economic variables. Ten years later they had their results."

Another dramatic pause from Sydney. Rory took the bait: "And?"

"And the chairmen managed to tie the garbage collectors, and the finance ministers finished in the cellar. But to make matters worse, the average prediction was more than 60 percent too high or too low."

"So why bother even trying to build a strategic plan then?" Rory's voice rose in obvious consternation. Not only was this task thrust upon him with no warning, but according to Rambo here it was next to impossible.

"Don't get your knickers in a knot. I never said you shouldn't try," Sydney barked. "You just need to do it right." The two exchanged a look, and Sydney went on. "Back at the gas station, I noticed you doused yourself with that hand sanitizer stuff instead of hittin' the head and washing your hands."

"Yeah, well that was easier, and I didn't want to waste time."

"Exactly my point. Most organizations put on hand sanitizer instead of washing their hands."

Rory rolled his eyes at this one, wondering what it meant and almost hoping some arcane historical references might be paraded out again instead of the homespun wisdom.

"Don't get it?" Sydney growled. "It was easier to put on the hand sanitizer than take the time and energy to wash your hands. But are your hands clean now, really clean?"

"Well, according to the bottle," Rory reached for the small plastic container beneath his seat and squinted at the tiny print, causing the car to veer into the left lane for a moment, "this kills most of the germs."

"Yeah, well I can still smell the gas over here. It's a short-term fix, Newman. To really get the gas off, you should have gone to the can and washed your hands, cleaning them completely."

"So what's this got to do with companies?" Rory decided to concede and move on.

"Like your company, most management teams get together, talk about what they already know, and make projections into the future based on that. They put on the hand sanitizer, rather than asking the fundamental questions that will lead to real breakthroughs."

"So they don't work hard enough to find the answers, is what you're saying?"

"It's not the answers, it's the *questions*. They don't ask the right questions," Sydney bellowed. "Instead of asking the critical few questions that can really help them, a lot of companies chase every piece of data and end up turning strategic planning into a fill in the boxes kind of exercise that results in plans that sometimes run over a hundred pages, chock-full of graphs, boxes, charts, arrows, and crazy diagrams. And you know what? They do nothing but give me MEGO."

"MEGO?"

"My eyes glaze over—MEGO."

Rory chuckled a bit at this but it was no laughing matter to Sydney.

"I'm not kidding, you could go blind trying to get through these things. In a lot of ways they're worse than the hand sanitizer versions of strategic plans that don't offer anything new. They're so full of analysis that they paralyze people and prevent them from taking any action, and that's deadly." Sydney punctuated this last point by using one of his cigar-shaped fingers to pull an imaginary trigger.

"Balance Newman, balance. The process doesn't have to be overly simplistic or ridiculously complex to be effective. Ask the right questions, which are always the most basic and fundamental, and you'll get an effective strategic plan."

Before Rory could ask about these mysterious questions, pangs of hunger announced themselves in his stomach. He

peeked at his watch—12:45 P.M. Rory had always been somewhat rigid in his eating habits: breakfast at seven, lunch at noon,
and dinner at seven. He liked the symmetry of the sevens, and
hated to miss a meal at the appointed hour.

"Are you hungry?" he asked. Sydney shrugged, and that
was enough for Rory. The Walnut Avenue exit for Greenfield
lay a mile and a quarter ahead and he steered the car toward
it. As they cruised the off ramp Sydney gazed at the distant
fields and said, "Salad bowl of the world. It's a two billion dollar
industry here." Rory just shook his head.

Operating literally on gut instinct, Rory turned right on
Walnut Avenue, oozed along the blacktop at about 15 miles an
hour, then took a left on El Camino Real. Two lights later and
it was a right on Apple Avenue. Ahead in the distance he saw it
radiating in the afternoon heat: El Mariachi.

8

What You See Is Not Always What You Get

The El Mariachi Restaurant, established in 1941 according to the hand-painted sign in the window, greeted Rory and Sydney with a full-on assault of the senses. Before they had opened the door the sounds of Ricky Martin's "Tu Recuerdo" reached them on the sidewalk. The soothing melody carried them like a wave through the restaurant's well-worn front door and suddenly the sounds were overtaken by the aromas: spicy salsa, sizzling carne asada, golden toasted tortilla chips, and the unmistakable vapor of tequila floating like a pillowy cloud over the entire mix.

Attempting to acclimatize to the dark and cavernous space before them, Rory and Sydney quickly removed their sunglasses. Rory squinted as he absorbed the surroundings: walls covered with musical instruments of all varieties and vintages, a diversity of crowded tables and booths all of which overflowed with an abundance of food and drinks. The floor was done in a checkerboard pattern of terracotta Saltillo tiles, and Rory was convinced he detected paw prints molded in several of them. In the center of the room sat an enormous three-tiered fountain that sent water splashing around its vast perimeter, providing a light shower to those seated at the surrounding tables.

This was clearly the place to be in Greenfield at lunchtime. After checking in with the hostess, whose efficient demeanor conveyed that she had things under complete control, Rory and Sydney stood wedged among a mélange of migrant farm workers, businesspeople, and young families all waiting patiently for a table.

As Sydney studied a menu, Rory noticed a tall man clad in a crisp white shirt and pants of a Darth Vader black. His good looks were well matched by the eye-catching blonde woman and two very cute kids—a boy about 10 and a girl in the vicinity of 6—standing next to him. They made an attractive package and could easily have been a TV commercial family. As the wait continued for all packed around the hostess station, the white-shirted man struck up a conversation with another man nearby. This gentleman with an enviable head of grey hair, wore a blue blazer with the top button clasped, and stood perfectly erect. Sticking to the TV metaphor, Rory thought he could pass for a soap opera actor with a name like Conrad Halliburton or Dylan Faust.

The whole scene was comforting to Rory for some reason and he quickly conjured a possible explanation: here were two men, probably professional acquaintances, taking time out of their busy days to share a meal with their families. Good old family values alive and well, he thought. A moment later the distinguished gentleman and his companion were summoned to their table. The first man waved a pleasant good-bye and no sooner had his hand descended than his son asked: "Do you know him, Dad?"

"Yeah, he works at the hospital," the father replied nonchalantly.

"What's he like?" inquired the son.

Without hesitation the father replied: "He's an ass."

A stunned expression washed over the boy's face and he replied, "Why?"

"I don't know, ask the man upstairs. He's an ass."

The little boy appeared totally perplexed at this point, as did Rory, whose image of the family patriarch was quickly shattered before his eyes. "Why would anyone say something like that to his young son?" The question rolled on a continuous loop through his head, until finally and mercifully, the hostess called him and Sydney to a table that sat immediately left of the enormous fountain.

"You give out raincoats with these tables?" Sydney offered playfully to the hostess. She simply smiled and spun away. There was little doubt she'd heard that line many times over the years.

With military precision a busboy appeared out of nowhere with ice-cold glasses of water, followed by a waitress who supplied a speedy hello while simultaneously sliding menus and producing a basket of warm and crispy tortilla chips. Before the wicker container had settled on the table Sydney's colossal hand met Rory's slender cake-white version in the middle of the chips and to their mutual delight, each came away with a bounty of golden delights. They munched in contented silence for a few moments, but then Rory glanced to his right and eyed the ass comment man and his family. Attempting desperately to get the sour scene out of his head he shifted back to the matter at hand: crafting a strategic plan.

"So what are these magical questions we need to ask to build a strategic plan?" he blurted out between mouthfuls of chips.

Sydney slammed his water glass down and barked: "Questions are for closers."

"What are you talking about?"

"Didn't you see *Glengarry Glen Ross*?"

Rory could produce little more than a bewildered look.

"Doesn't matter. The point is, you're not ready for the questions yet."

Silence descended over the table as "De Colores" boomed through the restaurant's ancient speakers mounted in each of the four corners of the room.

"So what—" Rory was interrupted by the sudden appearance of the petite waitress who seemed to weave at jet-like speed from table to table.

"What can I get you?"

Sydney didn't hesitate. "Chicken chimichanga and a Tecate."

Rory, despite his hunger and the deviation from his normal dining schedule, was less certain. He continued to study the menu for what seemed an eternity. With each accumulating second the tension mounted between himself, the waitress, and the quick ordering Sydney. Finally he began.

"Can I have the steak and crab?"

"The crab is an extra five dollars."

"Hmmm, well what steak do you recommend? Is the filet good?"

The waitress wagged her head as if to say, "Yes it's delicious, can we get on with this? I have 37 other tables . . ."

"Okay, the filet it is."

"Seven or nine?"

"What?"

"Seven or nine ounce?"

"Better make it nine." He smiled at Sydney, proud of his eating prowess.

"Do you want horseradish or blue cheese?"

"No, neither. Can you make it without?"

The waitress erased madly and scribbled anew on her pad while Rory picked up an empty glass on the table.

"Oh, and could you bring me a new glass, this one is a bit smudged."

The waitress nodded and grabbed the glass.

"What sides would you like?"

"Oh, are these the sides?" Rory pointed at the appetizers section of the menu.

With this, Sydney's patience had reached its limits. He exploded like Mount St. Helens, grabbed the menu from Rory's hand and cried out to the waitress: "Just bring him a steak chimichanga platter."

As Rory returned to the near empty basket of chips a clatter arose from the table of the ass man. It appeared that the young son refused to eat. The mother repeatedly implored, "Jack. Why won't you eat your taco, Jack?" But he remained steadfast, arms crossed in defiance.

Sydney cocked his head a few degrees, tuning in to the mild altercation, then turned to Rory and asked: "So, what did you think of that little father-son moment back at the door?"

"I was shocked to be honest. Why would any father talk that way in front of his son? Badmouthing someone like that. You could see the kid was upset by it, and now he won't eat his lunch."

"So what does that tell you?" Sydney asked as he rocked back in his seat, sending the two front legs several inches in the air.

"That the father's the real a—"

"No!" Sydney cried.

Rory sat back and contemplated what had happened, how he'd envisioned the family, drawn his conclusions based on what he thought he'd seen, and then discovered they weren't as perfect as he'd thought. Then it came to him.

"It tells me that I saw a superficial view of that family's situation, and based on that I quickly made some assumptions about them, but then I found out that those assumptions—in this case that it was a perfect *Leave It to Beaver* family—didn't match the reality of the situation."

"Give that man a contract!" Sydney gesticulated madly with his colossal arms, then continued. "Exactly right. You formed certain assumptions, jumped to some conclusions, and didn't challenge them. That's why you were so surprised by the father's little revelation."

The two clinked their water glasses in celebration of this minor breakthrough and Sydney sat back, nodding his head gently and eyeing Rory in the fashion of Harry Higgins taking the measure of Eliza Doolittle in *My Fair Lady*. He then lifted his fork, breathed heavily on it, rubbed it against his shirt to buff it and continued. "One of the most important things we can do in *any* situation—business, family, social, whatever—is challenge the assumptions about what we're thinking or feeling in that moment." He paused and then asked, "Have you ever done that, Newman?"

Rory could sense another rapport moment and didn't want to jeopardize the momentum by coming up blank. Plus, Sydney was on to something here, he could feel it and he wanted to learn more. "Ahh . . ." he thought and jerked forward, then just as quickly fell back in his chair. A false alarm. He sat with his eyes riveted on the table, feeling the intense heat of Sydney's gaze but had nothing to share. Fortunately, a reprieve came as the sprinting waitress arrived out of nowhere with Sydney's beer and two gigantic plates. Despite the speed at which she was operating she managed to place the plates softly and directly in front of the two diners.

"Can I get you anything else just now?" she asked.

Rory and Sydney shook their heads no in unison and grabbed for the cutlery. Just then the hostess sat another party at the table adjacent to them. Three men in their early 20s, all wearing drenched tank tops, wrinkled shorts, and running shoes, took their seats. It looked to Rory as if they'd just come from the track or trail, and he thought it was strange for them to finish off a run with a burrito. "To each his own," he thought as he dove into his deep fried chimichanga.

Just as the crispy treasure was hitting his mouth it dawned on him. He had challenged an assumption recently and it did make a big difference. Rory took great pleasure in hiking and jogging the hills near his house and made it a point to hit the trail at least three days a week. His regular route took him to a nearby rise he had dubbed "Fireman's Peak" because it was often used by firefighters in training. The trek began with a level dirt surface that after a mile or so gave way to a series of ascending switchbacks. About a half mile up was a straight incline of around five degrees that stretched a quarter mile or so. Rory challenged himself to run that portion whenever his fortitude permitted. His normal strategy was to zigzag up the steep hill, thereby steering clear of the clusters of calf-high chaparral that dotted the center of the trail and the many ruts that lay in wait to prey upon unsuspecting ankles. He reasoned that going through the chaparral and avoiding the ruts would slow him down considerably.

Recently, however, he had challenged the assumption that avoiding the chaparral and the ruts was the best alternative and decided to simply run straight up the incline, mowing through the ubiquitous wild plants and hopping over the partially concealed ruts. Despite the increased risk, he discovered after his very first attempt that by challenging the assumption he was able to shave a full 15 seconds off his time.

Rory shared this discovery with Sydney, who, to that point, had yet to raise his head from the now nearly empty plate beneath him. Sydney took a mighty swipe across his mouth with his paper napkin, and said: "Exactly what I mean. You challenge your assumptions and you see things, possibilities, that didn't exist before. And only then you can start taking the right kind of action."

"We need to do that at Kitteridge," Rory offered.

"Continue," Sydney directed.

"We think we know what customers want, we think we know where the market is going, we think we know what products are going to catch on, but we don't really test any of those assumptions before we launch into something."

"Can't build a strategy without it," Sydney quipped as he jabbed between his teeth with a quivering toothpick.

"Okay, so for me it was easy, running up the hill; the stakes are pretty low, a few seconds off my time. But how do we do it for Kitteridge? How do we challenge our assumptions?" Rory leaned in toward Sydney, who sat back in his chair once again and pointed to a poster on the far wall of the restaurant. Rory followed the finger, which led to a 1970s era Budweiser poster with Ed McMahon and the Clydesdales in their finest Christmas regalia.

"What's Ed McMahon got to do with this?" Rory asked, quite confused.

"Look again, Newman," Sydney commanded.

Rory studied the wall with renewed vigor and found another poster that featured a gaggle of vibrant-looking teen-agers gawking at someone overhead in a hang glider that was just about to go off a massive cliff. This did little to produce any lights for Rory who then stared at Sydney.

"Do you know where the hang glider comes from, Newman?"

"San Diego?"

"No! Leonardo da Vinci. He was sketching the predeces-sors of hang gliders, helicopters, and modern bridges almost 500 years ago."

"So we need to build bridges, not walls. I get it." Rory nodded his head several times in deep contemplation, quite proud of his philosophical insight. His reverie was quickly interrupted by Sydney.

"That's true and a lovely thought . . . if you're a beauty pageant contestant. But it's completely irrelevant to this discussion." Sydney cast a baleful glance Rory's way then continued. "Da Vinci once said he was a *discepolo della esperienza*." He offered this with quite an Italian flourish. "That means he was a disciple of experience."

"In other words . . ." Rory baited.

"In other words, he tested his assumptions through actual experience, he went out into the world and saw how things actually worked. Just like you running up the middle of the hill."

"Nice job fellas, did you save room for dessert?" The waitress again materialized seemingly out of thin air to resume her duties, which included adding Rory's and Sydney's plates to a small mountain of soiled tableware balancing precariously on her heavily burdened left hand.

"Can't hurt to have a peek at the menu," Sydney said with Rory nodding his head in agreement.

"Okey dokey, I'll be right back with it." And she was gone again.

"Ever been on a subway, Newman?"

"What?"

"A subway. You know, the underground transportation system." Sydney said with more than a hint of sarcasm.

"Yeah, a few times."

"Ever heard of Bill Bratton?"

Rory shook his head tentatively, the name rang a bell, but he couldn't place it immediately. He was also finding it a bit difficult to maintain his concentration above the din of clattering forks, spirited conversations, and Garth Brooks belting out

"Friends in Low Places," an odd choice for the El Mariachi. Sydney leaned across the table toward Rory.

"Bratton understood the power of tackling deeply held assumptions. In 1990, he was appointed chief of the New York Transit Police Department and one of his first priorities was cleaning up the subway. But nobody really cared or supported that because statistically subway crimes were just a tiny portion of the overall mess. Everyone assumed they weren't a big problem. He decided to shake things up a bit. Around that time the subway system was known as the 'Electric Sewer' because of the fear people felt, being accosted by bums and marauding bands of kids; it was nasty. Bratton had all of his team, including himself, ride the subway day and night, so they could get a whiff of the filth that regular New Yorkers experienced every day. They saw with their own eyes what was going on, they felt the fear, they smelled the effects of an overburdened, underpatrolled system. That blast of reality changed things in a hurry."

The story snapped Rory out of his post-Chimichanga funk and started his mind racing through the many so-called strategic sessions he and his colleagues had held at Kitteridge. When was the last time any of them had "ridden the electric sewer?" When was the last time they actually went out and had a meaningful dialogue with customers and got a true and revealing glimpse into how their products were being used? He was still cataloging the sessions when the waitress slid into the picture with their dessert menus.

"I recommend the *platanos machos*, it's my favorite." With no hints of recognition registering on either face, she translated. "Fried bananas. And we don't skimp on the butter, sugar, or Grand Marnier," she offered proudly. Rory and Sydney shared a glance, it sounded good, but on top of a plateful of chimichanga with rice and beans it could produce a nap on the 101, and that wouldn't be good for anyone. They decided to pass.

Rory returned to his critical examination of past strategy meetings at Kitteridge and realized that not only did they fail to confront the facts by challenging their assumptions, they frequently talked about the same old things, without any new information hitting the radar. "How could they possibly challenge their assumptions and learn about their environment without bringing new information into the picture?" he wondered. He turned this over in his head and then decided to share it with Sydney.

"So, to really go deep on our assumptions, first we've got to gather some information, right? Get a picture of what's going on, who thinks what, and then dig into that to see what it's telling us."

Was it the sun hitting the cascading water of the fountain, or did a glint appear in Sydney's eye? Rory couldn't decipher the expression with certainty but there was little doubt Sydney was impressed. He banged his massive hand on the table.

"Now you're gettin' somewhere Newman."

"So what sort of information is best?" Rory asked.

"Look out the window and tell me what you see."

Rory focused intently, looking beyond the cloudy glass, across the street, down an alley intersecting two modest store-fronts, past a sliver of weed-infested lot, until finally his gaze rested on a gently sloping hillside. Rory began to grasp desperately at the dictionary in his head. "Bucolic . . . idyllic . . . pastoral . . . rustic . . . pretty, no pretty's no good . . ."

After what seemed to Rory an interminable passage of time, Sydney jumped in. "You see that pretty hillside way out there?" "Rats!" Rory thought, "Pretty *was* good enough." With clenched lips he said, "Yeah, I see it."

"What does it make you ask or wonder?" Sydney inquired.

Rory stared at the tree-lined bluff once more and began his inventory of questions: "What kind of trees are they? They probably don't get much rain here, how much vegetation grows there? How long would it take to jog to the top?" A spent look on his brow, Rory turned to Sydney, awaiting his reaction.

"Okay, those are questions, and I like the one about how long it would take to jog to the top because it's creative, a little out of the ordinary. That's what you've got to do when you're gathering information Newman, look beyond the ordinary, get a fresh perspective."

"Okay, so what would you ask about?" Rory jabbed while gesturing out the window.

Sydney didn't hesitate. "How was the topography formed? How many, and what types of animals call it home? How has the landscape changed over the last hundred, the last thousand, years? If you looked hard enough could you find a nugget of gold or any precious metal there? What food would it accommodate growing? How fast did the fastest human and animal traverse it? Was it the site of any great battles? How many fires have ravaged it? How many planes fly over it in a single day?" Sydney drew a breath that suggested he was just beginning to get on a roll, but Rory got the point.

"Okay, okay. Nicely played. But we're not looking at hillsides, *pretty* as they may be, at Kitteridge. What should we be asking?"

"The same principle applies. Dig deep and find some questions that will really challenge you and illuminate your path. There are as many possibilities as there are boulders on that hill out there."

Sydney paused as he met Rory's expression across the table, a face reminiscent of a baby sparrow desperately seeking food from its mother. "Okay Newman, here are a few to whet your appetite: What are your most exceptionally successful products? Why are they so successful? Same with exceptional failures—what are they and why did they occur? What's the biggest hassle customers have to put up with when using your products? Which customers use your products in the most unusual ways? Could we still meet the needs of a majority of our customers if we stripped say 25 percent of the costs out of our product?" Sydney's delivery had the cadence of a machine gun and it seemed as if he could go all day on the subject, but sensing the rapid fire was overpowering Rory, he concluded, "That'll get you started."

The check spun to the table, flung by the whirling dervish of a waitress who left them with a wisp of "Thank you, have a nice day," as she sped off. A momentary standoff ensued as both eyed the simple white paper cautiously. Finally, Rory snatched it, flashed a smile Sydney's way and hopped from his seat. Without warning he collided with the ass comment man and his family, making their way to the door. They exchanged half-smiles, Rory spread out his arm directing the family to go ahead, and they were on their way. Rory then stopped and stared at the back of the man's crisp white shirt marveling at how much he, without ever exchanging a word with Rory, had taught him.

9

Getting to the Core

Rory and Sydney tramped heavily along the sidewalk then heaved themselves and their stuffed stomachs into the car. The interior, sun-drenched and cozy warm, was a veritable sleeping pill when combined with a heavy lunch. A splattering of cold water across his cheeks would have been the perfect antidote, but with that option unavailable Rory shook his head violently, in the manner of a cat or dog. This produced a portion of the intended effect, with the remainder arriving in the form of his buzzing phone, which alerted him to two new voice mail messages.

The first, left while he and Sydney were lunching, was from a somewhat frantic sounding Jim Tobin who, in short and deliberate bursts, said: "Rory ... it's Jim ... uh, we've been talking things over on this end, and we need that report on strategic planning sooner than later ... three days, not five. Can you deliver Rory? We've got to come out of the box swinging on this, need to make a splash for the new team, need some quick wins. Can you deliver? We're all counting on you. Call me if you have any questions, but the bottom line is we'll be expecting the report in three days. Thanks."

The chances of Rory somehow forgetting this message were less likely than Sydney being mistaken for an English butler, but he pressed 9 on his phone, saving it. Before he could process matters further his next message began.

"Hi, it's me. Where are you? You should always keep your phone with you. Henrietta just called to remind us the payment to the agency is due next week. She gave the old story about it being standard protocol but nothing goes forward until the check clears. Everything's okay at work, right? No problem to write the check?" There was a long pause and then, "We're going to pick up chairs now, call me tonight. Love you."

A torrent of thoughts raced through Rory's mind: three days . . . check due next week . . . problems at work. His preferred mode of processing difficult issues was to hit the trail, hammer it out in his head as he raced along a rocky path, but that was clearly out of the question. Trotting up and down Apple Avenue in Greenfield in his cordovan loafers was certain to produce confused stares but little in the form of insights. He stared straight ahead, his hands grasping the molten hot steering wheel when Sydney suddenly inquired: "Are we leaving or what?"

Back on the 101, only the rhythmic rumble of the car tires treading a straight path on the asphalt permeated the confines of the C230, as both Rory and Sydney tended their mental gardens in solitude. They sat quietly, barely moving a muscle. Rory's movements were confined to minor adjustments of the steering wheel while Sydney, succumbing to the marriage of an enormous meal and warm afternoon sunshine, demonstrated the unconscious twitch of the dreamer.

Of course he wasn't able to read his mind, but Rory was certain the current flowing within Sydney's noggin was considerably smoother than the waves thrashing about in his own head. A surge of envy reverberated through his bones but he shook it off as quickly as it appeared. "I can do this. I can do it." The cursory pep talk supplied only momentary relief and he was soon left scratching his head, asking, "But how?" He determined that in order to march forward he should first examine from where he'd come. What had he learned thus far? He drew several successive deep breaths, an attempt to accelerate the pace of his wits, and thought back to the events of the day as they had unfurled themselves in front of him. What a tumultuous six hours it had been! First came the news of the sale, Mark's strange gloating and veiled warnings, the news of this stranger who was to accompany him on his journey, their awkward beginnings, the adventure at the gas station, and, of course, the lessons Sydney had imparted.

What were those lessons, could he recite them to himself? Could he document them effectively to share with Jim Tobin? And so he began to enumerate the teachings: "You've got to start with a consistent definition of strategy, everyone has to be on the same page if the process is going to work. Good, okay, then what? The process itself is flawed in most organizations. They either create a hero sandwich of good intentions or produce hundred-plus-page documents with graphs, charts, and tiny fonts that lead to nothing but paralysis by analysis." Rory's train of thought was interrupted by a glance at the speedometer, creeping north of 80 m.p.h. "I should use the cruise control," he thought, but instead he opted to lighten his pressure on the pedal and continue with his inner monologue. "So how do you fix the process? You start with an open mind and a willingness to challenge assumptions about your business. And how do you do that? You test the assumptions, you ride the electric sewer like Bratton in New York. That opens your eyes. And then, before you actually build a strategy you gather information, ask creative questions that will shed light on the way things are and the way you'd like them to be."

An unquestionable surge of accomplishment and pride began to well up in Rory, he was making progress, he was on the right track, but where did he go from here? What was the next step? It had to be the fundamental questions about your business Sydney had suggested as being core to the process. Not the questions you develop when gathering information, those framed the process, but the basic, primary, and essential questions that would lead to the crafting of your strategy.

As Rory continued to grapple with the next step on his path, all of his attention was suddenly riveted on a new and urgent challenge when a large piece of driftwood came hurtling from the bed of a Toyota pickup traveling in front of him. Like a rampaging elephant, the enormous wooden missile barreled down on the car and would surely wreak untold damage in the matter of a second or less. Rory instinctively twisted the steering wheel violently to the right sending the car careening past the shoulder and on to a strip of gravel no more than two feet wide. He struggled mightily with the car, which now seemed to be divorced from his control and reacting like a beast pursued in the jungle. With equal parts brake and smooth manipulation of the wheel he was able to bring the vehicle under his command once again. The adrenaline was still coursing wildly through his veins as he chanced a look in the rearview mirror and caught a brief glimpse of the wayward log coming to rest in the middle of the road.

Sydney was now bolt upright in his seat, his erect posture causing his orange bandana to rub against the roof as the car surged forward. The two sat in stunned silence as they passed a congregation of signs announcing their arrival in King City. It was the customary combination of little block symbols signifying the presence of gas stations, restaurants, and other amenities, including in this case the King City golf course. Rory had always questioned these signs, not their functionality but their artistic rendering. Take, for example, the weary traveler sign, which always seemed to him the antithesis of a comforting image: a stick figure with a circle for a head and no neck connecting to his body, laying on what appears to be a sheet of concrete. Couldn't they come up with something better?

With Sydney regaining full consciousness courtesy of the rogue driftwood, Rory decided the time was right to continue the examination of strategic planning. He turned decisively to his passenger and said, "So, I know the next step." Sydney reacted to this proclamation no more than a marble statue of him might, so Rory continued, "It's time for the questions. We've sown the seeds so to speak, by getting a consistent definition of strategy, examining and challenging our assumptions, and gathering information. Now we hit the questions, correct?"

"Did you see that sign back there?" Sydney asked.

"The one for King City?"

"The one for the golf course."

"Yeah, so?" Rory's frustration bubbled close to the surface at this seemingly meaningless diversion, but it was lost on Sydney, who continued.

"A few years back I played in one of those celebrity golf tournaments out in Palm Springs. Man the wind was howlin' that day, must have been blowing 50 miles an hour. Anyway, our celebrity was Maurice the Mallet, remember him?" A vague hint of recognition registered on Rory's face, at least enough for Sydney to move ahead with his story.

"Man that guy cheats like crazy. He'd be driving up the fairway in his cart and he'd make up a score for the hole, simple as that. All of us tried to talk him out of it but it was useless. We had one hole on the back nine, we musta' had 18 putts, and he gives us a birdie. Thanks to the Mallet's creative scorekeeping we ended up shooting 56 and winning the whole thing. We got to the clubhouse, signed our card under tremendous duress from the Mallet, and the guy there says, "Maurice the Mallet, he cheats!" So they talk it over and put us third instead of first."

"What in the name of all that is good does this have to do with anything?" Rory murmured under his breath. He signaled right, and the car glided into the number two lane, passing an ancient RV, a veritable tenement on wheels, hogging the outside portion of the road. With the car back on course he cast a skeptical glance at Sydney who recognized the facial tone at once.

"Point is, there's one more thing before the questions." He stopped abruptly and ran his fingers over his unshaven face. "You've got to examine your core purpose, your mission."

"And what does that have to do with Morris with the mullet?" An exasperated Rory asked.

"*Maurice the Mallet*. I thought you knew who he was Newman?" A pause, then Sydney trudged forward in his narrative. "Every person and every organization is guided by a compass of some sort, its core purpose, its reason for being, its *raison d'etre*. Maurice's internal compass was way out of whack and that caused him to make poor decisions that ultimately cost him. It's more than just a golf game, too, I just read he got nabbed for investment fraud and is headed for the slammer. His compass was way out of alignment."

"I'm still not reading you on this one, Sydney."

"Mission and strategy always go together. You can't have one without the other. Before creating a strategy, you've got to ask: Why do we exist? What's our core purpose? What's the true north of our compass? Only then can you develop a strategy, your broad priorities, that will lead you toward your mission. Purpose is at the heart of strategy; it's the hub of the strategy wheel. It gives direction to everybody in the company and allows leaders to explain the relevance of the decisions they ultimately make. I used Maurice as an example because unfortunately his core purpose was clear—win at all costs. That led him to adopt certain priorities and actions, his strategy in other words, which consisted of cheating and cutting corners, and we know where that got him." Sensing a more positive message was necessary to reinforce his point, Sydney continued.

"That's a dramatic, and definitely negative, example but the vast majority of people and organizations use their core purpose for good. Look at John Browne. He used to be CEO of British Petroleum. He said their purpose was who they were. It represented what they existed to achieve, and what they were willing to do and not do, to achieve it." Sydney then adopted a pronounced magisterial air and said: "Find your true and noble purpose Newman, and the strategy will follow."

After a short pause, no doubt intended for dramatic effect, Sydney turned with eyebrows raised and said, "You do have a mission statement at Kitteridge, don't you Newman?"

Rory smirked and nodded his head as if to say, "Of course we do; what a ridiculous question." However, he was keenly aware that he had to summon said statement immediately because it was just a matter of time, most likely seconds, before Sydney demanded he recite it. What was it? It was like losing a set of keys in your house, you know you've seen them, but where? How could they simply disappear? He was sure the mission was on a poster in the reception area, and you could still find it on the odd mouse pad or coffee mug in the kitchen. Then, in a moment of insight, a flash of words and phrases appeared: increase equity, market share . . . productivity.

"So?" Sydney asked, right on cue.

Rory had given his share of spontaneous speeches and presentations over the years and wasn't out of place at the lectern, but there was no point in faking this, he just couldn't remember the company's mission statement. "It focuses on equity, market share, and productivity," he stammered.

"Geez, that's really inspirational, Newman, you'll have to give me a minute to rub down the goose bumps."

"What's wrong with it?" Rory snapped back instinctively, somewhat surprised at his own defensiveness.

"We passed Palo Alto a while back, what's it famous for?"

Rory tensed in his seat, not at all enthused at the prospect of another history lesson from Sydney, but ultimately determined it was best to play along. Plus, this was an ace for him, his roommate in college hailed from Palo Alto and was a walking town encyclopedia who was only too pleased to share his knowledge with anyone within shouting distance. Rory blurted out: "Joan Baez, Jerry Garcia, and Hewlett-Packard, of course."

"Very nice Newman, a student of music I see." After an affirmative nod from Rory, Sydney continued. "Let's focus on Hewlett-Packard. The company got started back in 1939 in a little garage in Palo Alto, on Addison Avenue I think." He stopped as if considering the geography of the city carefully, then began again. "Doesn't matter what street. Point is they built their first product in that garage, but they also started building something else, their core purpose. Years later, Dave Packard summarized that concept in a speech he gave. He said, *'A group of people get together and exist as an institution that we call a company so they are able to accomplish something collectively that they could not accomplish separately—they make a contribution to society . . . do something which is of value.'* A contribution to society Newman. Does your mission reflect your contribution?"

As Sydney pivoted in his seat to make this grand gesture his elbow collided with the glove box, releasing it and sending a couple of pens and a pad of Post-it Notes careening to the floor. He picked up the Post-it Notes, examined them like an anthropologist studying a native artifact, then stuck the packet in front of Rory's face, momentarily blocking his view of the road. "Ha, Post-it Notes!" Sydney exclaimed. "Get it, Newman?"

"What's with this guy?" Rory wondered. "He quotes German generals, is some kind of maverick business guru and strategy expert, but gets freaked out by a packet of Post-it Notes?" Rory took the measure of Sydney with a long gaze before returning his attention to the road, and said gingerly, "No, I don't get it Sydney." The way you might address a lunatic who accosts you in the street.

Sydney appeared completely oblivious to Rory's condescending voice and twirled the Post-it Notes in the air, taking great pleasure from the flipping pages. After one particularly vigorous toss the packet sailed through the car and landed smack dab in the middle of the rear window ledge. It was in the crosshairs of Rory's rearview mirror, driving him to near distraction. Yet another blemish on his perfect environment, first the grimy fingerprints, now this. Before he could dwell on the attack any further, Sydney, who couldn't care less about the location of the packet, continued.

"Post-it Notes come from 3M. You know what their mission statement is?"

Before Rory could offer a reply, not that one would have been forthcoming, Sydney carried on: "*To solve unsolved problems innovatively*. You know why I love that Newman?" It was obviously a rhetorical question because once again Sydney marched forward. "Three reasons. One, it inspires change. We're always going to have problems that need solving and this mission is sure to lead 3M into lots of fields that aren't even glints in their test tubes at this point. Two, it's written for the long-term, it could last over a hundred years. And three, it's easy to understand and communicate. No mention of—" Sydney drew a vast breath, "value-added, bandwidth, synergies, paradigm shifts, mindshare, core competencies, or bleeding edges."

Rory piped in with a dead on impersonation of Don Pardo, the venerable announcer from *Saturday Night Live*: "Time now for Buzzword Bingo!"

"Yeah," Sydney chuckled, "All I needed was proactive, outside the box, or results-driven to win the three-piece living room set!"

A giddiness bug is known to infect road trips, and Rory and Sydney were suddenly stricken with the gut-busting virus. The Don Pardo reference unleashed a surge of *Saturday Night* live memories and debates: Who was better on Weekend Update, Chevy Chase, Norm MacDonald, or Tina Fey? What years featured the best cast? Sydney argued tirelessly for the late '70s gang that included Bill Murray, Gilda Radner, and his personal favorite, John Belushi, while Rory was stuck on the Phil Hartman and Kevin Nealon era. What musical guest had the most appearances? Rory was adamant it was James Taylor but neither could say with certainty. As though it had been rehearsed a thousand times, the two closed their laugh fest with a pitch perfect recitation of "We are two wild and crazy guys!"

As the laughter receded like the scenery in the rearview mirror an uncomfortable twitch made its way into Rory's stomach. There was unfinished business at hand. "So, how do we create a mission statement like 3M, or something that would make Dave Packard proud?" he asked.

"Lots of options," Sydney replied. "But my favorite is something called the Five Whys."

"The Five Whys?"

"Yeah, you start with a basic statement, like we make this, or we do that, and then you ask yourself why that's important five times. A few iterations in and you start to see your true mission emerging."

Rory contemplated the exercise as he guided the car around a sluggish garbage truck rumbling along the inside lane. The brightly colored truck, remarkably clean given the enterprise in which it was engaged, grabbed the attention of Rory and Sydney who caught their reflection in the vehicle's gleaming chrome hubcaps as they sped past.

"What do you think their mission is?" Sydney asked.

Rory shrugged his shoulders. Beyond the obvious reply of "We pick up garbage," he was stumped.

"Try the Five Whys," Sydney prompted. "Pretend you're the CEO of that company."

"Okay," Rory acquiesced, "We pick up garbage."

"Why is that important?" Sydney pounced.

"To keep the city clean."

"Why is that important?"

"To help protect the environment."

"Why is that important?"

"Sustainability, economic growth . . ." Rory was stumbling a bit but the lesson was taking shape. He paused and mentally aggregated his whys, then offered: "How about: We contribute to a stronger environment by creatively solving waste management issues." He turned to Sydney.

"I like it. It could inspire change as environmental problems evolve, it's written for the long term, and I can understand it, no buzzwords. Most important, you can use it as the basis for building a strategy, for taking action and working toward it. Well done, grasshopper."

Rory smiled knowingly at the *Kung Fu* reference. Before long, however, his mind was otherwise engaged, running free across a vast prairie of possibilities regarding Kitteridge's mission statement. Sydney's insights had unlocked a storehouse of inspiration. Using the Five Whys would surely lead to a new and dramatically improved mission that declared their true purpose.

As was his custom, Rory's foot grew heavier as his head danced with the enticing opportunities this simple exercise unveiled, and soon the Mercedes was zipping along at more than 83 miles an hour. Suddenly there was a surge of red and blue light across the rearview mirror and a shrill sound approaching quickly in the distance.

10

Think Fast

"Nice goin' Andretti," Sydney muttered as a somewhat
flustered Rory directed the Mercedes to the side of
the road, his heart and mind racing. Glaring lights
and pulsating sirens never failed to elicit a heightened response
despite the fact that like most law-abiding citizens, Rory had
nothing to fear from the police.

As the menacing California Highway Patrol cruiser rumbled to a stop behind him, the first thing Rory noticed were
the enormous welded-on nudge bars used as battering rams
to force rogue offenders off the road. The ghosts of chases past
were plainly evident from the many deep scrapes on the unit's
thick black bars. Next, it was the lights that caught his attention; so bold and resonant, so blindingly bright when captured
squarely in the rearview mirror. He was lost in their glare
when the door opened and the officer uncoiled from his seat
to emerge on the shoulder of the road. Now it was the sound
that overtook him: a strange harmony of clinking keys, dangling

billy club and the thumping holster cradling the officer's deadly weapon, all affixed in one way or another to his wide leather belt. In his hand he carried a simple, black, zippered folder.

Rory was still processing the cocktail of sensory assaults when he heard a brusque tap tap tap on his window. He fumbled for the window control, first hitting the lock mechanism before finally lowering the glass to meet the officer's steely gaze.

"What's the hurry?" the officer asked nonchalantly.

"No hurry officer."

"You realize you were doing 84 in a 70 zone?"

"Was it that fast?"

The officer nodded. "I'm going to have to write you up. License, insurance, and registration."

Rory's right arm shot across to the glove box, knocking Sydney's elbow from the perch it had assumed on his knee. Organized as Rory was, the registration and insurance cards should have been easily obtained from a small portfolio resting at the left side of the box. However, as a result of the previous inadvertent opening of the glove box that led to Sydney's juggling act with the Post-it Notes, the portfolio had shifted almost out of Rory's reach. Even with the tumult of the speeding stop demanding his full consideration, Rory's fastidious tendencies propelled him to cast a disapproving glance Sydney's way.

He handed the documents to the officer who took them and returned to his car for what seemed an eternity. Rory stared into the mirror the entire time, monitoring the officer's activities, which appeared to consist mainly of tapping at his onboard computer. Finally, the officer returned to Rory's window and opened his folder. As he slowly undid the zipper, a thick assortment of papers were exposed. Sydney caught sight of one particular edge in the very periphery of his glance. Although it flashed for just a second or so he was certain he recognized the letters 'es' in a stylized script, along with the blue and white edges of ocean waves.

"We're headed for San Diego," he announced.

Rory's head spun in his companion's direction, clearly questioning the value of idle chitchat to this transaction. But Sydney continued.

"Hoping to catch the Friars . . . big three-game set with the Dodgers."

The officer stopped writing in mid-ticket and lowered his head, positioning it directly into the car, forcing Rory to descend deeper into his seat.

"You a Padres fan?" he asked.

"My dog's name is Trevor," answered Sydney.

"Favorite song?" challenged the officer.

"Always up for a little Hell's Bells!" Sydney returned.

Rory didn't know what to make of the exchange. To him it resembled some old black-and-white movie with shady characters exchanging passwords and secret handshakes to gain access to a speakeasy.

The officer stared in silent reverence, then said, "552 and counting." He looked down at his folder then pulled from it the piece of paper whose corner Sydney had spied. It was a San Diego Padres season schedule. The officer grinned, then ripped the ticket from the pad and tore it up. He smiled at Sydney then turned to Rory, their faces separated by about the thickness of a quarter, and said, "You just watch the speed limit alright, buddy?"

He turned, and then he was gone. Rory, still a little scarlet in the cheeks, turned to Sydney and asked the obvious question, "What was that all about?"

"When he opened his folder I thought I saw the edge of the San Diego Padres logo, so I took a chance that he was a fan."

"So what's AC/DC got to do with it?"

"They play 'Hell's Bells' over the PA system whenever Trevor Hoffman, the closer, comes into a game. Any real fan would know that."

As Rory returned the portfolio to its customary spot in the glove box, Sydney took the measure of the road stretching out beyond them and said, "It's like I always say Newman, you can think your way out of anything."

11

A Push in the Right Direction

"Y ou can think your way out of anything." Rory, who had now heard the phrase twice, mulled it over, contemplating the thinking he had done since meeting Sydney, and what was ahead of him if he was to get his report to Jim on time. As if on cue from a stage manager, his phone rang at that very moment. It was Jim Tobin.

"Rory, it's Jim. Where are you?"

Rory looked out the window, but a study of the scenery wasn't really helpful, given that it hadn't changed much for the last 100 miles or so. He didn't know exactly where they were. He whispered to Sydney, "Where are we?" Without hesitation Sydney calmly answered, "Bradley."

"Just passed Bradley, Jim." Rory said over the beep of his phone battery, informing him it was rapidly expiring.

The sound of clicking keys rattled over the phone line as Jim typed into his computer. "Let's see, B-r-a-d-l-e-y . . . perfect, you're close to Paso Robles." Then Jim paused as if grasping for the right words and asked, "Do you ride?"

"Ride? Ride what?"

"Horses. Can you ride?"

Rory shared a perplexed look with Sydney whose eyebrows were cocked to an almost perfectly inverted v-shape.

"It's been a while Jim, but, yeah, I guess so." Been a while was an extremely charitable estimation. In truth, he hadn't sat on a horse since doing a couple of laps at a petting zoo when he was about eight years old.

"Good. We've got a potential new customer, Ike Redmond, who's just crazy about horses and he wants to meet tomorrow morning at a ranch in Paso Robles. Getting access to his stores could be huge for us Rory. Normally I'd go down myself but since you're right there, and you know the company as well or better than anyone we thought it was perfect for you."

Jim followed with the details and the requisite corporate pep talk: big account, huge opportunity, great chance for you, and so on, which Rory embraced tepidly. He was all for landing a potential big fish, but why did the deal-making have to take place on the back of a horse? The conversation completed, Rory turned to Sydney and said, "Guess we're overnighting in Paso Robles." The bubble of words had scarcely left his mouth when Rory began to cringe in anticipation of Sydney uttering some pithy phrase in recognition of Paso Robles. Sure enough, he did not disappoint.

"Pass of the Oaks, home of great wine and rejuvenating hot springs."

The call from Jim had ratcheted up the levers of Rory's already elevated sense of urgency and once again he began to project across the screen of his mind the lessons Sydney had imparted: Start with a consistent definition of strategy; everyone has to be on the same page if the process is going to work. Most organizations either create a hero sandwich of good intentions or produce 100- page documents with graphs, charts, and tiny fonts that lead to nothing but paralysis by analysis. To fix the process you start with an open mind and a willingness to challenge assumptions about your business. And how do you do that? You test the assumptions, you ride the electric sewer like Bratton in New York. That opens your eyes. And then, before you actually build a strategy you gather information, ask creative questions that will shed light on the way things are and the way you'd like them to be. Then you either create or validate your mission, which will act as your compass.

Sydney took a peek at Rory and could swear, although he appeared practically catatonic, that his lips were moving. The peek transitioned to a full-on stare, but Rory was clearly in a zone and not to be deterred. Finally, he emerged from his self-imposed cone of silence and said, "Okay Mr. Wise, we define strategy, fix the process by testing assumptions, gather information using creative questions, then create or validate the mission. What's next? We build the strategy right?"

Rory's question was straight to the point, but if their brief history together was any indication, Sydney would not reciprocate with a simple answer; instead the response would be cloaked in some strange metaphor or enlightening story. Rory braced for the next mysterious rung on the ladder.

"That's right, you start building the strategy by focusing on the four fundamental strategy-building questions."

Rory was just this side of flabbergasted at the simple reply and, seeing that a crack in the obtuse armor had been exposed, was quick to pounce.

"Okay, great, so—" Before he could finish Sydney abruptly interrupted him.

"Hey, are those the kids we saw in San Jose?"

Sure enough, marooned again at the side of the 101 was the classic VW Vanagon they'd passed in San Jose a few hours earlier. The young man was circling the van in obvious distress, while his waif-like companion sat at the rear of the vehicle, surprisingly serene looking, in some sort of advanced yoga position.

"Stop the car!" Sydney shouted.

Reacting instinctively to the high decibel command, Rory slammed on the brakes and swerved to the shoulder. He backed the Mercedes up until it rested just a few yards in front of the Vanagon. Sydney shot out in an instant.

The young man took an automatic step back at the sight of this gigantic person, red ringlets bobbing along in concert with his long strides, barreling down on him. But upon hearing the sincerity in Sydney's inquiry, "What's the trouble?" he met the behemoth of a fellow near the front door of the decrepit van and shook his hand vigorously.

"I'm not sure. The engine started to choke and wheeze, then just died. I managed to glide to this point thanks to the paucity of traffic," the young man replied quietly. Rory had joined Sydney by this point, and they were quick to swap a confused look. Did he just say paucity of traffic? He looked like an extra on a Hollywood stoner movie but spoke like an Ivy Leaguer.

Sydney hovered over the steaming engine, but as enticing as the possibilities were, it had been a long time since his fingers bore the stain of oil and grease. He hmmed and hahhed, holding the collected crowd engrossed, but in the end could offer only: "Well, you're not far from Paso. If you can get there, you can get to a garage."

"And how do you propose we do that?" inquired the young man gravely.

All eyes were riveted on the paved shoulder as deep thought descended upon the group. The young man took to circling the vehicle again, apparently his preferred method for divining solutions. Unfortunately, three laps around the van managed to produce little more than annoyance for the others. Then, as if delivered on a veritable silver platter, or more appropriately a silver screen, a solution presented itself to Rory.

"*Little Miss Sunshine!*"

This exuberant utterance was greeted with nothing but blank stares, so Rory attempted to explain further.

"Didn't any of you see the movie *Little Miss Sunshine*?"

"Is that an American film?" the waif in white cotton asked, uttering her first words to the group. Before Rory could answer, she continued, "Because if it is, we haven't seen it. We watch only foreign films and mostly the masters: Fellini, Bergman, Kieslowski. How did you interpret *The Decalogue*?"

Considering the waif a lost cause on this point, Rory turned to Sydney and the young man. "In *Little Miss Sunshine* they have a van just like this, and it breaks down just like yours. So they push it, get it going around 20 miles an hour, pop the clutch, it starts and they all run and jump in."

"Capital idea!" shouted the young man, again causing Rory and Sydney to wonder. Rory ran to the Mercedes and with no traffic in sight, backed it to the rear of the Vanagon, clearing the way for a launch.

It was quickly determined the waif could offer little in the form of brute strength necessary to start the van rolling so she was situated in the driver's seat, hands clasped on the wheel, awaiting the ascent to 20 miles an hour. The other three took positions at the rear and with a "one, two, three, go!" from Sydney they began to heave. Within a second or two the wheels started to roll, slowly at first but gaining momentum with each successive push.

Like a flywheel in perpetual motion, the van gathered steam and was soon rolling free and easy along the shoulder.

At Sydney's prompting the young man zipped to the front, the waif scooted to the passenger seat, the clutch was engaged and the van, after emitting a series of eerie hisses and sputters, began gobbling up the 101. A furniture delivery truck was forced to maneuver around the van, but otherwise the takeoff was smooth. Two wildly gesticulating hands, one reaching from each side of the van, served as the pair's enthusiastic good-bye.

Like proud parents seeing their kids leave the nest, Rory and Sydney gazed in silence as the van gradually disappeared from view. "Nice kids," Sydney sighed. "Yeah," was Rory's simple reply. The two followed the invisible path of the van for another moment or two then walked back to the car, where Rory hastily collected the misplaced Post-it Notes from the rear window ledge, and soon they were on the outskirts of Paso Robles.

It doesn't take a detective to quickly discover that Paso Robles is wine country. The clues are everywhere: vibrantly painted billboards advertising wines and tasting opportunities, smaller and some might say more dignified signs for the boutique bottlers, and of course the acres of vineyards rising up on either side of the 101, their rows of luscious bounty sitting motionless, seemingly growing bigger by the second under the warm central California sunshine. "A Cabernet is going to taste good tonight," Rory declared, conjuring a comforting image of himself sitting in a restaurant, his nose perched over a wide-brimmed glass of swirling velvety perfection.

It took a neck-jarring shake of his head to bring him back to the moment and in doing so he recalled rapidly where he and Sydney had left off before their Good Samaritan deed. He was buoyed by the possibility that Sydney might simply launch into a recitation of the next steps of the strategic planning process with machine-like precision. After all, he'd answered Rory's last question very definitively: "Yes, the next step in the process is to start building the strategy by focusing on the four fundamental strategy-building questions." That's what he'd said. Rory decided to remind him.

"So Sydney, you said the next step is to—"

"You got your answer back there." Sydney once again butted in before Rory could finish his sentence, a habit that could grow old in a hurry he thought. Annoying proclivities aside, Rory was now faced with a bigger issue: yet another Sydney riddle.

Rory decided persistence was his greatest ally: "The next step is to answer the questions, right?"

"You got your answer back there. Remember, observe and think Newman." He paused and then repeated: "You got your answer back there."

Nodding his head dutifully, Rory replayed the scene in his mind, from the second he had asked the question to the point at which the van disappeared, and all points in between. The high point in the mini-drama was the unified push that got the van started again; Rory was convinced that was the key to this conundrum.

"Getting the van back on the road, right?" He glanced quickly at Sydney.

"Warm," was the curt reply.

"Pushing the van."

"Warmer."

In a frenzy of pure free association, a wheel of words began spinning in Rory's mind, but at which one should he stop the carousel? Finally he yelled out, as if trying to overcome a stutter: "Momentum!"

"Bingo!" Sydney's arms shot up jamming his knuckles into the sunroof with a pronounced thud. Literally shaking off the injury, his mallet-like hands creating a cool breeze in the front seat, Sydney continued: "What is it about momentum that would be the next step in the process?"

"Well, momentum means drive or thrust or energy, so I guess it's . . ." Rory hesitated. The dreaded concentration-induced lead foot had reemerged and the car was skating across the blacktop at over 75 miles per hour. He eased the pressure on the accelerator, no time for another visit with the California Highway Patrol, and resumed his pondering. "So, I guess it's creating forward motion of some kind . . ." his words trailed off as he considered their implication.

"Right," Sydney declared. "Think about it. Every organization is propelled in some direction, has momentum, or forward motion. At this point in the process you've got to determine what propels your business forward. Because when you do that it makes decision-making a whole heck of a lot easier. Makes deciding what to do, and what not to do, where to focus your resources, and where not to focus your resources, much simpler."

"Okay, that makes sense, but how do you know what propels you?" Rory asked.

"It's typically one of six things. Are you ready Newman? Got your finger over the red button on the old tape recorder in your head?"

"Yeah, I think I can handle it."

"Like I said, it's one of six things, six areas of strategic focus that propel you forward. The first is products and services. If your focus is products and services you're first and foremost occupied with trying to make your product or service better. You might sell to a bunch of different markets or customers, but it's always the same basic product. In the future you might have modifications or extensions, but there's always going to be a genetic connection among your offerings. Look at Boeing. It's all about aircraft. That's it. With their know-how and technology they could probably build trains or boats, but they don't. They focus on aircraft.

"Another potential area of focus is customers and markets. If this is your focus, you could sell different products, but you're always aiming at the needs of a defined set of customers or markets. That way you can offer greater value than, say, a product-focused company that is trying to build something for all potential customers. I'll give you two examples, at either extreme of the wholesomeness spectrum. The first is *Playboy*. Ever seen a copy of that Newman?"

Repeating a line they'd both heard a thousand times, Rory and Sydney uttered in perfect unison, "I only read it for the articles."

"Right, just for the articles. Anyway, *Playboy's* motto is 'entertainment for men.' Men, that's it. That's a customer group focus. So that allows them to branch out into lots of different product and service arenas: they have the magazine, the television channel, the clubs, and hotels. But it's all about entertainment for men. On the other end of the wholesomeness spectrum you've got Johnson & Johnson, which makes products for doctors, nurses, patients, and mothers. Band-Aids and talcum powder don't have much in common, except that a mom needs both."

Rory was diligently taking in Sydney's words but was somewhat preoccupied by the task of remembering them all. The examples were a great help, but he wondered if he could record Sydney, maybe using the voice recorder on his phone. "No, too complicated. I can never find the menu. I should always carry a voice recorder—note to self: buy a voice recorder."

"You with me Newman?" Sydney growled.

"Yeah, yeah, products and services and customers and markets, what else?"

"Alrighty then. Another possible focus that could propel you is capacity or capabilities. Think of an airline or a hotel, it's all about filling the seats and the rooms. The plane is going to take off with 50 or 150 passengers. They want to utilize their capacity. Keeping things running at full capacity is critical to their success. With capabilities, it's just that: focusing on your particular capabilities. When I was a kid there was a business in town called Atlantic Spring and Machine. My old man loved that place. I'm not kidding. He took everything from an old car bumper to a basketball hoop that he wanted to reinforce to that place. They had a certain set of capabilities that allowed them to work on a number of different things, as long as they matched their equipment and tooling.

Rory perked up at this last installment. "But anything for anyone is a dangerous recipe, right? Let's say I'm a consulting firm and my capability is marketing knowledge. I could cast the net to the entire world, but what really distinguishes me?"

"That's right." Sydney's glance at Rory conveyed a virtual tip of the hat. "You'd be better served by focusing your capability on a specific arena, maybe marketing for swimming pool companies, or funeral homes, or cement manufacturers. The point is to focus."

The Mercedes sped past yet another winery billboard, this one a tad out of step with the idyllic and cultured flavor of the others. It featured a tuxedo-clad lion holding a chalice of red wine. Apparently he'd already enjoyed the contents, as evidenced by the drops of red descending from his ample whiskers. The caption, in loud white letters read, "The Wine King." Rory was distracted by the unusual advertisement but also managed to catch a glimpse of a road sign advising that Paso Robles lay just 10 miles ahead. He was eager to capture the rest of the areas of strategic focus that propel a company forward before making camp for the night.

"Okay, keep going," he implored his passenger.

Sydney was only too pleased to comply, it was clear he enjoyed having an audience. "Some companies are propelled forward by a certain technology they have access to. Sometimes they don't even have a product, just the distinctive technology. They use that to develop a product or range of products that rely on the technology. They create their own demand. Look at DuPont. They discovered nylon back in 1935 I believe, and they used their nylon technology for everything from carpet to stockings to fishing line."

"Got it, technology," Rory said with more than a hint of urgency.

"In a hurry, Newman? This is gold I'm givin' you here. In the spirit of the locale, it's like a fine wine, to be savored, not gulped."

Rory simply nodded his head.

"But seeing as how you're such a willing student, I'll continue. You like this ring?" He thrust his sausage of a pinky finger in front of Rory's face.

Rory followed the ring as Sydney's arm took its position back on his lap. Despite its substantial size, Rory couldn't determine just exactly what was depicted on the setting. The best he could come up with was that it was a gaudy knockoff of something Keith Richards might wear.

"Yeah, it's lovely."

"The girlfriend gave it to me. I know it's a little tacky but it represents our love so I wear it with pride." He stopped, lost in thought, then continued. "Anyway, she got it on that shopping channel, QVC, I think."

"And this is relevant how?" Rory demanded.

"It's *relevant* because QVC represents another area of focus." A frosty glare was shot in Rory's direction. "They're not defined by their products, or technology, or customer group, or capabilities. With them, it's their sales channels. You can buy anything from jeans to Christmas trees but you do so through specific channels. My girlfriend bought this off the TV. Amway is another example of a company that's propelled by its sales and distribution channel. They move a lot of different products through the system, doesn't matter what, what matters is how.

"So that's five, what's the sixth way?"

"Raw materials. Like oil companies, if it comes from a barrel of oil, they'll make it. Mining companies are also good examples."

"So let me ask you this," Rory began. "We make products, we have customers and markets, we employ certain technologies, and we utilize sales and distribution channels. Are you saying we have to ignore all but one of these? That doesn't make sense."

"Hamlet."

"Give me strength. Here we go again!" Rory thought, digging his fingernails deeply into the leather steering wheel.

"To thine own self be true. That's what Polonius said in Hamlet, and that's what organizations have to do. Be true to themselves. One of the six areas I just told you about has to be primary and fundamental, your stake in the ground, the area you stay true to no matter what happens. Then you can make decisions about what to do, and just as important, what not to do. You can decide how to invest all your precious resources like money, time, and people. You'll still keep an eye on the other areas, of course, but you have to maintain a focus in one." After a pause, he added, "Make sense?"

"I wasn't an English major so the Hamlet reference is a bit of a stretch, but, yeah, overall, I understand. It's all about focus."

Rory had been to Paso Robles on two other occasions, spontaneous weekend getaways with Hannah that provided a deep reservoir of warm memories. They lodged at the same hotel during both trips and thus Rory directed the car toward The Vine View Manor, devoid of any real conscious choice in the matter. He parked between a pair of Ford Tauruses, rentals, he thought, and he and Sydney got out of the car. Like two cats emerging from a long nap in the sun, they stretched their arms to the sky and vibrated rhythmically, shaking off the long trip.

"You go ahead. I'll meet you in the lobby tomorrow morning at eight," Rory said as Sydney began to collect his belongings. With a shrug he headed for the lobby as Rory returned to the car, and began writing copious notes on what had turned out to be a day to remember.

12

One Night at the Vine View Manor

I t took almost three full pages on a trusty yellow pad (he never went anywhere without one) but after 45 minutes in the car, culminating with a deep breath in recognition of a job well done, Rory slipped the notepad in his case, and made his way across the parking lot. A freshening breeze cooled his cheeks as he climbed the three wide steps leading to the Vine View Manor's grape-themed lobby.

The reception area was quiet, just the shuffling of the balding mid-50s desk clerk and the slow whirring of an overhead fan providing a gentle background hum, as Rory completed his registration. "You've stayed with us before, haven't you Mr. Newman?" inquired the clerk. Rory nodded and smiled, "Yes, twice, with my wife." The clerk returned the smile and added, "Is she with you today?" As the words were floating from his lips, around the corner lumbered Sydney, striding with a definite purpose. Rory looked at Sydney, then at the clerk, and said flatly, "No, my wife isn't with me on this trip."

"Always like to conduct a tour of the premises," Sydney announced. His appearance was unchanged from the car with the exception of a large beach towel wrapped around his neck like a thick terry scarf.

"Heading to the pool?" Rory asked.

"Yep, that's the next stop."

"Where's your bathing suit?"

"*Birthday* suit, Newman, that's all I need. I'm hittin' the pool old school, just as nature intended."

The disturbing visual of Sydney parading naked around the pool made its way to Rory and the desk clerk simultaneously. Their faces were suddenly seized with contorted lines spreading like rivers in an atlas. The desk clerk began fumbling through a stack of papers below the counter, no doubt in search of a dusty hotel policy prohibiting nudity, while Rory flashed ahead to the cries of screaming children and mothers leaping to shield their little eyes.

"Gotcha!" Sydney screamed, then erupted in laughter.

"Yeah, good one," Rory muttered as he grabbed his key card, which was stuffed into a small paper holder announcing two-for-one drinks in the bar. He glanced down, saw "305" on the paper and trotted toward the elevator. Normally he would have taken the stairs but it had been a long day and the reward of a short elevator ride was warranted. Once in the elevator he pressed "3" and waited for the doors to close. Nothing. He pressed the "close door" button, and after another five or six seconds the doors slowly closed. Then began the slowest three-floor ride in the history of multistory buildings. It was as if the elevator was being lifted by a group of men huddled in the shaft. It jerked and creaked but eventually landed with a rocky thud at the third floor.

Rory didn't fit the mold of a seasoned road warrior, but he'd spent his share of nights in hotel rooms and had cultivated a routine over the years: place his suitcase on the bed and his briefcase next to the desk. Take out his laptop and check the Internet situation. Wireless? Good. Next, draw open the curtains and check for a view. This room didn't disappoint on that count, it hovered directly over the pool area. After that, he untied his shoes and began the unpacking process: first toiletries, then anything that needed to be hung, and finally socks and T-shirts. If the hotel was situated in a city or part of a city he deemed marginal, the protocol called for him to get down on all fours and check under the bed for intruders. A dramatic step, but he'd seen it on *The Today Show* in one of their hidden camera hotel investigations and the seed took root. If it was a really questionable venue he'd even yank back the shower curtain in *Psycho* fashion, lest an intruder be lurking.

Safely cocooned in room 305, Rory opened his laptop and began checking the day's e-mails. Because many of his colleagues had been in Napa with him, his inbox was mercifully small, but as always, there were a few notes that required immediate action. He started in on what he considered the most urgent matter, a recently discovered glitch in Kitteridge's budgeting software reported by one of his analysts. Then it arrived: the shrill screams of a baby echoing through the corridor. He sat in silence for a moment, praying the wailer wouldn't end up next to him. But a moment later he heard the click of the key card hitting what had to be 307 and suddenly there was nothing between him and the bellowing infant but a picture of the Tuscan landscape and two sheets of drywall.

Swiftly putting an escape plan in motion, Rory donned his swimming trunks and headed for the window to scope out the situation at the pool. He glanced down and his eyes were drawn immediately to Sydney's head of thick red hair, fully liberated from his bandana, flopping along beside a table. The queasiness associated with the birthday suit comment returned as he awaited Sydney's emergence from the shelter of the table. "Please tell me he's not in a Speedo!" Rory repeated to himself over and over, despite the fact he had seen Sydney in the lobby only moments ago.

Rory exhaled a sigh of relief as Sydney waltzed under his window in a moderately respectable suit featuring sharks and sailboats. Rory grabbed his flip-flops from beside the bed, their habitual position, and made his way to the pool.

The swim proved to be just what the doctor ordered for Rory. It dished out equal parts rejuvenation after a long day and soothing relaxation that would tee up a quiet evening back in the room. Once there he ordered a room service dinner of grilled salmon, mixed vegetables, and a glass of local Cabernet. After struggling with the decision, he also gave into a guilty pleasure and ordered the carrot cake. While waiting for his meal he phoned Hannah. Their lively conversation easily filled the 30 minutes that the room service operator had promised it would take for his dinner to arrive. He gave her a spirited account of the adventures he and Sydney had taken part in and used the opportunity to recite his lessons once again: ensure a consistent definition of strategy, do your homework, be willing to challenge assumptions, ask the right questions, develop or critically examine your mission, and the most recent pearl, determine what propels you. Hannah listened attentively, even breaking in with a few clarifying questions from time to time. When it was her turn to supply an accounting of her day it consisted of a hodgepodge of reunion-related activities: picking up vast quantities of soda, darting to the airport for pickups, working and reworking where everyone would stay. "A G7 summit can't be this hard to orchestrate," she noted. She then began a mild tirade about the challenges of acquiring appropriately sized plastic cups when two knocks and the call of "room service" filled Rory's room.

An hour later he placed the empty tray, save for a doughy half-eaten roll, gently on the floor outside his room. As a matter of fact, everything was done gently at this point, since the baby had long since ceased its laments, all was quiet, and Rory intended to do his part to keep it that way. He went through his pre-sleep routine, then slipped into bed when he realized he hadn't placed his breakfast order. Rory was a big believer in filling out the cards left in hotel rooms that allow you to order in advance by checking what you'd like, choosing a desired serving time, and hanging the card outside your door. Less margin for error this way, he reckoned.

He got out of bed, found the card stuffed inside the hotel guide, and perused the options carefully: "American breakfast," "Healthy Start," "Vegetarian Delight." Nothing suited his fancy, so he opted to fill out the "Special Requests" section at the bottom of the card. To draw the staff's attention to this choice he drew a bold square around the blank lines in that section, and to really reinforce his order, he decided to number his selections; leaving no room for interpretation. He wrote in bold and legible capital letters: 1. ORANGE JUICE. 2. COFFEE. 3. HALF GRAPEFRUIT (a big fear here because at least half the time they brought grapefruit *juice*, so he deliberately placed it third, hoping they would realize there was no way he'd want orange juice, coffee, and grapefruit juice), and finally he wrote, 4. WHOLE WHEAT TOAST. He then ticked the 6:45 to 7:00 A.M. box, circled it for extra attention and hung the card on his door. "Nothing left to chance," he thought as he tucked himself back into bed and soon dozed off into a deep and restful sleep.

Rory awoke the next morning at six A.M. refreshed and energized. The first order of business was to check outside his door and confirm the room service breakfast card had been retrieved. It had. "We're off to a good start," he thought, as he grabbed the copy of *USA Today* at his door. He then went about the rest of his morning routine: shower, shave, dress, read the paper, and check e-mail. At 6:52 A.M., a sharp knock on his door announced room service, and he anxiously bounced from the chair to answer it. "Right on schedule!"

The bubbly young blonde server greeted him enthusiastically and bounded into his room with tray in hand, asking where she should place it. Without even glancing at the tray or its contents he instructed her to put it on the coffee table, which she did. Rory expected a bill to be produced at this point, but instead he was surprised when she said, "I just have to go and get your other trays." She arrived with two more heaping trays and suddenly he realized what had happened. In misinterpreting his ordering scheme, something he fought so diligently to avoid, she delivered one glass of orange juice, two cups of coffee, three half-grapefruits, and four orders of toast. An order of toast is two slices, each cut in half, so for Rory's order that amounted to 16 pieces. They were piled so high on the plate the cover was unable to conceal them. Rory laughed out loud at this gaffe, taking responsibility for the miscommunication, but on the inside he was puzzled, thinking: "Didn't she take even a moment to consider this rather bizarre order?" The lessons of the previous day, teachings from which the room service staff could greatly benefit, were once again fresh in his mind: Challenge your assumptions, ask questions, think your way out of things.

13

Pucker Up

At precisely 7:59 A.M., Rory hopped down the stairs outside the Vine View Manor lobby and jogged to the car. To his surprise, Sydney Wise was leaning against the passenger door, coffee in hand, enormous duffel bag at his feet. The orange bandana was back, as were the boots and belt, but the shirt and shorts had been updated. Today he was sporting a silk Nat Nast shirt, very simple in design. It was inky black, with two white stripes flowing vertically on either side of the diamond shaped buttons. His shorts were earthy brown and fashionably distressed. Rory was comfortably clad in jeans and a white polo shirt, a change from his typical uniform of dress shirts and khakis, but he still appeared ultra-conservative next to Sydney.

Upon seeing his companion, a tonic of mixed emotions rushed through Rory. Sydney was there and on time, that was good, but he was leaning on the car, potentially spreading dust and possibly even scratching Rory's beloved automobile, that was not so good. But if he had to take one over the other, it was having Sydney waiting attentively, ensuring the day got started on schedule. In a flash, he determined the moment was a microcosm of his budding relationship with Sydney: there were things about his pseudo-mentor that he didn't care for, but overall, as he got to know the gruff giant, there was a lot to like and appreciate.

"Good morning," Rory chirped.

"Mornin'," Sydney replied.

They placed their bags in the trunk, hopped into the car, Rory started the engine, and then he just sat there, as if in some kind of meditative state.

"What are you waiting for?" Sydney asked.

"Thirty seconds in any weather," Rory said. It was his custom, he had many, to always provide the engine with thirty seconds to warm up before shifting out of park. He read the advice years earlier and couldn't even recall the source at this point, but it resonated with him at the time, and he continued the practice to this day.

Rory pulled his phone from his pants pocket and brought up a text message. "Okay, here's the plan. We meet Ike Redmond at 8:30 at the Travis Hill Ranch, which is located at 10038 Travis Hill Road. Here, you can navigate." He tossed a sheet of paper on Sydney's lap that contained the directions to the ranch. Sydney inspected the paper briefly, rolled it up, and filed it in a cup holder. "No problem," Rory responded, "I've memorized the directions anyway."

"According to Jim, Ike loves to ride horses, gets out whenever he can and says this Travis Hill Ranch has some of the prettiest country in central California. Apparently that's where he does most of his business, too, on the back of a horse." The clock in his head now well past 30 seconds, Rory pulled the gearshift into drive, and soon the two were cruising east, on the hunt for Jardine Road. As they rolled past gas stations, tack shops, small tasting rooms, and a variety of other entrepreneurial endeavors, Rory continued. "Should be a real feather in the old cap if I can get Ike to commit to carrying our products." He paused, and then added, "I mean *when* I get Ike to commit." A satisfied smile spread across his face, while his head nodded in the affirmative.

"Turn here," Sydney barked. Rory, still absorbed in his self-help moment, came to and yanked the steering wheel to the left, producing a subdued squeal from the car's tires. The scene became instantly rural, a two-lane road, bordered on either side by rickety fences of wobbly posts and tattered wire. Beyond them, lay fields of chaparral, interrupted by the occasional stand of oaks. "We follow this for two miles," Rory said. The road weaved back and forth like the contours of a wriggling snake, ensuring Rory never got above 30 miles an hour. Without any prompting from Sydney, Rory then turned right on Hog Canyon Road. He demonstrated his geographic prowess by flicking the right turn signal well in advance of the actual turn, but it failed to draw any reaction from a reticent Sydney.

"Three miles down here, then right on Travis Hill Road, and then the ranch," Rory said while stealing a glance at his watch: 8:15, still plenty of time. The terrain altered now, even blossomed, as vineyards emerged in every direction, with men and women in white shirts and wide-brimmed hats going about their daily work, kicking up dust as they moved languidly through the rows of grapes. If you looked closely you could see rabbits scurrying along the clods of brown earth, squirrels darting to and fro, while overhead birds were gliding effortlessly. It was magical. The bucolic images seemed to hypnotize both Rory and Sydney who drove quietly, absorbing this idyllic parallel universe with not a word exchanged.

Finally, Sydney broke the trance by stating flatly, "We've gone more than three miles." Rory hadn't checked the odometer, but a glance at his watch caused his heart to nearly skip a beat;

it was 8:30. He was going to be late. Could there be a more vile word in the entire English language? Late: the last bastion of the irresponsible, of the unaccountable, of unreliable scoundrels. He despised being late for anything. And now, at the dawn of a new era at his company, at the first opportunity to impress, he was about to show up late for a critical meeting. "Did we miss it?" he cried out in obvious panic. Before Sydney could respond, Rory jabbed at the cup holder, groping for the directions. He unfurled the map, eyes racing between the twisting road and the paper, searching for their error. Had they missed a turn? Impossible, he'd memorized the simple steps over his 16 pieces of toast during breakfast.

Without warning, Rory swerved the car violently onto a makeshift road that consisted of nothing but two tire tracks. He jammed the gearshift into reverse and stepped on the pedal, sending the car rocketing backward along Hog Canyon Road. Still not a word from Sydney. The scenery literally disappeared from his view; beyond the asphalt road was nothing but white space. He raced along, head bobbing from side to side, in search of Travis Hill Road. 8:39, his watch mocked.

"There." Sydney pointed a finger at a wounded post, leaning at about a 45-degree angle just off the shoulder of the road. Its faded sign dangled like a severed limb, and the words were barely visible, but as the car sped closer, it came into focus: Travis Hill Road with a tiny arrow. Rory hit the turn hard, shooting gravel up past the windows, before steadying the car on the hard-packed dirt road. They rumbled along the desolate lane, waiting for the elusive ranch to reveal itself, when Rory spotted a small hand-painted wooden sign announcing Travis Hill Ranch in bright red letters. He slowed the car, attempting to regain his composure and make what he hoped would appear a dignified arrival, but one infused with a sense of urgency, given the hour.

For some reason, when Rory had conjured images of Travis Hill Ranch, Southfork from the old TV series *Dallas* popped into his mind. He pictured a long and elegant drive framed by majestic cypress trees, with grassy fields spreading out on either side showcasing spectacular horses galloping along in carefree play. In his head, the drive would lead to a palatial manor with lusciously manicured grounds exploding in a Technicolor sea of flowers.

Southfork this was not. The house was probably about 30 years old, but by the measuring stick of wear and tear, the injured structure appeared to be of a far more advanced age. The windows were single pane and appeared to be in pain— just one tap away from shattering; and peeling paint littered the house like leaves from a windy autumn day. Everything screamed out for renovation. The sickly dwelling was surrounded by a group of equally neglected outbuildings including, to Rory's utter astonishment, a small and rickety wooden hut with a sign tacked on it that said, "Gift Shop."

"You think they sell snow globes in there?" Sydney chuckled.

Rory nosed the Mercedes up to a sparkling new Chevy Tahoe, very much out of place in this environment, and tentatively slid the car into park. He got out and nearly heaved at the sight of his beloved car, now cloaked in a sweater of dust and dirt from the morning's rally driving. He was busy calculating the next possible opportunity to give the car a bath when someone charged out of the barn. Bobbing along toward them was a chubby man in his 50s, with a round and red face, wide and friendly eyes, a bulbous nose, and thick dry lips. He licked those lips as he drew close to Rory and Sydney, and offered his hand enthusiastically. "Ike Redmond, and you must be Rory?"

"Yes I am, it's great to meet you Ike, and I'm so sorry I'm late—"

"No problem whatsoever," Ike interrupted, "We're on horse time here." He pointed back at the barn where the laid-back but inquisitive horses had craned their long necks over their stall doors to catch a glimpse of the visitors. Rory peered into the big soft eyes but his gaze was soon drawn once again to the ramshackle buildings surrounding them. Ike caught the diverted glance, and said, "It's not much to look at, but they take great care of their horses, and you're gonna just love the scenery. Speaking of the horses, let me find Marcy." Right on cue, a tanned and winsome young woman in her late 20s and decked out in full cowgirl regalia made her way from the tack room inside the barn. "This is Marcy, she's going to be our guide today," Ike said as he directed the young woman into the conversation. "And you are?" Ike shot his hand toward Sydney.

"Sydney Wise."

"You with Kitteridge, oops, I guess I should say Olivenhain?"

"No," was the extent of Sydney's reply.

After a flurry of handshakes acquainting the group, Ike said, "Well, let's get you fellas saddled up and hit the trail. Marcy, whaddya think?"

Marcy surveyed Rory and Sydney, neither of whom looked ready for a *Bonanza* moment, turned to the barn examining the available stock, then said calmly, "Buzz and Pucker." Ike grinned in agreement and Marcy retreated to the very darkest confines of the barn, emerging moments later with two big barreled and groggy quarter horses that looked so mellow that a bomb wouldn't arouse them. Upon seeing the two walking sofas, a wave of instant relief flowed through Rory, who approached them confidently and began stroking their warm necks.

Ike was right about horse time. The tacking up process for all four horses (Marcy and Ike chose to ride the more spirited Iris and Val), including the requisite brushing, blanketing, saddling, cinching, and bridling took close to an hour. Then came the moment of reckoning. A mounting block was brought from the barn, placed next to Pucker, and Rory was directed atop the plastic contraption. "Put your left foot in the stirrup, grab the horn and pull yourself up. It's as easy as pie," Ike said reassuringly. Rory, sensing the pressure of three pairs of eyes riveted on him, not to mention Pucker's placid glance, literally rose to the occasion and propelled himself up like John Wayne. Not to be outdone, Sydney followed in equally impressive fashion and before they could say "giddyup," Buzz and Pucker were walking slowly along the dusty path that meandered to the surrounding hills.

The facilities at Travis Hill Ranch may have left something to be desired, but the scenery was stunning. There were miles of trails cutting through endless hillsides, alive with a rich tapestry of oak trees, rugged native brush, and gently swaying grasses. But it was more than a visual feast, the sounds were equally magnificent: the wind dancing through branches, eagles whooshing above, creeks bubbling through ancient beds, and the rhythmic clomping of the horses' hooves. Even the feel of the leather reins, lightly cradled between his thumb and index finger, was soothing to Rory.

Marcy acted as proud tour guide; the property had been in her family for more than 100 years, and she boasted that she'd seen every square inch of it either on foot or on the back of a horse. "Know this place like the back of my own hand, I do," she said. Nobody in the group would dispute the claim. The farther they descended into the bush, the more Rory found his cares melting away, and he was almost disappointed when Ike said, "Well, I guess we should talk a little business."

"Right, right," Rory said, as he transported himself back to the world of commerce.

"I'm a simple man, Rory, so I'll keep this real easy. Why don't you tell me why I should start carrying your company's products?"

Although his job title didn't convey sales in any way, Rory was a veteran of Kitteridge and knew both the company and its products inside out. He prided himself, as did many employees, on being an ambassador for the company's wares. So he didn't hesitate. He launched into a passionate narrative of the company's founding, its history, the craftsmanship inherent in its products, the proprietary technology it employed, the loyalty of its customers, and the commitment and skill demonstrated by its employees. Rory's many years of toiling over a calculator and spreadsheets were readily apparent as he then began to regale his prospect with tantalizing visions of the revenue growth, value, and earnings that would result should Ike decide to stock Kitteridge products. The monologue went on for a good 10 minutes, absorbing the time it took to cautiously cross a vibrant creek bed, traverse a sandy and rutted portion of the trail, and weave back to a grassy hillside.

Ike stopped under the shade of a giant sycamore, starting a chain reaction of "whoas" and allowing the horses to graze on the lush grass at their feet. He took in the vast expanse around them and said in a measured tone, "I like your passion Rory, and I like your—" He was interrupted by the buzzing of his mobile phone, tucked deep in the recesses of his saddlebag.

"Shoot, I thought I left that thing in the car," Ike exclaimed. Sydney leaned across Buzz to Rory and whispered, "Then don't answer it." But Ike, like so many people, found the lure of a buzzing phone just too irresistible and overpowering. He dismounted from Val and extricated his phone from the saddlebag. "Ike Redmond here. Yes . . . yes . . . what time? Okay, tell them I'll be there." He put the phone back in the bag and looked up at the others. "I'm real sorry but I gotta' get back. You finish your ride with Marcy though, the view from that summit will take your breath away." He walked over to Rory and Sydney, shook their hands, then hopped back aboard

Val, spun to the west and was gone. From about 50 yards down the trail he turned slightly in the saddle, without breaking from a steady trot, and said almost as an afterthought, "I'll have to get back to you Rory."

Sitting slack-jawed on Pucker, Rory assessed what had just happened. One minute he was in rhetorical glory, with Ike apparently hanging on every word, and the next minute Ike was gone. What was he going to tell Jim, who would most certainly be calling for an update? In his state of intense focus he failed to notice Marcy and Sydney had gone on without him, and were rapidly climbing the knoll that led to the ranch's highest point. He shook the reins, gave Pucker's barrel a firm squeeze, and the two were on their way.

After another five minutes of campaigning the three reached the peak, and Ike was right; it took Rory's breath away. A commanding 360-degree panorama of vineyards, olive groves, secluded estates, and mile upon mile of ambling trails, all painted in the organic colors of nature. Even the air felt different, it felt alive, energizing, tangible. The three rolled off their horses and stood transfixed. After a few minutes of quiet reflection, punctuated by the crunching sounds of apples and trail mix, Marcy pointed out historical landmarks, old travel routes, and even hypothesized about the microclimates that impacted the growing season in the region. Finally, with a heartfelt sigh that betrayed how much she hated to leave this cherished spot, she said, "Well, I guess we oughta head back to the ranch."

Chatter was kept to a minimum as they ambled along the trails, swaying side to side on the horses' backs. Then, with Marcy out in front a ways, Sydney sidled Buzz up along Pucker, turned to Rory and said, "You know, you're going to get that account."

"What do you mean?"

"With Ike."

"Why do you say that?

"The way you talked about Kitteridge. A lot of people would have hit it hard with the numbers: Here's what you stand to make, here's what it'll cost you, and so on. But you painted a real picture, a meaningful picture, of the company in lots of dimensions. Ike responded to that. Hell, I responded."

They passed a tall stand of pine trees, the long needles tickling their elbows as they brushed by. Rory considered Sydney's words, his praise, stifled a proud smile, and said, "Yeah, well, we'll see what he says." He paused, then added, "If I'm so persuasive, maybe I can get Jim to buy my newfound strategic planning expertise."

"Well you already know the next step."

"What?"

"The next step, you already know it."

"Okay Sydney, all you did was rearrange your words, now tell me what you're talking about." Rory said this with a hint of irritation not so much directed at Sydney, but more as a result of a literal, and growing, irritation he felt in the saddle.

"What did you tell Ike?"

"I told him about the company."

"Elaborate," Sydney pressed.

"I talked about our people, how committed and knowledgeable they are, about the technology we use, about our customers, about the financial aspects of stocking our products."

"In other words," Sydney broke in, "you spoke about a number of dimensions."

Rory considered this and said, "I guess so, yeah."

"It's the same in strategic planning. The first of the fundamental questions you have to answer is what propels you. We talked about that after the Vanagon adventure, remember?"

"Sure." Rory spit the word out like venom. The chafing irritation against the saddle leather was morphing from an annoyance into a legitimate pain. Sydney peered at him, but everything looked okay so he continued.

"There are three other fundamental questions that underpin your strategy, but this is a good point to introduce what I call the four lenses." He formed his long fingers into circles and mimed the focusing of a set of binoculars. Rory followed the shape of his fingers but was more impressed with the fact that Sydney had the courage to drop his reins, although it appeared Buzz was oblivious to the momentary liberation.

"The four lenses?" Rory asked.

"Yeah, it's looking at things from multiple dimensions or lenses. Every decision you make about strategy should be examined through each of the lenses."

"Elaborate," Rory said, mimicking Sydney.

"I think you already know Newman, but okay. The first lens or dimension is social and cultural. When you're making decisions about strategy you have to consider the impact on your social environment, and your culture. You've got to start with the heart. Let's say you determine what propels you are products and services, but based on the research you've done and the discussions your team has had about the future, you decide you want to switch to a technology focus. Well, the first thing you have to ask is: Are we passionate about technology? Start with the heart. If your focus has always been products and services, chances are that's where your passion lies, and that's what your culture has been built around. Changing your focus could impact the whole fabric of your organization. You have to ask if you're prepared for something like that."

"Are you talking about values?" Rory asked.

"Yeah, values fit in there. Values are timeless beliefs shared by all employees. And again, they're going to be shaped over time by what propels you as a company. You change that focus, and you better be prepared for a cultural, social, and values shift."

Rory was fidgeting almost constantly in his saddle now, trying to alleviate the pain shooting from either side of his rear end. With each step Pucker took, his skin was blistering. There was no doubt, he had saddle sores.

"Everything okay Newman?"

"Yeah, yeah, fine. Let me see if I get this. I told Ike about our people so one of the lenses has to be people." He paused, awaiting Sydney's reaction, but as he had learned, silence meant he should press on. "When you think about your strategy you have to figure out whether you have the right people, correct?" Rory's intellectual exercise served the dual purpose of bolstering his strategic planning knowledge and briefly masking the lasers of pain.

"I call it the human lens," Sydney began. "Every decision you make about strategy will imply a certain set of necessary skills. You have to determine whether your people have the skills necessary to execute the strategy you're contemplating. If they don't, are you willing to make the investments in hiring and training to fill the gaps? Because if you're not, your strategy isn't worth the paper it's written on."

The horses cantered up a rise, Rory standing in the stirrups to minimize the agonizing discomfort. When they reached the top, the ranch, glimmering in gold at the horizon, came into view. Rory felt like an ancient explorer who's been at sea for months and then peers over the ship's rail one fateful day and spies land. The relief! But then reality fell over him like a thick net and he realized they were still a good mile from the ranch.

"You sure you're okay, Newman?"

"Yeah . . . the third lens is technology, right?" Bits and pieces of his speech to Ike were flashing across his mental sky and technology seemed a logical candidate for one of the lenses.

"Grasshopper strikes again. That's right. Every decision you make about strategy also has to be examined through a technological lens. Will the decision require an investment in new technology? What about the current technology you employ, will it become redundant? And as you can probably see for yourself, the lenses impact one another. New technology may require new skill sets, the human lens. And technology is one of the most threatening things you can introduce, especially to seasoned employees, so you better have a good grasp on your cultural and social lens."

Marcy stopped to let Rory and Sydney meet her at a wide swath of trail. "You up for a shortcut?" she asked. "Yes!" Rory gasped. "Follow me," she said. They tucked through a narrow opening between two fence posts and Marcy began to trot on Iris. "No, not more bouncing!" Rory thought. But the upside of getting back to the ranch even one minute sooner won out over the intolerable pain of every collision between backside and saddle.

Once again grasping at any means of occupying his mind, Rory managed to stutter over the horse's jarring gait: "Ssssooo, tthee ffourtttthhh llleeennnss . . ."

"Financial," Sydney shot back in a perfectly smooth cadence as if he were riding in the backseat of a Rolls Royce gliding over an airport runway. "Your strategic decisions will entail financial investments, whether in infrastructure, or people, or capacity, you name it. And, of course, you expect revenue growth and profit as well. The question is: will the revenue and profit compensate for the investments?"

Was it a mirage, playing the nastiest and most sinister of tricks on him? What was it? Rory and Pucker plunged ahead and with each plodding step the image took clearer shape. Finally, in high relief against the bright blue sky, it became clear to him. It was, in all its glory, the gift shop. As Sydney galloped past, making a heroic return to the ranch, he turned to Rory and said, "Maybe they sell Band-Aids in there, cowboy."

14

Charged Up in Pismo Beach

O ne of the first things Rory noticed when he test-
drove his C230 was the rigid and unforgiving driver's seat. The salesman took the opportunity to turn a
negative into a positive, as salespeople are wont to do, and
responded to his concern by noting that American cars often
camouflage performance deficits with seats that are as soft and
plush as living room sofas. "What do you want, a La-Z-Boy or a
performance automobile?" The salesman had barked. Rory at
first grudgingly accepted the unyielding leather, but over time
began to come around to the salesman's view and wore the discomfort as something of a badge of honor. Two hours aboard
Pucker, however, made him yearn for the soft leather of a recliner
on wheels today.

He contorted himself gingerly into the driver's seat, shifting
only as absolutely necessary to gain full access to the pedals and

steering wheel. Sydney jumped vigorously into his seat, producing a small earthquake within the car and causing Rory to wince in anticipation of the inevitable pain that was to follow. Rory caught a glimpse of Marcy leading Buzz and Pucker lazily back to the barn as he adjusted the rearview mirror before guiding the car past the gift shop and back to the road.

The alarm clock in Rory's stomach was not deterred by his throbbing rear end, and it began to sound a distress signal almost as soon as the two had reached the 101. He was about to acquiesce when he realized they were still more than 300 miles from San Diego, and even without another stop it would be close to 6:00 P.M. before they arrived. Judging by his slow and easy breathing and closed eyes, Sydney had drifted into a post-ride slumber, hence chatting to keep his mind occupied was out of the question for Rory. He decided to turn the dialog inward and once again played in his head the lessons he'd learned, weighing them for validity, and questioning their applicability to the new situation that had suddenly emerged at Kitteridge.

It's not that he was hoping to discredit what Sydney had shared with him, he was simply casting a critical eye, as anyone new to the subject should. But the more he rolled the tape, the more the teachings seemed perfectly suited to his, or any, organization. Specify your terms, do your homework by asking creative questions, and craft your mission—your core purpose as an organization. Then determine what propels you as an organization; what it is that drives you forward and will inform all your subsequent decisions. Finally, he came back to the four lenses of social/cultural, human, technological, and financial that must be considered when answering the basic strategy questions. The intervening minutes since the bumpy ride had added some perspective and he saw how vital each lens was to making strategic decisions, and how they could interact with one another, thereby enriching the strategic dialogue.

The reflection had distracted his mind from his discomfort, and Rory felt a deep satisfaction take hold of him. He was unquestionably pleased with what he'd learned and bordering on optimistic when it came to his chances of delivering a report that would be favorably received by Jim and his other new bosses at Olivenhain.

"Can't be," Rory thought as the car whizzed past a sign for Santa Margarita. "That's like 25 miles." Then he realized, "It's the car coma." Car coma: you're driving along, totally absorbed in thought and completely oblivious to the world outside your windshield. But like a person wrapped in the cocoon of a coma, you're still functioning. On some remote level your mind is processing what's taking place as the tires sing over the road and your motor skills are adept enough to act on what the brain is transmitting, but part of you just isn't there, it's lost in contemplation. Everything you pass while lost in the car coma—every building, every shrub, every other car—is one big empty void.

In his own powerful reverie, Rory had passed Highway 46, which if traveled about 19 miles to the west will lead to the Cabrillo Highway, and from there it's just a few miles north to one of Hannah's favorite places, Hearst Castle. The palatial estate of newspaper magnate William Randolph Hearst is a true gem, set on over 100 stunning acres. He'd also zoomed past Templeton, Atascadero, and Highway 41, a left turn on which would take you to Creston, a picturesque hamlet of wandering vineyards and horse ranches.

It was a ringing phone that finally jolted Rory and Sydney, who was clearly dissatisfied with the duration of his nap, back into full consciousness. Through the speaker, even before Rory could get out a greeting, Melville Bell began to clamor.

"Rory, you won't believe what Mark is doing!"

"Take it easy Mel, what's going on?"

"Well, it was lunch so I was in my office doing my Kettlebell Jerks, when I heard Mark making a ruckus in your office."

At the word Kettlebell, Sydney gave a quizzical look, prompting Rory to whisper, "It's an ancient Russian exercise." Sydney was clearly not convinced so Rory continued, "Basically like a cast iron cannonball that weighs about 35 pounds with a handle on it." Still nothing but skepticism from Sydney. "It's big in Hollywood," Rory offered. Sydney rolled his eyes, shook his head, and commenced taking in the passing scenery, marking his exit from the conversation.

"Rory . . . you still there?"

"Yeah Mel, sorry. Go on." He said this tentatively, suddenly recognizing that Sydney, who quoted German generals, American statesmen, and Shakespeare and who seemed to know the tagline of every city, town, and village in California, didn't know what a Kettlebell was. Rory's superior knowledge, at least on this one very arcane item, provided him with satisfaction beyond measure.

Mel continued: "So I go over to make sure everything's okay and Mark is lounging in your chair and has his feet all over your desk."

Rory shuddered at the incursion and the violation of his glass-top desk, one he burnished with Windex on a daily basis. The image of Mark's loafers on the pristine surface caused his stomach to churn violently.

"So I said to him: What do you think you're doing Mark?"

At this point, Rory's phone battery uttered a warning beep, signaling it was on its last legs, but the caveat was ignored.

"And?" Rory urged him to continue.

"And, he says: 'You want this chair Bell? How about that credenza? Newman's not long for this place, so consider it a corporate yard sale.'"

"That slimy bas—" Rory stopped short of a full-on profanity-laced tirade, calculating quickly that Mark's wickedness, the limits of which knew no bounds, could have somehow led to him threaten Mel with who knows what, and then forced him to make the call, with Mark right there in the office no doubt recording it for his later advantage.

"Don't worry about it, Mel," Rory said, now bathed in a veneer of calm.

"But what did he mean Rory?"

"I've got to deliver a report on how to develop a strategic plan and he's, well, let's just say he's skeptical about my chances of success."

"When is . . ." Mel's voice trailed off as Rory's dying phone battery emitted its final wailing beep, and then the car was quiet once again. Rory picked up the phone from the cup holder and inspected it closely, like some artifact from a cave.

"So charge it," Sydney croaked.

"Tried that. The battery is toast, won't hold a charge," Rory returned. "We're going to have to stop to get one, plus I'm starving." Rory took the next exit off the 101, which happened to be Price Street.

"Seventeenth longest pier in California," Sydney said calmly.

"What are you talking about?"

"Pismo Beach. It's got the seventeenth longest pier in California, about 1,200 feet if memory serves."

This savant-like knowledge of California trivia was beginning to wear very thin on Rory, who especially resented the timing of this particular tidbit, coming as it did on the heels of his own intellectual display.

"Who would possibly know something like that? What's with you anyway?" he demanded and then returned his attention to the road as they darted past two beachfront hotels and veered south.

Pismo Beach, unlike many of its small town brethren across the United States and around the world that have cultivated a taste for the big box retailer, has done an enviable job of maintaining an eclectic collection of locally owned establishments. On Cypress Street alone, the curious traveler will find a pleasing mélange of shops hawking everything from garden gnomes to hippie-era beads to, of course, all things surf. Rory and Sydney found their heads bobbing from side to side as if watching a tennis match, while they soaked up the blend of shops and restaurants, tourists and locals who make up this vibrant little coastal community. Fortunately for Rory, the medley of businesses included its share of mobile phone stores, and he soon discovered Bob's Mobile Mart beckoning less than a few hundred feet on his right. He flicked the turn signal, turned into the parking lot, then had to brake sharply for two teenage surfer dudes who appeared out of nowhere. Once the coast was clear he guided the car to a spot in front of the store's two glass doors.

"You coming in?" Rory turned and asked Sydney.

"Why not?"

As with many small businesses, the door to Bob's Mobile Mart was equipped with a bell that dinged upon opening, alerting employees to potential customers. Unfortunately, this particular bell didn't appear to provoke the intended effect from the store's single employee, a razor-thin young man, with spiky brown hair who sat slumped like a fern over a wooden stool behind the store's only counter, with, what else, a cell phone glued to his ear. He wore a muddy brown T-shirt with writing on it, but the letters were presently obscured by his posture on the stool. Black jeans and Vans completed his ensemble.

With the jangling of the bell fading behind them, the two walked into the center of the small square store and were surprised by the choice of music being played.

"Is that opera?" Rory asked with a quizzical expression.

Sydney hesitated, then said with an affirmative nod, "'Dove Sono,' from *The Marriage of Figaro*." Responding to Rory's immediate glare, he added, "What? It's Mozart, everybody knows that Newman."

The two parted, with Rory roaming left to inspect a wall lined with three shelves, each littered with new cell phones. The phones were scattered across the space in no apparent order or sequence, and appeared dull and lifeless thanks to at least a week's accumulation of smudges and fingerprints from would-be purchasers. Rory leaned in on one model but yanked his hand back when its greasy smears became visible. He was a little embarrassed by the instinctive gesture, but his fears were unfounded. The young man behind the counter remained oblivious to the pair's presence and, in fact, carried on his phone conversation with gusto.

"So who was there? No way . . . that's sick . . . hey did you show Matt that cartoon I sent you? Uh huh . . ." Unrestrained chuckling ensued at this point, and then, "What? No I can't, I've got to close tomorrow night. That'll be depressing."

Sydney's shadow crept across the stool and finally captured the young man's attention. He craned his long celery-like neck to take in the full measure of Sydney, then hissed into the phone, "I gotta go, I'll call you later."

"To what humiliations I am reduced by a cruel husband." The words tumbled out of Sydney toward the suddenly bewildered young man.

"What's that boss?" he asked haltingly.

"The song, that's what the Contessa is saying. But you already knew that, right? You being a big opera fan."

"Oh," he chuckled feebly. "That's Bob's stuff, not mine." He unfolded off his stool, allowing the writing on his T-shirt to come into view. In large yellow letters was the word "SARCASM," followed underneath by "One of my many talents."

"Nice shirt . . . corporate uniform?" Sydney asked.

"No."

Rory moved to Sydney's left, reached into his pocket, and retrieved his phone.

"I need a replacement battery for this, do you have one?"

The young man barely glanced at the device before returning, "Nope."

"What? You didn't even look at it."

"We don't have *any* batteries."

Rory looked around the store and swung his arms theatrically as if conducting a symphony orchestra, then said, "This a cell phone store, of course you have batteries." As he said it he looked triumphantly about the store to prove his point, but as his eyes explored the scant offerings he realized there were literally no accessories of any kind in the entire place.

"We don't have *any* batteries," the irritated young man repeated with a scowl.

"Where's Bob?" Rory demanded, surprising himself with his sudden indignation.

"Bob's sleeping."

"Well I guess you'll just have to go wake him up now, won't you."

"Look, I told you, we don't have any batteries. Why don't you try Beach Cellular on Hollister?"

"You live up to your motto don't you kid?" Rory said, glaring at the T-shirt. Then he shrieked, "What kind of a mobile phone store doesn't sell batteries?!"

Sensing a possible case of retail rage, Sydney stepped between Rory and the young man and said, "The kind of store that—" Before he could finish the young man interrupted him.

"It was Bob's idea. He used to sell everything under the sun: batteries, protective cases, service plans, car chargers, you name it. But last year he decided to sell nothing but new phones."

"And why did he do that?" Sydney asked the way a trial lawyer might when leading a witness.

"How the hell should I know? I make eight dollars an hour. The only reason I'm in this shitty job is I got pissed the night before my SATs. Now I can't even get into junior college, and I've got to spend every day listening to this heinous music and dealing with guys like you."

Sydney chose to ignore the 20-something angst and asked calmly, "What did Bob tell you about his decision?"

The young man stared at Sydney, sighed, and finally said, "Bob said every store in America is doing the same thing and he wanted to be different. He figured that with all the new technology, 3G and the like, that more and more people were going to be buying new phones in the next few years instead of accessories for old phones, so he figured he should just switch to selling nothing but new phones." He returned behind the counter, put his skinny elbows on the glass top, cupped his hands and dropped his chin wearily into them.

"Thanks," Sydney said flatly as he grabbed Rory's arm and led him out of the store, and back to the car.

The young man grabbed his cell phone, pecked out a number and was soon connected to one of his friends. "Dave, yeah I'm back. You wouldn't believe the shit I have to put up with in here." Then a pause and, "Do you think I could get into film school?"

"Where's Hollister?" Rory barked, as he backed the car up and turned back onto Price Street. They drove just two blocks and what appeared but Hollister Street. Rory spun the wheel to the right and within seconds a surfboard-sized wooden cell phone screaming, "Beach Cellular" appeared on the left. He wedged the car between two mopeds and a delivery truck, and then marched into the store. Apparently Sydney wasn't invited this time around. Two minutes later he marched back to the car, waved the phone at Sydney and hopped in.

"Piece of cake," Rory said as he placed the phone in the cup holder and eased back onto the street. He was trying to ignore it, but his hungry stomach was angrily protesting the hour, which had now reached 1 P.M. Without soliciting Sydney's input he drove south toward the beach, past more small shops and tourists of all descriptions lining the sidewalks, and found Wendell's Ocean Café. He parked the car and without looking at Sydney, said, "Look alright to you?" Sydney nodded and they headed for the beachfront café.

"Inside or out?" inquired the indifferent hostess, obviously numbed from the effects of asking the same question repeatedly. Rory and Sydney surveyed the restaurant and said in unison, "Outside." Sydney was motivated by the golden sunshine while Rory was tempted by the fluffy looking cushions on the outdoor chairs. The hostess grabbed two menus from a pile at her side and led the two through a labyrinth of tables, past the bar, and out a large set of double doors to the patio area, which consisted of a dozen or so round tables each adorned with a beer-sponsored patio umbrella flapping lightly in the ocean breeze. "Your server will be with you in a minute," the hostess said as she dropped the menus on the table, causing the napkin on Rory's side to take flight.

As they examined the menu, their waitress, a brunette who looked to be in her early 50s, with tanned leathery skin from years of shunning sunscreen, approached.

"What can I get you boys?"

Sydney glanced up at her, flashed a mischievous smile, and asked, "What's good here at Wendell's?"

"It's Wen-dells, honey, just in case you want to blend in with the locals," she said as she cast a suspicious glance toward the beach and at one particular metal-detector-wielding man in an unflattering Speedo.

"Wen-dells, huh? How's the burger?"

"Best in San Luis Obispo County."

"Bring it on. And let's wash it down with a Moosehead."

"Got a taste for the Canadian lagers, eh? And for you?" she asked shifting her pad and pen toward Rory.

"Tuna salad and an iced tea." Following a dubious look from Sydney, Rory added with an impish grin, "I've got to keep my boyish figure." The line failed to draw a laugh from either of the spectators.

As Rory fished a napkin from the adjoining table and placed it neatly under his well-worn fork and knife, Sydney leaned back over the chair and inhaled deeply, taking in the sea air and bathing his face in the warm afternoon sun. Still fidgeting with the utensils, attempting to place them directly in the middle of the napkin, Rory said: "I can't get over that Bob's place not selling batteries. What kind of a cell phone store doesn't sell batteries?"

Sydney's head remained craned back as he replied, "Why does he have to sell batteries Newman?"

"Because that's what cell phone stores do," Rory shot back.

"Apparently not all of them."

"So you think it's a good move?"

"I didn't say that."

"So what *should* cell phone stores sell?"

Sydney twisted his neck from side to side yielding an audible crack, and then replied, "Appears to me Bob's answered at least one of the fundamental strategy questions."

The knife Rory had been sliding gently along the napkin shot forward as the words hit him. He was about to respond, his lips were parted, when he stopped. Which question had Bob answered? Mission? What propels him? Had he used the four lenses in some creative way?

The waitress positioned a basket of garlic breadsticks in the middle of the table with a simple, "Enjoy," then hovered as if awaiting a response. Sydney picked one up, placed it under his nose like a fine cigar, laughed robustly, then took an enormous bite, engulfing half the stick. The waitress quickly departed.

Rory continued to ponder Sydney's last statement and revisited the episode at the store. What question did Bob answer? He ran through the conversation in the store and stopped when he came to the revelation from the young man that, "Bob said every store in America is doing the same thing and he wanted to be different." He picked up a fork and pointed it at Sydney.

"It's what to sell."

"What is?"

"The next question. It's what do you sell?"

"Now you know as much as Bob," Sydney said playfully. "Yeah, that's the next question. Once you know your mission, what propels you forward, and what kind of company you are, you need to consider exactly what products and services you're going to sell."

"And you use the four lenses for that, right?"

Sydney wiped a patch of garlic from the corner of his mouth and took a gulp from his frosty green beer bottle. "Yeah, you do. They'll help you answer two basic questions about what to sell." He stopped and grabbed the last breadstick, but before he inhaled it, he split it in two and tossed half on Rory's plate.

"So, what are the two basic questions?" Rory asked as he cut the bread uniformly into bite-sized pieces.

"Very simple. What products and services do we place more emphasis on, and which products and services do we place less emphasis on?"

"Let me take it from here," Rory said confidently. "Start with the heart. What products and services are we most passionate about? Then, which do we have the talent to produce better than anyone in the world?" He was on a roll now and the words came easily to him. "Next, which products and services best suit our technology? And finally, and maybe most importantly, which products and services are profitable and primed for growth?" He took an exultant swallow of his iced tea and slammed the tall plastic glass on the table, then continued. "If we answer all those we can determine which products and services to place more emphasis on and which to reduce emphasis on."

Before Sydney could respond their lunches arrived, served not by the over-baked waitress but placed gingerly on the table by an obsequious busboy clearly not accustomed to liaising with customers. After solemnly delivering the meals he skulked away without a word. Sydney and Rory shrugged their shoulders then dove into their heaping plates with vigor. What followed was a choreography of forks, knives, salt and pepper requisitions, beer and iced tea swilling that didn't end until both plates were emptier than the streets of Green Bay on a football Sunday.

Rory slid back from the table a little, swung his right leg over his left, and said, "Okay, I can see this question being really relevant to companies that are propelled by a product and service focus, but does it apply to the other areas of focus we talked about?"

"Which are?" Sydney demanded.

"Is this a test?" With no response from Sydney, Rory sensed it was just that. He closed his eyes and listened to the waves rolling gently on the beach. The serenity of that sound was balanced by cries of children playing and of mothers imploring, "Get back here . . . you're too far . . . do you hear me?" Finally he said, "Products and services, customers and markets, capacity and capabilities, technology, raw materials, and. . ." He grasped but there was nothing. What was it? Then, as Sydney shifted in his chair, the sun caught it, his gaudy Keith Richards-like ring, and the QVC conversation came back. "Sales channels," Rory bleated.

"Glad to hear you've been paying attention. The question applies regardless of what propels you. Can't help but notice you're taken by my ring here." He thrust his pinkie in the air. "Maybe we can get you one."

"Yeah, and a nice 'Mother' tattoo to go with it," Rory thought sarcastically to himself.

Sydney returned his hand to the table while maintaining his gaze on the ring, and continued, "Anyway, a company that focuses on a sales channel like QVC still has to determine what to sell, in fact, it's critical for them. Same with *Playboy* or Johnson & Johnson, which are propelled by customers and markets."

Satisfied with this reply, Rory decided to redirect. "Let's get back to Bob. Do you think it's a good decision only selling new phones? I mean, lots of people who get new phones buy accessories at the same time; a case maybe, a car adaptor. I know I do."

Sydney leaned in closer to the table, and replied. "First of all, I said it *appears* that Bob answered one of the questions. But he probably did it like most businesspeople and management teams, by accident. If he followed the whole process we're talking about he would have asked some creative questions at the outset, some of which would concern what customers want. If he'd done that he might have seen that, as you say, customers who buy new phones also buy accessories."

As Rory digested both his lunch and Sydney's words, a Frisbee flew toward them from the beach. The disc spun erratically and then plopped into Sydney's lap. With the tosser of the errant pass approaching from the beach, Sydney grabbed the Frisbee, drew back his forearm and unleashed a powerful heave that sent the Frisbee whizzing over the stunned tosser's head and coming to rest on the crest of a breaking wave. He sat and continued, "Strategic planning is a process, Newman. You can't do it in bits and pieces, you've got to go through the whole thing to get results." After a pause he added with a chuckle, "Maybe that's why Bob is asleep in the middle of the day."

15

You Know What Nietzsche Said about Groups

By 1:45 Rory and Sydney were back on the 101 with the waves of Pismo in the rearview mirror and the foothills of Arroyo Grande in their sights. To combat the post-lunch drowsiness, Rory turned to Sydney, but he was furiously engaged in a text message, his cigar-sized fingers attempting to daintily peck at the phone keys. Rory decided to take advantage of his now fully charged cell phone to call Hannah with an update on their progress. She was somewhat dismayed that it was closing in on two o'clock and they still had almost 300 miles to travel before reaching San Diego, but that paled in comparison to the plethora of reunion-related challenges that were surfacing at the event's last minute. Chief among them, the sudden decision by a branch of the family from the Northeast to attend, which had sent the organizers into a veritable tizzy: Who would collect them at the airport? Where would they sleep? Did anyone really know them? Rory soon found himself caught in a repetitive loop of "uh-huhs" and decided the conversation had gone about as far as it could go. He said goodbye and turned his attention back to the road.

It was south of Arroyo Grande, about halfway to Nipomo, a small town whose name is fittingly derived from the Chumash word "Nepomah," or foot of the hill, that a nagging question began to tap on Rory's shoulder. It was crystallizing when, closer to the town, they passed a field filled with families flying kites. "How odd," Rory thought, "you don't see that every day." There were big kites, small kites, every color on a painter's palette. They bobbed in the freshening afternoon breeze, with smaller children holding on for dear life to the long white string that connected them to the earth. The spectacle transported Rory back to the days of his childhood, dream-like Sunday mornings when his father would take him to the park to feed loaves of white bread to the ravenous ducks and afternoons spent running wildly with a kite riding the thermals above. Sadly, the soothing flame of the cherished memory was quickly extinguished when the nagging question bullied its way into his head, demanding an answer: "How do we do all this?"

Sydney kept telling him, "You can think your way out of anything," and he had certainly given him a much needed crash course in strategic planning, with more to come no doubt, but Rory was suddenly fixed on how they would do it—how they would orchestrate the actual process. He turned to Sydney, who had finished texting, donned his earbuds, and was now listening to who knows what on his iPod. Rory reached out and poked him above the elbow.

"What are you listening to?"

Sydney's chin jabbed forward and he put his hand to his ear, sending the nonverbal reply of "What?"

"What are you listening to?" Rory repeated slowly.

Sydney, only moderately irritated at the inconvenience, removed his earbuds and said, "Writer's Almanac with Garrison Keillor," great podcast, you know it? "Turns out I've got the same birthday as Frank Norris who wrote *McTeague*. You read that one?"

"No. Listen Sydney, I've been thinking . . ."

"That explains the smell of burning hair in here."

"Yeah, anyway, you've given me lots of good ideas, but . . ." He hesitated, and then continued, "But, how do we do it? I mean how do we actually answer the questions?"

"Tell me what you do now."

"What do you mean?"

"Well, for example, what you did up in Napa."

"We ate well," was the first thing that sprang to Rory's mind, the buffalo steak in particular leaving an indelible impression, but he didn't dare reveal that to Sydney. "I shot an 81 on the Pines course," was the subsequent recollection, but again, it was doubtful Sydney would ask about memorable eight irons into postage stamp-sized greens.

"Well?" Sydney asked impatiently.

Rory was unnerved by his inability to answer such a simple yet important question. He fidgeted in his seat, but that was short lived as it woke up the saddle sores he was trying so desperately to quiet. It wasn't that he didn't take the sessions seriously, but on deeper reflection he surmised that it was disappointment with them that caused his memory to cling to more pleasant diversions. Finally, he responded.

"About 15 of us sat around a table for 3 days with a creativity facilitator that Carson hired and tried to generate ideas."

"About what?" Sydney asked.

"About our business. The facilitator said there were no bad ideas, so we touched on everything from adding chilled beverage holders on our treadmills to painting the elliptical machines like animals to taking half-days on Fridays in the summer."

"And who did most of the talking?"

Rory hesitated, like a witness about to snitch on a mob kingpin and then blurted out, "Mark, Rick, and Heather. They always do 90 percent of the talking. Poor Mel, after the sessions he tells me about all his great ideas, but he can't get a word in edgewise with them, nobody can. I was shooting daggers at the facilitator, but he just kept on filling the flip charts and saying, 'keep it coming.'"

"Didn't anyone else talk at all?"

"A bit, but it was mostly to agree with what they were saying. Nobody likes to disagree with Mark, he tends to go ballistic. What a nightmare."

"What materials did you have going into the sessions?" Sydney asked this while neatly wrapping his earbuds in a perfect circle around his fingers. Rory was shocked by this show of near-fastidiousness and had to be prodded again by Sydney before answering. "Newman, what materials—"

"Yeah, sorry. Well, let's see, we had our financial statements from last year, and . . ." He paused. "That's about it."

They had nudged into Santa Barbara County now, with the City of Santa Maria, the largest in the county, flashing by on their right. To their left was a panorama of verdant vineyards covering the undulating hillsides. Sydney stared at the pastoral landscape for a long time, and it continued to hold his gaze when he began to speak.

"I'm giving you an F, Newman, but I'd give 90 percent of the organizations around the world an F, too, so don't sweat it." Then he tilted his head toward Rory and said, "You know what Nietzsche said about groups right?

After yet another you've-got-to-be-kidding expression from Rory, Sydney completed his quotation of the nineteenth-century philosopher. "He said that 'madness is the exception in individuals and the rule in groups.'"

Still no reaction from Rory, so Sydney moved on. "Where do I start? Let's keep it simple, what to do before the meeting and what to do when you get there, sound okay?"

"Sure."

"We'll start with before. You can't expect to have productive strategy discussions armed with nothing but your financial statements. The first thing you've got to do is have provocative materials distributed to your team in advance. Gets back to the creative questions we talked about at the El Mariachi, remember? Questions about your markets, your customers, about trends, about technology, and of course, about financial considerations. Interview your team, talk to customers, ride the electric sewer, and assemble a fact book you can use to tee up specific questions at the retreat. The fundamental questions we're talking about."

"So we give this fact book out at the retreat?"

"No!" Sydney barked, straining his gravelly voice with the feral cry. "You give it to people in advance and you make damn sure they read it before they get there. In my companies, when we had off-sites, I personally inspected the fact books of my team before they came in the room, looking for margin notes, highlighted passages, dog ears, evidence they'd done their homework." Responding to Rory's skeptical expression at this seemingly draconian measure, he forged on. "Sure, you'll get people who might mark it up five minutes before, but their lack of preparation will show up pretty quickly in the meeting, and I showed no mercy for a lack of preparation, I'll tell you that." Sydney practically vibrated with reverence.

The lecture was temporarily halted as Rory coasted past a bright yellow bus rumbling along the inside lane. On its side, flapping wildly between duct-taped edges was a sign that read, "LA or Bust, Garey Youth Soccer." The cacophony booming from the bus easily drowned out any road noise and even silenced Sydney's rich baritone. It took about half a mile to erase the racket, but when quiet returned, Sydney was left with a suitable metaphor for his next point.

"Can you imagine being in that bus? Every kid yelling at once, screaming for attention, and telling a different story. In a way that's what your meetings are like, Newman."

"How so?"

"Your meetings sound unfocused and undisciplined. Probably because your facilitator said there are no bad ideas, so you're like those kids just yelling out the first thing that comes to your mind. That's not how you develop strategy. With strategy you *focus* the questions, you know what outcomes you want to achieve. That's why the questions I'm sharing with you are in a definite sequence. They build on one another so you stay focused but are constantly getting closer to a tangible strategy."

"More specific please," Rory pressed.

"I thought I was. Geez, whaddya want, me to come and run your sessions for you?"

Rory thought about this for a second. Sydney growling out commands, the veins under his bandana exploding as he marched around the room in his cargo shorts and boots, the business end of which would likely meet the soft behinds of those unwilling or unable to keep up. A pleasing vision of Mark being catapulted into the air came to an untimely end when Sydney continued.

"Okay, study the fact book before the meeting, and in the meeting use it, and the four lenses, to stimulate discussion and generate responses to the fundamental strategy questions I've given you. No more, no less."

With Mark fresh on his mind Rory then asked, "Okay, but even if you have the right questions, how do we get everyone involved?"

"Easy, split the group up. I think large group brainstorming is a bad idea. What happens with you guys happens everywhere, you get two or three loudmouths who dominate and like to pontificate from their little thrones. Meanwhile, people with meaningful ideas, like your buddy Melville, get shut out. So here's what you do. If you have 15, split them up into teams of 3 or 4."

"But 15 isn't divisible by 4," Rory said playfully, but the nuance was lost on Sydney.

"Anyone ever tell you you're a little too literal, Newman? Like I said, split them up. When people are in groups of three or four the social norms of participation kick in and everyone will feel like they have to cooperate, so they'll talk more. Plus this way, instead of generating one idea at a time, you can have three or four, or as many as you have groups. And, in my experience, these small groups are great at introducing effective and nonthreatening conflict, the kind you need to move the agenda forward and get results."

"More on that last part . . ."

"Conflict. It's critical to getting to real answers. You said your team mostly agrees with what's said. Most people don't feel comfortable questioning their peers, especially in public, but you've got to have some disagreement in order for people to really dig deep on their assumptions, so that they can truly examine their beliefs. The lack of conflict is why most meetings are deadly boring. I love spicing things up in my meetings with tough questions and open disagreement. But I never do it in a personal way, I never attack a person. I force them to articulate what they believe; give them the chance to convince me. Your CEO has to set the tone for that, he's got to make it clear that constructive conflict, a little sandpaper, is a good thing, but you never get personal.

Rory contemplated this, zeroing in on Sydney's point about conflict overcoming the boredom factor, so high in most meetings. He thought back to the sessions in Napa, and remembered his young colleague, Karen. In the morning she was the epitome of youthful energy, bright eyes, engaged expression. But as the day wore on, especially after lunch, she literally degenerated before them: sagging eyes, puffy face, pale skin. In the span of a couple of hours she morphed from a motivated and attractive young woman to looking like Macaulay Culkin's mug shot.

"Does each group answer the same question, or do you give them different questions?" Rory asked, moving swiftly to the next subject while the question was fresh in his mind.

"Nice, Newman. It's up to you. You can have each group work on a different question, then have report outs to the big group, but I think it's best if all groups work on the same question. Then you look for commonalities and points of divergence before you finalize. Plus, this way everyone has involvement and ownership on every question, and if you want your strategy to succeed, you need everyone to feel ownership in it. Oh, and one last thing on the groups. Put all the big talkers like Mark in the same group. It's like *Lord of the Flies*; you'll love it."

The torrent of words was still flowing as Rory passed a sparkling bronze colored Toyota Camry. An older man of late-60s vintage joined the driver, a man of about 40, in the front. Both were sitting stoically, while in the back an animated and spry grey-haired lady appeared to babble incessantly. Also in the back sat a woman who was about 20 years from a perfect resemblance to the chatterbox. The younger woman gazed contentedly out the window at the broad, black highway disappearing beneath her.

Sydney surveyed the group, and while staring intently at the garrulous older woman, said, "You could do everything we just talked about to have better meetings, build a great strategy, and be a great success, or you could just off the CEO's mother-in-law."

"What?" came the response from a flabbergasted Rory.

"A study in Denmark found that company profitability goes up an average of nearly 7 percent for the two years after the CEO's mother-in-law buys it."

"As *my* mother-in-law used to say, you're an odd duck Sydney."

"Takes all kinds."

16

Two Thumbs Up

"We're making good time now," Rory assured himself as they zipped past Los Alamos, with the 101 beginning its southward bend en route to Buell-ton. In Rory's estimation, the scenery had evolved from beautiful to absolutely stunning, truly awe-inspiring. He studied the landscape as it rolled past, wondering why this portion of the trip always had such a powerful effect upon him. Finally, he decided it was the contrasts: the leafy green tendrils extending from the gnarled grape vines; the interplay of light and shadows on the Santa Ynez Mountains that bathed some portions in brilliant light and created deep channels of darkness in others; and the curves in the road provided a final contrast to the long stretches of arrow straight blacktop further north on the 101. Here, from Los Alamos through to Gaviota, one had not simply to steer but actively drive. Rory loved it. His fingers gripped the steering wheel tightly as the car hugged the turns, and all through his body there was the pleasant tension one feels when fully engaged in a challenging, yet pleasing, task.

His mind completely occupied with navigating, Rory was quite unprepared when a previously, and uncharacteristically, subdued Sydney shouted, "Turn here, here, here!" at the junction of the 101 and the 246. Rory responded to the primal cry and yanked the wheel hard to the right, sending the Mercedes on a wild skate up the off ramp. The speedometer was still registering over 60 when Rory saw a red light less than 50 yards ahead. He pounded the brakes, causing the car to swerve to the right, and came to rest inches from the grazing gazelle vignette that adorned the back of an enormous RV.

As the car shuddered from the sudden stop, Sydney twisted in his seat, frustrated in his attempts to see past the Great Wall of RV in front of him. Then, as the light turned green and Rory inched forward, the first glimpse came into view. And when the RV trundled through the turn, the lethargic blades were fully exposed and Sydney gesticulated madly: "There!"

Rory smiled as he crossed the intersection, went down a gentle hill, and entered the parking lot of the Buellton Days Inn motel, its signature windmill revolving at a leisurely pace. He drove past the office, further into the property, while Sydney intensely patted down the pockets of his shorts, exclaiming, "Where's that damn camera!"

"So you liked *Sideways*, huh?" Rory asked teasingly. It was a reference to the 2005 film about two friends sharing a road trip through wine country before one is to take his fateful trip down the aisle. Portions of the movie had been filmed at this very hotel. Rory didn't really like the movie, and he was shocked that Sydney would enjoy such sentimental fare.

"Are you nuts? Gimme *From Dusk Till Dawn*, gimme *Planet Terror*, heck, anything by Robert Rodriguez, but *Sideways*? Nahh." He paused, and then added, "If that wimp in the movie, that Miles guy, was my friend I would have kicked his ass from here to Santa Barbara."

"Then why did you make me pull that kamikaze stunt on the off ramp to get here?"

"My girlfriend loved it. Saw it three times and dragged me, kicking and screaming, every time. If she knew I drove by this place and didn't get a picture, there'd be hell to pay."

Rory wasn't convinced. "Okay, let me get this straight, you saw it three times, you can offer commentary on the motivation of one of the main characters, but you hated it. So if you detested it so much, how did you know exactly where the hotel was?"

"Umm, common knowledge, Newman. Where's that damn camera?" He continued to mine the contents of his pocket but was unable to find the missing camera. "Guess the phone will have to do," he grumbled as he stepped out of the car and gawked at the second floor of the building. He then lifted the phone and swept it past a section of second floor doors. As he barked, "What room was it?" a maid emerged from room 204, glanced down, then continued about her business, clearly accustomed to the attention the small hotel had garnered since the movie's release.

"Why don't you go up there, and I'll get a shot of you," Rory said. Sydney didn't hesitate. He bounded up the stairs to the second floor with the exuberance of a 10-year-old on the playground at recess. When he reached the top he began to prowl the floor, still searching for the exact room from the movie, and looking for the best angles for a photo opportunity. Finally he stopped in front of 206, perched his canoe of a right foot up on the wooden railing and struck a catalogue pose for Rory who took several pictures before Sydney growled, "Okay, that's enough," and clomped back down the stairs.

Grabbing the phone from Rory, he grimaced, smirked, and half-smiled his way through a review of the pictures. Walking back to the car he stopped abruptly as if on hallowed ground and said, "This is exactly the spot where Stephanie beat Jack with the motorcycle helmet. Man was she pissed." He chuckled at the reflection and added with an air of sanctimony, "But he had it coming."

This second commentary was enough for Rory. He said accusingly, "Admit it, you loved the movie as much as your girlfriend."

"What did you think, Roger Ebert?" Sydney redirected.

"We're not talking about me, but as long as you asked, I wasn't crazy about it. Why won't you just admit you liked it? There's no crime in that, after all, it won an Oscar."

Sydney jerked open the passenger door, began to bend down, then stopped and popped back up to face Rory who had moved toward his door. "You know, there's a strategy lesson in this," he said furtively. Rory squinted back, catching the playful gleam in Sydney's eye and responded: "You think you can distract me with shiny beads and trinkets?"

"Let's hit the road and I'll tell you all about it." Rory smiled across the glossy roof but Sydney had already ducked in and was waiting patiently for the trip to resume.

Two easy right turns later and they were back on the 101 south. Rory had momentarily forgotten the dangling possibility of another strategy lesson and was absorbed in a missed opportunity of his own that also involved the 101 and the 246. Just a few miles east on the 246, and you'd reach the town of Solvang. The charming town was founded in 1911 by a group of Danish educators who, like many before and since, beat a path to California in search of better weather. To this very day, their heritage has been cherished and well-guarded. Danish restaurants, Danish shops, and everywhere Danish architecture greet the visitor. Hannah grew up under the spell of writer Hans Christian Andersen, and a picture under his statue was a customary part of every trip the two had made to Solvang. Rory couldn't help but think that a call from Solvang, while he was standing in the shadow of the statue, would bring a little joy to Hannah's day.

It was too late for that, however, and the pressing issue of his report to Jim rekindled. As they railed through a sweeping twist in the road, one that seemed all the narrower thanks to a thick border of brush on either side of the freeway, Rory said sarcastically, "So I'm dying to know, what's *Sideways* got to do with strategy?"

"Did you like it?" Sydney repeated his earlier solicitation from the parking lot.

"I told you, no, I didn't."

"My girlfriend loved it. Saw it—"

"Three times, I know," Rory interrupted.

"Okay, she loved it, you say you didn't like it, so?" Sydney asked while he continued to gaze longingly at the low resolution pictures on his phone.

"So, that's movies. Not everybody's going to like the same movies."

"You're getting warmer."

"What am I, four?" Rory thought. He hated this little warmer/colder game but knew Sydney was unlikely to let up, especially if Rory protested. Finally he said, "Preferences, it's about preferences."

Sydney put down his phone and pantomimed the cranking of an ancient movie camera aimed straight at Rory. "You think when they make a movie, they're expecting everyone to like it, Newman?"

"I'm sure they'd love that, but no, of course not. They've got an au—" Rory stopped as the emerging lesson quickly took shape in his mind. "An audience, they've got a target audience in mind." Sydney was quiet, he could see the wheels were turning.

"So you're talking about choosing target customers, right?" Rory offered as he scanned the links of the strategy chain in his head: mission, then the driving force that propels you forward as a company, then what we sell, and now, who we sell to. The progression made sense, and customers were the next logical link. He snuck a peek at Sydney, looking for affirmation and the latter straightened up in his seat, tossed his head back royally, and drew his lips apart. Before he began Rory quivered as the thought raced through his head: "Here it comes, another quote . . ."

"I can't give you a surefire formula for success, but I can give you a formula for failure: Try to please everybody all the time." Sydney concluded the sentence with a triumphant tip of his broad and stubbly chin.

"That doesn't sound like Shakespeare or something a German general would say. Was that a Sydney Wise original?" asked a relieved Rory.

"Oh, Newman." Sydney chuckled heartily, causing a frown to form on Rory's face. "You're a piece of work." When the giggling subsided, Sydney continued: "No, but thank you for attributing the words of the very first recipient of the Pulitzer Prize to me. No, that wasn't Sydney Wise, it was Herbert Bayard Swope."

It was all Rory could do to restrain himself from careening into the shoulder to send his smug passenger crashing into the door. It's miraculous how fast the mind can work when engaged in villainy. He had it all planned, "Oh, sorry," he'd say, "I had to swerve to avoid a bunny." Or, if only he had an eject button for the passenger seat a la James Bond. He could see Sydney vaulting into the air and then freefalling from a thousand feet. Fortunately, maturity reigned and Rory absorbed yet another swipe at his intellectual ability with dignity, returning to the subject at hand. "You're . . . I mean Herbert, was right. You can't be all things to all people. You've got to focus on a set of target customers."

"So how do you do it at Kitteridge?"

"We do a lot of competitor analysis then look for gaps we can exploit."

"Oh," Sydney responded, clearly underwhelmed.

"What?" Rory demanded.

"So you look at competitors first?"

"That's right," Rory scowled, "You don't believe in competitor analysis?"

"You ever buy a book from Amazon, Newman?"

If you looked close enough you could see little rockets of contempt firing from Rory's eyeballs. "Why can't this guy give a straight answer?!" he wondered. But Sydney was orchestrating the rules of this game so Rory played along, as usual.

"Yes, many times."

"You know the CEO of Amazon?"

"Sure, it's Jeff . . . Jeff, uh, Jeff Bezos."

"Right. He's got a great philosophy that I think fits this discussion perfectly. He's always telling his team to be afraid of their customers and not their competitors, you know why?"

"Why?" Rory acquiesced.

"Because customers are the folks with the money. Competitors are never going to send you money."

Rory let the words sift like sand through a prospector's pan, looking for the nugget of gold in Sydney's advice. The basic idea appealed to him, but it seemed overly simplistic, not hard-nosed enough for the full-contact world of modern business. As if sensing his apprehension, Sydney said, "Look, I know it seems too simple to be true, but think about it. What happens when you focus on your competitors first? I'll tell you what, eventually you start to imitate them, and then they imitate you, and all the players in the market chase after the last piece of existing demand and it becomes a zero-sum game that ultimately drives down margins for everyone."

"So you don't think you should pay attention to your competitors?"

"There's a Grand Canyon of difference between paying attention to and focusing on, my friend."

The Grand Canyon reference snapped Rory's attention back to their route as they descended from the Gaviota Pass through a narrow canyon that completely obscured the sun and plunged them into a sudden darkness. To the west, on the northbound 101, travelers would be passing through the 420-foot Gaviota tunnel, a famous landmark that Rory quickly recalled had also been featured in *Sideways*, the film that sparked this entire discussion.

"You with me, Newman?"

They passed a particularly steep and muscled canyon wall, one covered with netting to protect the roads from rockslides, and Rory slowly drifted back to the conversation.

"So you say we should keep tabs on our competitors but not focus exclusively on them, is that it?"

"Correctomundo," Sydney said with an indistinguishable accent. "Read their annual reports, listen to news reports, keep an ear tuned to what industry groups are saying, sure. But don't ever let competitor actions tempt you to take your eye off of the folks that really matter, the ones that send you money, your customers."

Conversation ceased as the Mercedes emerged from the corridor of canyon to reveal the grand Pacific, laid out like a colossal and shimmering blue blanket before them. "Look at that," Sydney whispered in awe as they regarded the sweeping panorama glowing in the mythic California sun.

The 101 twisted sharply to the left now and would mostly trace the sandy coastline for the next 60 miles, all the way to Ventura. Although it was after three in the afternoon, Sydney hastily removed his forearm from the window, which instantly conducted the sun's fire. Rory adjusted his visor, diverting his attention from the road for just a split-second, and in that time a seagull dive-bombed the windshield causing Sydney, and a rattled Rory, to jerk back in their seats the way you might from the jutting jaw of a monster in a 3-D movie.

Sydney followed the wayward bird's path and said, "Place is true to its name."

"Yeah," Rory responded, having no idea what Sydney was talking about. He decided to nudge Sydney back to the topic of customers before he gave a lecture on the origins of Gaviota. "Okay, we focus on customers first. So is it the same idea as products and services? Determine which customers to place more emphasis on and which to place less emphasis on; use the four lenses?"

"Uh-huh, same drill. But to do that you've gotta start by really understanding your customers. You think you know your customers, Newman?"

Like a political candidate, Rory chose not to answer the question directly, but said instead, "This gets back to riding the electric sewer, experiencing things from the customer's perspective, right?"

Having lost sight of the seagull, which had joined a committee of others on the beach a couple of miles back, Sydney was now riveted by a couple of inept surfers trying with little success to catch a wave. Without looking at Rory he said, "You got it." He laughed uproariously as one of the surfers toppled clumsily into a breaking wave, then continued. "You know, on the plane out here, during those rare moments I could concentrate between the ministrations of the flight attendants, I read an article that said less than 25 percent of management teams agree with the statement, 'we understand our customers.' That's pretty frightening."

"You'd think it would be fundamental," Rory replied.

"You would, wouldn't you?"

"So how do you overcome that? What do you do beyond getting out there and experiencing things from their point of view?"

"Research, ask questions. Look at the basics like customer profitability, market share, retention, satisfaction, loyalty. But then go beyond, and ask some different questions, like: Which customers' needs are shifting most rapidly and why? Does our direction align with that migration? Or, who uses our product in surprisingly large quantities? That's a great question," Sydney said in a self-congratulatory way before continuing. "Answering it can not only help you focus on specific customers but can even lead you to selling in new places or even to entirely new businesses. That's what happened to Ray Kroc. You know who he is don't you Newman?"

This time Rory was prepared. Big Macs were a guilty pleasure of his, and he knew Kroc was responsible for taking McDonald's from a single restaurant in San Bernardino to a global fast-food behemoth.

"I do. McDonald's," Rory said, with the thought of a Big Mac triggering a Pavlovian response in his mouth.

To Rory's chagrin, there was no acknowledgment from Sydney, who simply picked up where he left off. "Before he became hamburger royalty and owner of my favorite baseball team, Kroc sold milkshake machines, and he wondered why these two brothers in California were buying so many. That led him west, and the rest, as they say, is history. So, asking who uses our product in surprisingly large quantities can yield some tasty results."

"Tasty . . . Big Mac . . ." Rory needed to change the subject pronto. "Any other questions we should ask?" he blurted.

"Yeah. Always look at noncustomers, cause you'll always have more of them than you will customers. Which groups does your industry choose not to serve and why not? And who doesn't use your products or services now but could if you made some adjustments?"

The concept struck Rory immediately. While he absorbed the road ahead, scanning from the lonely telephone wire to his left to the coastal sagebrush at his right, it was clear he had lapsed once again into the Car Coma. How did he know the concept? An unlikely spruce tree, one perfect enough to adorn Rockefeller Center at Christmas, started the chain reaction that led to the answer. From spruce tree, to pine trees, to Pines golf course at Napa, to golf in general, to Callaway, the club maker. He recalled hearing from a golf pro that Callaway developed the Big Bertha driver to attract nongolfers to the sport. Callaway surmised, rightly, that many people were intimidated by the challenging level of skill required to hit the ball with even a modicum of proficiency. Going out and driving the ball about 10 yards per whack is not the most enjoyable way to spend an afternoon. Therefore, Callaway developed the Big Bertha, with its signature large head, to make striking the ball relatively easy and attracting newcomers to the game.

The Car Coma worked its spell with Rory driving competently but caught under the magic charm of a reverie that had him transported from the Callaway Big Bertha to Augusta National Golf Club where the Masters is played (he saw himself hitting a perfect little seven iron to the center of the green on number12, much to the delight of the ever-chirping feathered spectators) to McDonald's for a Big Mac.

He reemerged from his trance with an overwhelming desire to hit a small bucket of golf balls and scarf down a burger. With the road bordered by ragged hills on one side and the broad expanse of ocean on the other, the first desire was out of the question, but ahead, a gas station and snack shop held the promise of satisfying his second craving.

17

Sandy Resolutions

"I'm going to stop for a minute," Rory declared as he flicked the right turn signal and made his way toward the exit.

"What for?" Sydney replied.

Ever vigilant regarding his gas consumption, Rory flashed through the screens of his onboard display until the range page appeared. According to the computer, the car had another hundred miles in the tank, rendering the gas excuse out of the question.

"I need a snack, and we might as well fill up on gas, too. That way we'll be good all the way to San Diego."

"Can't you wait? Santa Barbara is just down the road. One of my favorite places."

Santa Barbara was about 10 clicks away so, despite his hankering for a snack, Rory deferred to Sydney and kept the tires singing along the freeway.

A few minutes later and they were sailing along the 101 in Santa Barbara, past Hollister Avenue, then Storke Road, then by Los Carneros. Rory awaited a signal from Sydney. This being one of his favorite places he was sure to pick a place to stop. Wasn't he? Fairview Avenue came and went, then it was Patterson Avenue waving good-bye in the rearview mirror, followed soon after by Turnpike Road and State Street. Not a peep from Sydney. The 101 snaked to the right and they passed Las Palmas, then Las Positas. West Mission flashed by, still nothing. The freeway straightened out as they whizzed past West Mission, with West Carrillo fast approaching. Rory's nerves were being severely tested: "Did he forget we were going to stop? Did he black out on his memory of Santa Barbara?" Finally, with a simple gesture of Sydney's right hand and a flat, "take Castillo," Rory could exhale once again.

"Now where?" Rory asked impatiently as they reached the top of the ramp. Sydney thumbed right and Rory steered the Mercedes in that direction. As the car nosed past Cliff Drive, Sydney said, "There," and motioned to a small rustic building that looked as if it had been yanked right off the set of an old Western movie. The façade was whitewashed, and in front of the structure's creaky wooden awning, supported by two ancient beams, there was an actual hitching post. If a tumbleweed had rolled lazily past the front door, Rory wouldn't have been surprised. He parked on the street then extended his neck toward the passenger side window to take in the curious sight, which seemed all the more foreign given its neighbors: a 7-Eleven and an Arco gas station. Rory's gaze panned from the distressed front door, up over the awning to a long, rectangular, and very weathered sign that read: "Joad's Coffee Emporium."

"Best coffee and apple strudel in Southern California," Sydney said almost proudly as he left the car and marched like a conquering hero through the front door.

A part of Rory expected a chorus of "Sydney!" to greet them as they walked in, the way the denizens of the bar on the old TV series *Cheers* did when barfly Norm Peterson burst through the door. But, on this occasion at least, not a head was raised in the dark, and by Rory's estimation, somewhat drab, little coffee shop. The western motif didn't extend inside the shop, which was dominated by two large leather sofas and a scattering of wingback chairs. A large tabby cat with huge white paws occupied one of the chairs. He was coiled contentedly and snoozing soundly. Over the bar, in assorted handwriting, were coffee-related quotes like: "Grab life by the beans," and "Chocolate, Men, Coffee—Some things are better rich."

As he walked up to the bar, Sydney said, "I'll get this, Newman," oblivious to what Rory might actually want.

Rory, his saddle sores still barking, eased gently into a vacant chair next to one of the sofas and picked up a crumpled *Biking* magazine. Over the lazy drone of the restaurant, he settled into an article on how to pack for cross-country bike trips. He was halfway through the second page when Sydney nudged his left shoulder with a cauldron-sized cup of steaming coffee and a warm apple strudel. Sydney pulled a chair next to Rory and the two set in on their bounty. As Rory was taking a king-sized bite of his strudel he overheard an interesting question from the direction of the sofa.

Two men in their late 20's, both dressed in button-down shirts and khakis—Rory's customary uniform—were sitting with legs crossed and sipping espressos when one asked the other: "What do you do to challenge life?" Clearly not prepared for this sudden segue from idle chitchat to life philosophy, the second man said, "Huh?"

"What do you do to challenge life?" the first man pressed. "You get up, you go to work, you pay the bills. What do you do to challenge life?"

Rory gently placed his half-eaten strudel on a napkin in his lap and took a drink of his coffee. He didn't want the sound of chewing to drown out the upcoming response to this fascinating question. As he awaited the second man's answer he decided this was a great question. No, a brilliant question. And it could be answered a million different ways. Maybe man number two would say, "I'm compiling the definitive history of denim," or "I'd like to teach monkeys to play the guitar," or "My plan is to translate all the classic Russian poems of the eighteenth century—but just the dirty parts." It could be anything! Rory leaned in as the second man finally drew a breath, let out a satisfied sigh, one resulting no doubt from sincere introspection, and then said, "I'd like to go back to business school."

What was left of the strudel went "splat" on the floor from the jerking of Rory's entire body upon hearing this response. The two men glared over their shoulders at him and he smiled politely when he said, "Slippery sucker." They turned their backs once again and Rory fell back into his solitary criticism. "Go back to business school. That's the best he could come up with? This guy looks like he has it going on—he's young, nice-looking, seemingly intelligent, and from what he overheard of their earlier conversation, he's already got a good job." Rory had nothing against business schools, except, of course, the kind that produced the Marks of the world, but as an answer to life's call to arms, this response, "Go back to business school," left him flatter than the remnants of strudel being brushed from the floor by a sour barista.

Rory's face took on the expression of a forlorn puppy as he watched Sydney gobble the last of his strudel, the concluding bite accompanied by a satisfied "Mmmm." Sydney then daintily, for him at least, wiped the corners of his mouth with a napkin and said, "Let's hit the beach." Rory looked at his watch, which read 4 P.M. and said, "Nah, we better get back on the road."

"Come on. Five minutes. I'll even give you the last of the four strategy questions."

They were back in the car and headed south along Castillo when Sydney instructed Rory to turn right on Shoreline Drive. Just past the Santa Barbara City College football field Sydney said, "Park here." He was solemn but smiling as he crossed the street, took off his boots and socks, and sunk his bare feet into the luxurious sand of Leadbetter Beach. Rory followed gamely, the barefoot sand walking and saddle sores combining for a curious gait. After several painful steps he caught up with Sydney and could see that his eyes were inward on pleasing memories. Rory stood quietly until Sydney said, "Spent the summer of '85 here. What a time." He inhaled the salty air deeply and continued, "Skimboarding with my buddies all day, bonfires with the girls at night. Time of my life."

"Skinny dipping!"

"No. Skimboarding!" Sydney shot back, agitated at the intrusion into his warm recollection. "It's like surfing, but you take your board and run *into* the wave from the beach, and . . . ah, never mind!"

Sensing the moment had been lost for Sydney, Rory said, "I hate to cut your trip down memory lane short Sydney but we really should get going. Hannah's going to kill me if I show up too late."

"You want the last lesson or don't you?" Sydney growled.

"Right. Of course I do, but can we do it in the car?"

Sydney sat in the sand, drew up his knees, and said: "No. I feel inspired here." Rory mimicked the pose and both stared into the endless Pacific until Sydney spoke again.

"How do you challenge life, Newman?"

"What? You heard that? Could you believe what that guy said?" With some disdain, he added: "Go back to business school? That's the best he could come up with?"

Silence descended once again and they sat, digging their toes into the soft sand. Rory was equal parts waiting for the

lesson and skeptical about how Sydney could concoct a strategy lesson out of the conversation from the coffee shop. Finally,
after dusting a patch of sand from his ankle, Sydney spoke.

"I think if you asked the guy, he'd tell you that by going
back to business school, he could do some great things, he could
add value, to use business speak."

"Not comprehending."

"Let me cut to the chase and we can loop back if we have
to. The last fundamental strategy question you need to ask is,
how do we sell?" Sydney looked to Rory and saw nothing but
a blank face with squinting, questioning eyes. "By that I mean,
how do you propose to add value for your customers? How do
you stand out in their eyes?"

"But didn't we already do that with the second question?
The one about what products or services we'll sell."

"That question was about what specifically you're going to
offer. Which products and services you'll place more and less
emphasis on. Then we talked about what customers you'll offer
those products and services to, and now, now we're talking
about how you'll offer them."

"Like offering good service?" Rory asked as he followed a
gaggle of teenagers skittering along the water's edge, the boys
kicking water at the screeching girls.

"Yeah, but a bit broader. It's simple really. There are two
basic ways to sell. You can offer the lowest total cost to your
customers, that's one way. Or, you can focus on differentiation."

"Low cost I get, but what do you mean by differentiation?"

"You sure you get lowest total cost?" Sydney challenged.

"Sure, give the lowest price. Simple as that."

"But how do you do that?" Sydney shot back. When Rory
failed to defend his point, Sydney continued. "If you're going to
offer the lowest total cost you've got to have processes in place
throughout your company to do that. It's all about formula,

about everything the customer doesn't see. Everything you can do to wring costs out of the business."

"Wal-Mart!" Rory snapped in a sudden epiphany.

"Yeah, Wal-Mart. They have standardized operations, world-class supply chain systems, and maybe most important, a culture that demonizes waste and rewards efficiency. Same with McDonald's. You go into a McDonald's anywhere from Boston to Beijing, the experience is pretty much the same. It's all about a standardized formula to keep costs down and offer low prices to customers."

"Okay, so what about differentiation then?"

"There are two camps of differentiation. One way to differentiate is by focusing on your relationships with customers. Some people call it being customer intimate."

"Customer intimate?" Rory asked with eyebrows raised.

"Easy, Newman. It just means you're not focused on single transactions but are cultivating relationships over the long term by offering the best service and best *solution* to the customers' needs. You probably charge a bit more, but the customers are willing to pay because you understand their needs better than anyone else, and you'll go the extra mile to fulfill those needs. A good example is—"

"Nordstrom," Rory interrupted.

"Sure, Nordstrom. Their service is legendary. They're not the lowest price option, that's Wal-Mart, but they offer industry-leading sales and support. Their salespeople are experts in their field, stay with the company a long time, and work to foster relationships with customers so they'll come back again and again.

It was Rory's turn to challenge: "But McDonald's and Wal-Mart want people to come back again and again, too."

"Of course they do, but it's how they get them back. At Wal-Mart they've got the greeters, and sure they're friendly, but that's not why people come back. They come back because the price is right. At Nordstrom they come back because of the level of service and the relationship they have with the store. At Wal-Mart all operations are geared toward low prices. Nordstrom's systems would focus on understanding customer needs, changing tastes, and offering the best solution at any given time."

"Okay, you said there were two camps of differentiation, what's the second?" Rory said as he glanced at his watch.

The ticking clock element wasn't lost on Sydney, but it wasn't respected either, as was evident by his reply: "Take it easy. Fill your lungs with that ocean air. Do ya good." After a few more deep breaths that would make an osteopath proud, Sydney conceded and went on with the lesson, but in his unique fashion of course.

"You ever read those in-flight magazines on the plane, Newman?"

There was zero upside in questioning either the origin or purpose of this question, so Rory simply said, "Yeah, so?"

"Ever see an advertisement for that crazy-looking exercise machine? The one that costs about 14 grand?"

"Oh yeah," Rory said with a chuckle, "looks more like a medieval torture device to me."

"That's the second kind of differentiation in action. They're selling by offering what they consider to be the best product, period. Companies that sell with this focus try and create a product that has the newest and best features that people will be willing to pay extra for. They're on the cutting edge of design and innovation always striving to introduce the next big thing."

"Like Apple. That's how they differentiate themselves, right?"

"Right on!" Sydney exclaimed as he punched Rory's arm, toppling him into the sand. "They've always made cool stuff that pushes the design and performance envelope. Years ago it was Apple II, then the Mac, and now the iPod and the iPhone. An iPhone isn't cheap; Apple definitely doesn't compete on cost, but they're betting their future on new products that people will pay extra to have. That's differentiating on product."

While brushing the sand off, Rory said: "If I've heard this once, I've heard it a thousand times. We live in an era of hyper-competition. Change is happening faster than ever. Don't we have to sell in all three ways? I mean we have to have a low price, offer outstanding service, and put out great products, right?"

"I'll grant you that good service, reliable products, and a fair price are table stakes in any business. But what I'm talking about is a commitment to how you sell. How you're proposing to add value for your customers. Wal-Mart, Nordstrom, Apple, they've invested deeply in certain capabilities and hard assets to deliver on their promises. They can't do all three things in a pure way. Not without going broke in the process. And neither can you or any other business in the world. Plus, when they're faced with a decision, companies that have made a choice know how to react. At Apple they know that when push comes to shove, they're always going to focus on the product. Companies that don't have a focus will have managers running around like chickens with their heads cut off. They don't know how to react."

Rory was about to move on, but Sydney wasn't quite finished. "We've talked about Wal-Mart and Nordstrom. One is low cost and the other focuses on relationships, customer intimacy. Now look at Sears. They've had a split personality for years. Are they low cost, product leaders, or customer intimate?" Rory shook his head. "Right. Nobody knows, and their sales have been essentially flat for almost two decades. You've got to commit, Newman."

"So how do we decide which area of focus is right?"

"It's not which area is right; none of them are inherently more appropriate or correct than the others. It's which is right for *you*. Start with your mission and the first three fundamental strategy questions. The mission and your answers to those questions should fit one another, should reinforce one another. You'll probably find that the answer to, 'how do we sell' will be a natural consequence of working toward your mission and your answers to the first three questions. Plus, you've always got the old reliable lenses to help you. What you're passionate about, what you've got the talent to do, what infrastructure investments you've made, or are willing to make, and what the numbers say."

The sun had started its lazy descent toward the horizon now, and beachgoers were rolling up their towels, folding up their squeaky chairs, and heading back to their cars. Rory and Sydney wordlessly followed the quiet migration.

18

"KISSin" Cousins

The two retraced their route past Joad's Coffee Emporium and made a short stop for gas. "Hopefully the last stop we'll make," Rory thought as he squinted at his watch, protesting the advancing hours. His eyes performed a constant scan of the gas station's periphery while he pumped, slightly cautious and on guard lest there be a sudden appearance from their old nemesis, Mister Leather. An overtaxed mother in a minivan was the only other patron, however, and soon Rory and Sydney were back on the 101 and rolling past Santa Claus Lane.

Rory's lips parted as he was about to engage in some light banter, questioning why there would be a street called Santa Claus Lane in Santa Barbara. But he quickly and savagely bit his lip, sucking the words back with the realization that Sydney would surely know why there was a Santa Claus Lane and wouldn't hesitate to offer a detailed description. Rory stole a furtive peek Sydney's way to see if he'd noticed the curious sign, but his passenger was otherwise engaged with his phone.

"Missed two calls from Maggie when we were on the beach. But no messages."

"Who's Maggie?" Rory asked.

"Dog sitter. Can't be anything serious or she'd have left a message." He contemplated a return call, rolling the phone through his massive fingers while he considered it, but finally returned the device to his shorts' pocket, and sunk deeply into his seat.

The Pacific was a deep blue diamond as they rolled on with the miles passing imperceptibly beneath and both men retreated into private refuges of thought. Rory felt a welling of confidence stirring within him. Modest at first, then bolder as he reflected on all he had learned in the past day and a half and how seemingly well prepared he was for his report.

He allowed himself the luxury of playing out the next several days in dreamy detail. Tonight he would arrive at the reunion, be reunited with Hannah, and meet relatives of hers he hadn't seen in years, and some he'd never met. Later, as the clan became chummier around the crackling campfire, they'd talk, laugh, and maybe tell a few tall tales. It would be like a Norman Rockwell painting. After the good-byes and promises to keep in touch, he and Hannah would drive back to the Bay area, passing the hours with debates about what books their new daughter should read, where she should go to college, and how old she'll be when she becomes the first president to be born outside the United States.

Back at the office he'd record all he'd learned from Sydney, create a dazzling PowerPoint presentation and accompanying narrative, then deliver it flawlessly to the suits at Olivenhain. He saw himself at the front of their boardroom, in full oratorical sail with his new bosses sharing occasional nods in obvious appreciation of their intelligent choice for this task. So vivid was his reverie that he could see the expressions on their spellbound faces and hear the cadence and rhythm of their questions, all of which he would answer masterfully. It was during this rehearsal that he suddenly envisioned a rumpled character in a stark gray suit asking drably from a dark corner of the room: "What is the outcome of this process?" That's when his throat seized.

He knew the importance of a mission, had the prework required to develop a strategy to a tee, was well-versed in the four fundamental strategy questions, and equally schooled in the lenses to be applied in answering them. But after squeezing all of that through the metaphorical grinder, what magical nugget emerged on the other side? That he didn't know. Was it a paragraph? A 1-page document? A 50-page dissertation? Still there in his mind was the old rumpled man and his now legions of Olivenhain followers bearing down on Rory, who was pitifully armed with nothing but a cheap plastic remote for advancing slides. Like ghouls in the night they tramped forward, relentless in their pursuit. He saw them surrounding him, a ravenous pack of corporate wolves in their worsted wool suits, chanting mummy-like: "What is the outcome . . . what is the outcome?"

"Where's the fire?" Sydney asked casually.

It took a few seconds for the words to penetrate as Rory shook the invisible phantoms from his subconscious. Then he caught sight of the speedometer: 83, 84, 85 and felt the tension burning from his hips through his thighs, knees, and ankles all the way to his foot that was glued to the accelerator. He quickly lifted his foot, easing the pressure on the engine, and soon the car was traveling at a leisurely pace once again.

"Where were you there, cowboy?" Sydney asked.

"What's the outcome?" The words tumbled out of Rory's mouth in a heap.

"Outcome of what?"

"The process? You do the prework, you answer the four questions, then what? What comes out the other side?"

"Gimme a kiss," Sydney said nonchalantly as if requesting a napkin or a pen.

A bevy of options unfurled themselves to Rory. He could opt for the cliché response of "I don't think I'm your type," or the equally tired, "I'm not that kind of guy," or simply feign ignorance and wait for Sydney to explain himself, as he inevitably would. He chose door number three and shared a knowing look with Sydney who then said, "Not that kind of kiss. I mean capital K, capital I, capital double SS—KISS. Which we all know stands for Keep It Simple Stupid."

"Simple is a relative term, Sydney."

"True enough. By simple, I mean your final strategy statement should be a paragraph, maybe two, that basically strings together your answers to the four questions. It doesn't have to be eloquent, it doesn't have to be wordy, it just has to be simple and sincere. It doesn't even have to be all words. You could have a picture that combines images and narrative. The key here is communication. Get your point across in a straightforward way that people can understand, and more important, act on." He paused, then added somewhat indignantly, "But be creative, too. People are always looking for a fill-in-the-blanks, paint-by-numbers formula. Answer the questions, then communicate in a way that fits with your culture, your way of doing things. Simple as that."

"But if you do all the prework, and you answer the four questions, you're going to generate a lot of discussion material in your meetings. What do you do with all that?"

"Good question. You definitely want to keep that as supporting material for your final answers, but it's not what you're going to distribute or print on your mouse pads. Maybe post it on your intranet. That way when people read the final strategy statement and they want to know how your senior leaders arrived at the decisions they did, they can find out. I've always done that. I want transparency and this way anyone can look at what and how the leadership team developed what they did. It also shows your team dug deep and did the hard intellectual work that's necessary to build a strategy. And, one more thing, it's a great historical record when you go back to update your strategy."

"Do you include your mission as part of this statement?"

"Separately, but on the same page, sure. Like I said before, it's about communication, and communication should be simple and clear."

In a role-playing exercise that would have made a corporate change facilitator grin ear to ear, Rory transported himself back in front of the suits at Olivenhain and channeled the rumpled old man. What would he ask? What's missing from all of this? The old man hoisted himself from his chair, stepped boldly forward and then demanded of Rory: "What about vision? Where is the vision?" Rory lashed at Sydney, expecting an immediate response to the question, forgetting he had failed to verbalize the old man's question.

"What?" Sydney asked.

"Well, what about it?" Rory frothed.

"You're loopy, Newman." His voice trailed off to a whisper as he muttered, "White line fever."

"What are you talking about, white line fever? I'm just fine and dandy, thank you. Now where was I? Oh yeah, the vision statement? Don't we need a vision, too?" Rory said all this while stiffening in his seat and straightening his back, adopting a pose worthy of an English gentleman.

"Like I said, loopy." After a moment of wagging his head in affirmation of this discovery, he said," So, how would you define a vision statement?"

"You're not going to make me call people are you?" Rory asked with mild distress.

Sydney shot back with, "Don't you have unlimited minutes?" He soon relented. "Nah, you don't have to call anyone, just tell me what you think it means."

Rory pulled back all the curtains in his mind, but the old rum-pled man had apparently gone off to have tea somewhere because he was nowhere to be found. On his own for this one, he hemmed and hawed and then said, "Well, if mission is your core purpose, like your compass, the vision is more concrete, right?"

"Some people call it a word picture." Sydney stopped to consider this, then went on, "I like that—word picture. A word picture of what the organization ultimately intends to become. Maybe 5, 10, or 15 years out. And yeah, it's more concrete than the mission. A vision typically includes specific numbers, maybe revenue numbers you hope to achieve or customers served, that sort of thing."

"Sounds like it fits right in with what we're talking about, were you saving it for bonus rounds or something?"

"Yeah, for the Showcase Showdown, just like on *The Price Is Right*." Sydney then twisted toward Rory and spoke in a deep and earnest tone when he asked, "Who do you like more Bob Barker or Drew Carey?"

"Well," Rory began, "Drew is hip and I loved him on *Whose Line Is It Anyway*, but Bob is an institution, and . . . and . . . can we talk about this some other time? What about the vision?"

"Comes later," Sydney said matter of factly. "Look, if you have a burning desire to create a vision at this point in the process I won't stop you. But I think it's better served once you've taken the next step in the process."

"Which is?"

"Looking forward from the strategy to its execution. You ask yourself, 'Okay, if we're going to execute this strategy, what will it mean?' If you've followed the advice I've given you, then you've decided what propels you, what you sell, who you sell it to, and how you sell. *Now* you determine where that will lead you. I just think if you try and create the vision before the strategy it's like putting the cart before our old buddies Buzz and Pucker."

The mere mention of the horses awakened Rory's saddle sore memories, and he shifted uncomfortably in his seat as Sydney plunged ahead. "Think about it. If the vision is concrete about revenue or customers or markets, don't you first have to determine what you're going to sell and to whom? And, I'll go you one better. I don't think you necessarily have to even use the word 'vision' when you get to that point. It's just more terminology in an already jargon-stuffed business world. Why not just engage people in your story by saying, here's our mission, here's our strategy to get there, and if we do all that, this is what you can expect. KISS Newman. KISS."

The pair fell silent once again as the 101, described by John Steinbeck in *The Grapes of Wrath* as the "mother road," exercised its maternal prerogative and curled the car softly east into Ventura. To their right, bidding a twinkling adieu was the Pacific Ocean, whose path they would not cross again until San Clemente. Rory held the shimmering jewel in his rearview mirror until the urgent ringing of his phone broke its spell.

19

Every Dog Has His Day

I n the span of a few short moments the scenery had altered
dramatically, from bucolic countryside, accented by the
melodious tune of the ocean, to the tune of a different
sort—the relentless urban pounding produced by cars, people,
and the vibrant thrum of industry. The transition occurred so
rapidly, it took Rory three rings before he was able to press the
phone button. In a final jab he slammed it and spat out a desperate "Hello."

"Rory?" came the confused reply.

"Yes, this is Rory."

"It's Jim Tobin. How are you making out?"

As he looked in surprise at a tract of farmland barricaded
between two industrial parks, Rory replied, "Great, Jim. I'm in
Ventura."

"Beautiful country down there, been there many times." He waited a beat and then said excitedly, "Great news. Actually, let me rephrase that. I've got good news and good news, which would you like first?"

After the requisite feeble chuckle, Rory said, "The good news I guess."

"We got the Ike Redmond account." Another pause, once again causing Rory to wonder if Jim was expecting some spontaneous corporate cheer.

"That's great, Jim."

"Yeah, it's thanks to you Rory. I don't know what you said to Ike on that ride up in Paso, but he's definitely on board the Kitteridge ship. And speaking of ships, we'll start shipping to him in a month or so. Oh, and he said to tell you he's sorry he had to run out, but he's looking forward to working with you."

"Fantastic, I'm looking forward to working with him, too."

"So you want the other good news?"

"Bring it on!" Rory said in a jubilant tone, the adrenaline of a closed sale now coursing giddily through him.

"I'm going to meet you in San Diego tonight, in fact I'm boarding my flight now. Ike's going to a horse show in Del Mar tomorrow, and after that he's heading to Spain for three weeks, so we want to make sure we get the contracts signed before he heads out of the country. I volunteered to fly down, and he agreed to meet tomorrow morning."

"Great Jim, but what's that got to do with meeting me?"

"Well, I know it's only been a little over a day since we gave you the strategic planning challenge, but I was thinking we could meet tonight, and you could give me a verbal update, then I could report back to the guys at corporate. They're very interested in this Rory." He paused, and then played his trump card, "Plus, you *did* commit to having something in three days, so this shouldn't be a problem, right?"

At that very moment, an emergency vehicle went wailing by in the next lane. It was big and powerful and a streak of pristine white. As it blurred past, Rory was able to read the bold scarlet letters on its side: "VENTURA COUNTY MULTI-CASUALTY DECONTAMINATION UNIT." What a fitting metaphor. It was his career that was about to be a casualty and require decontamination.

"Rory? You still there?"

"Yeah, Jim. Still here." He tried to project confidence in the reply but it sounded flat and Jim recognized it.

"You *can* give me a report tonight, can't you? You know how much we're counting on this. I don't want to put any pressure on you, but you're going to find that things will be moving a lot more quickly now that Olivenhain is at the helm. You can keep up, can't you Rory?"

Jim was in charge, that was undeniable, but Rory couldn't help but think that Mark was somehow pulling strings in the shadows, helping to orchestrate his demise. He blurted out, "Did Mark suggest this briefing?"

"What's Mark got to do with this?" Jim asked with a tone of sincere curiosity. "I've got news on Mark. I'll fill you in tonight."

The muscles in Rory's forearms rippled as he grasped the wheel and nodded his head mechanically toward it. He could see Mark in his office at that very second, shredding all evidence of Rory's existence, dancing gleefully on his glass desk, and barking orders at a helpless Melville Bell.

Sydney had kept his gaze fixed straight ahead during the corporate drama playing out on the speaker, but now he turned to Rory, and his eyes were calculating. When Rory returned the glance he could see in Sydney a measuring of him. Was he up to the challenge?

"I'll be ready, Jim."

"Great!

And then began the venue haggling. Rory suggested he meet Jim at his hotel, they could find each other in the lobby, Rory could give his report and that would be the end of it. But Jim insisted that he didn't want to put Rory out and cause him to miss any family time. He said he'd be happy to come to the reunion and promised he'd be "in and out in 10 minutes." The soft volleying continued back and forth until Rory realized it was pointless to argue any further; Jim was coming to the reunion for his update. It was as if Jim sincerely believed that he was doing Rory a favor by crashing the reunion. "Hannah's going to love this," he thought. "Just your typical down-home family reunion—some singing and dancing, a little croquet maybe, and a dissertation about strategic planning to a guy in a suit."

"I'll see you tonight, then." Jim said enthusiastically.

"Okay, Jim, see you then."

Rory tapped the END button gingerly, and when Sydney looked at him he saw a face like three rainy days.

"What's gone askew with you there, Old Shaver?" was his strange way of opening Rory up.

"You heard it," Rory snorted back.

"What's the problem? We've been talking about this stuff since yesterday. You should be able to give your report to this Jim dude with your eyes closed, one hand behind your back, and the other hoisting a margarita."

Rory grumbled, "First it was five days, then three days, and now they want it tonight. It's nuts."

"Sorry amigo, but Jim's right. It's the way of the world now—speed, speed, speed. Everything's coming at you faster and you've got less time to react and less margin for error."

"Is that your idea of a pep talk?"

"It's better than a pep talk, it's the truth. Maybe not the part about the margarita, you'd just spill it, but the part about us spending the last day talking about strategy. You asked a lot of good questions, made lots of great points. You can do it, Newman." The words hung in the air, suspended by the sincerity of Sydney's delivery. As they finally dissipated, he added, "Feel better now?"

"Much." The words were delivered with a mist of sarcasm, but Rory did feel his spirits climbing back from the edge a bit. He *had* spent the better part of the last day and a half in a crash course on strategic planning and could definitely hold his own on the topic at this point. He knew how to define strategy, he was well versed in developing a mission, he also knew the four fundamental questions to ask, and the four lenses that help answer the questions. But more than his own budding cerebral dexterity on the subject, he had Sydney, a veritable planning guru, right at his side, ready to ride to his rescue or bail him out of any tricky situations that might arise from Jim's presence tonight.

Ventura vanished behind them, making way for Oxnard, then Camarillo where they climbed 1,800 feet to the top of Conejo Mountain. Without warning they were carried on a great wave of traffic, a riptide of hurtling metal on all sides. Greater Los Angeles, The Southland, was just beyond the summit and its titanic automotive tentacles had reached them. Rory had negotiated Los Angeles traffic many times, but each new visit required a momentary transition to adjust to the volume, the velocity, the sheer madness of a century-old car culture.

The current carried them swiftly along the 101 toward Calabasas, its McMansions sparkling in the sinking rays of light. Enormous tracts of land had been assaulted to build these symbols of upper middle-class achievement, and Rory beheld them with ambivalence. They represented the American Dream of home ownership, but he couldn't help sense that if the land had any choice in the matter it would disdain the SUVs and trampolines and revert back to unmolested chaparral.

"You like LA?" Rory asked his companion. Nobody he had ever known answered that question with an "It's okay," or "Sure, it's alright." LA is the kind of place that evokes strong feelings one way or the other. People plant a flag for loving it or hating it, but there's no middle ground. He was interested to get Sydney's reaction and looking forward to a softball diversion for the next chapter of their drive.

Sydney raised his left hand, formed a fist like a mallet, and was about to speak when his *My Sharona* ringtone filled the car and brought an end to the grand gesture. He dropped his hand, retrieved his phone, and answered.

"Maggie . . . what? Slow down . . ." He became very erect in his seat and pressed the phone close to his ear. "When did it happen? Did you take him to Doctor Pressfield? Okay, yeah." He looked at his watch and said with great authority, "I'll be there in three hours." With that, the phone call was over.

"What's wrong?" Rory asked with cars darting from lane to lane around him and adding to the sense of panic and drama he felt unfolding before him.

"Take the 405," Sydney barked as he scrolled frantically through the address book on his phone.

"I would anyway, that's how you get to San Diego. What's going on?" In Sydney's eyes he saw the smolder of pain but before he could ask again his own phone rang. He was rattled, Sydney was still pawing maniacally at his phone, Rory's phone was squawking, it was chaos. Hannah was calling, for an update no doubt, but he sent the call to voice mail and returned his attention to Sydney.

"What's wrong?"

Sydney didn't respond, but raised the phone to his ear and began a new conversation. "Michael, it's Sydney . . . Good, listen I don't have a lot of time to talk. Trevor's in surgery and I need to get from LA to Denver ASAP." He sat, his face as stiff as wood, listening, then said, "6:45 out of LAX on American, perfect, book it."

Rory was busy weaving the tidbits of information in his own mind. "Who's Trevor?" Didn't Sydney know about the surgery? Flight out of LAX at 6:45? It's 5:45 now and we're in Encino, LAX is more than 20 miles away, and it's rush hour; there's no hope."

"LAX, Newman, and hustle." Sydney said with somber urgency.

"Who's Trev—" Before he finished the sentence he remembered. Trevor was Sydney's dog, named after Trevor Hoffman from the San Diego Padres. The episode with the Highway Patrol flashed before him, and Sydney's deduction that the officer was a Padres fan that led to the avoidance of a sure ticket.

"What's he having surgery for?"

"Got hit by a car a few hours ago, that's why Maggie called twice. She was at the vet's office but it didn't look bad so she didn't want to worry me. But then, when they were fixing his hip they discovered internal bleeding, and found out his spleen was ruptured. He's in surgery now. Can you go a little faster please?"

Rory turned up his hands and shrugged his shoulders in deference to the forest of vehicles surrounding them. The notoriously clogged 101/405 interchange lay ahead and traffic was slowing to a crawl.

"Do you really need to rush back to Denver for this?" The words escaped from Rory's mouth, a surprise to even him. Before he and Hannah had begun adoption proceedings, their world revolved around Jock their golden retriever. Pets had always been in Rory's orbit, since he was a boy, and he'd sobbed over the graves of enough goldfish, cats, and guinea pigs to understand the bond between people and their pets. He was about to apologize when Sydney interrupted.

"Yeah, I do." he said solemnly.

"Sorry Sydney, I just meant . . ."

Sydney jumped in, "Thanksgiving four years ago, I've got 12 people at my house, including 4 little kids. We're having a great time, watching football, talking, it's chilly outside, there's a turkey in the oven, it was perfect. Then Trevor barges in the room, barking his fool head off. I'm thinking, 'This is nice, my dog goes nuts in front of company.' I try to calm him down, but I can't. Then he keeps going back and forth to the back door. Finally, I followed him and then I smelled it. Gas. I scrambled the party like a SWAT team and we were out of there in about 30 seconds. I call the Fire Department, they rush over, and sure enough, there's a leak. They said if Trevor hadn't warned me the place could have gone up like it was the Fourth of July. A pretty sad Fourth of July."

Sydney turned to Rory and spoke once more. "So I owe that ball of fur, and win or lose today I'm going to be by his side and do whatever I can for him. He'd do it for me."

With steely resolve, Rory fixed his gaze on the maelstrom of traffic before them and said, "We can make it."

A Red Sea-like parting of vehicles would have been the fairy tale next step, but the LA traffic refused to configure itself to the wishes and preferences of these two, who instead remained, like thousands of others, marooned on the unforgiving asphalt of the freeway.

They squirmed through the junction of the 101 and the 405, each revolution of the tires an eternity in the process. Then, light appeared from the end of the tunnel, as the flow of vehicles suddenly jumped to life: 40, 50, 60, 65 miles per hour. They zipped along the blacktop, gobbling up asphalt acreage at an ever-increasing pace—70, 75 miles per hour. Then a violent screech of the tires, a horrible union of rubber and asphalt as Rory slammed on the brakes. Phantom traffic had appeared from nowhere, once again grinding their progress to a halt.

"You think we should try surface streets?" Rory asked.

"Nah, no better," was Sydney's terse reply.

It continued that way for the next 10 miles, uplifting starts and devastating stops, the tachometer rising and falling like a jittery stock market. When the vice was loosened for even a moment Rory would swerve between lanes, zigging and zagging wildly, employing every rodeo driving practice he cursed on his normal commute.

The Getty Center sat like a crown to the west as they approached the 10 Freeway, inching closer to LAX. Under normal circumstances, the Getty, like its host city, could easily spawn a colorful conversation. Their vast collections of priceless antiquities, its revelatory architecture, even its commanding view, were all fodder for opinion and discussion. Today, however, it was ignored, a spurned jewel sitting lonely atop a hill.

Sydney saw the digital display on his watch melt from 6:19 to 6:20 as the Mercedes finally escaped the 405 and torpedoed through the La Cienega off ramp. Not a word was exchanged as they raced along West Century Boulevard, yellow lights offering little more than an engraved invitation to continue the rampage.

"What terminal?"

"Four."

Rory navigated deftly through the porridge of rental car shuttles, hotel courtesy vans, and passenger vehicles that clogged the lanes abutting the terminals. At 6:24 he jerked to a stop at the sidewalk outside Terminal Four. Sydney leaped from the car and tapped impatiently on the trunk as Rory grasped for the release lever. He yanked it, and the trunk popped open, narrowly avoiding a collision with Sydney's chin, reminiscent of the one that had taken place when they met just yesterday morning. "Was it only yesterday?" Rory thought as he spun around the car and hoisted one corner of Sydney's mammoth bag to the sidewalk.

Sydney stuck out his hand, and Rory grasped it, tight as he could muster.

"Still like a fish," Sydney said with a grin. Before Rory could respond Sydney turned and marched briskly to the door. When he reached it, he turned and said, "Give 'em a great story." With that, Sydney Wise was gone.

20

The Reunion

Rory sat and stared blankly at the vacant passenger seat, its warped leather bearing testament to the punishment of accommodating Sydney's whopping frame for almost 400 miles. He smiled, but his expression quickly morphed into confusion when a violent thumping occurred on his window. An airport traffic officer, as granite-like as anything mined from a quarry, warned sternly: "You want a ticket buddy? Move it!" Rory obeyed with a shake of his head and made a hasty exit from LAX.

A few minutes later he was back on the 405 South, the San Diego Freeway, just another piece of polished flotsam riding the wild surf of Southern California traffic. He was regaining his car bearings when his phone rang. Hannah. "Damn," he thought. "I forgot to call her back." He struck the button.

"Hi." He offered the two simple letters in a breathless tone as if to imply more, to intimate, "Wait till I tell you . . ." But Hannah had an agenda of her own.

"Where have you been? Did you get my message?" she asked, a vein of frustration running just under the surface.

"Sorry hon, it's been nuts. I'm just leaving LAX."

"LAX?"

"Yeah. Long story. Trevor got hit by a car, and . . ."

"Who's Trevor?"

"Sorry. Sydney's dog. He got hit by a car, and now his spleen is ruptured, and Sydney caught a flight back to Denver to be with him."

"Is he going to be okay?"

"I don't know."

"So Sydney's not coming to the reunion then."

"No."

A hush fell over the call, the sort that makes you wonder if the other person is thinking about something, contemplating their next sentence, or if the connection has fallen into the black hole of dropped calls. Finally, Rory broke the silence.

"You still there Hannah?"

"Who's Jim Tobin?"

"He's . . . well, I guess he's my new boss."

Hannah interrupted, "Why is he coming to the reunion?"

"How did you know?"

"He called me."

"What?" Rory said, then mumbled to himself, "Must have got the number from my file at work."

"Rory! Don't mumble, I hate it when you do that! Speak into the phone."

"Sorry. That's another long story, anyway he won't be there long, just long enough for me to give a preliminary report on strategic planning."

Another interlude of quiet. Rory knew Hannah well enough to know that she was processing this information and determining whether it warranted a follow-up. Apparently, when weighed against the chaos of a reunion in full swing, it didn't.

"When will you be here?"

Rory took the measure of his surroundings, his gaze shifting from billboard to billboard, as if one might suddenly announce his arrival time in San Diego. When no such pronouncement was offered, he said, "Probably in about two, two and a half hours."

"Okay, just hurry, but drive safely."

"I will. Love you."

"Love you, too. See you soon."

It was around Long Beach, just past the 710 freeway, that the urgent blur of vehicles subsided, permitting Rory to devote a portion of concentration to his upcoming presentation to Jim. Suddenly a low-grade anxiety rose up from the pit of his stomach and soon blossomed to a full-on panic with the realization that he had no way to properly or concisely summarize what Sydney had taught him. He hadn't even had the chance to really think it all through himself. His plan was to take everything, all the lessons and anecdotes, back to the office then collate, summarize, synthesize, and create a comprehensive presentation. That opportunity could still present itself in the future, but most likely only if he passed this initial test with Jim. And make no mistake, it was a test.

"Focus, Newman!" Rory barked the order to himself as he sailed, fittingly enough, past Seal Beach. If ever there was a time to test his intellectual mettle, a time for stern concentration, for intense deliberation, this was that occasion. It was certainly *not* the time for sloughing off responsibility, for daydreaming, or prancing down memory lane. So what did he do? He guiltily excused himself from the pressing matter at hand and went jauntily along the gilded path of recollection. His mind traced the road back to the previous morning and the awkward meeting with Sydney. He laughed at the thought of his trunk almost clipping Sydney's chin. He marveled at their adventures: overcoming Mister Leather, then rescuing the shipwrecked couple in the Vanagon. Their lunch at the El Mariachi where his lessons really began to take shape, the fabled ride at Travis Hill Ranch, the chilly encounter with the angst-ridden kid at Bob's Mobile Mart in Pismo Beach, Sydney's glee at finding the Days Inn in Buellton. He was swept away in nostalgia, the warm cocoon of what had been acting as a comforting substitute for what lay ahead at the reunion.

No detail was spared in Rory's reminiscence, as entire passages of dialogue streamed through his head like a transcript. This pleasurable Car Coma had absorbed a healthy chunk of mileage and it was near Fountain Valley when the string of events playing in his head reached their conclusion, his terse farewell with Sydney at LAX. The exchange flowed easily in his mind, "Still like a fish," Sydney had said when shaking Rory's hand, and when he reached the door, "Give'em a great story."

"Give'em a great story," Rory clung to the words, repeating them mechanically, and as he did, they slowly transitioned before him from Sydney's parting, and seemingly innocuous, greeting to his final, and most important, lesson.

"That's it!" Rory cried as he rained celebratory blows on the steering wheel. "Strategic planning isn't supposed to be a dry, clinical ooze of facts and figures; a plodding march of drab rhetoric. It should be alive, dynamic; it's the *story* of the company's success!" He realized that when Kitteridge did develop a new strategy it would have to sell it to its employees. Dishing out 100-page binders of competitor analysis, strengths and weaknesses, and enough acronyms to make the military proud, wasn't going to capture the hearts and minds of his colleagues. The strategy had to be a story, one in which every employee took center stage. They had to see the world before them in living color and understand with exacting clarity why the strategy as proposed was the best course of action. Only a story can convey things so powerfully. Rory understood that his task was the same: Tell Jim the story of how they would develop a strategic plan.

He committed to spending the remainder of the trip creating his story for Jim, the narrative that would compellingly show why the steps Sydney had shared with him were right for Kitteridge or any organization for that matter. From that point forward, the car seemed to glide effortlessly over the surface of the freeway, almost hovering. By Costa Mesa he had created his story's chapter on the importance of defining strategy, in Lake Forest as the 405 merged with the 5 South, asking creative questions was cultivated in his mind. And on it went, each landmark spurring new associations, every mile giving rise to exciting possibilities for sharing his story. The rush of tires and thought merged as one and the miles passed, completely undetected. In San Clemente he was reunited with an old friend, the Pacific. Darkness was upon it, but the black expanse welcomed him warmly and ushered him into San Diego County. He was less than an hour from the reunion.

The freeway was dark and eerily quiet as Rory continued south, now surrounded on both sides by the massive 125,000-plus acres of mostly open space that comprised the Marine Corps base, Camp Pendleton, just outside Oceanside. The cloak of night was no match for his morale, however, which was bordering on stratospheric, owing to his discovery of story when discussing strategy, and the sheer adrenaline rush one feels as he nears his destination after a long journey.

From the 5 South he merged east on the 56, following it to the city of Poway. He trudged east, and soon the modest city gave way to its rural roots, developments of identical tract houses being replaced by rustic ranches of 4, 6, 10 acres and more. At precisely 8:45 he pulled onto a well-worn gravel drive, continued past two Redwood-like poles that supported a post announcing the "Yearsley Ranch" and followed the handcrafted signs, work of the junior family members no doubt, toward the reunion. Wild bunnies skittered across his path as the headlights led him to a makeshift parking lot, and then, with a deep, triumphant, and utterly satisfying sigh, he put the Mercedes in park and turned off the engine.

Uncle Frank's property spanned six acres of mostly level ground, and Rory could see the dim lights of tents spotted about him at all points in the distance. To his right, about 50 yards away, sat the nexus of reunion activity, the so-called "Main Lodge." It was a veritable hive of activity, with glowing tiki torches, raucous music, and a cacophony of chatter rising to the sky.

A great clatter arose as Rory made his way from the clearing into view of his extended family. Very soon he was the recipient of the sort of greeting that is customary at family reunions: warm, spirited, and completely oblivious to whether the person being greeted is actually a member of the family or not. Jack the Ripper could have advanced from the shadows and received an indistinguishable reception. Amidst the passionate welcome, Rory could hear the odd voice ask, "Who is it? Who? Hannah's husband?"

Hannah led the welcoming party and enveloped Rory in a warm and very welcome embrace. The two shared nary a single word before Rory was then engulfed by the familial horde. A dizzying succession of hugs, kisses, and introductions followed.

"Great to see you!"

"I'm your cousin Matt."

"Are you the one that can get treadmills at cost?"

"Give me a hug big guy!"

"Oh, you're even better looking than Hannah said!"

With that, Rory had been initiated, was one of them, and could recede into the mass of men, women, boys, and girls spinning giddily about him. He reveled in the sights and sounds of pure joy ricocheting through the room. Every spoken name preceded by aunt, uncle, or cousin. Every conversation accentuated with hugs, kisses, or backslaps. Even Jim Tobin was into the act! Rory caught the corporate heavyweight skipping around the room like an ingénue, while behind him, in hot pursuit, were teenage cousins Ben and Jeff wielding scissors, no doubt with necktie homicide on their minds.

Hannah found Rory once again and dragged him through the party to a corner of the room. A mysterious look flashed across her face when she said, "I heard from Henrietta at the adoption agency again."

Rory didn't hesitate, "The check, I know, the check. We'll get it out first of next week." He paused, catching sight of Jim who was making a beeline for him, having evaded, for the time being, cousins Ben and Jeff, then continued, "Depending on how the next 10 minutes go, it should clear."

A quizzical look washed over Hannah but she was unable to give voice to it as Jim had stretched to reach Rory's hand. He clutched it and said, "Some party."

"Having fun?" Rory replied.

"Yeah, great people. That Uncle Duke, the one in the pajamas, he's quite a character."

Rory nodded as they admired Uncle Duke, passing by in his paisley satin pajama bottoms, beer in one hand, *Wall Street Journal* in the other.

"So, I'm really looking forward to what you've got to tell me," Jim said expectantly.

"Me, too," Rory said with a self-effacing smile.

The scrum of revelers had stumbled to the lodge's ample wooden patio, when someone yelled out, "Stand by Your Man!" The request was greeted by a chorus of "woo hoos" that echoed across the acres and up into the star-filled night. It was clear that happy hour here at the Yearsley Ranch, at least under the auspices of a reunion, started early and ended late. Uncle Frank made his way to the stereo, CDs were flipped, tossed, and thrown in a heap, and then seconds later the twangy voice of Tammy Wynette serenaded the appreciative and swaying crowd:

> And if you love him
> Oh be proud of him
> 'Cause after all he's just a man
> Stand by your man . . .

The song droned on, but the mass of family members obviously weren't big country music fans because they were stuck like an old 45 on the same line, repeating "Stand by Your Man" over and over and over. Above the mournful whine, Jim stood with eyes fixed on Rory, who moved apprehensively toward the crowd and cried out, "Sorry, everyone, can you keep it down just a bit, I need to have a conversation with Jim, here."

Uttering the request in Swahili, or directing it at one of the palm trees bordering the patio would have been as productive. The tipsy group went on with their melancholy rendering of *Stand by Your Man*.

Tomorrow, Rory would realize the prudent response would have been to take his conversation with Jim to another corner of the property, but in the moment, in his zeal to both get it over with and share his new convictions, that avenue never revealed itself to him. No, they were going to have their showdown right there. He marched defiantly at the group and screamed, "Keep it down!"

The shocked cluster of partiers abruptly stopped their feral rendition and stared at Rory. Then, from deep within the mob a voice cried out, "Can someone please remove the stick from cousin Rory's butt?" A refrain of unfettered, gut-busting laughter followed, with the laugh riot building on itself to the point of near explosion. Hannah stepped bravely from the group, breaking ranks, and said, "Just for a minute."

The effect was magical. The unruly group dissipated immediately, with some dissolving into side conversations, others retreating to the bar, and a few sitting quietly on wicker chairs dotted about the patio. Rory dispatched a stunned thank-you to his wife and turned to Jim.

"Jim," he said with effortless poise, "Let me tell you a story. This is a story about *telling your story*."

Rory then embarked on his dissertation. He told Jim about the importance of defining strategy, why it was critical for everyone to be on the same page with the definition so they could then communicate effectively. "Every story needs research," he explained. He discussed the necessity of doing prework before ever debating potential strategies. He talked about asking creative questions and exploring the present and anticipated future environment to provide a backdrop for the creation of strategy. Jim was nodding eagerly so Rory continued. He provided his rationale for developing or confirming mission, the organization's core purpose, at this early stage in the process, and elaborated on how it plants a stake in the ground that guides all future decisions.

From the corner of his eye Rory felt someone approaching. It was Hannah. He was a bit self-conscious delivering this oratory with her by his side, but then he felt her confidence in him, and its power overwhelmed any potential embarrassment. With renewed vigor he shared the next chapter in the story, determining what propels you forward as a company. He then strode on with confidence, enumerating the four lenses that can be used to help answer the fundamental strategic planning questions.

Uncle Duke had sidled up to Jim, and Aunt Gwen, and then cousin Sara quickly joined him. The growing crowd seemed to kindle Rory's confidence and he spoke with great conviction and passion about the next step in the process, which is deciding exactly what products and services to sell, which to place more and less emphasis on.

Rory was in full control as he reached the story's next chapter, agreeing on the target customers. His rhythmic cadence barely broke stride as the group around him continued to swell. At his elbow, stretching her tiny ears to hear, was little cousin Holly, who was being clutched lovingly by Aunt Kit, both of them adorned head to toe in pink. Rory reached his crescendo with his convincing argument on the critical nature of deciding how the company will sell, and outlining the cost leadership and differentiation schools of thought.

They were standing shoulder to shoulder around him now, hanging on his every word. After a dramatic pause that would make Sydney proud he concluded by saying simply and humbly: "So Jim, that's how we'll develop a winning strategic plan for Kitteridge." Every eye in the room swung to Jim, his reaction now possessing the power to galvanize the group into full frenzy or send them to their canvas tents bemoaning the fate of poor cousin Rory.

"Fantastic!" Jim cried. "I knew you could do it!"

The room erupted in cheer. Glasses meant to be clinked gently, were smashed together in celebration, every human patch on the family quilt joined together in celebration, and the children, who had absolutely no idea what just happened, danced with glee on their wobbly legs.

"Stand by Your Man!" someone shouted. Without warning, and for no reason, it had suddenly become the anthem of the reunion and the jubilant gang danced their way back to the wooden patio. Rory was left, awash in adrenaline, with Jim and Hannah.

"We can work on a formal presentation next week," Jim said.

"Great, great."

"I'll introduce you to Abby on Monday. She'll be point with you on this."

A haze of confusion fell over Rory who reluctantly accepted Mark's role in all things strategic. "What about Mark?" he asked.

"This will be official on Monday, but . . ." Jim looked around cautiously, but seeing only Hannah and Buddy, Uncle Frank's intrepid Pomeranian, he continued, "Mark's gone. Ethical issues." He shook his head as he concluded, "Don't know how Carson didn't know."

Jim bid goodnight to Rory and Hannah, carved his way through the family, and disappeared into the dark. Finally, Rory and Hannah were alone.

"I'm so proud of you," she said as she burrowed into his chest.

He reached around her waist, lifted her off the ground and sang out, "I love you!"

Hannah, her voice muffled, said, "I heard from Henrietta today. She sent me a text with an interesting attachment."

Like the air from a balloon, Rory felt instantly deflated. "The check, I know."

Hannah put her fingers over his mouth, reached into her pocket and retrieved her cell phone. "No," she said.

She scrolled through a series of photos on her phone and stopped at the image of a baby girl, a tiny angel with a face you'd dream of when wishing for a baby girl. Rory looked at the photo, then at Hannah who was giggling deviously now, and said, "Is that . . ." Hannah nodded. They spun in embrace until their legs would hold them no longer and then fell to the floor in ecstasy.

"Let me see it again," Rory pleaded as his own phone rang. He was going to ignore it, the enormity of this moment, one he would never forget, was not to be interrupted by something so trivial as a phone call. But instinct nudged out sentiment, and he reached for the phone. It was Sydney.

"Sydney! How's Trevor?"

"He pulled through, he's going to be okay. He'll be out controlling the squirrel population again in no time."

"That's great."

"How about you? How'd it go with Jim?"

Rory, all the while staring at the grainy cherubic image on Hannah's phone, began by thanking Sydney for the lessons, especially the most recent revelation of "giving them a story." He then regaled Sydney with his own story of the evening's events, guiding him through the entire conversation, and capping the review with Jim's enthusiastic response.

There was quiet on the line, until Sydney said: "It's like I always say, you can think your way out of anything."

Roadmap Strategy Process and Model Summary

R ory did it. With Sydney's help he devised a simple process for creating a strategic plan, and you can, too. As Rory learned, a strategic plan doesn't have to be complex to be robust and effective, it just has to answer basic questions that are fundamental to the essence, nature, and success of any organization.

In Exhibit S.1, you'll find a graphic that represents the process described in the fable, which I'm calling "Roadmap Strategy," based on the book's title.

In the steps that follow I'll review that process and in doing so, provide a summary of the key points and questions our two travelers discussed on their trip down the 101.

Step 1: Have Your Team Read This Book

Is this a desperate attempt to drive book sales and rack up frequent flyer points by conducting book signings around the world? Not at all. If you're going to use this process it's critical that the

Exihibit S.1   Roadmap Strategy

team developing the strategic plan—your senior management—understands the method you'll employ. Therefore, reading this book should be the first step in the process so that all members of the team comprehend the model and are on the same page before you embark on creating the plan.

It's difficult to present this suggestion without it sounding self-serving, but it really isn't. In fact it's an attempt to save you time and money and help you avoid frustration. I've been consulting in the Balanced Scorecard arena for over 10 years and in that time have been part of many engagements that fall prey to a debilitating syndrome. It works like this: One member of the senior team reads a book on the Balanced Scorecard, maybe one of mine, maybe one of Kaplan and Norton's. He loves the idea, advocates for it, and the next thing you know I'm on-site ready to facilitate the development of a Scorecard system. Some members of the team have embraced the concept, others have been dragged along reluctantly, and some have simply acquiesced in apathy, but in any case they typically have failed to perform their due diligence of really understanding what the model is all about. In those cases, we're clearly not all on the same page. The Balanced Scorecard is a very prominent and mature methodology most senior executives would be loath to admit they are unfamiliar with so they simply say, "The Scorecard, sure I know it," and waltz into a workshop with no real understanding of the subtleties or intricacies of the system. Valuable time and effort is wasted because much of the early work in the engagement is spent erasing the team's misconceptions about the system and educating them on its many details.

It's the same with the model I'm promoting here. Sure, on the surface it's simple, but to derive value from the process, it's vital all members of your team truly understand it. For example, they must be willing to challenge assumptions, experience their products and services from their customers' perspective, accept the fact that mission and strategy are inextricably linked, comprehend how the core questions fit together, and understand how you can use the four lenses to assist you in answering those questions.

Step 2: Determine Why You're Developing a Strategic Plan, and Define the Word Strategy

Bring your senior team together for this session, the purpose of which is twofold. I believe one of the most important questions we can ask ourselves about any endeavor we undertake is why. Why are we doing this, and why now? The answers to these questions create our purpose for engaging in the act and guide our future actions, create a sense of urgency when complacency threatens to bully its way in, and help us communicate the rationale for decisions we eventually make.

Assemble your senior team and have each member share his or her opinion on the purpose of developing a strategic plan, why you're engaging in the considerable time and effort necessary to craft a strategy, and why now. Additionally, they can share what they hope to achieve from the process, and how they see it benefiting the organization going forward. I'd be shocked if at least one member of your team has not, at some point in their organizational past, had a bad experience with strategic planning. Now is the time to exorcise those demons and create a united front, not 9:00 A.M. on the first day of your planning retreat.

The second, and equally vital, agenda item for this session is to agree on the definition of the word strategy. You'll recall when Sydney challenged Rory to define the word and then have two colleagues do the same it resulted in three different definitions. Try it at your organization; my guess is you'll experience a similar result. If each member of your team arrives at a planning workshop with a unique definition of the word, they will obviously come to different conclusions and recommendations on the road you should follow. In this step you're setting ground rules and boundaries with your definition, creating an intellectual and mental box within which to operate.

If you're following the Roadmap Strategy model, the definition of strategy will be: *The broad priorities adopted by an organization in recognition of its operating environment and in pursuit of its mission.* Those broad priorities are determined as a result of answering the fundamental strategy questions posed in the model. Committing to this definition creates a shared understanding of what lies ahead, what you're focusing on building together during your subsequent sessions.

Step 3: Challenge Your Assumptions and Experience Things from Your Customers' Perspective

When I was in the eighth grade, a science teacher gave us a lesson one day that I've never forgotten. I can't recall the impetus behind it, but he strode to the blackboard, and wrote the word "ASSUME" in bold capital letters. He stared at the word for a moment or two, and then turned to his class of stunned preteens, none of whom had any idea what he expected us to do. Finally, he spun back to the board and said, "When you assume you make . . ." and he began to write as he spoke, "An ASS out of U and ME."

You've probably already heard that one, and in retrospect, the lesson probably stuck with me not only because of its practical resonance but as a result of the shock value of a teacher actually writing and uttering the word "ass" in class. In any case, it remained with me and I call upon it often, especially when encountering a new and unfamiliar situation. I won't suggest I've perfected the technique, but I've become quite adept at slowing myself down a bit and asking, "What am I assuming about this situation?" That simple question has helped open a lot of doors when solving problems over the years, and it's a vital state of mind to carry into your strategic planning efforts. You've got to be willing to question the way things are, or more appropriately, the way they seem to be to you. Unearthing hidden assumptions, particularly when working in group settings, allows all participants to learn from other points of view, question perceptions, and ultimately tap a much broader pool of potential responses to any situation.

Intellectual interventions are somewhat effective, but the best way to challenge assumptions is to get out and actually experience things, see a situation from another point of view. In the fable, Sydney tells the true story of Bill Bratton, former chief of the New York Transit Police Department. He understood that in order to bring about change in the minds of his people it was necessary for them to challenge the deeply held assumptions they had regarding the subway system, the so-called "Electric Sewer," and the only way that was possible was to direct them to actually ride the Sewer. Seeing, hearing, feeling, touching, and dare I say, perhaps even tasting what was taking place below ground opened their minds to what was really occurring on their watch and motivated them to move toward bold change.

The iconic design firm IDEO, responsible for breakthroughs in everything from egg beaters to CD players, adopts this hands-on, practical, see things from the customers' perspective approach whenever they work with a new client, and do so regardless of the industry. At New York's Memorial Sloan-Kettering Cancer Center, for example, IDEO closely observed patients, how they actually moved through the system, and quickly busted a long-held assumption that patients disliked long waits for treatment. It turns out that they found other worries more stressful, for example, waiting for the results of a blood test that determines if they are strong enough to be given treatment on that day. This and other experience-based findings led to significant changes. When IDEO worked with Mexican cement company Productos Cementeros Mexicanos, its first step was to have executives ride in cement trucks and visit with customers.

Don't ever hold the assumption that you know exactly how your customers feel about your products or services, or you know precisely how they use them. Get out into the field and perform your due diligence; observe, listen, and ask questions.

Only then will you free the cognitive space necessary for strategic breakthroughs to occur.

Step 4: Conduct Senior Leadership Team Interviews to Create a Fact Book

Before you can create your desired future, you need to understand your present and learn from your past. In this step, each member of the senior leadership team will be required to complete a questionnaire that helps you do just that.

On the pages that follow in Exhibit S.2 you'll find a multitude of questions you can choose from when creating your own questionnaire. There are queries to help you assess your current and anticipated future environment and questions that focus on the four fundamental building block questions underlying the Roadmap Strategy model. My goal in crafting the list was to give you a buffet from which to choose, but I strongly urge you not to ask all of these questions of your executives. There are 26 questions in Exhibit S.2, and if you were to ask your executives to answer all of them it would require a huge investment of their time, likely engender some significant antagonism, and ultimately lead to more of a "fat" book than a "fact" book. My recommendation is a maximum of 15 questions, and even that might be pushing it.

When choosing which questions to include, I would suggest you look for those you haven't asked before or that are perhaps phrased in new and engaging ways. Regarding the questions that relate to the four fundamental Roadmap Strategy "meta" questions, consider including your favorite one or two in the interview. That will provide you with fodder for your strategy workshops, and you can always facilitate a discussion of those not used in the interview at the session itself.

Exhibit S.2   Roadmap Strategy Questions

Question	The Question Relates To	Notes
Think back 10 years ago, and consider what has transpired in the world since that time. Did you envision the iPod, the popularity of hybrid automobiles, another war in Iraq? Those were some of the events in the world at large, but what happened in our business environment in those 10 years; were there revolutionary changes? Now, look forward 10 years into the future. Please outline what you feel may impact us in the next 10 years; the major trends, customer and stakeholder expectations, technological changes, demographic, political, or economic issues, and so on.	Environmental scan	This is a biggie, and a long question I grant you, but in my experience the interviewee's energy and patience tend to wane as the questions mount, so let's start with guns a blazing, and ask a question that forces them to really think about all of the critical areas that may impact your environment.
The previous question (looking into the future) challenged you to look into a crystal ball and foresee the future. You most likely envisioned a number of things that will be different from today. Changing your perspective for a moment, look into the future again, but this time, what do you see as stable in our environment? In other words, what will not change over the next several years?	Environmental scan	Another long question, but also essential. This one relates to points of stability in your environment. We're all hypersensitive to change, as we should be, but it's also important to be cognizant of those things that may remain stable, as they may impact our strategy.

Question	Type	Description
How could a newly formed organization, with significant human and financial resources, make us irrelevant? What would they have to do to ensure our demise?	Environmental scan	This question focuses on perceived vulnerabilities.
What are our organization's unique strengths?	SWOT	This is the first of a number of questions based on the venerable "SWOT" (Strengths, Weaknesses, Opportunities, and Threats) model. When considering strengths it is customary to look internally at your organization (skills, process, capabilities, etc.).
What special traits, skills, or talents do we possess that may become strengths in the future?	SWOT	There may be untapped and situational strengths residing within your organization, and this question challenges you to enumerate them.
What are our organization's unique weaknesses?	SWOT	Typically, this question focuses on internal weaknesses.
Do we have any processes, skills, or capabilities that may lead to weaknesses in the future?	SWOT	As with the similar strengths question, this one asks you to project into the future.

(Continued)

Exhibit S.2 (Continued)

Question	The Question Relates To	Notes
What opportunities may exist for our organization?	SWOT	Generally, the perspective with opportunities is external, i.e. looking outside your walls. It may prove useful to ask for opportunities to be delineated by time frame; short-term, medium, and long-term, for example, as that may impact the strategy you create.
What threats does our organization face?	SWOT	As above, it may prove useful to delineate threats by time period.
How can we creatively combine any existing strengths and opportunities?	SWOT	This question focuses on the "analysis" component of a SWOT analysis by challenging your executives to consider how you may combine unique strengths with existing and emerging opportunities.
How might we mitigate the combined impact of weaknesses and threats?	SWOT	The inverse of the question above. Here, you're combining weaknesses and threats that may work together to damage your organization and challenging your executives to determine how you might mitigate any deleterious outcomes.

Question	Fundamental question	
What drives our revenue and profitability?	What propels us forward?	This, and the two questions that follow, are focused on the first of the four fundamental strategy questions, "*What propels us forward?*" You might also consider including a question that outlines the six choices presented in the book, and ask interviewees to choose one. However, that would likely require some additional space for explaining each option. I'd suggest you save that exercise for your actual strategic planning workshop. The questions here will provide background for that discussion.
What things do we do better than anyone else in the world?	What propels us forward?	If you do something(s) better than anyone else they may indicate what propels you forward.
What specific skills or competencies do we possess that it would be difficult for our competitors to copy?	What propels us forward?	Roadmap Strategy does not focus on competition, but this question focuses on attributes you can use to differentiate yourself.
Have we had any exceptionally successful products or services? If so, what are their characteristics?	What do we sell?	Your task with the question "What do we sell?" is to primarily determine which products and services you'll place more and less emphasis on. Therefore, it's important to determine which products and services have been most successful and why.

(Continued)

Exhibit S.2 (Continued)

Question	The Question Relates To	Notes
Have we had any exceptionally unsuccessful products or services? If so, what are their characteristics	What do we sell?	The inverse of the question above.
Do any of our customers significantly modify our products and services for their own use?	What do we sell?	This question helps identify product and service modifications.
Which products and services produce the highest profit margins?	What do we sell?	Self-explanatory.
Which products and services produce the lowest profit margins?	What do we sell?	Self-explanatory.
Where do we sell now (geographic markets)?	Who are our customers?	This question, and the next challenge respondents to examine current customers and the determinants of success.
Where do we sell and why?	Who are our customers?	As above.
Do we have any very unsuccessful user segments? If so, why have we been unsuccessful in serving these customers?	Who are our customers?	The inverse of the two questions above.

Are there any customers our industry prefers not to serve? If so, why not?	Who are our customers?	This question seeks to identify potential new customer groups.
Do any customers groups require significantly more or less support than others?	Who are our customers?	This question relates to customer profitability.
Which customers' needs are changing most rapidly and why?	Who are our customers?	This question can be used to match changing customer behavior with your unique strengths.
Why do our customers choose to do business with us?	How do we sell?	Determining whether we focus on cost leadership or some form of differentiation is the focus of this, the only question for this specific strategy building block.

197

Step 5: Distribute the Fact Book to Your Leadership Team

The California Gold Rush that began in 1848 was a bit before my time, and I've never panned for gold, so I probably shouldn't be using prospector analogies, but here goes. It's vital that the members of your leadership team critically review the fact book prior to the strategy setting workshop so that when they arrive they're well versed in the facts of your situation and are ready and able to advocate their position based on reason borne out of a careful review of those facts. Here comes the gold part— when you're on the river prospecting you'll sift through beaches of sand to find that one nugget, but when you find it you know there's more where that came from, and you've struck it rich. Same idea here, you'll mine through a lot of information when reviewing the fact book, but when it leads you to the gold of better strategy, it's well worth the time and effort.

Step 6: Create or Confirm Your Mission

When discussing mission, the core purpose of an organization, Sydney says to Rory: "*Purpose is at the heart of the strategy wheel . . .*" Well, if you've looked at the Roadmap Strategy diagram you'll see that it most certainly does reside at the very center or heart of that wheel.

The mission statement defines your reason for being as an organization beyond succeeding financially, which, for a profit-driven enterprise, is a given. A nobler calling, your contribution to society and your team's motivation for engaging in its work, is reflected in the mission.

Strategy outlines the broad priorities you'll adopt in recognition of your operating environment and in pursuit of your mission. In other words, the mission helps guide the development of strategy by acting as a beacon for your work. In addition to providing direction for your work, the mission allows your leadership team to explain the relevance of the strategic decisions they ultimately make by demonstrating the linkage back to your core purpose.

Outlined below are some characteristics of effective mission statements. If you already have a mission statement, use these attributes to determine its efficacy. If you don't have a mission, the items below will assist you as you craft your statement of purpose.

- Inspires Change. While your mission doesn't change, it should inspire great change within your organization. Because the mission can never be fully realized it should drive your organization forward, stimulating change and positive growth. Take, for example, the mission of 3M, which is "To solve unsolved problems innovatively." Such a simple and powerful mission is sure to lead 3M into many new and interesting fields as it attempts to solve the innumerable problems we face.
- Long-term in Nature. Mission statements should be written to last 100 years or more. While strategies will surely change during that time period, the mission should remain the bedrock of the organization, serving as the stake in the ground for all future decisions.
- Easily Understood and Communicated. Buzzwords have no place in a mission statement, which should be written in plain language that is easily understood by all readers. A compelling and memorable mission is one that reaches people on a visceral level, speaks to them and motivates them to serve the organization's purpose. You can actually consider your mission a valuable recruiting aid in attracting like-minded individuals to take up your cause.

If your organization doesn't currently have a mission statement, consider using the "Five Whys" method that Sydney introduces to Rory. Start with a descriptive statement such as "We make X products or deliver Y services." Then ask, "Why is this important?" five times. A few "whys" into this exercise and you'll begin to see your true mission emerging. This process works for virtually any product or service organization. For example, a market research organization might transition from "Provide the best market research data" to "Contribute to customers success by helping them understand their markets" after a couple of rounds of questioning. You'll find that with each round of "why" your true reason for being as an organization will emerge in higher relief, and the value or contribution you strive to create or make will become evident.

Step 7: Develop the Strategy by Answering the Four Fundamental Questions Using the Four Lenses

The four fundamental strategy questions and the four lenses you'll use to help you answer them, are shown once again in Exhibit S.3, Roadmap Strategy.

In the sections below I'll review the questions in the order they appear both in the book and in the diagram, working clockwise from "What Propels Us Forward?" In the fable, the four lenses are introduced after the first question. However, here in the summary, in the quest for continuity, I've placed the lenses after the final question.

Fundamental Strategy Question 1: What Propels Us Forward?

Every organization, whether it is consciously aware of it or not, is being propelled in a certain direction as a result of its actions.

Exhibit S.3   Roadmap Strategy

Your task when answering this first of four strategy questions is to determine what is propelling your organization forward now and whether that is appropriate given your mission and what you've learned from answering the interview questions that constitute your fact book.

The six potential areas of propulsion are:

1. *Products and services:* Companies propelled by products and services may sell to many different customer groups, using a variety of channels, but their focus is on a core product or service. Sydney uses the example of Boeing, the aircraft company. With its technology and skills it could probably

design and build a multitude of things, but Boeing remains committed to the aerospace industry.

2. *Customers and markets:* Organizations dedicated to customers and markets may provide a number of product or service offerings, but they are all directed at a certain core audience. Johnson & Johnson's diverse wares have one thing in common: they're aimed at the needs of the company's core market—doctors, nurses, patients, and mothers.

3. *Capacity or capabilities:* Hotels focus on capacity. They have a certain number of rooms available and their goal is to fill them, it's as simple as that. Airlines operate on the same premise, filling available seats. Organizations propelled forward by capabilities possess expert skills in certain areas and will apply that toolkit of skills to any possible product or market.

4. *Technology:* Some organizations have access to a proprietary technology that they leverage to a number of different products and customer groups. In the fable, Sydney cites DuPont, which invented nylon in the 1930s. The company went on to apply the technology to a varied range of offerings including fishing line, stockings, and carpet.

5. *Sales and distribution channels:* The operative word with this focus is "how," not "what" or "who." Organizations that are driven by sales channels will push a diverse array of items through their selected channels. TV shopping networks are a great example. Where else can you buy makeup one hour and DVD players the next?

6. *Raw materials:* If you're an oil company, everything you sell is going to be derived from that black gold you pumped from the ground. You may have the skills and technology to mold the oil into a number of things, but all will be directly descended from the original raw material.

Some recent studies have cast a discerning and ultimately disparaging light on the topic of multitasking, long the best friend and closest ally of the Type-A personality. It turns out that most of us simply aren't gifted or mentally agile enough to handle numerous challenges at once, and when attempting to spin multiple plates we end up smashing more than our fair share. There is a finite boundary to our attention and focus, and organizations are subject to the same limitations. Some may review the options presented above and declare with bravado, *"We can do all of those!"* They think that if they can balance all six plates they'll be able to serve everyone by any means and come out a winner every time. But reality doesn't support this, and, in fact, such a lack of focus—multi-tasking on corporate steroids—is sure to lead to diffusion of effort, confusion, and skepticism from already change-weary and over-taxed employees, and ultimately result in suboptimal outcomes. Determine what propels you forward and focus on optimizing it.

Fundamental Strategy Question 2: What Do We Sell?

Regardless of what propels you forward as an organization, you have to sell something to your customers to keep the cash register ringing and the financial stakeholders pacified. For example, customers and markets propel *Playboy*, and its target market is men, but the company must still determine exactly what to sell. QVC is propelled by a unique sales channel, but once again, it must decide exactly what it will run through that system.

The challenge with this question is to critically examine your current product and service offerings and determine which you'll place more emphasis on in the future and which you'll reduce your emphasis on. The four lenses (discussed in an upcoming section) will aid in your decision, as will the interview responses summarized in your fact book . . . you know, the document that every member of your planning team should have studied before coming into the session.

Fundamental Strategy Question 3:
Who Are Our Customers?

As with the question, "What do we sell?" when determining your target customers, the ultimate aim is to decide which customers (and geographies) you'll place more emphasis on in the future and which merit less of your attention. The starting point in this deliberation is gaining a clear understanding of your current customers by examining the usual suspect metrics such as: customer satisfaction, customer loyalty, customer profitability, customer retention, and market share. Of course, you'll also need to walk in your customers' shoes by experiencing things from their point of view.

Beyond the metrics noted previously, you should ask the questions Sydney provides in the fable: Which customers' needs are changing most rapidly and dramatically and why?" "Does our direction align with that migration?" "Who uses our product in large quantities?" And consider noncustomers: "Which groups does the industry choose not to serve?" "Who doesn't use our product or service now, but could if we made some adjustments?" Combining these more unique questions with the common metrics above will undoubtedly yield some interesting insights.

Many organizations settle on their target customers by closely examining the moves of their competition and reacting accordingly. My proclivity is to monitor competitors, but always make customers, and noncustomers, the focus of your analysis and decision-making. In the fable, Sydney quotes Jeff Bezos as saying, "Competitors are never going to send you money." I know none of mine have ever sent me a dime, have yours? Also on the competitor topic, Dave Balter, the CEO of the word-of-mouth media company, BzzAgent, says: "Most companies consider their internal presentations confidential; we publicly post our PowerPoint decks about sales presentations. . . . If a competitor wants to see our slides, so what?" Such chutzpah! But it's true, scrutinizing your competitors, losing sleep over what they'll do next, poring over their every move will most likely lead you to copy their decisions in order to thwart any advantage they have. Multiply this by time and numerous players and you end up with an industry devoid of innovation, and one in which every player is mercilessly chasing the last fraction of market share, even if that means razor-thin or negative margins.

Fundamental Strategy Question 4: How Do We Sell?

You've determined the mission that outlines your core purpose, agreed upon what propels you forward, decided what to sell, and who to sell to, now you're left with one final question: Why should anyone buy from us? That is the essence of the fourth fundamental strategy question. You must clearly demonstrate your value to customers and potential customers in order to: first draw their attention, hold it through the initial transaction, and retain it for, hopefully, a lifetime of repeat purchases. The choices are limited and basic: You can either attempt to offer the lowest total cost of ownership to your customers, or you can put forth a *differentiated* product or service.

Companies that compete on lowest total cost, Wal-Mart being the poster child for such paragons of efficiency, have invested deeply in capabilities, processes, and assets that allow them to standardize their operations and create a repeatable formula that results in low prices for the consumer. McDonald's follows the same approach in the quick service restaurant industry. You're not soaking up a lot of ambience with that Big

Mac, but the price is definitely right when compared with the little French bistro downtown.

If you choose to compete based on differentiation, there are two paths you can follow. The first is differentiation based on cultivating deep and rich relationships with customers, so that your focus is not on a single transaction but building something that last years, maybe even decades or a lifetime. You charge more for your product or service, but your knowledge of customer requirements, your service, and your know-how are so superior that your clientele is willing to pay more to experience it. Think of Nordstrom. Its customer service is legendary and keeps customers coming back for years.

A second path of differentiation is competing based on the superior functionality of your products. Companies traveling this road focus on innovation and design, crafting breakthrough products that feature the latest and greatest functions, often pushing the technological envelope. Apple may be considered a product leader, given its history of creating exciting new products, most recently the iPhone.

For years I've been asking clients in my workshops to tell me which of the three avenues they pursue: lowest total cost, customer intimacy (great service, fostering relationships) or product leadership. After the inevitable awkward silence and furtive glances to the CEO, a brave soul will emerge and offer a tepid choice typically followed with, "But we really have to be all three." This is generally greeted with ritualistic head nodding from the others. If you're nodding, stop it. Immediately. You can't be all three, at least not purely. I think Sydney said it best:

"I'll grant you that good service, reliable products, and a fair price are table stakes in any business. But what I'm talking about is a commitment to how you sell. How you're proposing to add value for your customers. Wal-Mart, Nordstrom, Apple, they've invested deeply in certain capabilities and hard assets to deliver on their promise. They can't do all three things in a pure way—not without going broke in the process. And neither can you or any other business in the world. Plus, when they're faced with a decision, companies that have made a choice know how to react. At Apple, they know that when push comes to shove, they're always going to focus on the product. Companies that don't have a focus will have managers running around like chickens with their heads cut off. They don't know how to react."

All of the questions posed in the book are vital, but if I had to choose one that is most critical for your team to achieve consensus on, this is it. In many ways it represents the aggregation of your responses to the previous questions, and it will directly impact, in a significant way, every decision and investment you make going forward.

The Four Lenses

So how do you answer these strategy questions? On the outer ring of the Roadmap Strategy diagram you'll find what I call "the four lenses." Think of each of these as just that, a lens through which to consider the question you're pondering or a different perspective to adopt as you deliberate on your alternatives.

As you work through each of the fundamental questions you can turn the dial on the outer ring to a different lens. I like to think of it as clicking the dial on a safe, although when you're rotating a safe's dial there is only one correct combination. With the four lenses, every combination of question and lens is a winner, because each challenges you in a new and enlightening way.

I've already discussed the importance of challenging assumptions during the strategic planning process, and this is another tool to assist you in doing that by examining each strategy question through a variety of lenses. Each is summarized below:

- *Social/Cultural:* As Sydney puts it to Rory, "You've got to start with the heart." When discussing and debating the strategy questions, and developing possible responses, consider which potential answer most resonates with your passion as an organization. For example, if you're propelled by a proprietary technology, have a long and proud tradition of technological achievement, one which your employees are justifiably proud of, it may not make sense from a social and cultural standpoint to shift your focus to customers and markets or any other alternative. The evidence suggesting that such a shift will lead to profound success had better be substantial to override what's in the hearts of your people.
- *Human:* When debating alternative responses to the strategy questions it's vital to be ruthlessly realistic about your team's skills and talents. You may wish to sell surfboards because three members of your team are avid surfers but if your sales associates have never been to the beach you've got very little chance of succeeding. In that case, to make the transition, you'd have to be willing to invest in training, perhaps consultants (surfing dude consultants?), and new hires to bridge the potential skills gap.
- *Technological:* Technology has become a critical enabler of virtually every industry, and thus it must be carefully considered as you answer the four fundamental strategy questions. Will the answer you're contemplating require an investment in new technology? What about the current technology you employ, will it become redundant? And, it's important to realize that the lenses impact one another. New technology may require new skill sets, the human lens. And technology is one of the most threatening things

you can introduce, especially to seasoned employees, so you better have a good grasp on your cultural and social lens.

* *Financial:* Perhaps the most basic of the four lenses, but certainly not to be overlooked. Every decision you make when answering the four questions will most likely entail the allocation of resources, for example: training your people to cover a skills gap (human lens), investing in new technology (technological lens), or creating a communications campaign to support your chosen direction (social/cultural lens). And on the opposite side of the ledger, each decision must be examined in light of the potential revenue and profit that will result from pursuing that course of action.

Step 8: Create the Strategy

When I was writing the fable I envisioned a vignette during which Rory gave Sydney a copy of the Kitteridge strategic plan, a paper behemoth that Sydney regarded with great disdain and promptly tossed out a window of the moving car. Unfortunately, I wasn't able to squeeze it in, but such is my contempt for giant-sized plans that I felt great anguish in leaving it on the cutting room floor as they say in the movie business.

The value of a strategic plan should never, I repeat never be judged on the basis of its weight. You'll undoubtedly sacrifice a lot of trees during this endeavor, from the interview fact books, to the flip chart pages in your sessions, and I recommend you catalog everything you've discussed over the course of the entire process, but that should not represent the end product. The final result of your intense deliberations should be a simple statement, perhaps only a single paragraph, which weaves together the answers to your fundamental strategy questions.

Could you do that right now, before answering the questions in the book? I often tell the story, perhaps apocryphal, of Mark Twain, who settled in one day to write a concise letter to a friend, a task that was easier said than done. He recounted in the eventual missive: "I tried to write a short letter but it was too hard, so I wrote a long one." The same applies to strategic planning. Most organizations fail to confront the basic and fundamental issues they face, and produce mind-numbing plans of dizzying charts and graphs that offer no concrete resolution whatsoever. Dare to be different. Producing a concise statement of strategy is not an indictment against vigorous thought and debate, but is in fact a logical outcome of such an enterprise.

Regarding the composition of the strategy statement (or whatever you ultimately decide to call it), you'll notice I suggested it should weave together your answers to the four fundamental strategy questions. It doesn't have to be Shakespeare, but there should be a narrative flow to the statement, a lyrical quality that shows it's not simply four sentences bolted together haphazardly. In my hometown there was a car dealership that did TV ads when I was young. Now, my father was not a man quick to laugh, but whenever the boss of this dealership was on the tube, Dad would bust a gut. The pitchman, apparently sponsoring the ad to drum up business, would stand in front of a gleaming row of new cars and utter with the cadence of a zombie on Prozac, "We . . . waaaant . . . your . . . biz'ness." It was a robotic chant with all the emotion of a fence post. That's what your strategy statement will sound like to your employees if you simply staple the answers together, so take the time and exercise the creativity to craft a statement that clearly communicates your strategy in a compelling way. Here's an example:

New Bloom Floral provides freshly cut rose bouquets to those consumers who desire the beauty and elegance of roses at a discount price.

Our focus is on the Southern California market where we derive a significant cost advantage that we can pass on to our price-conscious customers from local growing and short-haul distribution to high-volume retailers.

That's it. Fifty-nine words. But they speak volumes, and answer the four questions with precision and economy. We can see that New Bloom is propelled by products (flowers), and they sell only roses, not all-occasion bouquets, not vases, just roses. They focus on Southern California because they grow their flowers locally and can leverage cost advantages which they can pass on to their target market of price-conscious customers. Thus, we know that low cost is the answer to the final question of how they sell to their customers.

New Bloom's strategy statement, with its admirable brevity, also provides a solid stake in the ground for future decision-making. Leaders now have a filter through which to judge opportunities that will inevitably arise in the course of their day-to-day operations. Does the prospect ensure low costs for their target customers? Will it allow them to leverage the advantage they have by focusing on the Southern California market? Does it involve rose bouquets, their chosen product focus? With such a prism at their disposal, managers and employees at all levels of the organization can make informed, and more importantly aligned, decisions that ensure they remain true to their strategic choice.

A final word on the strategy statement: Despite what I said previously about weaving the responses together, your statement should ultimately be constructed with deference to your unique culture. If a picturesque paragraph would do nothing but raise eyebrows because for as long as anyone can remember you did everything in lists or bullets, and that's worked, then by all means stick with it.

Step 9: Review and Vet the Strategy

Developing a new strategy is hard work, no doubt about it, but it's also invigorating and exciting, as you tunnel through your assumptions, examine information in a new light, and ultimately craft a statement you feel will vault you to great success. An important caveat to be cognizant of during the intense process, especially as you begin to reach conclusions, is the possibility that your objectivity may take an unscheduled leave of absence. This can make your team vulnerable to the corrosive effects of "group think," with constructive conflict beginning to shrink and consensus appearing swiftly and easily.

To guard against this, it's important to have an independent group, the members of which were not involved in the actual strategy setting process, review and vet the outcomes you've reached. The goal of this panel is not to rewrite the strategy, but to ask the difficult questions that even seasoned executives may be unwilling or uncomfortable raising in the strategy workshops. Nor should the work of the panel be considered a savage inquisition, attempting to ensnare strategy creators for minor defects in the document. Again, it's simply a third-party review whose mandate is to ensure all assumptions have been challenged, difficult questions have been raised, and perhaps most important, that the team creating the strategy is given the opportunity to passionately, articulately, and credibly defend the statement they've created. Independent board members, retired executives, and even known corporate curmudgeons are all potential members of the vetting panel.

Once your strategy has passed the review process it's time to communicate, communicate, communicate. In my workshops I share a statistic that suggests that only 5 percent of the typical workforce understands the organization's strategy. Once that sobering number has begun to sink in I query the group as to why such an abysmal percentage is possible. Over and over I have heard respondents suggest it's because the strategy is never widely communicated. Audiences from small firms, large corporations, government agencies, and nonprofit associations have all provided this answer, so although I'm not conducting any kind of scientific study, their responses must have merit.

In the past, part of the problem for this paucity of communication may have been the result of strategy documents that are thicker than the permafrost in Alaska, and thus virtually impossible to share without some form of translation. Or, as some of my more mischievous and skeptical workshop participants have suggested over the years, could it be that the executives themselves never truly reached agreement over the strategy and therefore are unable to articulate it clearly?

Roadmap Strategy, as presented in this book, allows you to overcome both of those sinister possibilities. The process ensures all executives confront the facts before them, challenge their assumptions, see things from the eyes of your customers, and ultimately create a document that reflects their shared understanding of the road ahead. Additionally, the outcome of the process is a simple statement, devoid of corporate speak, that clearly and easily outlines your strategy.

Step 10: Execute Your Strategy

Congratulations! You've got a freshly minted new strategy, forged from vigorous debate and discussion, vetted by a crack team of trusted examiners, and communicated ceaselessly to your employees. Now what? Now the real work begins: making it happen, executing that simple statement, stamping it on everything you do, every day of the year.

We've come full circle back to the book's introduction now. I wrote it largely as a result of my frustration with the current state of strategic planning and the impact that had on my work as a practitioner and consultant of the Balanced Scorecard. But if you've followed the advice on these pages you're now prepared to fully harness the immense power of the Scorecard system to bring your strategy to life. I invite you to take advantage of the books I've written on that subject and also to stay tuned for more from Rory and Sydney. The adventure continues.

Roadmap Strategy Online

I invite you to visit www.roadmapstrategy.com for more helpful resources, including a series of guided exercises to help you create your own strategy. There you'll find tools and resources that will facilitate your journey by working through the Roadmap Strategy Process, allowing you to chart your progress along the way.

In addition, there are links to other helpful sites you can visit as you embark on creating and executing your strategy.

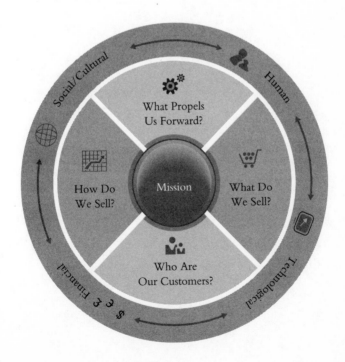

References

Introduction

Page viii: "A hero sandwich of good intentions." From: Peter F. Drucker, *Managing the Nonprofit Organization* (New York: Harper Business, 1990), 5.

Page viii: McKinsey study on satisfaction with, and use of, strategic planning. From: Renee Dye and Olivier Sibony, "How to Improve Strategic Planning," *McKinsey Quarterly*, August 2007.

Page ix: Folding business units into other SBUs to avoid strategic planning. From: Henry Mintzberg, *The Rise and Fall of Strategic Planning* (New York, The Free Press, 1994), 100.

Chapter 4: The Red Zone Is for Immediate Loading and Unloading Only

Page 20: "Sure a few of them had their eccentricities, like Uncle Duke who took to wearing pajama bottoms in public because, as he put it: "The Chinese do it." From: Ray A. Smith, "The New Pajama Look: Better in Bed?," *Wall Street Journal* (Kindle Edition), September 4, 2008.

Chapter 5: Who Is this Guy?

Page 29: "Yeah, but if China . . ." This was drawn from www.fxcm.com/if-china-revalues.jsp and accessed on September 5, 2008.

Chapter 7: Ask a Silly Question

Page 42: "Kissinger said that what passes for planning is frequently the projection of the familiar into the future." From: Henry Mintzberg, *The Rise and Fall of Strategic Planning* (New York: The Free Press, 1994), 179.

Page 44: "Back in 1984, *The Economist* conducted an interesting study." From: Michael E. Raynor, *The Strategy Paradox* (New York: Doubleday, 2007), 104.

Chapter 8: What You See Is Not Always What You Get

Page 55: *Discepolo della esperienza*. From: Michael J. Gelb, *How to Think Like Leonardo da Vinci* (New York: Bantam Dell, 2004), 78.

Page 56: "Electric Sewer." The story of Bill Bratton and the Electric Sewer is drawn from: W. Chan Kim and Renee Mauborgne, *Blue Ocean Strategy* (Boston: Harvard Business School Press: 2005), 153.

Page 58: Sydney provides Rory with some creative questions to use during the process. Some questions were drawn from:

Kevin P. Coyne, Patricia Gorman Clifford, and Renee Dye, "Breakthrough Thinking From Inside the Box," *Harvard Business Review*, December 2007, 70–79.

Chapter 9: Getting to the Core

Page 67: "[Purpose] is the hub of the strategy wheel." From: Cynthia A. Montgomery, "Putting Leadership Back Into Strategy," *Harvard Business Review*, January 2008, 54–60.

Page 68: David Packard quote. From: James C. Collins and Jerry I. Porras, "Building Your Company's Vision," *Harvard Business Review,* September–October 1996, 65–77.

Page 70: *Saturday Night Live* debate regarding which musical guest had the most appearances. According to Wikipedia the answer is Paul Simon with nine. James Taylor has six.

Page 70: The Five Whys. From: James C. Collins and Jerry I. Porras, "Building Your Company's Vision," *Harvard Business Review,* September–October 1996, 65–77.

Chapter 11: A Push in the Right Direction

Page 83: Here Sydney begins to instruct Rory on the importance of determining what propels you as a company. Over the years, many theorists have discussed the importance of this topic using a variety of descriptions and phrases to articulate it. I have drawn primarily from two sources:

Robert W. Bradford, J. Peter Duncan, and Brian Tracy, *Simplified Strategic Planning* (Worcester, MA.: Chandler House Press, 2000), 137.

Michel Robert, *Strategy Pure & Simple II* (New York: McGraw-Hill, 1998), 63.

Chapter 14: Charged Up in Pismo Beach

Page 113: "Seventeenth longest pier in California." According to www.vaughns-1-pagers.com/local/california-piers.htm, it's actually the eighteenth longest at 1,250 feet, although the official site for the City of Pismo Beach, at www.pismobeach.org, lists it at 1,200 feet.

Page 121: The questions regarding emphasis were drawn from: Michel Robert, *Strategy Pure & Simple II* (New York: McGraw-Hill, 1998), 62. But, as with all topics in the book, many writers, researchers, and practitioners have offered this advice in various forms over the years.

Chapter 15: You Know What Nietzsche Said about Groups

Page 127: "You know what Nietzsche said about groups, right?" Drawn from: James Surowiecki, *The Wisdom of Crowds* (New York: Doubleday, 2004), xv.

Page 129: Portions of Sydney's advice regarding meeting management were drawn from: Kevin P. Coyne, Patricia Gorman Clifford and Renee Dye: "Breakthrough Thinking from Inside the Box," *Harvard Business Review*, December 2007, 71–78.

Page 131: Danish study regarding profitability and the death of CEOs' mothers-in-law. From: Mark Maremont, "Scholars Link Success of Firms to Lives of CEOs," *The Wall Street Journal*, September 5, 2007.

Chapter 16: Two Thumbs Up

Page 136: Information regarding the origins of Solvang, particularly the immigration of Danish educators, was drawn from the wikidpedia.org entry for Solvang, California.

Page 138: The quote from Herbert Bayard Swope is drawn from: Timothy Ferriss, *The 4-Hour Workweek* (New York: Crown Publishers, 2007), 29.

Page 139: The section on Jeff Bezos' philosophy regarding customers is drawn from: Julia Kirby and Thomas A. Stewart, "The Institutional Yes," *Harvard Business Review*, October 2007, 74–82. Also in this article, Bezos mentions that everyone at Amazon, from himself on down, has to spend time in fulfillment centers and every two years they do two days of customer service. Sounds a bit like the Amazon version of "Riding the electric sewer." Bezos says it's not a chore, and in fact is "Quite entertaining, and you learn a ton."

Page 141: Less than 25 percent of managers agree with the statement "We understand our customers." From: Chris Zook, "Finding

Your Next Core Business," *Harvard Business Review,* April 2007, 66–75.

Page 143: The story of the Big Bertha golf club is drawn from: W. Chan Kim and Renee Mauborgne, *Blue Ocean Strategy* (Boston: Harvard Business School Press, 2005), 102.

Chapter 17: Sandy Resolutions

Page 150: Here they begin to discuss the question "How do we sell." Sydney then provides three possible responses: lowest total cost, customer intimacy, and product leadership. These are drawn from: Michael Treacy and Fred Wiersema, *The Discipline of Market Leaders* (Reading, MA: Perseus Books, 1995). However, as Michael Raynor points out in his book, *The Strategy Paradox* (cited above) these ideas have been around for many years and have been advocated for by a number of scholars and practitioners under different labels. For example, the idea of low cost has been explained as: Cost Leadership (Porter), Operational Excellence (Treacy & Wiersema), Exploitation (March), and Defender (Miles and Snow). Differentiation goes by many names as well: Product Differentiation (Porter), Product Leadership/Customer Intimacy (Treacy & Wiersema), Exploration (March), and Prospector/Analyzer (Miles and Snow).

Chapter 19: Every Dog Has His Day

Page 166: Fans of The Brothers Grimm will recognize the following passage, ". . . when Sydney looked at him he saw a face like three rainy days." "Now then Old Shaver, what's gone askew with you?" This is drawn from The Bremen Town-Musicians in: Jacob and Wilhelm Grimm, *The Complete Grimm's Fairy Tales* (New York: Pantheon Books, 1944).

Roadmap Strategy Process and Model Summary

Page 190: Experiencing things through the eyes of your customers. The IDEO reference is drawn from: Phred Dvorak, "Businesses Take a Page From Design Firms," *Wall Street Journal*, November 10, 2008.

Page 199: The characteristics of effective mission statements and overview of the 5 Whys method are drawn from: Paul R. Niven, *Balanced Scorecard Step by Step: Maximizing Performance and Maintaining Results (Second Edition)* (Hoboken, NJ: John Wiley & Sons, 2006), 73–75.

Page 205: Quote from Dave Balter of BzzAgent, from: Dave Balter, "Conversation: Marketing CEO Dave Balter on Achieving the Corporate Full Monty," *Harvard Business Review*, October 2008, 33.

Page 212: Reviewing and Vetting the Strategy. Portions of this section (the importance of a vetting panel) are based on material presented in: Paul B. Carroll and Chunka Mui, "7 Ways to Fail Big," *Harvard Business Review*, September 2008. PP. 82–91.